The Men Who Flew
the Heavy Bombers

The Men Who Flew the Heavy Bombers

USAAF Four-Engine Heavies in the Second World War

Martin W. Bowman

Pen & Sword

AVIATION

First published in Great Britain in 2022 by
Pen & Sword Aviation
An imprint of
Pen & Sword Books Ltd
Yorkshire – Philadelphia

ISBN 978 1 52674 631 3

A CIP catalogue record for this book is
available from the British Library.

Typeset by Mac Style
Printed and bound in the UK by CPI Group (UK) Ltd,
Croydon, CR0 4YY

MIX
Paper from
responsible sources
FSC® C013604

Pen & Sword Books Limited incorporates the imprints of Atlas,
Archaeology, Aviation, Discovery, Family History, Fiction, History,
Maritime, Military, Military Classics, Politics, Select, Transport,
True Crime, Air World, Frontline Publishing, Leo Cooper, Remember
When, Seaforth Publishing, The Praetorian Press, Wharncliffe
Local History, Wharncliffe Transport, Wharncliffe True Crime
and White Owl.

For a complete list of Pen & Sword titles please contact

PEN & SWORD BOOKS LIMITED
47 Church Street, Barnsley, South Yorkshire, S70 2AS, England
E-mail: enquiries@pen-and-sword.co.uk
Website: www.pen-and-sword.co.uk

Or

PEN AND SWORD BOOKS
1950 Lawrence Rd, Havertown, PA 19083, USA
E-mail: Uspen-and-sword@casematepublishers.com
Website: www.penandswordbooks.com

Contents

Someone was praying hard for us today. Left England at 1230 – 28,000 feet – 44 degrees below zero. Spit escort twenty minutes before the target our #4 engine ran away and we couldn't feather it. Couldn't hold our altitude or stay in formation. We dropped down and turned back. Three minutes later four Me 109s picked us up. We dove down to 12,000 feet trying to get away. Got into all the clouds we could. Vertical backs, dives, climbs, etc. the fighters came in at 5, 6, & 7 o'clock on our tail making several passes. Riggs said he saw one explode and another go down in smoke. Couldn't get much speed having only three engines and a head wind. We dropped all our bombs in a field near Arras, France, in order to get more speed. We zigzagged for the coast. Flak picked us up and followed us for two or three minutes but did not hit us. We finally hit the coast and twenty minutes later hit the English coast. Our tail gunner Faber was wounded. A 20mm hit the tail. Bullets in his leg, buttocks and side. Not much bleeding so no first aid necessary.

Turned north up the coast for home but our #4 engine was burning so we landed at the nearest field, Detling, an RAF Spitfire field, five miles south of the Thames near London. When we stopped rolling on landing the engine was really spurting out fire. Tried to put it out with fire extinguishers that we had but couldn't. The field fire truck finally put it out. One tyre was flat when we landed – bullet through it. Plane was riddled with holes. Must have been 200–300 holes in it; 20mm cannon holes (maybe 7 or 8) in it. Can't see how the tail and waist gunners got back alive. Holes within inches of them – dozens of them. One 20mm went through our bomb bay with our 12 incendiary bombs still there. Nose was not shot up much as they all attacked from the tail.

Skinny Fryer turned back ten minutes after we did and evidently went down as they haven't heard from him. He was in our squadron. Three gunners in our group died on the raid from anoxia. Their oxygen tubes came loose and they didn't know it.

Moral: stay in formation, even if you have to get out and push.

Mission #7 Duren, Germany, 20 October 1943, 2nd Lieutenant Joel D. Punches, navigator, born Wymore, Nebraska 1915, on Robert M. 'Tex' Taylor's B-17 crew, 549th Bomb Squadron, 385th Bomb Group, Great Ashfield, Suffolk. (All ten crew on 1st Lieutenant Lyle Vermont Fryer's crew on Shack Bunny *were taken prisoner). On 21 February 1944 when Punches was shot down on B-17* Crazy Horse *and was one of three men who evaded capture, returned to England on 15 September 1944. He died in Santa Maria, California on 26 April 2004.*

Acknowledgements

A book of this magnitude includes so many personal stories kindly given over to me by the veterans and their offspring over the past forty years that I have lost count of actually how many have kindly taken me to their hearts and have reached into the deepest corners of their souls to share their reminiscences with me and my readers. Of course it goes without saying that they and their sacrifices must never be forgotten and I hope that this book is a lasting reminder to men the like of whom we will never see again. I hope that I have not left anyone out of their rightful place of honour on this page. I will start with the oldest veterans first, a few of whom are still with us at the time of writing, but of course very few are left.

I am most grateful to Gordon W. Weir for his story; part of which Truett Lee Woodall Jr. and I featured in *Helton's Hellcats: A Pictorial History of the 493rd Bomb Group* (Turner Publishing, 1998) and which is now featured in full on http://www.arizonahandbook.com/8thAF.htm. Gordon died on 5 October 2011, just four days short of his 89th birthday. I corresponded for many years with the late Judge Ben Smith Jr., author *Chick's Crew: A Tale of the Eighth Air Force* and extracts are reprinted here with his kind permission. Particular mention must also be made of the contribution by Lawrence 'Goldie' Goldstein over many decades of correspondence and visits to each of our homes in Norwich, England and New York City. I was just finishing writing this book in spring 2021 when Larry had just celebrated his 99th birthday and on 10 February 2022 Larry celebrated his 100th birthday. Equally, I am indebted to the late Jack Rude of Amarillo, Texas another nonagenarian who died in June 2020 at age 97. Jack served in the 493rd Bomb Group and was a frequent visitor to these shores over many years when he would accompany me on many visits to his former stomping grounds in Suffolk and Norfolk.

I must also make special mention of Jim Hanson whom I first met on his and his family's pilgrimage to Norfolk and Suffolk in October 2016 and our ongoing correspondence since then has resulted in his telling of the story concerning his uncle, Oscar T. Hanson and it being recorded here for the first time. Thanks also to the 100th Bomb Group Foundation and Norm and Melanie Bussel of the 447th Bomb Group Association.

I am equally grateful to the following veterans for their unstinting support that began in the 1970s and continued until their passing in recent years: Wesley J. Bartelt; Donald L. Becker; John M. Bennett; Richard Bing; John E. Borg;

General Harold Webb Bowman; Marvin Somerset 'Red' Bowman; Bob Browne; Clarence F. Cherry; Alan S. Cook; Hubert Raymond Cripe; Harry H. Crosby; Jasper Clyde Crowley; Hayward F. Deese Jr.; Robert H. Densmore; Forrest S. Clark; Stephen Fecho; 'Dick' Ghere; John Gibbons; William L. Gibbons; Harry D. Gobrecht, 303rd BGA historian; Jackson Granholm; Sam Halpert, author of *A Real Good War*; Cliff C. Hatcher; Joseph M. Hoffman; Celesta B. 'Red' Harper; Charles E. 'Chuck' Huston; Richard R. "Dick" Johnson, author of *25 Milk Runs*; Carlyle J. Hanson; John D. Kettman; Alfred R. Lea; 'Ed' Leighty; John McClane; James H. McMahon; Glenn R. Matson; Philip H. Meistrich; Kenneth C. Micko; Cornelius 'Ed' Miller; Paul M. Montague; Ralph Munn; Raymond R. Newark; John R. Parsons; Wallace Patterson; Stanley A. Peterson; Joel D. Punches; Ernest J. Richardson; 'Rosie' Rosenthal; Doug Sharp; Doyle Shields; Bob Shoens; Paul A. Shull; Jack Spencer; Thurman Spiva; Russell A. Strong; Glenn Tedford; Marshall J. Thixton; Joe Urice; Bill Varnedoe; Lowell Hoyt Watts; Henry 'Hank' Wentland; Henry 'Hank' K. Wetherhold; Ray Wild; Edward F. Wittel and Joe Wroblewski.

And, also, the late Roy Cholchester; Bob Cossey; Patricia Everson; Robert M. Foose; Brian Francis; Chris French, Historian/Archivist, 447th Bomb Group Association, who was crucial in making all requested information and more, available to me; Peter H. W. Kamin; the late Paul Knight; Friedrich J. Kowalke; Ian MacLachlan; and last but by no means least, Paul M. Andrews and William H. Adams for their invaluable work entitled *Heavy Bombers of the Mighty Eighth: An Historical Survey of the B-17s and B-24s of assigned to the 8th Air Force August 1942-June 1945*.

I can think of no better written epitaph than Laurence Binyon's famous words: *Age shall not weary them, nor the years condemn. At the going down of the sun and in the morning. We will remember them... They mingle not with their laughing comrades again; They sit no more at familiar tables of home; They have no lot in our labour of the day-time; They sleep beyond England's foam.*

Martin W. Bowman, Norwich, England, January 2022

Introduction

The train chugs its way through the English countryside, stopping every ten minutes at and often between, each little station along the way.

 'This here's worse than a sardine can and I don't know where the hell we're going.'

 'Bassingbourn, the 91st' I remind him.

 'Isn't that where they sent ol' Clark Gable?' He squints his eyes, puckers his mouth and in a real bad imitation of Gable says, 'Frankly my dear, I don't give a damn...'

 'Well at least it ain't the Bloody Hundredth.'

A Real Good War by Sam Halpert, who's fiercely authentic, autobiographical novel (first published in 1997 by Cassell Military Paperbacks) was a remarkable fiction debut at the age of 77. Born Brooklyn in 1920, after enlistment Sam gave up his job as an apprentice typesetter in Buffalo and was trained as a navigator on the B-17.

During the war years, 1942-1945 the United States 8th Air Force stationed its bomber and fighter bases in Eastern England and the villagers and townsfolk shared a close attachment that only wartime can create. England then was a battlefront. All the civilians were involved in the war effort: as shipyard and factory workers, Red Cross and Land Army volunteers, farmers and firemen. Above all they were determined fighters who had already endured more than three years of war. Into their lives came the sights and sounds – particularly the jargon – "flak leave, R&R, and pubbing missions" to name but a few choice phrases – of the men from the big cities and the backwoods, upstate and downtown: from California to Connecticut, Delaware to Dakota, 'Frisco to Florida; Midwest to Maine, the mighty Mississip' to Missouri; New York, New England, Ohio and Hawaii; the Pacific, Philly and the Rockies to the Rio Grande; from Texas to Tallahassee; Wyoming, Wisconsin, the 'Windy City' and way beyond. The English locals and the Americans themselves were in for a culture shock. The impressions they made were profound. Some things though never change. Boston, Cambridge, Ipswich, Manchester and Norwich were the same in any language, on both sides of the 'pond'.

 American troops, or 'GIs' as they were known because of their own derisive term of 'Government Issue', began arriving in war-weary Britain in the months immediately after Pearl Harbor. Bomber and fighter groups made a particular impact. The young Americans, with their well-cut uniforms, new accents and money, created a colourful and heroic chapter in the lives of the British people that is still remembered today though for many, the building of so many bases in rural Norfolk and Suffolk and further afield often brought upheaval and often danger. For one, Teddy Whybrow, a former porter and clown from Sangeres Circus, who was bombed out of his London home in 1942, bought "Little Awe" farm in Suffolk in the hope of peace and quiet, only to find out that within a year, his house would be in direct line with the main runway of Mendlesham airfield and the 34th Bomb Group B-24s and B-17s would be skimming his property on take off by only a matter of feet!

In all, some 67 airfields in Eastern England provided bases for US bombing raids over Germany. About 200,000 US personnel served in East Anglia.

The Combined Bomber Offensive in World War Two resulted from the RAF nocturnal onslaught and the American unescorted precision attacks on targets throughout the Reich until the P-51 Mustang escort fighters enabled the 8th to assume the mantle of the leading bombing partner in theatre. February and March 1945 saw the most intense bombing destruction when Nazi defences were minimal or absent and the war was all but over.

Final victory in May 1945 came at a high price indeed. Half of the U.S. Army Air Forces' casualties in World War II were suffered by 8th Air Force, with in excess of 47,000 casualties, with more than 26,000 dead. RAF Bomber Command lost 55,573 men killed out of a total of 125,000 aircrew and 8,403 wounded in action while 9,838 became Kriegsgefangenen, or prisoners of war. RAF and American bomber crews could therefore be forgiven for thinking they had won a pyrrhic victory; one that had taken such a heavy toll that negated any true sense of achievement, though, if nothing else, the human effort spent by RAF Bomber Command and the 8th Air Force did pave the way for the Soviet victory in the east.

Chapter One

In At The Kill

As a lad, living about 3 miles from Grafton Underwood in Northamptonshire my first recollections of the 8th Air Force was cycling a few miles to Deenethorpe airfield to watch the return of the 401st Bomb Group B-17s from their missions, sometimes noting the damaged planes as they came in to land and observing that when two red flares were fired from an aircraft it signified that there were wounded aboard or perhaps something even worse! Ambulances racing to a plane as soon as it turned off the runway, to attend those injured. In 1944 all the local children (me included) were transported to the base by US trucks for a Christmas party. Bananas, ice cream, oranges and turkey were all on the menu. Quite a treat for us kids. We were each given a small toy made by the GIs to bring home. How could I ever forget generous Yanks?

When the wind was in a certain direction I could hear the B-17s' engines being run up prior to a mission; then quiet for a short time. Then engines revved again, followed by the sound of brakes being applied as they began to taxi to the runway; engines roared again about every thirty seconds as they took off. Watching the B-17s forming up prior to missions was a most spectacular sight to see and hear. Planes from several airfields began the climb out and into formation before setting off. Even my headmaster allowed us to watch this event even at 0900 hours when we should have been in school, commenting that this was "something you will never see again." Sadly, there were a few crashed that occurred near home. Some were takeoff crashes and some, mid-air collisions with many fatalities among the crews. I visited a few of the crashes and it was a very sad sight to see. I always thought that it was some mother's son who had died so far from home.

Paul Knight, Northamptonshire schoolboy.

One Saturday evening in sleepy Suffolk in September 1942 there was excitement and high tempo in 'The Dog' public house in Grundisburgh (if you lived there long enough you called it 'Grunsbra'), a compact village of brick cottages, with a church and a general store-post office all surrounding a triangular green, through which flowed the brook. By 8 o'clock there was standing room only as farm workers in their rough clothes and elderly couples began to arrive. By 9 o'clock the dark, narrow hall between the front room with the dart board, the 'saloon bar' and the back room with the piano was full too and the old pub rocked with a carnival spirit and excited conversation as the old gaffers and their evil-smelling pipes filled the air with blue smoke and the smell of burning seaweed. The 'Yanks' had arrived!' As one local put it, 'We were going to have a great new bomber aerodrome and thousands of American soldiers and airmen! And bombers flying right over Berlin to pay those Jerries back! Surely the tide of war was turning today!'

During the war years, 1942-1945 the United States 8th Air Force stationed its bomber and fighter bases in Eastern England and the villagers and townsfolk shared a close attachment that only wartime can create. England then was a battlefront. All the civilians were involved in the war effort: as shipyard and factory workers, Red Cross and Land Army volunteers, farmers and firemen. Above all they were determined fighters who had already endured more than three years of war. Into their lives came the sights and sounds – particularly the jargon – of the men from Idaho, New York, California and the rest, as they went on flak leave, R&R, and pubbing missions. The impressions they made were profound.

Construction of a bomber airfield at Debach (pronounced Deb-itch) for the 8th Air Force had begun in September 1942 by a white construction battalion. On 9 May 1943 when the 'drome was only 26% complete, the work was taken over by the black troops of the 820th Engineer Aviation Battalion. This caused something of a culture shock in the surrounding areas. However, they were very soon accepted by the locals. The days began early and by 2100 hours the men were tired. By that hour the lights were often out, though they were allowed to have them on until 2230 hours. At 11 o'clock the air-raid siren would sound. They all stayed in bed, listening to the moan of the sirens and then to the hum of the Luftwaffe overhead and then to the crump-crump of the ack-ack and the shuddering boom of the bombs. If the raid sounded near, one of the GIs went to the door to give a play-by-play description to the others. Not always was the sound of engines German. On winter nights when the lights had been turned off and they lay in their beds, the distant hum of four-engined bombers could be heard on high, far away, hanging in the sightless sky, moving eastward towards Germany. The sound would grow and then fade and then grow again and pass overhead, with a lingering insistence and then gradually fall silent. Before disappearing, another would come and then two and three at the same time, in different corners of the sky. Men would lie awake and try to count them from the sound and say, 'RAF is out again. RAF is out tonight and it sounds like a big one.'

The sound of the passing bombers would continue for perhaps an hour as the unseen hundreds throbbed slowly eastward and the Americans would be asleep before it ended. Perhaps three, four or five hours later, if they awakened they would hear the bombers returning, lower and louder; often limping home just above the tree-tops with an engine missing or the rough sound of planes in trouble. Not fully awake, they would be aware of the roar of the engines. They would hear the other men stir and think to themselves 'Well, there's one who got back... The fire's gone out... It's raining again...' And then they would sleep.'

In 1943 when Peter H. W. Kamin was just 10½ years old and his brothers were aged 15, 7 and 5 and his sister was two months old, they lived in a house that had rooms in the cellar in the suburb of Neue Mühle, about three kilometres from the town of Königs Wusterhausen, south east of Berlin. One of these rooms was reinforced with thick planks across the ceiling, supported by thick wooden props. Their father was Bürgermeister of their town and also the administrative Bürgermeister of Senftenberg/Niederlausitz in the brown coal district. He came home only at weekends and sometimes could not come for official reasons. Peter and his 15-year-old brother Klaus went to the Friedrich Wilhelm Grammar School and at the end of the year Peter was sent to a school in Dingelstedt in Thuringia. 'It was run on military lines. We were often woken up during the night and made to march in all kinds of weather. There was a railway embankment not far from the little town. We always marched there and were forced to run up and down it many times. At the start we enjoyed it, but I remember that some of my fellow classmates couldn't manage it. Suddenly they disappeared and we were told that they were only weak mummy's boys and were of no use to the school. They should have been sent home. I remained there exempt from air raid sirens until shortly before Christmas 1944 and never returned because the Americans were advancing. Older pupils were often discharged to the front or for building fortifications.

'When I returned home my father had been called up into the armed forces as a wireless operator in Sudetenland. My brother Klaus was also not at home. He was serving as a gunner with an anti-aircraft detachment in the west, helping to defend the 'Fatherland'. My mother was now on her own at home with us four children and the conscripted home help girl Hedwig. My grandfather Karl Kamin visited us often; he looked after the large garden, planted vegetables and kept the house in good order. Grandpa had taken over the role of my father, who I didn't see again until 1952.

'I carried on again at the Friedrich Wilhelm Grammar School in Königs Wusterhausen. Most of the original teachers were now in the armed forces. We now had teachers who had been recalled from retirement. Some of them were very old and also sometimes very strict and thorough. Today I realise that I learned a lot from them, even if it was sometimes not so easy. This school was on the bombers` return flight path after dropping their bombs on Berlin. Many of the schoolgirls and schoolboys came to school from outlying districts and came either on bicycles or by train. Because the school's air raid shelters couldn't accommodate all the pupils, any pupils who lived in the town or nearby suburbs had to run or cycle home as soon as the warning sirens started. This meant that the American planes were often flying over us before we reached home. I actually felt exhilarated and excited by this, as overhead the aerial combat raged between the bombers and the German fighter planes or flak. Sometimes after an attack, long silver strips that looked like tinsel lay scattered all around. They were probably used to disrupt radio communications. Propaganda leaflets were also often dropped. My parents and teachers had often said that it was strictly forbidden to pick them up or read them. Draconian punishments awaited anyone who did.

'If the bombers came late in the morning we didn't need to return to school because of the long distance involved. The other pupils who had stayed in the school air raid shelters, or who lived nearby carried on at school. This always made us very happy, to have finished school early.

'The air raids had become more violent and took place many times, both during the day and at night. Sometimes we fell asleep at school due to exhaustion or had to be shaken awake in the morning. In the air raid shelters we were not allowed to lie down only to sit. According to my mother this was because if one was lying down, one would be trapped at once. Less of a target area was presented if one was sitting. I often thought during that time how marvellous it would be if I could only lie down and sleep, sleep, sleep. We were no longer alone in our shelter. Two families with children, from our neighbourhood but without shelters of their own had joined us. Sometimes the little children and babies cried. My mother often held us tightly, but never cried, I never felt afraid, because a German boy didn't feel fear, also I wanted to eventually become a brave soldier and win the 'Knights Cross'.

'The RAF bombers attacked at night and the American bombers came during the day. Very high at the start and one could see only vapour trails. At the end of the war they flew much lower and I could recognise their national emblems the white stars. I remember a Focke Wulf 190 fighter-bomber climbing steeply to attack a US bomber squadron and it shot up an engine on one of the bombers forcing it to jettison it`s bombs. I saw the bombs glinting silver in the sun and I heard bangs. The bomber had dropped its bombs on the neighbouring district of Zernsdorf. I and my friends rode over on our bikes and we saw bomb craters and damaged houses. A pipe was sticking up out of a bomb crater and spurted flame; it was probably a gas pipe. I can`t remember if any people were killed or injured. At the time I was very proud of the German pilot, who was a hero in my eyes. I wanted to be like him some day.

'There was a prisoner of war camp for RAF officers in Zernsdorf. Some of them probably came from Australia or Canada. At the time I had no idea just how large the British Empire was. As boys we often roamed through this area and we were very interested in this camp. I remember that the German guards didn't mind us going close up to the fence. The prisoners called out 'hello boys' and asked after our names. I thought our enemies were very likeable. In any case they always appeared well groomed and ran around with towels and kept themselves clean and well shaven. I also remember that some of them wore scarves and looked very elegant. Some of them carried sticks, I never knew why or for what purpose. I also saw a British officer offer one of the guards a cigarette. It made me wonder why these nice men had dropped bombs on us in order to kill us.'

To Berlin the appearance of American planes for the first time was a sharp warning that it was possible for the daylight raiders of the fast growing US air forces in Britain to carry into the daylight hours the heavy pounding which the RAF was giving the capital at night. Air Marshal Sir Arthur Harris was of one mind in this respect. 'When precision targets are bombed by the 8th Air Force in daylight the effort should be completed and complimented by RAF attacks against the surrounding industrial area at night' he said. 'This gave me a very wide range of choice and allowed me to attack pretty well any German industrial city of 100,000 inhabitants and above.'

On 4 January 1944, B-17s of the 8th Air Force flew their last mission under the auspices of VIII Bomber Command. On 6 January both the 8th and 15th Air Force in Italy were placed under a unified headquarters called 'US Strategic Air Forces, Europe' (USSTAF – the overall USAAF command organization in Europe) at Bushey Hall, Teddington, Middlesex. General Carl 'Tooey' Spaatz returned to England to command the new organization, while Lieutenant General James H. Doolittle took command of the 8th Air Force from Lieutenant General Ira C. Eaker, who moved to the Mediterranean theatre to take command of the new MAAF (Mediterranean Allied Air Forces). Spaatz and Doolittle's plan was to use the US Strategic Air Forces in a series of co-ordinated raids, codenamed Operation 'Argument' and supported by RAF night bombing, on the German aircraft industry at the earliest possible date. However, the winter weather cause a series of postponements, and the bombers were despatched to VI rocket sites in northern France.

Good weather was predicted for the week 20-25 February and so Operation 'Argument' – which quickly became known as 'Big Week' – began in earnest. The opening shots were fired by the RAF which bombed Leipzig on the night of Saturday, 19/Sunday, 20 February. Next morning the 8th put up 1,003 B-17s and B-24s and 835 fighters, while the RAF provided 16 squadrons of Mustangs and Spitfires. In all, 12 aircraft plants were attacked on 20 February, with the B-17s of the 1st Division going to Leipzig, Bernburg and Oschersleben, while the unescorted 3rd Division bombed the Focke Wulf 190 plant at Tutow and the Heinkel 111 plant at Rostock and 272 B-24s in the 2nd Bomb Division were assigned aviation targets at Brunswick. At Deenethorpe Colonel Harold W. Bowman the 401st Bomb Group CO led his Group, which led the 94th Wing, which led the 1st Air Division, which led the 8th Air Force. "So we like to think that I led the 8th Air Force in the biggest mission of the war up to that time" Bowman has written. "In fact, this stretches it a bit. Each Division had its leader, and each subordinate unit had a specific aiming point assigned. I led the stream and had authority to turn the 1st Division around if advisable. This was done only when weather made penetration impossible, which seldom happened, once the formation was airborne. The only time I ever ordered a turnaround was once when units ahead of us in the stream created so much con-trail formation that a solid bank of clouds ahead of us made it impossible to continue.[1]

"Our target was the Erla Maschinenwerk aircraft production factories at Leipzig. Because the weather was uncertain, we were provided with a PFF crew, especially trained for instrument bombing. Weather en-route to the target was indeed bad and preparations were made for aiming by instrument means. However, as we approached the target area, the clouds opened up to "scattered" and a visual sighting was made. The result was, for our Group, 100% of our bombs within 1,000 ft of the aiming point (the means of scoring accuracy)."[2]

Losses were light – the 8th was missing 15 bombers and four fighters – and the raids caused widespread damage. Their impact caused Albert Speer the German minister for armaments to order the immediate dispersal of the German aircraft industry to safer parts of the Reich while in the higher echelons of the 8th Air Force the results were of course welcomed. "When Major General Robert Williams, 1st Division Commander, called his subordinate commanders to his headquarters for a critique – the usual custom in order to air mistakes and complaints, etc, there were the usual gripes and suggestions for improvement" recalled Colonel Harold Bowman. "When my turn came, I reported, "Nothing unusual to report, sir. The mission was run as briefed". He replied, "No, nothing unusual, except that it was the most successful mission ever run by the 8th Air Force". "Whereupon Williams descended from the platform and he pinned on Bowman the Silver Star for his "gallantry, tenacity of purpose, and brilliant leadership on that date while leading a heavy bombardment division of Flying Fortresses which dealt a "crushing blow to the enemy's war effort".[3]

"Lest my boasting get out of hand, let me confess a failure (on 24 February). Our target was Dijon, France. Due to weather combined with navigation problems, we failed to locate the target, so were forced to find and bomb a "target of opportunity", per SOP. (I was leading the mission). Nothing seemed suitable until we approached the coast, when we spotted the airfield at Caen, loaded with German planes. We bombed it with excellent results. How were we to know the super-secret fact that the strategists were carefully avoiding the assignment of targets in that area, in hopes that the enemy would conclude that we were saving it for the D-Day landing? I guess no harm was done, since it was later determined that the enemy was, indeed foiled, in spite of my ignorance."[4]

On Monday, 21 February, 861 B-17s and B-24s and 679 fighters set out for the two M.I.A.G aircraft factories at Brunswick and other targets. H2X blind-bombing equipment was used at Brunswick when heavy cloud prevented visual bombing, and some groups bombed targets of opportunity. Sixteen bombers and five fighters were shot down, but the B-17 and B-24 gunners claimed 19 German fighters shot down. One of the four bomber losses in the 91st Bomb Group was *Lightning Strikes*, piloted by 27-year-old 1st Lieutenant William F. Gibbons, of Tuchahoe, New York, which was shot down by fighters just after the

IP (Initial Point of the bomb run). "We were doing exceptionally well, a good formation, a tight high box as we came to the target area" recalled Tech Sergeant John R. Parsons the engineer-top turret gunner. "Since we were all a little bit to the south and to the east of the target, we were instructed to make a 180 and then drop. It sounded like a good idea, and it was, except the lead navigator, who was somewhat of a cowboy, turned too short, and of course it completely scattered the formation. We were in flak like mad – a helluva lot of flak – we were hanging out to dry, so to speak; there were nine airplanes behind ours and I saw two of them blow up right off. I looked at the damnedest mess of fighters you ever saw – they swarmed in like bees. Of course, there were a lot of them shot down, but we were in a position where we had to fight for our lives.

"They would come in close and one would be attacking the rear, and another would be attacking the right or left side. Most of them came in from the left and, oh God, we had a Focke Wulf 190 come in right over the tail gunner, Paul M. Gorcke. I told Paul to fight for his life. Everybody was shooting everything they had, and this guy comes in and I think he was the one that really hurt us – a 20mm explosion in the No.3 engine blew the whole cowling off, and three of the jugs in the engine were blown out; you could look down and see the guts just flying around in the engine: Of course you couldn't feather the darn thing, and when they all started going, it didn't help us at all. Also we had one helluva big hole in the No.3 reserve tank, and burning gas was coming on board. The attacks kept coming.

"I saw tracers fly through the airplane, and I don't know how or why they didn't kill anybody, but they didn't. I got down out of the top turret because the plane was going to go. Paul rang the 'bail-out' bell, and I felt air come up through the bottom so I knew that the bombardier and navigator were already out. I grabbed Clyde McCallum, co-pilot, and said, 'Mac – go!' We all went out of that airplane at about 20,000 ft."

The mission by the 385th Bomb Group to bomb the airfield at Diepholz in North West Germany cost the Great Ashfield outfit two B-17s and a PFF crew on *Crazy Horse*, a 482nd Pathfinder ship under command pilot, Captain Gerald D. Binks the 550th Squadron Operations Officer. *Crazy Horse* fell out of formation after bombing the target when two engines gave trouble and he was unable to feather the props and it was later attacked by FW190 over Zwolle forcing Binks to ditch in the Ijsselmeer, 9 kilometres SW of Harderwijk. Two of the extra navigators and the waist gunner evaded capture but Binks could evade only until captured near Liege, Belgium on 27 May. The body of 1st Lieutenant Ralph W. Holcombe the pilot was washed ashore on 4 May. On the return, *Sleepytime Gal II* piloted by 24-year-old Captain John Neal 'Hutch' Hutchison Jr. from Avon, Washington County, Mississippi, who was on his 25th mission, the completion of his tour, was involved in a mid air collision over the Reedham marshes near Great Yarmouth with the B-17 piloted by 21-year old 1st Lieutenant Warren Jay Pease who apparently lost control in cloud. Both crews were killed. Pease, born on 19 March 1922 at Juniata, Adams County, Nebraska grew up on a farm outside of Farragut in Freemont County, Iowa and graduated from Farragut high school in 1939. He left a widow, Maria Kraschel who he had married in 1943. He had been on 11 missions over Germany.

On Tuesday, 22 February, 101 heavies bombed aircraft production centres at Bernberg, Halberstadt and Oschersleben in conjunction with a 15th Air Force raid on Regensburg. The majority of the 8th's bomb groups were forced to abort because of bad weather over England, and 35 bombers were shot down. Next day, bad weather kept the 8th Air Force heavies on the ground. On 24 February Doolittle despatched 266 B-17s of the 1st Bomb Division to ball bearing factories at Schweinfurt. Eleven B-17s were lost on the attacks on the Vereinigte Kugellagerfabriken AG's VKF-Werk I factory in the centre of the city, the VKF-Werk II factory south of the main rail yard and the Kugelfischer-Georg-Schäfer industrial complex north of it. Only five Forts were lost from just over 300 B-17s of the 3rd Bomb Division that were despatched to bomb targets on the Baltic coast but attacks on targets at Gotha and Eisenach by 239 B-24s of the 2nd Bomb Division saw 33 Liberators fail to return. On the 25th very considerable damage was caused to the Bf 109 plants at Regensburg-Prufening by 290 B-17s of the 3rd Bomb Division, which arrived over the target an hour after the 15th Air Force (who suffered high losses) and met only token fighter opposition. The Messerschmitt experimental and assembly plants at Augsburg were bombed by 268 B-17s of the 1st Division and aviation plants at Fürth and the VFK ball-bearing plants at Stuttgart were hit by almost 200 Liberators. In just one week of sustained operations RAF Bomber Command and the USAAF dropped 19,000 tons of bombs on the Reich. Generals' Spaatz and Doolittle believed that the USSTAF had dealt the German aircraft industry a resounding blow but losses were high with 224 American and 157 British bombers failing to return in just one week of sustained operations.

Another tough nut that the 8th was hoping to crack was 'Big B'. A raid by the 8th Air Force on Berlin had been scheduled for 23 November the previous year but had been postponed because of bad weather. RAF Bomber Command had been bombing the capital nightly for some time but Berliners had never before been subjected to the round-the-clock bombing which had devastated so many other German cities. 'Round-the-clock? Well you can imagine' said Ray Wild, a B-17 pilot in the 92nd Bomb Group at Podington in Bedfordshire known as 'Fame's Favourite Few'. 'Say you lived in Berlin and you were bombed all night long. Then, the next morning, you were bombed again and the next afternoon. The next night, you were bombed again. You lived in an air-raid shelter. Boy, after a while, this would wear you down.'

When Ray Wild had arrived in England one of his first actions was to look up an RAF pilot who had been a classmate during training in the States. 'He and I went out' said Wild, 'and had a couple of beers with some of his buddies. They felt that we Americans were out of our minds. They had tried daylight bombing and it just wasn't feasible. They said we'd get the hell shot out of us. They were right: on the first few raids we did get the hell shot out of us. But those limeys did something that sure would scare me – night bombing. They'd come in over a target a minute apart, one guy this way, another guy from another point in the compass. This would scare me to death. They had tremendous intestinal fortitude. They were also realistic in that they couldn't bomb by daylight. Those Lancs were built to carry bombs and not to protect themselves, while we could. So long as we stayed in tight formation, we could throw a lot of lead out in the right direction at the right time.'

It was on Wednesday, 1 March 1944 that the *New York Times* proclaimed that 'The long-predicted 'round-the-clock' bombing of Germany is at last apparently under way. Bad weather may from time to time set the clock back. But Allied air superiority is now so great that henceforth we may expect a fairly regular schedule of American raids by day and British raids by night."

'The very thought of making a raid on Berlin was almost terrifying', recalled Captain Robert J. Shoens, pilot of *Our Gal' Sal'* in the 351st Bomb Squadron, 100th Bomb Group at Thorpe Abbotts in Norfolk. Born in Detroit, Michigan, Shoens' father served in the Navy during World War I and his mother volunteered on the World War II draft board. His love for aviation began when, as a young schoolboy, he saw the 'Dare Devils' perform. In 1941, during his second year of junior college, he decided that he wanted to serve and become a pilot, considering it his patriotic duty. Denied by the Navy recruiter, he walked down the hall to the Army Air Corps recruiter's office and enlisted as a private in the United States Army. At the age of 20, Shoens began training, after which he received his commission. He married upon completion of Flight School in Roswell, New Mexico in May 1943. 'Rumours began flying thick and fast several weeks before the day of the Berlin mission arrived, adding to the apprehension and anxiety. Each day we would walk into the briefing sessions wondering if the tape on the wall map would stretch to 'Big-B' that morning. A great sigh of relief could be heard from the crews when the briefing officer pulled back the curtain and the tape went somewhere else.'

At Snetterton Heath it had taken Staff Sergeant Ernest J. Richardson, the radio operator in 2nd Lieutenant Sherman Gillespie's crew in the 96th Bomb Group a little time 'getting lined up with his crew because they were all doing their own thing. "But eventually our crew started to come together" recalled Richardson, who was born in Long Beach, California on 17 November 1922. 'There wasn't any mention of Berlin but I think we were all aware that this one particular raid would come up.

"Finally, at the Friday, 3 March briefing we were informed: 'This morning, gentlemen your target is Berlin!' Some crews stomped their feet in protest, others just groaned and there was lots of swearing. 'No! Let the RAF take care of it, they're doing OK. It's better to bomb it at night.' They'll scrub it.' The S-2 [Intelligence] officer tried to seem nonchalant; he had to know everyone hated the thought of going there. No one laughed at his jokes that morning. There was plenty of tension in the air. After briefing it seemed to me there were longer lines in front of the religious personnel than usual but it may have been my imagination.'

At Flixton on the Norfolk-Suffolk border crews in the 446th 'Bungay Buckaroos' Bomb Group were awakened at 0400 hours and caught the 6 × 6 tarp-covered-trucks to the mess hall. After chow they went to the combat crew locker room to get into their flying gear. Briefing was scheduled for 0600 hours. When the curtain was pulled back the ribbon reached all the way to Berlin. There were gasps, low whistles, moans and groans as the crews realized where they were going. It was snowing, but the weather officer said that the weather would be better over the Continent. The target was the Heinkel Flugzeugwerke at Germandorf, 16 miles northeast of Berlin where Heinkel 177s were being built. The Friedrichstrasse station in Berlin proper was to be the secondary target. All Divisions of the 8th Air Force were to hit targets in the capital and its suburbs. It meant flying more than 1,000 miles. Twenty-six Liberators loaded with M-47s would be dispatched from Flixton.

The crew of *Hula Wahina II* in the 'Buckaroos' piloted by 22-year-old Second Lieutenant Ernest Warren Bruce from Utah was slated to lead a three-plane element flying to the left and below the Group lead plane. The first *Hula Wahina* had lost all four superchargers on the Frankfurt mission on 29 January and ran out of cloud cover over Belgium, fighting off repeated enemy fighter attacks while flying 75 ft, Bruce performed a wheels-up landing at RAF Detling with two wounded crewmen aboard and *Hula Wahina* had to be written off. In March 1944 when a new B-24 was delivered to Lowry Field for the flight to England it was assigned to John T. Goss, a 19-year-old first pilot and a native of Honolulu who had decided to join the Air Corps after Pearl Harbor was bombed on 7 December 1941. Goss had crew chief John Minturn find an artist to paint a Polynesian hula wahine below the cockpit. "It was kinda reminder of home" and it was in the perfect position for him to stroke her okole ('butt') while taxiing out to take-off.

At Seething about 9½ miles southeast of Norwich, the Liberator crews were briefed at 0500 for Berlin. A newspaperman when war began, Lieutenant Wallace Patterson, bombardier on 23-year-old Lieutenant Albert B. Sanders' crew in the 448th Bomb Group, was having trouble writing up his diary. His fingers were sore from the freezing cold temperatures he had endured at altitude. Without oxygen, a man would be unconscious in thirty seconds. After two minutes he'd be dead. 'It was to be the first time the AAF had ever hit the 'Jerry' capital' said Patterson, painfully (a raid on Berlin had been scheduled for 23 November 1943 but had been postponed because of bad weather) 'and a feather in the cap of everyone to participate. We were scared to death but anxious to go to Berlin. The city was ringed with anti-aircraft guns that could fire high explosive shells to a height of 45,000 ft, much higher than the ceiling of Libs and Forts. Flak towers over 120 ft high and six levels underground could fire a salvo of eight shells that would explode simultaneously covering an area of 260 yards across. They could do it every 90 seconds. Any bomber caught in that pattern was kaput.

'The target actually was Oranienburg, a heavy bomber factory and airfield 14 miles from the centre of Berlin. The route over put us in Germany near Hamburg after a long over water hop and return was routed entirely over land, which was German-held. Fighter support would leave us at the German coast and pick us up again over two hours later, leaving us unsupported over the most hotly defended sectors of the Reich.'

At every base whistles and groans greeted the news as briefing officers pulled back the curtains to reveal the red tapes reaching like groping fingers all the way to 'Big-B'. The three Divisions were dispatching 748 bombers and they would be escorted by 730 fighters in the 8th and 9th Air Forces. The primaries were industrial areas and aviation industry plants at Berlin and Oranienburg and the Vereinigte Kugellager Fabriken ball bearing plant at Erkner, in the Oder-Spree District of Brandenburg on the south-eastern edge of 'Big B'. VKF was a subsidiary of the Swedish company SKF or Svenska Kullagerfabriken AB. Sweden was Germany's largest trading partner and OSS (Office of Strategic Services) agents had infiltrated the SKF plant in Göteborg and were monitoring shipments to Germany. Ball bearings reduced friction and wear in the machinery that was being produced at breakneck speed and were critical to the manufacture of aircraft, vehicles, tanks, guns and submarine engines. Ball bearings were also being manufactured at the factories of the Norddeutsche Kugellager Fabrik at Lichtenberg.

'What a birthday treat,' thought 2nd Lieutenant 'Cliff' C. Hatcher, co-pilot in the crew in the 94th Bomb Group captained by Lieutenant John E. Pyles as they sat through the briefing for 31 crews at Rougham on the outskirts of Bury St. Edmunds. Only the day before Cliff had celebrated his 21st birthday. When the target was announced there were gasps from 360 throats.

Notes

1. Harold Webb Bowman was born in Waverly, Nebraska on 12 February 1903. He graduated from the University of California in 1928 with a reserve commission from Air ROTC. In June of that year he was appointed an Air Corps flying cadet, and after graduating from primary and advanced flying schools, he was rated a pilot. He received his regular commission as a second lieutenant of the Air Corps on 4 September 1929. In June 1943 he was ordered to Geiger Field, Washington to take command of the 401st Bomb Group shortly after its activation, and six months later he took the group overseas to become a unit of the 1st Bombardment Division of the Eighth Air Force.
2. Correspondence between the author and Brigadier General Harold Bowman, 8 November 1979.
3. Ibid. "The 401st Bomb Group (Heavy) was cited in the name of the president of the United States for extraordinary heroism, determination, and esprit de corps in action against the enemy."
4. Ibid. Harold Bowman died on 23 October 1994.

Chapter Two

The Tour

Another 11 hour flight and the return to base made in late afternoon haze. I think we landed with only fumes in the fuel tank. All of us are dragging our ass at this point.

Staff Sergeant Larry 'Goldie' Goldstein, radio operator, 1st Lieutenant Belford Jan Keirsted's crew, 388th Bomb Group, diary entry, Thursday, 24 February 1944.

On Saturday, 19 February, 27-year old 1st Lieutenant Belford Jan Keirsted of Pittsburgh, Pennsylvania and the members of his B-17 crew at Knettishall had been able to relax after a hectic two day pass. Almost a year earlier over a period of about three and a half months, he and his crew, each from different parts of the USA and with different likes and personalities, had, with each flight at Moses Lake Army Air Base in Washington State and at Geiger Field, Spokane and Pendleton, Oregon, formed a mutual respect for one another while finding the time to enjoy each other's company that it was as if they had known each other for many years. Until the operational removal later of the ball turret there were ten members on a crew. Now there were nine. Staff Sergeant Edward W. Kozacek the 32-year-old engineer/top turret gunner was born in Horseheads, New York and was residing in Coeymans Hollow in Albany County when he enlisted. Staff Sergeant E. V. 'Pete' Lewelling (22) was born in Zolfo Springs, Florida and had enlisted at Starke while domiciled in Hardee County in October 1942. He and Tech Sergeant Jack C. Kings who was from Virginia were paired as the two waist gunners on the crew and Robert Miller of Chicago, Illinois was the tail gunner. Tech Sergeant Lawrence Goldstein, the 22-year-old radio operator, was a former trainee draughtsman with the US Coast and Geodetic Survey. On 7 December 1941 'Goldie' was lying on his bed at home in Brooklyn listening to a radio broadcast of a football game when the broadcast was interrupted by a news flash that the Japanese had bombed Pearl Harbor. Within two weeks 'Goldie's draft number was called and in 1942 he enlisted at Fayette County, Pennsylvania. Just before entering the Army, 'Goldie' had met Rose Mandel, his first real serious romance, and the girl that he wanted to marry when his service was over. 'While we trained in the US we were impressed by our importance as combat crew members' he wrote 'and wore the silver wings as a crew member. My first view of the B-17 Flying Fortress was awesome. My first thought, can this mighty looking plane fly? As I sat in the radio operator's position for the first time I wondered if I could manage this position; could my fellow crewmembers count on me? Then again, did each of my crew have the same thoughts about their position?

After training ended and Keirsted's crew and 29 others were alerted for a move to "some place" overseas. When, on a typically English rainy, dark and cold November night, Keirsted's crew finally arrived at their quarters at Knettishall (Coney Weston) in Suffolk to join the 388th Bomb Group they found that they were to share their Quonset hut in the 563rd Squadron area with five other crews of enlisted men. But on arrival there were just six men lying around on their bunks. The men were gunners on *Pegasus*. The other thirty beds were vacant with their mattresses rolled up. When Goldstein asked 'why the empty beds?' one of the gunners said: "They all went down a few days ago". "The next sound was our egos crashing to the floor. We suddenly realized that we were in a combat zone. Flying a combat mission was serious business. We thought that we had trained for this but reality took over and every man wondered how he would handle this. We unpacked our bags and each of us suddenly began to think of what combat flying might be like."

In another hut in the 563rd Squadron area on the base slept Keirsted and the three 2nd lieutenants on his crew. Clifford E. 'Ace' Conklin the 23-year-old co-pilot was from New Paltz, in Ulster County about 80 miles north of New York City. With leadership from 'BJ' and 'Ace' the crew worked well together and there was always time for some good natured banter. Phillip Brejansky the 24-year-old navigator, who was born in Brooklyn, had once got the crew lost during a cross country training exercise in the States and Kent J. 'Cap' Keith the 22-year-old bombardier, the third of four children, from Ekalaka, Montana, never let him forget it. The joke was that there was a dog on Kent Keith's father's 50,000 acre ranch that could find his way home better than Brejansky, who always thereafter was known as 'Bloodhound'! 'Keith had a quick wit" recalled 'Goldie' Goldstein. "In the intense blackout in London on pass he met a 'Piccadilly Commando'.

'How much honey?' he asked.

'Four pounds' (about $24 dollars American) was the reply.

'I only want to borrow it' the cowboy said; 'I don't want to buy it!"

On 14 January 1944 Keirsted's crew had flown ten missions and two aborts. All except two round trips had been in a B-17 that had come off the Douglas production lines in April 1943 and one they intended naming 'The Worry Wart'; but they never got around to it before the battle-weary 'F' model[1] was transferred to the RAF on 21 January.[2] "In 1943 a combat tour was 25 missions" wrote Goldstein.[3] "To finish 25 would be a miracle but at the start of our tour 'BJ' had said: 'We will make it; you can mark it down. Keirsted was a strong, quiet man from Uniontown, Pennsylvania, a tough coal town and he had a 'dark, brooding look about him. He and his sister Dorothy had toured the country before the war as the ballroom dance team of 'Jan and Janis" – hardly the credentials to lead a combat crew but his promise that they would complete their tour still held true. The crew's next nine missions, 21 January to 10 February 1944 were flown in B-17Fs and Gs. They included *Dry Run* aka *Screamin' Red Ass*; *Patty Jo*; *Cock o' the Walk* and *Pegasus Too*. The latter was a replacement for *Pegasus* (which in mythology Bellerophon had been allowed to ride in order to defeat the monstrous Chimera but had fallen from the back of the winged horse while trying to reach Mount Olympus). Attacked by fighters on the Brunswick mission on 23 March, the beast's namesake and 2nd Lieutenant Donald B. Filler's crew had fallen too. Filler, who was from Oklahoma and four crew were killed; five men being taken prisoner.

Up to and including 10 February Keirsted's crew had taken their mission tally to nineteen. After a lull of nine days missions would come thick and fast. When, on Saturday the 19th the skies began clearing slightly and an extensive high pressure area appeared to be moving south-east across Central Germany, the weather situation looked promising enough for the generals to signal the start of an almost continuous offensive against aircraft factories in Germany and 'Big Week' as it became known, was given the green light. At the bases in eastern England just over 730 B-17 and 272 B-24 crews and 835 fighter pilots were placed on the battle order for attacks on primary targets, targets of opportunity and last resort targets throughout the Reich.

Keirsted's crew was awakened very early that Sunday, 20 February; which coincided with their 20th mission of their tour if it went ahead. "OK you guys" the CQ announced; "there is a mission this morning; breakfast at 0400, briefing at 0500. Flying today!" Then he listed the pilot's names. "When our crew heard our pilot's name" said 'Goldie' Goldstein "we tumbled out of bed into a very cold winter morning. Winter in England was brutal. There was never enough heat provided in our living quarters. We slept in our clothes under several blankets. Water never got warm enough for a decent shave, considering that an oxygen mask was so tight to our face that the least bit of stubble would itch and chafe under it. Still dark the GI trucks waited to take us to the mess hall. Breakfast was important because a mission would take many hours to fly and it would be many hours until we would eat again. Then it was back on to the trucks for the short trip to the briefing building for this, our twentieth mission. Five more and we could go home.

"We were briefed that the target was Poznan, Poland. This would be a long flight, mostly over the Baltic Sea. Each crew member left the briefing with an individual task, the co-pilot to pick up escape kits, the navigator for his maps; the bombardier for his bomb load, me as radio operator for the codes of the day. The rest of the crew assembled in a locker room. It was here that we all came to dress for the flight. Over our winter underwear we donned the blue electrical heated suit, our heavy fleece outer wear. We carried our flight helmet, oxygen mask and our heavy gloves and then checked out a parachute along with our life vest and parachute harness. The GI trucks were waiting to carry us out to our assigned airplane. The cold dark winter morning was very evident. Even though we were dressed warmly we were never warm; were we nervous about this first flight? At various areas around the airfield the B-17s were parked waiting for their crews. At 6:45 we boarded *Cock o' The Walk* loaded with 5,000 lbs of bombs, maximum fuel load and thousands of rounds of ammunition. In the dark of the winter morning the B-17 looked ready to fly. The question remained; were we ready to fly?"

Cloud would have prevented bombing at the 3rd Division targets so they were switched to Rostock and other targets of opportunity. 'There wasn't much flak and very little enemy fighters" said 'Goldie' Goldstein. Eight B-24s were lost on the mission to Brunswick and thirteen B-17s in the 1st and 3rd Bomb Divisions also failed to return. A total of 198 bombers in all three Divisions bombers returned badly damaged and five aircraft declared Category 'E' (beyond economical repair) were written off. Two of the losses were from the 388th Bomb Group but Keirsted's crew was not among them. 'The worst part of this mission was the flight time of 11 hours" said 'Goldie' Goldstein. "We landed OK but very exhausted.[4] Most of us passed the mess hall for supper. We dined in the barracks on packages from home. Only twenty missions completed...do we dare to think of more and hope for easy flights?

On Monday morning, 21 February Keirsted's crew was awakened early. After the long mission the day before they were hoping for a short one but the target was Brunswick, one of the toughest in Germany. Just the thought of attacking this place made the crew get uptight but, as Goldstein said, 'the actual mission [in *Heaven Can Wait*] wasn't as bad as expected. The flak was off target the enemy fighters attacked other groups. It was extremely cold and the use of oxygen tired me out. I believed that the Germans were feeling the might of the 8th Air Force. We landed OK after eight hours in the air but again very exhausted.[5] The crew did not talk about 21 missions completed. It was almost like preventing anything happening if we didn't talk about it. Tuesday, 22 February we were up early again; three in a row. All of us were feeling the pressure now. Briefing was delayed for some reason, but we were briefed on Schweinfurt, the worst possible target for a crew with 21 missions. After takeoff and three hours in the air the mission was scrubbed. The weather was our friend; it was awful. It was back to the barracks and thankful for that. Most of us just rested; the last three days had been gruelling and mentally exhausting."

On Wednesday, 23 February Keirsted's crew were called again for an early morning briefing. "Getting up at 0330 hours is not the way to start the day" noted 'Goldie' Goldstein in his diary. "The target was Regensburg but the weather prevailed, and before we even left the briefing room the mission was scrubbed. They keep getting us up for a raid and then have to cancel it because of the weather. Winter weather here is miserable, snow, cold, generally low clouds and rain. It keeps us on the ground. These last few missions are evading us. As a crew we do not dare think about them. I personally have not allowed it to enter my mind. Even before going to sleep, the exhaustion sets in and I fall asleep fast.

"Who can I blame for applying for flying status?" his diary entry on Thursday, February 24 began. "Again we were awakened early for a mission. The target was Poznan, the second time we were briefed on this Polish city. After a very long flight, the bomb group leader could not locate the target because of cloud cover. This after flying many hours, a second target called Rostock, a German sea port was chosen and we bombed through the clouds. The flight home was a long one and 'BJ' and 'Ace' nursed the gas consumption. The enemy action was light. I think they were as confused as we were. Another 11 hour flight and the return to base made in late afternoon haze. I think we landed with only fumes in the fuel tank. All of us are dragging our ass at this point.

"At this point we as a crew figured that the next three missions to bring us to the magic number of 25 would, by the law of averages be simple, light missions. How wrong we were. For the sixth consecutive day we were awakened for our 23rd mission on Friday, February 25. The target was Regensburg Germany. This was a very long flight 12 hours and we had heavy flak and enemy fighter attacks all the way to and from the target. The weather was clear and we bombed with no weather problems. Our fighter protection was great our pilots are not afraid to engage the enemy. The mission was very scary because of the long flight and time on oxygen. CAN THIS BE TRUE, ONLY TWO MORE MISSIONS? Our crew wonders if we can continue at this pace but so far everyone is standing up to the pressure."

On Saturday, 26 February 'BJ' Keirsted's crew were up early again for a mission. A few days earlier they were wondering what were causing the long stretch between missions; now they were flying almost every day. The briefed target was Friedrichshafen, Germany. This looked like a very tough flight but the weather helped them and the mission was scrubbed before they got out to their plane. None of them complained because they all needed a rest and so it was back to barracks and the sack. On Sunday the weather again turned bad and it meant another day of real rest which was enjoyed by all. The extreme cold, being on oxygen for long periods and the general pressure of flying into combat had taken its toll on most of them. They were in bed early and there was not so much conversation. 'Goldie' Goldstein really relaxed, read some and went to a movie and into bed early. Next day crews could spend the day reading, writing letters and looking for incoming mail. That night it was to the movies again. But it was back to the war on Tuesday, 29 February. "The extra day of the year made no difference to our schedule" said Goldstein. "Up early again and the target is Brunswick that awesome target. Our takeoff was OK but soon after *Pegasus Too* had engine trouble and 'BJ' and 'Ace' aborted this flight. Better safe than sorry. The crew had mixed feelings about missing out on our 24th mission. However we never tempt fate and we have always looked up to 'BJ' to make the correct decision. This was our first abortion in 21 straight missions and 'BJ' gets credit for that from the Command people. Wednesday, March 1 was a quiet day for a change. No flying just relaxation time. Weather not good. I used the rest to catch up on reading and mail writing." On the morning of Thursday, March 2 when the 388th was called for mission Keirsted's crew remained on the ground and several of their friends completed their 25th mission. Goldstein was happy for them but got his crew thinking "can we do it?" "It must be a great feeling to have combat behind you" he said. "Today's mission was an easy one, sorry that our crew missed it. Actually there is no easy mission, something can always happen. Early to bed, because we are alerted for a mission tomorrow.

'That Friday, 3 March we were called out to a very early briefing. When we entered the briefing room the chaplains were very visible. This made us uneasy and we thought it must be something big. Our 24th mission, and it looked like it would be a long flight and dangerous. When our crew heard that the target was Berlin – 'Big B' we looked at each other in amazement. As a crew we prepared for this flight in *Pegasus Too* with a heavy heart. What a terrible break for our crew, possibly the worst selection of a target. When the route and the target were explained to us there was not one man in the room who thought he would be sleeping in his own bed that night. As we waited for our chance for takeoff I tuned to Radio Bremen which spoke in English. Here we were waiting to take off for a raid over Germany and Radio Bremen was saying, 'American bombers are on their runways in England now, waiting to attack north-west Germany.' How did they know?"

The B-17s began taking off in marginal weather conditions. 'We finally got into our takeoff position and rolled down the runway' continues 'Goldie' Goldstein. 'Takeoff was at 0730 hours. Soon after forming the group was on its way. We used a tricky route in to the target and were to bomb and get the hell out quickly. The weather was our friend. It turned bad and the mission was finally scrubbed after our target was socked in.'

'I recorded the recall in my log and after many repeats I called to 'BJ' on intercom. One very sharp operator somewhere in the force acknowledged receipt of the recall even though he was not authorised to do so. Then over the VHF system someone in authority ordered a recall. Non acknowledgement of the recall could have been disastrous. We turned about and headed for home. As we were well over enemy territory and flew in and out of heavy flak we received credit for a mission. We brought our bombs back and returned okay despite a bad engine.

'When we landed and pulled into our revetment, a communications officer drove up in a jeep, confiscated my radio log and ordered me to report to a Group Communications meeting immediately. It seemed that the mission lead and deputy lead radio operators never heard or acknowledged the recall. I was on duty, recorded the recall and was not one of those reprimanded.'

In the 96th formation the weather got so bad that crews could hardly see their wing men. 'Or for that matter', recalled Ernie Richardson, 'any ships at all. It's a hell of a feeling flying through clouds that thick, especially when you know there are about 800 planes in the same vicinity. We were all tensed up.

'Let's try and go over it, everyone keep their eyes open.'

'It was Gillespie. It was good hearing someone. We were climbing for about five minutes when we finally broke out into a small clearing. I wished it could have been a couple of minutes later because just as we broke through the clouds, off to our left, two B-17s came together head on. All it left was a big blotch of black smoke in the air; a grim reminder of the event. I didn't say anything about it over the interphone; I didn't want to make anyone any more jumpy than they already were. It was strange; almost everyone else saw it and didn't mention it for the same reason. It came up later after we landed back at our base during interrogation. We climbed to about 30,000 ft and never did make it over the clouds. The mission already had been cancelled. I heard someone say the temperature was 70 degrees below zero. Everyone had their heated suits turned up as far as they would go. I stood with my legs straddled because there seemed to be too many heating wires in the crotch, we almost froze. Finally we went down to just above the water and all my radio equipment turned white with frost. We worried all the way back to England as I'm sure many other crews did that day.'

The real purpose of bombing Berlin, not disclosed to the bomber crews, was in fact the beginning of a strategic effort to draw the Luftwaffe up so that the American fighters might reduce enemy strength in preparation for the coming invasion. 'Intelligence had called early this morning' – a big mission was on – it was the long-awaited show to Berlin" said 29-year-old Lieutenant Colonel Jack S. Jenkins of de Leon, Texas commanding the 55th Fighter Group at Nuthampstead in Hertfordshire. He was destined to pilot the first USAAF combat aircraft to approach Berlin thus far in the war, in P-38J Lightning *Texas Ranger IV.* "We went straight in and were pretty well shot up by flak over Magdeburg, Hanover, etc. We kept calling the bombers but could not contact them. We circled the edges of Berlin for about fifteen minutes waiting for them, but could not see them. The ground was covered with snow and it was very cold around Berlin. It sure looked cold here for people to be running to air-raid shelters. We caught some flak from other cities we passed, but none from the big town and did not get a single fighter scrap coming or going. The toughest part of the trip was the stiff headwind on the way home and the intense cold which seemed to get worse with every mile of the 560-mile trip out and back. I got so cold that my crew chief had to help lift me out of my cockpit. For two hours after I got back I could not even feel my feet with my fingers. I learned later that the bombers had actually turned back at Hamburg and we did not get the word. Therefore we were the only Allied planes to reach Berlin."[6]

Wallace Patterson saw the B-17s returning. 'Heavily loaded for the 1,400-mile trip, we just barely got off the ground and after forming, started across the North Sea. Our formation was very poor and all around, above and below us ships were aborting like mad. Our group practically disappeared and we tacked onto the 93rd for mutual protection. Every ship left long vapour trails, which were visible for miles. At Heligoland, where they started throwing flak at us, we met the B-17s coming out. That was queer because they were supposed to return by land. Then the fighters had to leave us. We could see the smoke rising over the clouds from Hamburg, which was the B-17 target. Luck told us his turret was inoperative, leaving our rear unprotected. I think I was praying in a way and 'Rod' [2nd Lieutenant Rodney E. Webb, navigator] was muttering something about murder. About ten miles in front of us were the contrails of hundreds of 'Jerry' fighters waiting for us. And just then we were recalled. We caught a little more flak on the way home. It is still undecided whether or not we'll get credit for a mission, because we threw no bombs. But we should. We all agree none of us would have come back if we had continued.'

'It was not a CAVU (ceiling and visibility unlimited) day' said Thurman Spiva, a B-24 navigator in the 446th Bomb Group who was from Los Angeles County, California. 'The clouds continued to build higher and higher over northern Germany. The 26-plane formation tried to get above them, but it was a losing battle. You barely saw your wingmen through the thickening clouds. A fully loaded B-24 at high altitude reached a point where you were just 'hanging on by your propellers.' It was not the most stable or the easiest aircraft to fly under such conditions. The day was cold and dry… a stinging, piercing cold. The needle on the outside temperature gauge read minus 50 or 60 degrees Centigrade. Then the recall for the entire 8th Air Force was received. We headed back toward the North Sea. It was a relief to let down where it was a little warmer and have our first cigarette in over four hours. The crews were unhappy about the recall – we were within 150 miles of the target.'

Aboard *Hula Wahine II* radio static interfered with communications so John Goss turned it off. The clouds were getting thicker in front of them. Not wanting to fly under a formation of planes inside a cloud system he climbed above it still flying to the left of the lead element. His wingmen, both new to the Squadron, kept hanging in with him flying nice and tight. Other planes were dropping out of the formation. Then they hit the front. *Hula Wahine II* was bouncing and they could not see the tips of the wings. The Group was gone. The wingmen were gone. With maximum power and a full rich mix and what seemed like an eternity, they popped out of the clouds at 25,000 ft. It was not a recommended altitude for a B-24. 'Lo and behold, there were his two wingmen and puffs of flak. Goss asked Calvin Hanlyn, the navigator, for a heading to Berlin. The first heading was more like the way to Sweden. Quickly corrected, they were on course to Berlin. The three-plane element was quite alone. In the distance they saw fighters with Me 109 profiles. They salvoed their bombs somewhere in Germany – thought it might have been Hannover. Starting to head into the clouds, they saw the planes they thought were 109s were P-51s. They wished they had been more attentive during the aircraft recognition class. Heading for home, they dropped lower and saw the cloud cover disappear as they left the enemy coast. After six hours and being listed as MIA they touched down at Flixton. The ground was covered with snow, runways were clean. Goss taxied the *Hula Wahine* to the hardstand. The disappointed crew felt they had missed enduring fame as the first USAAF crew to bomb Berlin in daylight.[7]

Three Fortresses in the 447th Bomb Group had aborted over England due to mechanical problems. The rest of the formation went on at 26,500 ft toward Denmark. The weather began to thicken. In route the contrails from the B-17s ahead were heavy. All of a sudden the Wing headed west and a tragic accident occurred midway in the stream at Wesermünde where the B-17s tried to climb above the fog and cloud and it was hard trying to stay in formation. Unfortunately, the 3rd Division Groups had not got the recall signal until after the 1st Combat Wing in front and they just did a 180° to return on the same course that they had flown inbound and they flew through the 4th Combat Wing formation. Suddenly, Cliff Hatcher in the 94th Bomb Group looked up and saw what looked like hundreds of B-17s heading straight for them. The B-17 in the 94th Bomb Group piloted by 20-year-old Lieutenant Donald Leo Ahlwardt from Danbury, Woodbury County, Iowa collided head on with a 91st Bomb Group ship with no survivors on either bomber. In the 447th Bomb Group *Paper Doll* piloted by 25-year-old Lieutenant Francis R. Graham and *Morning Star* captained by Lieutenant Donald E. Ralston were hit by debris and became collateral damage as a result. Eight crew on Ralston's aircraft were drowned. All ten crew on Graham's ship were killed. Johnny Pyles' and Cliff Hatcher's B-17 flew right through the middle of a black cloud. 'I could feel the heat from the explosion' Hatcher recalled. 'We bounced all over the sky and I thought we had had it but, incredibly, we survived and began heading back. We were maddened by the wasteful and needless collision.'

Morning Star in the 447th Bomb Group piloted by Lieutenant Donald E. Ralston of Spokane Washington was also damaged and went down in the North Sea. Ralston and seven of his crew were washed away and drowned. Tom McKiernan the 22-year-old co-pilot and Chas Horak the ball turret gunner were picked up. The 94th Bomb Group disrupted into chaos after the recall and aircraft flew home in twos and threes, dropping their bombs en route. Johnny Pyles dropped his bombs on Heligoland. 'Coming back we ran into horrendous weather again" said Cliff Hatcher. "Half way across the North Sea we saw a front ahead of us. We were at 30,000 ft. The temperature was about 60-70 degrees below outside the aircraft so we decided to go over the front. We thought maybe we could find a hole between the thunderheads. We climbed and climbed and we still couldn't see the tops. We thought we'd have to go under it. We got down to about 15 ft off the water but ice built up and we got slower and slower. All our de-icer boots had been taken off the B-17 when we had entered combat because they slowed the aircraft down. It was thought that the chances of icing up were negligible but this was one time they were wrong. We even used some flap to keep her airborne because we were so close to stalling. The only de-icing equipment we had was for the propellers. If we hadn't got that we wouldn't have made it. Eventually, we broke clear and just made it back. It was hell after the mission to have to fly like that. When we got back to Bury we looked the aircraft over and it was covered in burn marks. It was a miracle. How lucky could we get?'[8]

At Knettishall there was no word from *Little Willie* and a new crew led by 23-year-old Flight Officer Bernard Michael Dopko of Valley Forge, Pennsylvania, whose enlisted men shared the same hut as the five EM of 'BJ' Keirsted's crew. Replacement crews like Dopko's always had brand new equipment plus they had a much cherished item; custom-made leather boots from Africa that they had picked up on the way over to England. 'Goldie' Goldstein was lying on his bunk when someone in the barracks said, 'Dopko's crew went down today on their first mission'. There was a mad scramble as 25 men reached for the brand new equipment and the custom-made leather boots from Africa that they had picked up on the way over to England. 'Later that evening after chow' continues Goldstein 'one of our barrack members said, 'Guess who I saw having late chow – Dopko's crew!''

Harold Rosenn the Squadron Intelligence Officer had spotted *Little Willie* and immediately rode his bicycle to the briefing room and quickly began to interrogate Dopko's crew who were laughing and joking about their madcap trip home from Berlin after a propeller ran away and the supercharger on another engine went out by flak hits over the heart of 'Big B'. Rosen was delighted to see that the plane had made it back with no one injured aboard. "My first question to Dopko was, "Dopko, where have you been?" Dopko's response to me was, "Rosenn, you s.o.b., you should have been with us." We all had a good laugh, and from there on, he and his crew gave their report in vivid detail."

The stricken ship had fallen out of formation and was immediately attacked by two German fighters. Staff Sergeant Robert McClintock Haydon Jr. the 20-year-old tail gunner of Madison, Wisconsin returned fire and they broke off the attack almost as soon as it started. Then the fun began. To keep from being attacked again, Dopko pointed *Little Willie*'s nose to the ground and screamed down to 50 ft, where he levelled off and started dodging rooftops. They skimmed chimneys down main streets of German towns and never more than 100 ft off the ground. They roared between two church steeples and went down the main road of one place so low that 2nd Lieutenant William G. Kelly the bombardier of Burlington, Iowa yelled to Dopko, 'Look out for the kerb'. They whistled and waved at a German girl cycling down the street of one town and finally shot up all their ammunition at the German defences on the Dutch coast.

'Coming over another city we were flying along a road and came upon a man riding in a cart,' said Lieutenant Glenn Roger Cederstrom, the 25-year-old navigator of Minneapolis. Minnesota. 'When he saw us he jumped and dived into a ditch. If he hadn't we would have knocked him off, we were that low.' Approaching a German machine-gun emplacement, the crew spied a soldier running to his gun position. Then, apparently thinking better of it, he ducked quickly to the cover of a nearby ditch. Every member of the crew joined in shooting up German defences. Thoughtfully, Dopko rocked his big plane from side to side to give his gunners better view for strafing. *Little Willie* hobbled across the last stretch of the North Sea at the height of 10 ft and made it back to East Anglia.

'We were embarrassed' said 'Goldie' Goldstein. 'Each of us who had taken some piece of equipment attempted to put it back. Unfortunately, we could not remember where all of the items went so they were just piled on one bed. When Dopko's crew walked into the barracks the quiet was astounding. Although one of Dopko's crew complained to the CO, nothing ever came of it. It seems this was an accepted way of life.'

One more mission to go and Keirsted's crew could join the order of 'The Lucky Bastards'. '…God be good to me on the next one!' Goldie'Goldstein wrote in his diary. It came on Saturday morning, 4 March. The crews were awakened at 0330. Keirsted's crew went to briefing with fingers crossed.

At Seething Wallace Patterson felt that they would have a stand down and so he decided he would go to Norwich to get some tyres for his bicycle. However, 'Big-B' was splashed all over the target maps at nearly all the bomber bases once again and Patterson was not alone in feeling disgruntled. 'Like hell we got a day off. At 0430 we were aroused to go fly, to Berlin again, this time over land.'

At the 95th Group's base at Horham in Suffolk the 37-year-old CO, Colonel Chester P. Gilger from Logan, Beaver County, Oklahoma closed the briefing with the words, 'Another great chapter is being written in the annals of the United States Army Air Forces on this day. You men are sharing part of history … Good luck and carry on.'

At Thorpe Abbotts 2nd Lieutenant John Phillip Gibbons, a pilot in the 350th Bomb Squadron recalled that at briefing 'it shocked us all as the ribbon reached all the way to Berlin!" Gibbons was born on 2 November 1919 in the small Kansas town of St. Mary's in Potawattomie County that had survived dust storms and the great depression. He never got further than Salina, Kansas to the west or further than Kansas City, nor Missouri to the east. Probably he would not have travelled that far if he hadn't learned to hitchhike. Now he was seeing Europe. While in the States on the way to his next phase of flight training, Gibbons was reading Lieutenant Colonel Beirne Lay's article *I Saw Regensburg Destroyed* (about the "Bloody Hundredth" and Major Gale Cleven's ordeal on 17 August 1943). Gibbons' recollections were 'I am not this type of guy'. Three months later, he was assigned to the 350th Bomb Squadron (Cleven's old squadron) and his first mission was to Regensburg, on 25 February 1944!

'Our crew would not be flying with the 100th, but as a composite group and we would be low squadron for the 95th Bomb Group. Great! My first mission with my crew and I would have to find them, or hopefully they would find me.' Earlier that morning he had been awakened by 'his favourite corporal', with the 'loud reveille', he had first heard on the morning of 25 February when he was called upon to fly his first mission: 'drop cocks and grab your socks Gibbons; you are going on a mission!" He was to be co-pilot to Johnny Lautenschlager, pilot of *Half and Half,* so named because half of crew were from the North, half from the South. 'I went to the briefing and heard everyone moan as they pulled back the curtain and the red tape reached to Regensburg. I wasn't much help to Lautenschlager, but I did become indoctrinated."

At Alconbury in Huntingdonshire when 1st Lieutenant William V. Owen of Columbus, Ohio and his lead crew in the 482nd Bomb Group got to the briefing room after struggling out of bed at 3 am they saw the route mapped out on the wall. That the target was Berlin came as no surprise to them because the Pathfinder Group had been briefed for Berlin the day before and would have led the mission had it not been 'scrubbed' on account of weather. Their Group was the only 8th Air Force radar-equipped pathfinder heavy bomber outfit in England. The Group used H2S 'Stinky' and H2X, the first generation radar equipment developed at the Massachusetts Institute of Technology Radiation Laboratory which could see land shapes on the scope through thick cloud. When Rabo first saw the B-17's equipped with the hand-built retractable H2X units under the nose of the aircraft at Grenier Field, New Hampshire, he was simply heard to say "that radome looks "Mickey Mouse". The nickname stuck and subsequently, it was shortened to "Mickey".

The Group had been removed from combat to focus on training pathfinder aircrews and develop tactics, although its developmental work occasionally required it to fly combat missions. Owen's crew said that the thought of Berlin did not create any special excitement. 'After you had been flying a few missions you didn't think what the target was but how far. Berlin was a 'DP' deep penetration raid and any time you saw a 'DP' on the briefing room map you started sweating it out' recalled Owen. 'We were not particularly afraid. We all had been a bit nervous and wished someone else had tested out the flak first. But as the briefing went on, we found we were getting good fighter escort and the setup 'looked pretty good'. All we were worried about was the flak and our four engines.' For five of the crew this mission was No. 12-B; which was what fliers called the 13th mission. 'We drew a good ship. The Fortress hadn't a name but it had been on eighteen straight missions without turning back and we knew that we couldn't let her down.'

At Rattlesden crews were awakened at 0400 hours. As they walked toward the mess hall their hands were in their pockets; shoulders hunched over and pulled together in an effort to ward off the damp cold. There was the noise of engines being run up. Lieutenant Isaac Doyle Shields, navigator on Lieutenant 'Hamp' Morrison's crew could see that the constellation Cassiopeia was dimly in the northeast sky. Born in Calvert, Texas, 12 December 1922, Shields' parents were of German, Welsh and German-Dutch and Scots-Irish ancestry. Math was his strong subject in school. The numbers involved in navigation intrigued him more than being a pilot and at his request he was classified navigator. He was awarded his navigator wings from the Advanced Navigation School at Hondo, Texas on 16 September 1943 as a second lieutenant and was sent to Moses Lake, Washington where he was assigned to Morrison's crew. 'Hamp' was from

Memphis, Tennessee. This was the crew's first combat mission. After they had completed their breakfast of fresh eggs and bacon they headed for the briefing room for the 0530 briefing. When the curtain was removed from the map there was a gasp. The target was 'Big B' again.

'Everyone was hoping they would call off all future raids to Berlin' recalled Ernie Richardson in the 96th Bomb Group at Snetterton. "However, we weren't the ones making the decisions, so we again heard the S-2 officer say.'This morning gentlemen, your raid is to Berlin.' After the cat calls, yelling and shuffling died down he went on to tell us about our route in and out, fighters, flak, how long we would be on oxygen etc. We were sure we would get there this time. No one liked the unnecessary route we were to take. It seemed to cover half of Europe. We had heard the 8th Air Force was trying to force the Luftwaffe into the air so we could eliminate them. We felt sometimes it was the other way around.'[9]

When he got out to his ship Wallace Patterson found that it was covered with snow and the turret was full of it, both vents being broken. He would have frozen to death in an hour. 'It was snowing so heavily that we couldn't see a 100 ft and while some of the other ships tried to taxi out onto the runways, most pilots said they would have faced court martial rather than risk their crews on slippery runways with ceiling and visibility zero. Fortunately the mission was scrubbed at zero hour. It snowed over six inches in the last 24 hours.'

At Alconbury there was a 15 minute delay before take off because of a snowstorm and for a while William Owen's crew thought they were not going. 'Then we took off and soon were in sunshine. Even though we see little sunshine in England we were not particularly pleased to see it now. We were the wing ship and deputy leader of our Division. But our Division was not the first for when we got over the Continent there were B-17s stretched out in front of us as far as the eye could see. Certainly we never thought we'd end up leading the parade to Berlin. The weather turned nasty.'

At Knettishall 'Goldie' Goldstein in 'BJ' Keirsted's crew, who were down to fly *Pegasus Too* again, had noticed that the extra early briefing was attended by all three chaplains: Jewish, Catholic and Protestant. 'This gave added importance to the destination. We hoped for a 'milk run', the term for a quick, easy mission. That was wishful thinking. We heard the briefing officer say 'the target for today is the first full attack on Berlin. Today we make history! It was the worst possible news that the 'Worry Wart' crew could hear. We looked at each other without a word being said. Each mission had seemed worse than the last but for the 25th we had hoped for an easy run and then home to the good old USA. Needless to say our crew went to our aircraft thinking about the danger and the possibility of completing our combat tour. The briefing was a duplicate of the day before. Conversation between us was short and the morale was very low. At each area the crew chief had erected a tent for his ground crew. We entered the tent, it was warm and immediately our crew settled in to soak up the wonderful feeling of heat. Start engines was scheduled at 0700, it was about 0630. Every few minutes one of the crew stepped outside the tent looked toward the control tower for a possible red flare indicating a scrubbed mission. It never came.

'Takeoff and assembly were normal but we were a little more on edge. Over France and into Germany we had flak and fighters but no damage or injuries. As the mission progressed and the weather worsened my crew kept calling me with 'Goldie' did you hear a recall? This was continual until 'Ace' Conklin called on the crew: 'Goddamit; if there is a recall we will know....' Then, just before we reached the target, on my radio in code for the second straight day there was a recall of the formation. I knew that meant the mission was cancelled. Decoded it read: 'Abandon ops. Return to base.'

'When I called 'BJ' he had just received the MSG on his command radio. It was the best possible news. The fact that we were going home was sweet music to our crew when I told them of the recall but just before the bombers reached the French-German border Kent Keith our cowboy bombardier from Montana said on intercom, 'BJ, are we going home with our full bomb load on our last mission?' 'BJ', normally a very conservative guy, agreed that if he could find a target we could unload on it. 'Montana' reported a very large, busy railroad yard just ahead. As a crew we made a decision by vote over the intercom to drop our bomb load on it. We dropped out of formation, now many miles ahead and the bombardier unloaded the salvo of bombs and turned for home. Our bomb bay doors were closing and according to 'Montana', they were closed. My job was to check those doors visually. I did. They were open. Several more attempts to close them were futile so 'BJ' gave the order for Jack Kings to leave his top turret and hand crank them closed.

'We were at about 25,000 ft. I watched to make sure he did not pass out. Suddenly, there was a loud explosion. A Me 109 must have seen a straggling Fort and fired several 20mm shells at us. 'BJ' and Conklin took evasive action by falling off to the right. Every time we came out of the clouds the German fighter was there with a couple of shots across our nose. We levelled off in the clouds before taking a head count. We took several hits but none to affect the aircraft's ability to fly. 'Ace' was flying the plane and he immediately dove to the right and into cloud cover. As we were to find out, this saved us as the enemy aircraft broke off the attack. Our pilot said, 'He evidently had no ammunition or ambition.' No-one reported any battle damage or injury. Little did we know that we were severely damaged."

Doyle Shields remembered his first mission very well: 'East of Lille, on return, the No.4 engine quit and then shortly thereafter the no.3 engine quit. With two engines out we could no longer keep up with the formation. I had been told in orientation that for the first ten missions, I would be worried more about self preservation than where I was. They were right! Now I had to set course for home. I thought we were near Lille and if I was right we should take a heading of 330° and as the British said, 'You *caun't* miss it' We salvoed our bombs on some farmer's outhouse – a standard characterization when we dropped our bombs away from the target – and threw out everything that was loose. Morrison was so busy trying to keep the airplane in the air with two dead engines on the same side, that when he got off course he didn't have time to explain that he had to go the long way back to the heading I had given him. I got on the interphone and shouted and repeated 'Three, Three, Zero'. We kept losing altitude. Through a break in the clouds, we saw water below. We made ready to ditch. When we broke through the clouds, there were the beautiful White Cliffs of Dover and we were still flying. The English gave us a shot across our nose. That didn't stop us. Morrison spotted Eastchurch, a grass RAF fighter field on the Isle of Sheppey on the south side of the mouth of the Thames and made a safe landing. This is an example of what caused a lot of losses among new crews. When Morrison tried to pull the valve to release the fuel in the 'Tokyo tanks'[10] into the main tanks, the valve was frozen and the engines just ran out of fuel.'[11]

Well into the mission, Ernie Richardson had looked out his side window and off to his left the sky was black with burst of flak. 'Not being turned in on interphone, I naturally thought it was Berlin, so I got my parachute, shoes and other essentials ready in case I had to bail out. I didn't think an aircraft could go through that flak without being hit. I'd just about given up on our chances of finishing 25 missions. (Short time later they changed the number you had to fly to 30). To my surprise we veered to the right, away from the flak. Naturally I was happy, but I couldn't figure out why we weren't going where the flak was so heavy. I was certain it was Berlin. The next day the *Stars and Stripes* reported the Air Force bombed northwest Germany. Also in the article it mentioned there was one group that managed to reach Berlin.'

One wing composed of two squadrons from the 95th Bomb Group and one from the 'Bloody Hundredth' (so-called because of the Group's continually high losses in the ETO) either did not receive the call signal or chose to ignore it and had continued to the capital alone. Lieutenant William V. Owen's crew in the 482nd Bomb Group saw clouds piled up as far as they could see. 'It didn't look as though we would get through' recalled Owen, who was from Columbus, Ohio, 'so the Bomber Command signalled each wing to use its own discretion about whether to proceed. Soon the other wings started to turn off, heading for secondary targets other than Berlin. Pretty soon we realized we were the only wing still going to 'Big B'. Then it half dawned on us that if anything should happen to the lead ship, we'd be the first American heavy bomber over the German capital.'

'I started as 'tail end Charlie' (the last ship in the Group – that gets all the prop wash) and wound up #2 on the lead', said John Gibbons. 'The weather was awful. Halfway through the mission, my radio operator heard a recall. Our leader, however, kept taking us through the clouds to Berlin. We were warned not to break radio silence. I wondered what he was doing. Then, there was Berlin in a blanket of flak like I have never seen before.'

'The Hundredth's code-name at this time was 'Fireball' recalled Captain Bob Shoens. 'And my squadron (351st) was part of 'Fireball Yellow'. 'We received the recall and brought our bombs home. It wasn't until we landed that we learned that 'Fireball Orange' (the second group of aircraft in the wing) had not received the call and had somehow made their way to Berlin. Fourteen minutes from the capital, 'Fireball Orange' was attacked by German fighters. Fortunately, some of the Mustang escorts were still with the wayward bombers and provided support in the target area. There is no doubt that their appearance prevented a debacle.'

Bill Owen's crew pretty soon ran into their first spot of trouble – flak – over a city they had often bombed before. Now they really began to sweat. A little later they reached the IP and they saw what looked like a heavenly cover of P-51s. It was not it until the first few had made a pass at them that they realized they were Messerschmitt 109s. 'Luckily none of us was hit' said Owen. Just as they were about to swing onto the bomb run, 26-year-old Lieutenant Colonel Harry Griffin 'Griff' Mumford of San Jose, California, the 95th Bomb Group Air Executive piloting *I'll Be Around*, the command bomber, signalled the Pathfinder ship's crew to take the lead. Mumford's bomb-bay doors had iced up and were stuck fast so he couldn't bomb! Owen's crew hadn't time to realize that this accident made them the first American bomber over Berlin. 'There wasn't time to think of anything except making a good run' Owen said. 'Luckily we did. We couldn't see what was happened because of a cloud below us.'

Second Lieutenant Marshall J. Thixton the bombardier on Owen's B-17, recalled: 'Almost as quickly as it happened before the clouds once more closed up. On we flew, courageously, brave and scared as hell. We wondered if our P-51 escort knew that a small number of struggling B-17s were still heading for Berlin and whether the '51s would be at Berlin when we got there – or if the German Air Force fighters were waiting for us at Berlin, in which case it would be another 'Battle of Little Big Horn'.' Born in Texas in 1924, Marshall Thixton had been sent to the state orphans' home in Corsicana at age 9 after the death of his father. He graduated from the state orphan home in May 1941 and with $6.50 in his pocket, went out into the world. Like most people of his generation, the Japanese surprise attack on Pearl Harbor changed everything. Now he had the honour of dropping the first American bombs on Berlin. At 1342 hours Thixton made the release and 29 B-17s unloaded the first American bombs on 'Big B'.

'When you're over the target even in good weather, you don't get much of a picture. There are too many other things to think about. This time it was fighters. They hit us right after 'Bombs Away'. Somehow we managed to avoid being hit and started home' said Owen.

'We flew over Berlin at 26,000 ft, mushed over the target, dropped our bomb load and headed back to England' continues John Gibbons. 'The B-17 doesn't fly well at 26,000. From a pilot's point of view, it's like dog paddling in a pool of oatmeal. I almost became a citizen of Berlin when a German fighter jockey knocked out my windshield at 19,000 ft. It was 55 degrees below zero. Now that's cold! I hit the deck and was escorted back by a P-51. We flew over a Nazi flight school with the troops in formation. Our gunners opened fire. I do recall at the debriefing it was concluded we were attacked by 121 German fighters. That bothered me. I wondered who was counting them and not shooting at them! From the French coast to Berlin it was air to air killing! I understand our leader received the Silver Star for that mission. I would have thrown the book at him for disobeying orders.'

'Griff' Mumford, who did indeed receive the Silver Star, recalled: 'Going in wasn't tough; the weather was pretty bad; clouds were broken. And it was cold – damn cold. As we got near to the city the clouds were still broken. We caught some ground checks, even though we were nearly five miles up. The navigator, 1st Lieutenant Malcolm M. Durr of Alton, Illinois deserved all the credit – he saw enough ground points to set us up for a visual bomb run. But the clouds closed in again and the bombing was done through clouds. I'm sure we hit the place.'

'It was a tough trip back' said William Owen. 'We hit solid cloud banks three different times. For a quarter of an hour at a time we couldn't see more than a tiny piece of the lead ship wing tip. Colonel Mumford and his navigator did a beautiful job getting us back. Credit for the show goes to him. When we broke out from the clouds for the third time we saw the French coast. There, waiting for us was our withdrawal escort of Spitfires. A lovely sight.'

Nobody's Fool and *Double Trouble II* aka *Northern Queen* in the 94th Bomb Group failed to return to Rougham. Battle damaged, a fire broke out in the radio compartment of *Nobody's Fool* so 2nd Lieutenant Delmar 'Bud' Pollock, the 26-year old pilot from Texas peeled off, out of formation, and the B-17 went into a dive. By attempting to recover from a tight spiral, Pollock stayed with the ship while five crewmembers managed to bail out before it exploded and crashed in the Calais area. The flight engineer/top turret gunner evaded and the other four survivors were taken prisoner. Pollock left a widow, Kathleen in Laredo, Webb County, Texas.[12] *Jeanne* aka *Li'l Opportunity* piloted by Lieutenant Charles E. Johnson of Philadelphia, Pennsylvania could easily have suffered the same fate as *Nobody's Fool* and *Double Trouble II*. The right waist gunner, Staff Sergeant Robert J. Thornton of Youngstown, Ohio recalled: "On this, our fourth try to reach Berlin, we got as far as Kiel and then had to be recalled. This was the day that two groups collided. One group turned the wrong way. The soup was so thick that visibility was nearly zero. We lost the #3 engine – oil pressure zero – couldn't feather the prop. Estimated outside temperature was -70 degrees. Oil was piling up on the cowling and the prop was wind milling. This didn't constitute a problem as long as we were in sub zero temperatures but our problems started as we departed the enemy coast and came down out of altitude. The warmer air made the oil liquid, the wind milling prop caused friction and set the oil on fire. The fire extinguishing system was inoperable. Conditions worsened. We had to get down fast. The coast of England came into view. A frantic search for an airfield was everybody's job. A new strip was located about one mile inland. It was just a strip; the field hadn't been started. We dropped fast and missed the strip the first time. After one go-around we landed. We were the first and only plane there. Construction people treated us like kings. Our base sent out a truck for us. The ship's wing was badly damaged from the fire and the plan was no longer operable. We were transported back to our base with a few belongings. Now we were out of the bombing business – or so we thought. We thought wrong."[13]

'BJ' Keirsted's crew had finally broken out of the clouds over France. Brejansky was unable to plot a course and 'Goldie' Goldstein was asked to get a heading. "Our 'G Box' was out of order so I contacted the RAF distress channel for help. God bless them because they answered immediately in the clear with a course for England, but the Germans immediately jammed it. A friend of mine, Tech Sergeant Wallace Gross, was flying as the alternate radio operator. Normally he was radio man on *Hulcher's Vultures* named after the pilot, Wendall Hulcher but somehow he was one mission behind his crew and volunteered to fly the ball position. He was not eager to be there for the whole flight and was sitting on the radio room floor. He was a crackerjack radio man and immediately set up another frequency. Again I transmitted and again the receiver message was jammed. We began to panic but Wallace put in a third unit and we received a heading which I gave to the navigator and when we broke out of the cloud we were over the Channel.

'The rest should have been routine – but it wasn't. There still was flak, enemy fighters and danger. At 25,000 ft, there was a sudden loud explosion. A fighter must have seen a straggling Fort and fired several 20mm shells at us. 'BJ' and Conklin took evasive action and we were lucky that the fighter broke off the attack. As Kent Keith said, 'He's not going get two more Jews.' He was referring to me and Brejansky.

'When we came out of the clouds over the English Channel and saw the White Cliffs of Dover it was the most beautiful sight that I could ever hope to see. *Pegasus Too* was probably the last aircraft to land. Everybody had seen us get hit and figured that we were lost. As we came over Knettishall our landing approach was normal until touchdown: no brakes. We went off the end of the runway and did a slow ground-loop coming to a halt in a farm field and there was a collective sigh of relief. The fire trucks all rushed to our aid but they were not needed. The medics wanted to know if the radio operator was hurt. When someone on our plane said I was okay one of the fireman pointed to a tremendous hole in the right side of the radio room. It was then that I realized that we had flown like that for three hours. I was probably too scared to realise how dangerous it had been. Nevertheless, it was 25 and home. We walked away from the plane and said our own individual prayers of thanks. We were going to make it back to the USA! Besides relaxing in the barracks there was no way to celebrate. The feeling of relief was enough. We all slept soundly that night. A few days later, 'BJ' came into our quarters and ordered us all to accompany him to the base chapel and there we really became one crew that was thankful for completing our missions without a major injury.'[14]

Eleven B-17s in total had been shot down on the Berlin mission. The 95th bore the brunt of the attacks and lost four of these including *Slightly Dangerous II* that crashed at Rostenburg after both waist gunners on Lieutenant Melvin B. Dunham's crew had been killed and the eight others had bailed out. The Hundredth, which the day before had lost three Fortresses on the abortive raid on Berlin, lost only one Fortress: *Seaton's Sad Shack* piloted by 1st Lieutenant Stanley Moler Seaton, who had been Shoens' best man at his wedding. A short time later, news was received that Seaton and eight crewmembers had been taken prisoner. The tail gunner had been killed. The 100th laid claim to the first fighter shot down by a bomber over Berlin when Sergeant Harold Stearns, the top turret gunner on *Rubber Check* got a Bf 109 in his sights at 800 yards, boring in fast from 12 o'clock high to level'. Stearns waited until he was about 400 yards away and then 'nailed him with 150 rounds'. It was last seen on fire as it spun into the clouds. Upon arrival back at Thorpe Abbotts John Gibbons' squadron commander told him that he had been through enough and his tour was over. In all the Kansan went to Berlin nine times during a tour spanning 49 missions up to and including 7 April 1945. Gibbons argued that he really wanted to fly his 50th mission, but the answer was 'no' and he was ordered on leave and not to return until the war was over. Gibbons left for the beaches of southern England "where he lost his pallor, drank some scotch and gained 10 lbs".

The Sunday newspapers made the most out of Saturday's raid on Berlin, although the Germans were quick to refute the American claims. Returning crews were now well aware that the German defences in and around the city had now been fully alerted and a rough reception could be expected next time the heavies ventured to 'Big-B'. The Germans knew only too well that any target which was not bombed because of a recall could be expected to be hit again at the earliest opportunity.

On 5 March Lieutenant Ralph G. Cotter, a 23-year-old bombardier in the 'Bloody Hundredth' who was born on 31 July 1920 to Gabriel and Jeanette Cotter in Taunton Massachusetts, wrote a letter to his mother. In part, it said: *"Well, today is Sunday and I am sitting in the club. We did not have a raid today, but it was such a nice day we went up and practiced bombing all afternoon. I had a very good day. I guess that is why I feel so well. Oh, Mom, I want you to look carefully in the Gazette and the Boston papers, because they gave our crew a write-up over the St. Omer raid. It starts off about Lieutenant William Terry, my pilot and all our names are mentioned. Enclosed you will find a clipping on my 16th raid. Just think only nine more raids and then I will be home. It will take about a month or more after I finish my 25 missions, but there is nothing to worry about. Well, Mom, everything is fine and I will say goodnight until tomorrow.*

Love, Ralph."

Notes

1. B-17F 42-30241/A.
2. It went to RAF Oulton in Norfolk where 214 Squadron began operating a number of Fortress B.IIs (including 42-30241, now SR378 BU-D) on RCM duties over enemy territory. See *Confounding the Reich: The Operational History of 100 Group (Bomber Support) RAF* (PSL, 1996, Pen & Sword, 2004) by Martin W. Bowman. 42-30241/SR378 was SOC on 11 March 1947.
3. In January 1943 General Ira C. Eaker had said that within 60 days many of his bomber crews would have to be taken out of combat 'by reason of having completed their operational tours.' By that time he said, the 8th Air Force would have many men who 'will be tired, war weary and punch drunk and will have to be relieved whether there are replacements or not.' Some men might be relieved even sooner... after 25 missions and 150 hours if circumstances warranted such action.
4. *Cock o' the Walk* was lost on 29 February with a 452nd Bomb Group crew captained by 2nd Lieutenant Jake S. Colvin. Both pilots and the ball turret gunner and one of the waist gunners were killed by flak. The six others were taken prisoner.
5. *Heaven Can Wait* and 2nd Lieutenant George K. McFall's crew FTR on 23 March. All ten crewmembers were taken prisoner.
6. Jenkins was shot down by flak flying P-38 42-67825 *Texas Ranger* on 10 April 1944 and crashed near Coulommiers. He was taken prisoner.
7. *Hula Wahine II* and Lieutenant Emil Berry Junior's crew were shot down by flak on 31 July 1944 when the target was the I. G. Farben chemical plant at Ludwigshafen. Berry, his co-pilot, Lieutenant John B. Good and tail gunner Staff Sergeant Lewis E. Pulsipher, along with four other men from the squadron, were executed by three SS officials who were later tried before a general military government court of the War Crimes Office, European Command, found guilty and were executed in October 1948.
8. Johnny Pyles, Cliff Hatcher's pilot, was killed on the Bremen raid on 26 November 1943 when his B-17 *The Sweetest One* and a Messerschmitt 109 were involved in a mid-air collision. Hatcher and two other regular members of Pyles' crew had been replaced by three new crewmembers for their combat indoctrination mission.
9. *History: 447th Bomb Group* by Doyle Shields Jr. and Marvin Lubinsky (Published by the 447th Bomb Group, 1996).
10. Tokyo tanks were internally mounted self-sealing fuel tanks. Although nicknamed "Tokyo" tanks to dramatically illustrate the significant range they added to the B-17 (approximately 40% greater with combat weights), it was also an exaggeration in that no B-17 ever had the range to bomb Japan from any base in World War II.
11. *History: 447th Bomb Group* by Doyle Shields Jr. and Marvin Lubinsky (Published by the 447th Bomb Group, 1996).
12. See MACR 2998.
13. Correspondence with the author via Robert M. Foose.
14. *Pegasus Too* was lost on 23 March 1944 on the mission to Brunswick when it was rammed by a heavily armoured Sturmgruppen Focke Wulf 190A flown by 24-year old Oberfeldwebel Willi Maximowitz and crashed at Steyerberg, 9 miles SW of Nienburg, Germany. 2nd Lieutenant Lloyd L. Wilson and six of his crew were KIA. Three were taken prisoner. Maximowitz was wounded and he bailed out near Wuppertal. Appreciation is due to Dan Case on Facebook.

Chapter Three

Black Monday Blues

Another heavy raid on Berlin; this time in broad daylight. For the Americans are now bombing too and their planes can fly higher than the British. Day raids are even worse than the night raids, as everybody is in town or on the move. It is said that the U.F.A. film studios in Babelsberg were destroyed. I fear that Potsdam, which is nearby, may also have been hit.

Twenty-seven-year-old Marie Illarionovna Vassiltchikov, diary entry, Monday, 6 March 1944. 'Missie', as she was known, was an anti-Nazi émigré from Russia and worked for the Information Department of the Foreign Ministry headed by her detestable superior, SS Brigadeführer Professor Doktor Franz Six. Through her contacts she had some advance warning of impending raids but having friends in high places did little to help her. 'Missie' moved to London after the war where she died in 1978.

'BJ' Keirsted's crew in the 563rd Squadron at Knettishall lay comfortably in their beds at 4 am that Monday morning when the orderly room GI or more familiarly, CQ (charge of quarters) burst through the door of their chilled hut, turned on the light and called out the other names on his list for combat briefing. 'It was the most beautiful morning of my life" said Larry Goldstein. "I awoke to a new world. It was a great thrill and some satisfaction to all of us to just turn over and go back to sleep. Relaxation was the order of the day. It was almost like a dream." Over in the 562nd Squadron area crews had only a rude awakening and thoughts of the nightmare to come. It preyed on the minds of 24-year-old 1st Lieutenant Montgomery 'Monty' D. Givens, born Browder, Kentucky and the three other officers on his crew and doubtless those of 23-year-old 1st Lieutenant Lowell Hoyt Watts and his co-pilot, bombardier and navigator on *Blitzing Betsy*. As he pulled on his clothes in the inky blackness of early morning Watts, born at Fort Collins, Colorado, thought perhaps he should have had a premonition of disaster. "If not then, maybe the briefing would leave me anxious and worried. We were all set for our final combat mission; one which would relieve the strain of combat and give us at least a month at home with our friends and families. How we looked forward to going home again. That trip was almost within our grasp."

At Rougham Staff Sergeant Robert Thornton was startled to be awakened early and told to get to briefing. "My reply was something like 'I have no ship and no equipment – you have the wrong guy! Wrong again. This was a maximum effort and every plane that was flyable [including *Jeanne* that had been repaired and would participate]. I was told that a composite group had been made up and that I was part of it. This was to be my 24th mission. I had 25 to do.[1] My crew was split up. We had a great deal of combat experience but the crew that was assigned was foreign to me. All of the equipment was assembled in a hurry. I was given a parachute harness and made the mistake of not adjusting it properly. Our job would be to lead the composite group." Charles Johnson would pilot the plane with 25-year-old 2nd Lieutenant James T. Howes filling in as co-pilot. Born in New Jersey, Howes had entered active service as an enlisted man in the cavalry of the New York National Guard at age 21. He was soon called up to federal service on 27 January 1941. When war was declared he had applied for transfer to the Army Air Force where he was granted cadet status. He was then married in 1942. The Berlin trip would be his ninth mission.[2]

At Seething in Norfolk at 0400 hours, the CQ had told crews in the 448th Bomb Group that a mission was 'on'. The village was on the North end of the airfield. Living accommodations, mess halls, hospital, clubs and other facilities were nestled in among farms, trees, barns, cow pastures and thatched cottages. Crews were impressed by the neat, compact countryside. There was every shade of green one could imagine and the tranquillity it conveyed belied the anxiety and apprehension that was always prevalent. Even the Seething control tower was code-named 'Brightgreen'. Crews were again impressed with the airfields about five miles apart in every direction; there was an airfield about every 36 square miles. They were not so impressed to be woken up at such an early hour. Staff Sergeant William 'Billy the Kid' McCullah, a 20-year-old aerial gunner from Springfield, Missouri fumbled for the name on Staff Sergeant Kenneth L. Dyer's bunk. Awakening the sleepy eyed radio operator, the CQ informed him he was the replacement radioman on *Hello Natural*. Dyer told McCullah he'd see him after the mission and McCullah went back to sleep. It was the last time he would see him.[3]

At Old Buckenham a CQ sleepily made his way down the wet and muddy walk that led past a row of Nissen huts where combat crews in the 734th Squadron were sleeping. Already there were sounds of activity. One of the B-24s was being tested for a sour mag that dropped 100-rpm. It was supposed to be fixed at 50-rpm but some crew chief was off the ball and it got worse. The orderly opened the door of one of the huts, turned on the light and called, 'Lieutenant Cripe?'

'Huh' was the only sleepy response that came from the lips of the 24-year old pilot from Bader, Schuyler County, Illinois.

'Breakfast at 3 o'clock, briefing at four.'

And with that the orderly left and went on to call other crews.

Lieutenant Hubert Raymond Cripe got up and shivered as the cold night struck him. He now knew how his father felt when he called him and his brother on a cold winter morning, only more so. Cripe called his co-pilot, 23-year-old

2nd Lieutenant Russell 'Russ' Anderson, of Minneapolis, Minnesota and his 23-year-old navigator, 2nd Lieutenant Homer W. Dallacqua. 'Spike', as he was more familiarly known, had been born in Chicago but was living in Detroit, Wayne County, Michigan when he enlisted in 1942. Cripe got his crew up with lots of grumbling and cuss words. They put on their helmets, oxygen masks, coveralls and parachute harness in a C-3 bag, dressed and got into the backs of waiting 6 x 6 trucks for delivery to their combat messes for breakfast. Combat crews throughout the region were given 'the works': greasy bacon which looked like oily rags, that would slide off a gravel driveway, orange juice, fresh eggs (if they had a good mess sergeant – some groups had to eat powdered eggs, cooked three tons at a time and prepared by being whipped into a great sticky emulsion; then apparently fried in axle grease left over from the needs of the motor pool; resulting in a well-vulcanised plastic lump of lukewarm goo. Powdered milk, toast, fruit and steaming black coffee with hot cakes and hard English rolls, pancakes and S-O-S (shit-on-a-shingle, creamed beef on toast) were available if one's digestion system had not already been ruined.

Breakfast over, at each base operations trucks delivered crews to their briefing rooms. Immediately on arrival they drew their bright blue electric suits and put them on. The outsize Nissen huts with enough folding chairs for about 250 men arranged in rows on a concrete floor, facing a low platform, filled rapidly. Someone bawled 'Ten-hut-ttt! as a lieutenant colonel entered the back of the room, flying crews quickly coming to attention. The officers and sergeants were a motley bunch, in coveralls or leather jackets, the officers wearing hard caps or leather flying helmets with earflaps turned up and the gunners wearing fatigue caps or flying hats or black woollen skull caps – each to his own taste, a ragtag mob altogether, sleepy, bad tempered, curious but not zestful-curious, mumbling, elbowing, with no sense of drama at all, just a dull ache of wishing the whole world-wide mess was over."[4]

'Seats, gentlemen' the Commanding Officer said, stepping onto the wooden platform. Checking his watch, he began, 'Synchronize watches on the hack.' Establishing the exact time of day, starting from the count of ten, he counted the seconds backwards, 'Five, four, three, two, one, hack.' Flying officers and radio-operators pushed watch fobs in on the 'hack'. The colonel indicated the target with a wooden pointer.

Three operations officers stood on an elevated stage at the front of the room. On the wall behind them two white sheets or a black cloth covering up a length of red twine stretched out on bright-headed push pins over the course of the target and back were draped over a large map of Europe. At some bases the spare twine at the end was rolled on a bobbin, which hung down and kept the line on the map under tension. Crews had long since figured out that if there was a lot of twine left on the bobbin there couldn't be much on the map and they'd have a milk-run... or at most a shallow penetration of France; but if the bobbin was almost empty...[5] Their fears were confirmed. At all three Bomb Division bases, Operations officers pulled aside the coverings with a flourish to reveal a jagged line of red yarn leading to 'Big B' again. A green ribbon showed their return route.

At Old Buckenham the briefing room had soon filled and at the far end of the room Major Edward F. Hubbard directed the route he put on the large map of England and the Continent. A hush ensued as two S-2 men thumb-tacked a thin sheet of plexiglas in such a way that a red crayon line on the sheet disclosed the route. Groans went up as the red line stopped at BERLIN! S-2 took over then and the first words they said were: 'Gentlemen, OUR target for today is Berlin.' Specifically, the target for two dozen crews was an electrical plant on the south side of the city. Cripe's crew would be flying *Betty Boop* off the wing of *Lonesome Polecat* piloted by Lieutenant Robert B. Witzel. Cripe's position was No.2 in the hi-right element – 'Purple Heart Corner'.

At Rattlesden at the briefing for thirty crews at 0530 hours 'Ed' Leighty, waist gunner on 'Bill' Greenwell's crew remembers: 'The Intelligence Officer pulled back the curtain over the wall map and there was the route to the target marked out in wool. 'Men' he said pointing with a stick, 'today you will bomb Berlin.' I didn't know any men being there in the room. I do know that there were a lot of frightened boys!'

'We were thinking that perhaps they would give up the idea of ever reaching the German capital' said Ernie Richardson. 'We found out differently on 6 March. This time the route was to take us directly in and out although everyone was once again disgusted that we would be trying to go there again, the route did lift our morale a little. At least we wouldn't be going all over the continent to get there. By now everybody was sure the Germans knew the 8th was going to bomb Berlin, we expected a really rough raid. We wouldn't be disappointed.'

The 8th stood ready to dispatch 226 B-24s and 504 B-17s and around 800 escort fighters to Berlin to make a bomber stream of over 90 miles long. The 1st Division in the van of the formation was assigned the VKF ball-bearing plant at Erkner, the 3rd Division, filling in behind them, were to bomb the Robert Bosch works at Klein Machnow south west of Berlin, which made ignition equipment for vehicles and aircraft. The Liberators of the 2nd Division, who as usual, would 'trail the parade', filling in behind the five B-17 wings, were to bomb the Daimler-Benz aero-engine works at Genshagen, 20 miles south of Berlin, the largest of its kind in Germany, turning out more than a thousand engines per month. If cloud concealed any of these targets the bombers were to make radar bomb runs using the Friedrichstrasse Hauptbahnhof in the centre of Berlin as their aiming point. 'How will it be over Berlin for half-an-hour with 600 guns?' said one crewmember under his breath.

At Tibenham in Norfolk 20-year-old 1st Lieutenant George H. Lymburn and his Liberator crew in the 445th Bomb Group had experienced the usual 4 am awakening they had 11 times before; ate the usual breakfast and took the usual position in the briefing room. Three crewmembers known as the 'Hard-

Assed Luck Boys' had even composed a song about the Group, one verse of which summed up the early morning departure: *We stumble to the mess hall to see what we can beg and what do you think we get boys, good old powdered egg… Next comes the briefing to answer to roll call. Will it be Berlin or is it a No-ball?*[6] Lymburn, who was born and raised in South Waymouth, Massachusetts, had given up his job in a department store after the attack on Pearl Harbor and had been sent to Montgomery Field, Alabama where he went through pilot training. After graduating, he had joined the 445th Bomb Group cadre in Orlando, Florida. At age 19 he was checked out as a first pilot of the 'magnificent' B-24. Following training, his crew had arrived in England in November 1943. For the Berlin raid Lymburn's crew was assigned *God Bless Our Ship* (formerly *Little Milo*). They hoped it would be a good omen, but the crew really felt ill-at-ease that they were to fly a replacement aircraft.

"Just a few more combat hours; that was all," Lowell Watts had said to himself. "But now those hours were to be spent deep in Germany over Berlin – defended in full force by the Luftwaffe and hundreds of flak guns manned by some of the best gunners on the European continent – a city the 8th had twice before tried to bomb without success. On the previous recalled missions to 'Big-B' a dog-leg route had been planned. There would be no bluff on this mission." *And,* not only would he have to fly *Blitzing Betsy* straight in and straight out but also he was the low squadron lead in the low group of the second section of his combat wing. "In short, our squadron would be the lowest and furthest back and therefore the most vulnerable spot in the wing to aerial attack. It was a grim prospect.'

Watts' squadron commander, Major Goodman, patted his young lead pilot pat on the back and gave him his good wishes. Watts and his 38-year-old co-pilot, 2nd Lieutenant Robert M. Kennedy; Lieutenant Edward J. Kelly Jr., the 24-year-old bombardier and 2nd Lieutenant Emmett J. Murphy the 22-year-old navigator warmed to the major's morale boosting assurance that *Blitzing Betsy* would be back on the line that evening. "And if not' he added, 'it would have cost plenty to bring her down.' No such assurances were received by 'Monty' Givens and his co-pilot 2nd Lieutenant Harry James Teat, nor Kenneth Hanley Betts the 25-year-old navigator from Warren, Pennsylvania or Lawrence Herman McMillan, the bombardier from Jackson, Mississippi. They, and no doubt the EM members on the crew, were dejected to discover that *Quarterback*, their regular B-17, was still being repaired from battle damage suffered on the 4 March Berlin mission and their replacement aircraft went by the somewhat titillating title of *Suzie-Sagtitz*!

Watts walked under a faded white half moon through the pre-dawn darkness to the equipment room thinking that 'the stars seemed cold and unfriendly'. 'We had arrived at that mental state where one more extra long, extra tough raid, meant almost nothing to us. It was just another raid. As for myself at least, I had grown calloused to many of the dangers of combat. The tougher the raid now, the better I liked it. Sure, the fighters and flak brought out the sweat and a tinge of nervous energy, but the thought of actually being shot down seemed like something that just wouldn't happen. Still, there was one thing certain, no chances would be taken on this last mission. I was deadly serious in checking over every detail of our 'plane and equipment. The sun crawled up and peeked over the eastern horizon, casting a pink tinge on the fluffy, scattered clouds that seemed to forecast a clear day. Had we known, could we have seen a few hours into the future, we would have taken that pinkish tinge as a portent of the blood that was to be shed above those clouds. But then, it just looked like another day with better than average weather. Still, I could show plenty of confidence when I told Master Sergeant 'Harry' Allert, our crew chief, to expect a first-class buzz job over his tent when we got back.' Harry Walter Allert had been born at Racine, Wisconsin on 30 October 1909. He first enlisted in the AAC on 19 November 1928. When he re-enlisted on 18 June 1942 he was working for the Guy F. Atkinson Construction Company and lived in Mud Mountain Dam, Washington.

Berlin was the third mission for 2nd Lieutenant Charles A. Melton's crew on *Paddlefoot* in the 458th Bomb Group at Horsham St. Faith on the outskirts of Norwich. They had flown their first Berlin mission three days' earlier. Staff Sergeant Glenn R. Matson the tail gunner recalled: 'Originally our target was to be the Heinkel Aircraft Factory at Oranienburg, north of Berlin. The 2nd Bomb Wing would lead with the 14th and 96th Squadrons composite [and the 20th Bomb Wing] to follow six miles behind them, bringing up the rear of the three Bomb Divisions of B-17s and B-24s. Temperatures at altitude were near 60° below zero F. We were to stay below 21,000 ft to prevent contrails and make it harder for the German fighters to spot us. At Horsham St. Faith at take-off, visibility was below 1,800 ft and patches of fog, with completed cloud cover between 3,000 and 6,000 ft. This meant going up through the soup for assembly, forming at 10,000 ft.

'About 1030 we departed England and headed for the North Sea and across Holland. Thirteen of our 33 B-24s aborted or failed to make the mission. The remaining twenty bombers joined up with the 14th and 96th Bomb Wing to form a composite Wing. We picked up our first fighter escort, the 56th Fighter Group, somewhere over Holland. We were following the 3rd Division B-17s when they got off course between Enschede and Osnabrück. The B-24s and part of the B-17s saw the error and stayed on the planned route. Temperatures at altitude were near 60 below zero F. We were to stay below 21,000 ft to prevent contrails and make it harder for the German fighters to spot us.'

Casualties came early on 6 March. On takeoff from Wendling in Norfolk *Carol Ann*, a B-24 Liberator in the 392nd Bomb Group ran into a patch of mist struck a tree at Church Farm, Great Dunham about 2,000 yards from the end of the runway. The entire bomb load exploded and the aircraft burst into flames killing all ten men on 28-year-old 1st Lieutenant Paul F. Shea's crew. In August 1943 the day after this Liberator arrived at the 392nd in Tucson, Arizona the crew had had to make a forced landing due to mechanical failure.

At Knettishall Lowell Watts considered his take-off was perfect. 'We slid into our formation position without trouble, the rest of the squadron pulling up on us a few minutes later. Everything was working perfectly: engines, guns, interphone. Every man on the crew was feeling well and in good physical condition. We were all set for this final and greatest combat test. I wondered then if all this was a harbinger of a smooth mission or the calm before the storm. The question was to be answered very definitely within a very short time. While we were assembling the wing and division formations over Cambridge, the lead ship of our section of the wing aborted. Our group took over the wing lead. I felt better then; at least we weren't in the low group now. We crossed the English coastline and the gunners tested their .50 calibres. The Channel passed beneath us and then the Dutch coast dropped under the wings and fell away behind us.'

The 3rd Division formation was led by Brigadier General Russell Wilson flying in a 482nd Bomb Group radar-equipped Fortress code-named 'Chopstick G-George'. It was flown by Major 'Fred' A. Rabo, whose crew included Lieutenant John C. 'Red' Morgan who had been awarded the Medal of Honor for his heroism on 26 July 1943.

One of the Liberators on the raid was *Reddy Teddy*, a B-24J in the 93rd 'Travelling Circus' Bomb Group at Hardwick, which was named for the pilot 1st Lieutenant Glenn Elwood Tedford by his crew. Born 5 January 1923, in Shallowfield, Texas, he had graduated from Wichita Falls High School in 1940. After their fourth mission they had decided to stay together and fly every mission because Sergeant William D. Wahrheit the tail gunner was killed after being put on another crew that never returned from the mission. Tedford's crew had started out for Berlin on 2 March. It was the coldest weather the young pilot from Wichita Falls, Texas had flown in with an outside air temperature hovering around 62° below zero. Missions to Frankfurt and France followed. Then, on 6 March *Reddy Teddy* took off at 0905 for the mission to Berlin. Glenn E. Tedford's brother Clois was a gunner's mate in the US Navy in the South Pacific. 'It is hard to distinguish who had the most dangerous assignment' Tedford wrote 'but the first mass daylight attack on Berlin was as bad as it could get in the ETO [European Theatre of Operations].

Enemy fighters could hardly miss the column of bombers heading for Berlin. The 94 mile long stream of 730 B-17s and B-24s sailed over the Zuider Zee and were almost over the German border when the storm broke. Over the Dummer Lake enemy fighters concentrated on the leading 1st Division groups and the 91st, 92nd and 381st were given a thorough going-over. The 457th Bomb Group, otherwise known as the 'Fireball Outfit', was met by head-on attacks. A Me 410, which did not pull out in time crashed into *Flying Jenny*, 2nd Lieutenant Eugene H. Whalen's Fortress in the high box and the combined wreckage fell on 2nd Lieutenant Roy E. Graves' B-17 in the low box. All three fell to earth. Only Sergeant Eldon A. C. Williams the tail gunner on Graves' aircraft survived from the two Fortresses.

Next it was the turn of the 3rd Division groups to feel the weight of the enemy attacks. The leading 385th at the head of the Fourth Combat Wing came in for persistent fighter attacks. Just as the formation approached the Berlin area the flak guns opened up and bracketed the group. In the leading formation Brigadier General Russell Wilson's aircraft was hit by three bursts of flak but continued on the bomb run with one engine on fire. Major 'Fred' Rabo gave the order to bail out when the bomber began losing altitude but before the dozen crewmembers could put on their parachutes, the aircraft exploded, killing eight men. Rabo and the two waist gunners survived, as did 'Red' Morgan, who was somersaulted out of the aircraft with his parachute pack under his arm. He managed to put it on after several attempts and was saved from possible injury when a tree broke his fall. After capture he was sent to Stalag Luft III. In England Morgan's fiancée, 2nd Lieutenant Helene Lieb, a nurse from Minneapolis, waited anxiously for news.

In the 447th formation 2nd Lieutenant Bryce B. Smith's left inboard engine supercharger was wrecked and shell splinters punctured two tanks causing fuel to run into the wing and flow out the trailing edge. He aborted the mission and headed for home. At 1240 hours, north of Hanover and Brunswick, the stream began to turn to the east southeast in order to go south of Berlin where the targets were located. An 88 mm anti-aircraft shell hit *Dottie Jane* piloted by 26-year-old 1st Lieutenant Arthur R. Socolofsky from Chicago. The crew were flying their 13th mission. A few seconds after the bombardier, Staff Sergeant Worley dumped his bomb load on Berlin, a burst of flak exploded inside the B-17. The *Dottie Jane* shuddered and careened out of formation. Staff Sergeant Robert D. Benjamin the 20-year-old waist gunner of Arcadia, Wisconsin suffered flak wounds to his right leg and buttocks. The tail gunner, Lyman Enrich, whose 23rd birthday this was, recalled: 'The shell blew the hatch above the radio compartment. This sucked Alton Moore, the radioman out without a parachute, taking nine bombs and most of the fuselage in this area. The shell cut a wing spar causing both wings to drop down. There was no intercom or hydraulic power. There was no way for Socolofsky to know the condition of the crew members. He managed to keep control of his airplane as he returned home.' Sergeant Herbert Morris the 20-year-old top turret gunner of Pirent, California, cranked down the wheels but found one tyre shredded. The crippled Fortress bounced onto the runway, settled on the flat tyre and finally careened to a stop. The ball turret had jammed and its twin machine guns fired into the runway, sending up a shower of sparks. Inspection showed the damage also included: bomb bay doors cut in half; its side wing nearly severed; hundreds of holes; and a mass of twisted wreckage with ends of severed cables, wires and tubing hanging limply inside. Enrich, who was wounded in the left buttocks and leg and Benjamin flew no more missions. Co-pilot Howard N. Barr was killed on 29 April 1944 along with 1st Lieutenant Hayden T. Hughes the 26-year old pilot of Washington, Iowa and six others.

'Shortly after crossing the Zuider Zee, reports started coming in' recalled Ernie Richardson in 2nd Lieutenant Sherman Gillespie's crew in the 96th Bomb Group.

'Fighters 12 o'clock. Our level.'

'Fighters 9 o'clock; keep your eyes peeled.'

'Seventeen going down 12 o'clock one, two, three, four, five ... five chutes open.'

'Fighters coming in 12 o'clock.' That followed by a burst of machine gun fire from our plane.

'Take him ball-turret. He's yours.' More gun fire sounded.

'We had enemy fighters all the way to the target. It was a mixture of fighters, bombers and parachutes going down as far as you could see. Of all the raids we had been on this was undoubtedly the worst.'

Of the 504 B-17s and 226 B-24s that had set out, 474 Fortresses and 198 Liberators attacked their primary or secondary targets in the Berlin area. None of the Fortresses in the 1st Bomb Division bombed the primary target at Erkner, dropping their bombs on the Kopenick and Weissensee districts of the capital instead. Only the B-24s of the 2nd Division released some of their bombs on their primary target; the rest of the attack fell on secondary targets in and around 'Big B'. The 3rd Division also missed the primary target and bombed the Steglitz and Zehlendorf districts.

'Over the target it looked like the Fourth of July – flak bursting in red flashes and billowing out black smoke all around us' recalled 1st Lieutenant Vern L. Moncur a 27-year-old pilot in the 303rd 'Hell's Angels' Bomb Group at Molesworth in Cambridgeshire. He had attended school in Rupert, Idaho. Following college, Vern taught high school in Eastern Idaho for four years. It was there that he met Alice Neeley and they were married on 4 June 1941. Moncur's seventh mission on 29 January 1944 was his crew's first in the brand new *Thunderbird* that he would fly on twenty of her first 24 missions and it had a wing shot up so badly it had to be replaced. 'The flak over Berlin was the most accurate and most heavy flak we ever got into" recalled Moncur. "It seemed almost thick enough to drop your wheels and taxi around on it. The Krauts were practically able to name the engine they were shooting at. We received hits in the No. 1 engine, the No.2 engine and the No.4 engine. The hit in the No.2 engine knocked out one cylinder, though the engine still gave us partial power and continued to operate on our return flight to England. Our left 'Tokyo tanks' were shot out. (We had transferred the gasoline out of them before this hit.) The plexiglas surrounding the left cheek-gun was shattered by a chunk of flak. The horizontal stabilizer had a big hole shot through it and the vertical stabilizer received a jagged hole in the top of it. We also picked up another hole in the right side of the fuselage, near the tail wheel. A piece of flak came through the cockpit and cut the left sleeve of my leather flying jacket but didn't touch me. Our ship received the heaviest damage of any of the 27 planes in our squadron. On our way back from the target, we had a few passes made at our group, but the P-51 fighter escort very quickly took care of these Me 109s. Our fighter escort was really swell on this mission.' Moncur would complete his combat tour on 10 April 1944; *Thunderbird* would fly 112 missions without any crewman ever being injured.

'One day you are roaming around London, but thinking about what is in store for you for the tomorrow" wrote 24-year-old 1st Lieutenant Edgar Cornelius 'Ed' Miller, co-pilot on the crew captained by 1st Lieutenant Earl Newton Thomas in the 'Hell's Angels' Group. "The next day you are a part of the largest armada of B-17s and B-24s ever to attack the City of Berlin. What a jolt to you "mental system" to walk into an early morning briefing, after getting back from London and see "Big B" as the target. Since the 3rd of March we had been trying to reach Berlin – to let Hitler know that the 8th Air Force does exist. Today we made it but the bombing results were not too good. Photos indicate that no bombs hit their assigned targets. And we paid a huge price in human lives and aircraft. The briefing officers said that Berlin would be defended with the largest array of enemy fighters and anti-aircraft artillery known to man. They were right. The losses were staggering – at least eighty aircraft (53 B-17s, 16 B-24s and 11 fighters), a new 8th Air Force record for any one mission. This may have been due to the fact that we were at a much lower altitude than our usual bombing. But it was necessary as the trip in and out took almost nine hours. We were barely able to get home. I was sure one of those enemy aircraft bullets had my name on it – but not today.'

'As we neared Berlin the sky was the blackest I'd ever seen with flak bursts" remembered Ernie Richardson. "At most targets the flak was right around our altitude, here at Berlin it was quite a ways above and below us and tremendously heavy at our altitude which was about 23,000 ft. We made history; it being the first time in daylight that Berlin was bombed with the full force of the 8th Air Force but both sides paid a heavy price.'

Ten minutes after the IP, 100 miles from Berlin, Lieutenant Bob Witzel in the 453rd Bomb Group formation suddenly pulled *Lonesome Polecat* out of the formation, feathered No.3 and Hubert Cripe at the controls of *Betty Boop* followed. At the target was the most concentrated flak barrage Cripe had ever seen. It was almost a solid black cloud with red bursts of exploding shells that could be seen fifty miles away and it filled him with dread. Suddenly they were in the flak. Spent pieces of flak bounced off *Betty Boop's* metal skin and a burst directly to one side rocked the plane. Instantly, 2nd Lieutenant Maurice A. Dinneen the 22-year old replacement bombardier of St. Louis, Missouri, hit his bomb release before *Betty Boop* glided down, out of 'gas and the crew bailed out over Noord-Holland and into the sea. Seven of the crew drowned in the ice cold water but 'Spike' Dellacqua and Cripe and Russ Anderson survived. Dellacqua was immediately arrested by the crew of a small sea patrol boat, one of a flotilla used by the Wasserschützpolizei (German water police) and commanded by SS general Hanns Albin Rauter, the leader of the SS in the Netherlands. Barely any regular German policemen were left on these boats. Mostly they were crewed by brutal Waffen-SS volunteers. Dutch fishermen pulled Cripe and Anderson into their boat, warmed them and gave them dry clothes. After they docked the Wasserschützpolizei announced that two of the fishermen were to be sent to Westerbork prison and thence to a death camp at Durchgangslager in Germany and they were given an hour to go home to say goodbye to their families. Luckily, the burgomeister of Edam persuaded the Wasserschützpolizei to release them. The three Americans meanwhile were taken into captivity.[7]

The B-24H flown by Lieutenant Elmer B. Crockett, from Grafton, Virginia had also been ditched. Five men died. Crockett, 2nd Lieutenants' George T. Nacos the navigator from Dubuque, Iowa and Orvis C. Martin, and Staff Sergeants' William T. Talbott and Max A. Martin survived.[8] *Shack Rabbit* piloted by 28-year old 1st Lieutenant Patrick D. Tobin Jr. of Birmingham, Michigan had gone down over enemy territory too, shot down by fighters near Plantlüne during the return flight. The Liberator exploded after four of the crew had bailed out and went down in a small wood at Biene after Tobin had pulled up the B-24 to avoid crashing at Lingen/Ems. *Lillie Belle* had been ditched in the sea by 21-year-old 2nd Lieutenant Herman Joe Meek and he was drowned. The bombardier, 2nd Lieutenant Joseph G. Cyr of Old Town, Maine was the lone survivor. Attempts by Lieutenant Richard C. Holman to tag onto passing formations after he lost two engines to flak over the heart of Berlin failed so he dropped to the cloud level, chased by six or seven FW 190s. With only the top turret and waist guns in operation the crew claimed two and possibly three of the enemy fighters. Evading their attackers the crew ran into flak over Amsterdam but Holman put the crippled Liberator through violent evasive action. Desperately short of fuel, he finally reached the enemy coast after guns, ammunition boxes, flying equipment and all other equipment that could be detached were tossed overboard. Despite serious damage the "two engine" bomber brought Holman and his crew home "without so much as a scratch".[9]

In the 445th Bomb Group formation *God Bless Our Ship* flown by George Lymburn had taken its position in the formation, climbed to 22,000 ft and approached Berlin from the south. Helpless, Lymburn had witnessed the destruction of the 100th Bomb Group in front of him. Now the 445th Bomb Group headed towards the centre of Berlin on the bomb run. 'Wham!' Almost immediately, a cluster of flak bursts caused the Liberator to break into flames. One shell exploded under the B-24 and drilled a hole right through the wing. Staff Sergeant Walter J. Downey Jr. the top turret gunner of Hamburg, New York was hit on the head by a piece of red-hot shrapnel from another burst of flak above the B-24. Fortunately, Downey was wearing a flak helmet, which saved him from serious injury. Another shell tore into the tail section, damaging the controls and causing the rudder to flutter. The final shell burst directly in the bomb bay, starting a fire. The damaged wing was losing fuel, which ignited to form a stream of flame from the wing back to the tail section. Downey swung his top turret to face forwards and saw the trailing edge of the wing melting in the intense heat. Lymburn ordered the crew to bail out. All made it except 2nd Lieutenant Frank R. Serpico the 28-year-old navigator from Kings County, New York who was dragged by his 'chute into a large tree stump and he was killed on impact. Lymburn left the flight deck and made his way to the bomb bay to bail out but once there he could see the ground one minute and the sky the next. At this moment he lost his nerve and found that he could not jump, so he made his way back to the cockpit and hoped that he could put the Liberator down somewhere. He picked out a 'green field', 'crash landed and was astonished to discover that the tail gunner, Staff Sergeant Francesco P. 'Frank' Cittadino from Inwood, New York, had come down in the back of the B-24. The nine survivors were captured and would spend the rest of the war in prison camps.

There had been instances of bomb doors of Liberators inching closed during bomb runs. If they went too far, a safety switch operated to prevent the bombs releasing. Until the B-24s could be modified to cure this fault the radio operators had to position themselves over the front of the bomb bay and press the lever to hold the bomb doors fully open. As he did so 23-year-old Tech Sergeant Donald V. Chase from Jersey City on Lieutenant Perry's crew in the 44th Bomb Group looked down hoping for a glimpse of Berlin. He remembered seeing a lot of clouds and flak bursts – there were some great rifts in the cloud – but he didn't remember seeing anything of the city. 'It was a long day...' he wrote later ... "8½ hours in flight... sucking in your breath as shards of 88s and 110s pierced our ship's thin, olive-drab skin... checking the fighters to determine if they were bandits or 'little friends'... hoping that the oil pressure of No.4 engine didn't drop any lower and possibly force your ship to be a straggler for enemy aircraft to prey on – all that kept the adrenaline surging. The flak over the city was intense and accurate and many aircraft received flak damage. As I straddled the catwalk during the bomb run and pressed the bomb bay anti-creep lever, a chunk of shrapnel ripped through my 'blue bunny' suit, nearly making an instant soprano out of me as it shorted out my suit. It was a cold flight home. The 2 oz shot of 86-proof which hit my empty stomach like an exploding star was especially welcomed at the end of that difficult day.'

The 458th Bomb Group had taken a course southeast after passing between Brandenburg and Magdeburg to the Initial Point to start bomb run on the Heinkel Aircraft Factory at Oranienburg and had then swung north into the wind to the target. 'The worst flak hit us as we approached Oranienburg' recalled Glenn Matson in the tail gun turret of *Paddlefoot*. 'There may have been kids firing those 88 mm flak guns, but they were good. It was bad enough riding that flak road in and out of Berlin, but as we arrived at the IP we were on a collision course with a B-17 Group on their bomb run. Our Group leader, Lieutenant Colonel Isbell, had to abort our bomb run, change course and close bomb bay doors and set up for another run. Again we were off our target and he turned us 360 over Berlin instead of away from it. That put us in almost constant flak for over thirty minutes. He wasn't satisfied with our other two runs; he wanted to hit the rail station and yards, not just 'Big-B'.

'We were flying in the lower left three plane element in the position of 'Purple Heart Corner'. The guy leading our element took us under the main Group formation. By now our bomb bay doors were open again and we were in a very precarious situation. We didn't like looking up at those open loaded bomb bays directly above us. Melton decided to leave the element and slid back up in the formation where we belonged. Our element leader and the other wing man were two of our five losses that day. We feared at the time that our own Groups bombs fell on them. It was on this third bomb run that our navigator, 2nd Lieutenant Charles C. Weinum stuck his head up in the navigator's dome in front of the pilots and thumbed his nose at them. He noticed a dog fight and got down inside to get a better view through the side window. After he had left, a chunk of flak made a hole through the dome about the size of a fist. If his head had been there; Pow! No head. He stuck his head up there again, saw a flak hole and got the surprise of his life.

'We had to divert to an alternate target [the Daimler-Benz Motor Works at Genshagen]. By then we had heavy cloud cover and ended up dropping our bombs near Potsdam. With the target no longer visible, we had to resort to PFF and the results were very poor. Shortly after leaving the target area, we were attacked by two FW 190s without causing any damage. Our Group had been badly shot up by flak, one aircraft lost over the target. This was *Ford's Follies* flown by 2nd Lieutenant Guy C. Rogers of Missoula, Montana whose crew was on its first mission. They crashed west of Berlin; eight men were killed, two bailed out when the plane exploded. The next to go down was flown by Captain 'Jack' L. Bogusch the 753rd Squadron Operations Officer of Jersey City, New York who flew as pilot for the crew of 2nd Lieutenant Lloyd B. Andrew, who was ill. Four men were killed and six survived the crash and were taken prisoner."

Roll Call aka *Belle of Boston* piloted by 27-year old 2nd Lieutenant Thayer Hopkins, whose home at 34 Maple Street, San Francisco was a world away from Berlin, the centre of which he bombed from 20,000 feet. *Roll Call* was then hit by flak about one hour after the target. "It went off beneath our starboard wing" remembered 2nd Lieutenant Samuel W. Roberts Jr., the 23-year-old navigator of Norristown, Pennsylvania. "Number 4 engine quit and was feathered quickly. As we flew on, number 3 coughed and died, but would not feather. Now we had to crab onward on two engines and full left rudder! Both number 1 and number 2 were running with throttles to the firewall. The exhaust manifolds were white hot!" Hopkins turned back towards the Dutch coast escorted by three P-47s to the coast of Holland after distress signals were fired. "Finally, near the North Sea the last two engines quit and it was time to leave and leave we did" said Roberts who jumped from 5,000 ft. Hopkins gave the order for the crew to bail before making a forced landing near Nijkerk, Holland. The co-pilot, 1st Lieutenant Ernest Thompson Herndon of Dallas, Texas broke his ankles on landing and

Sergeant Earle L. Knight the wounded flight engineer of Andrews, South Carolina suffered a broken hip and a lacerated lip when he hit the ground. They and Sergeant James William Peterson the radio operator of Zanesville, Ohio; Sergeant James Walker Hobson the ball turret gunner of Detroit, Michigan; Sergeant Harold P. Lambousy the waist gunner of Crowley, Louisiana and Sergeant Bewel Ellis Warren the top turret gunner of Ennis, Texas were captured by the Germans. Sergeant Eric J. Hilditch the tail gunner of Trenton, New Jersey, who had been an aircraft inspector before enlistment, buried his parachute under some bushes and took off. Roberts paired up with Flight Officer Robert Cleveland, the 20-year old bombardier of Sapulpa, Oklahoma and they hid in irrigation ditch until sunset and then they went to a farm house where they told their story and were fed and given warm milk and allowed to sleep in the hay loft. Next day they were picked up by the Dutch escape organization and were reunited with Hilditch. Later, all three were driven to Amersfoort and the home of the Resistance chief, HAGr4 Gelius 'Gerard' Ottens, a police officer. Two days' later they met Hopkins. All four men were hidden by members of the Comète line at a score or more different addresses until they were liberated south of Liège by the 3rd Armoured Division prior to the Battle of the Bulge on 6 September 1944. Hopkins kept his tobacco tin, cigarette roller and a spoon made from a Dutch coin, Belgian newspaper and Dutch war coins, razor and razor blades and a tooth brush as souvenirs of his long journey through Holland and Belgium to freedom.[10]

'450',[11] the B-24H piloted by 2nd Lieutenant Beverly E. Ballard Jr. of Suffolk, Virginia, whose crew were on their first – and last – mission was the next to go down. Flak knocked out their hydraulics and possibly punctured a fuel tank which forced the crew to bail out about ten miles north of Amsterdam. One of the crew, instead of jumping, may have attempted to fly the plane back to base, lost control of the aircraft and three of the crew perished in the crash. Ballard and five others were taken prisoner. The ball turret gunner, Sergeant Victor W. Kruger of Milwaukee, Wisconsin, evaded capture for 14 months when the Dutch Resistance found him and hid the evading American until the British troops rescued him in April 1945.

During the second bomb run at the target 27-year old 2nd Lieutenant Jesse Lee McMains' ship was damaged. Losing power, McMains, of Hooker, Texas County, Oklahoma dropped out of formation and was attempting to 'hit the deck' when German fighters found them. At 1353 hours 23-year old Oberleutnant Hermann Greiner of 11./NJG 1 flying a radar-equipped Bf 110G pulled up and fired a short burst which knocked off the entire tail unit of the Liberator which went into a steep dive, spinning out of control without catching fire and crashing beside the Army munitions factory at Münsterlager near Uelzen.[12] "With the assistance of Sergeant Clarence Daw the top turret gunner" stated 2nd Lieutenant Robert Dean the 28-year old bombardier of California, "McMains held the ship steady while seven of the crew bailed out." Staff Sergeant Harvey Hofstott the radio operator remained at the radio sending a call for help. He and Daws (22), one of five brothers from Pensacola, Escambia County, Florida to enlist during WWII, did not have time to get out before the ship exploded and crashed. The 25-year old co-pilot, 2nd Lieutenant Casimir J. Kolezynski of Cleveland, Ohio was the last man out of the ship through the bomb bay and he saw these three men at their stations. As the plane was burning fiercely, he sustained severe facial burns. Dean also had a recommendation for his pilot. 'This man's family deserves an award for their son who gave his life that we who escaped might live. He gallantly fought to keep this burning airplane in straight flight until we all were out. Then it was too late for him.'

'As for our crew' continues Glenn Matson, '*Paddlefoot* experienced a bit of flak damage, but no one on the crew was injured and our return to England was uneventful. This was a very costly mission for the 8th Air Force as well as the 458th, which lost five bombers and three returned with minor battle damage – the most ever for one mission throughout the remainder of the war. Approximately one out of every ten bombers was lost on this mission, the greatest on any separate mission for the 8th Air Force. We knew we had been on a big one. Yes it was a big one – 'Big-B'.'

Immediately south of the Olympic stadium where, much to Hitler's chagrin, Ohio State's Jesse Owens won 200 metres gold in the 1936 summer games, the 20th Wing turned west. The 128 mm guns of Heavy Flak Abteilung 123 on the Humbolthain and Zoo bunkers loosed off 91 rounds at the B-24s of the 93rd Bomb Group, famously known as the 'Travelling Circus'. 'The bombers were engaged with repeated salvoes from all eight128 mm guns' Oberleutnant Maschewski. directing the fire from the Humbolthain bunker, later reported. "During the course of the engagement the altitude of the targets reduced from 6400 metres to 6000 metres, velocity 130 metres per second. Tracked by the Em 10 metre R 43 (optical range finder) the formation flew without taking any evasive action, from the south-southwest to west. Fire was opened at maximum effective engagement range and soon after the detonation of the initial salvo a machine in the middle of the formation began to trail dark smoke from both outer motors.'

It was *De-Icer* in the 93rd whose 11-man crew was captained by Lieutenant Jack D. Harris of Huntington Park, California. The B-24J was at 23,000 ft when it was hit by flak in the #2 propeller just after 'Bombs Away'. 'The prop came off and spun through the cockpit making a huge hole' said 2nd Lieutenant Harry Lee Howie Jr., the navigator of Pinebluff, North Carolina. 'The pilot was not in his seat. If he had been the prop might have thrown him out the hole. The windshield and oxygen in the nose were out, on fire and half of the left vertical stabilizer was torn off. Also the interphone was out from our nose. We immediately went out of control although I could see the co-pilot [2nd Lieutenant Sanford W. Fish of Orange County, New York] doing all he could to keep us flying. As it fell away from the formation the pilot gave the order to bail out.'

Only Howie and the two waist gunners made safely out of the bomber. Breaking up, *De-Icer* spun to the ground and crashed in the Spandau district, narrowly missing a house. Seventeen-year-old Oberhelfer Hans Ring, serving with Heavy Flak Abteilung 437 who was concentrating his attention on the main formation being engaged by his battery, was suddenly astonished to see a complete B-24 fin and rudder assembly coming down like a falling leaf near his gun site. At Oberursel, 13 km north-west of Frankfurt-on Main the "Durchgangslager der Luftwaffe" or "Transit Camp of the Luftwaffe" (which was called Dulag Luft by the PoWs), a Luftwaffe officer informed Harry Howie that his plane spun to the ground and crashed into a house and that five bodies were found in it and that they identified three of the men. One of the bodies was identified as Staff Sergeant Walter Springer Jr., the 28-year-old tail turret gunner. He left a widow, the former Hazel Othea Polson. They had one child, Wayne, born in 1942. Staff Sergeant Hyman Waxler of Bristol County, Massachusetts died trapped in the nose turret of the Liberator. He had been hospitalized for several days and was trying to catch up with his regular crew when he flew three of his final four with Jack Harris and his crew.

Staff Sergeant James H. McMahon of St. Albens, New York, tail turret gunner of *Baggy Maggy* in the 93rd 'Travelling Circus' looked down on Berlin with hate in his heart. He should have been as 'nervous as hell' (his plane was in the high element and 'coffin corner') but he thought of his brother Thom in a PoW camp and all the other fellows he had seen go down.[13] 'The sky was perfect, no clouds, which meant that the German fighters were going to come up and that the flak would be accurate. I figured if I came back, OK, but if I went down it would be for Thom. Thinking this I felt glad. I believed that I was going to die and was fully prepared to die right over the target. I felt that what I was doing was the most important thing I had done on all my nine previous raids. All of the men felt the same way. We felt that if we could hit Berlin and survive we would probably survive to go home. Of course, this was rationalising but it worked for a lot of us. Well, all the way in to the target the flak was bad and the 'Jerry' fighters sure played hell. Our fighters sure gave them hell too. I didn't get any shots at fighters till the target. I saw one Focke Wulf 190 shoot down one of our B-24s, which went into a dive and went straight down. Then all hell broke loose. The flak was terrible at different places going to the target and coming out. It was very heavy over Berlin itself. It looked like we had flown through a black thundercloud as we were going away from the target area. The plane shook and was buffeted like we were in air turbulence and you could hear the shrapnel hitting the ship like a tree branch whipping a metal roof. German fighters were everywhere. The group behind us was catching hell with fighters and I got in about ten squirts at them.

'We kept flying through the flak and made two runs on the target (I believe that we went directly over the centre of the city). It took twenty minutes. All this time I could see Berlin and there were B-24s and B-17s all over the place. Our bombs hit smack on the target and my heart bled for those damned krauts down there. The whole lousy place was on fire. Everything was blowing up. Well after that for 100 miles I could see the fires and smoke. It looked like all Berlin was on fire. Boy did I feel good. I was laughing like hell for some reason. I guess it was because I was still there. After I got back to base (after squirting those 'Jerry' fighters all the way home) I got to sleep and dreamed about Thom. All the time over the target I was thinking about him and Dad and Mom and Sis. Everything was going through my mind at once. I sure felt good because we knocked the hell out of them. We didn't even get a scratch on the plane either and that sure was something for the books. I saw many, many planes burning on the ground and pieces of aircraft flying past my turret from ships that had exploded somewhere ahead of us. I remember many chutes floating down and watching some ships going down in flames after head-on fighter attacks. Most of the planes exploded into three or four balls of fire like Roman candles before they hit the ground. Typically they fluttered to the ground like falling leaves or spiralled into a ball of fire or just disintegrated. I saw many, many German fighters passing under my turret and sometimes just above it. It was like a fast speed movie. Lots of the time I didn't get a chance to squirt them. Fighters going away were the hardest to hit.

"Returning to base, we were on the same path as when we went in and the fires were still burning on the ground. Some of them were ours and some of them were theirs. I had a feeling of hate for the Germans and I wished that I could have gotten a clear kill. I felt that we had killed many Germans and that perhaps our raid would pay them back in some way for the comrades and innocent people they had killed. I hoped that that raid would terrorise them as they had terrorised us. It was the beginning of the end for them and they knew it. We lost six planes on this raid.'

The crew of *Reddy Teddy* in the 93rd formation had crossed the enemy coast at 22,000 ft at 1121 and at 1213 they encountered flak for the first time on the flight. About an hour later Messerschmitt 109s and 110s and FW 190s and Stukas appeared in the sky but they sailed though and began the bomb run at just after 1330 hours. 'There was very heavy flak by extra heavy guns and rockets" recalled Glenn Tedford. "As we began the bomb run flak was brutal from 88 mm guns and we guessed 150mm guns because of the size of the bursts. Two engines were out leaving Berlin. I feathered one prop for good and feathered the other off and on and was able to transfer gas' to the engine giving us some power. Our altitude dropped from 22,000 ft to 20,000 ft and 'Ken' Keene, co pilot, called in escort fighters to drive off the Me 109s attacking us. Finally we were at 18,000 ft, out of formation and on our own. We could have gone to Sweden or Switzerland. If we went to either we would lose our crew. On the crew's advice we brought *Reddy Teddy* home. We crossed the Dutch coast at 14,500 ft at 1516 and landed at Hardwick at 1600 hours. After this experience we were sent to a 'Flak House' in southern England for a two week rest. Our plane had the two engines replaced.'

"The weather was considerably better than the past few days" wrote Lieutenant Thurman Spiva, bombardier on *Lil' Max* in the 446th 'Bungay Buckaroos' named after the 'Little Max' comic book character. Spiva had the feeling that his crew would make it all the way to Berlin this time. (On 3 March they were one of the crews who were recalled when they were within 150 miles of the target). 'The take-off, climbing into formation and departing the English coast was routine. We were a little behind schedule at departure, but were back on schedule by the time we crossed the Dutch coast near the Zuider Zee. Every minute it took to make up lost time cut into the scanty fuel reserve. We could see the black patches of flak ahead in the Dummer Lake areas. The 1st and 3rd Divisions preceded us. Our turn at the target came just after noon and was followed by scattered enemy fighter attacks. Fortunately, most made only single passes through the formation and there were no losses. At the bomber stream breakup point north of Magdeburg, the 446th made a turn to the right. Berlin was abeam to the left just about fifty miles away. You could see the 3rd Division ahead as they made their turn at the IP, heading almost due north toward Kleinmachnow. The air around their formation was filled with vapour trails as the battle reached a climax. Then the bombers entered the flak area around the target. The 446th had seen flak many times, but few times could compare with the sight before the Group. Whistling shrapnel burst into coloured balls of purple orange, green and gold. Shrapnel hitting the planes sounded like hail on a tin roof. Being the last Division in the bomber stream, the Group looked into a great black sea of smoke as it turned at the IP and headed toward Genshagen. It was a sobering sight. Flak was dreaded more than enemy fighters. You could shoot back at fighters; there was nothing you could do about anti-aircraft fire. Maybe take evasive action and drop 'Chaff' to attempt to foul up their radar. You just had to sit there and let them shoot at you. Many times we were told at briefings that most of our losses would come from fighter attacks. The losses from anti-aircraft fire were estimated to be less than one percent. All that information meant little when you had to penetrate a flak area like that defending Berlin.

'As we levelled out after the IP turn, our troubles began. The prop on our No.2 engine ran away. The pilot reached for the throttle to cut it back. Unfortunately, this was our first mission in the latest model B-24J. The throttles were ganged together on a bar to make it easier for the pilots to fly in formation. By the time our pilot had the power reduced on the engine it had blown a cylinder. One dead engine and worse, the propeller had failed to feather. The plane began to shudder from nose to tail.

'It was apparent, with the vibrations; we were not to get much farther unless the situation could be corrected. The pilot worked feverishly to feather the prop. The crew readied themselves for possible bail-out. There couldn't possibly be a worse place to bailout. We were over the edge of Berlin and it was the 8th Air Force's first full raid over the German capital. If forced to hit the silk, it would have been a very warm reception when we hit the ground. Finally, after what seemed like an eternity, the pilot by using the starter on the dead engine it turned enough to feather the propeller and we settled down to normal flight. Although all this took only a few minutes, when it was over we had dropped 12,500 ft and found ourselves alone in the sky. We could see the tail end of our formation miles ahead as it approached the target. Simple arithmetic told us we could not regain altitude and rejoin our formation by the time they reached the target. It was also obvious we were having to use high power settings and were burning a lot of fuel just to carry our full load of bombs. The pilot decided to head north and drop our bombs on the first target of opportunity and hope to rejoin the formation as it made its homeward turn northeast of Berlin. Our bombardier, Adrian Perrault, soon found a small railroad marshalling yard and he salvoed our 12 500-pounders there.

'We soon found the formation was leaving us. It was a lonely feeling as we were still about 400 miles from home. Fortunately, everything went well until we reached the Wittingen area. Our right waist gunner reported enemy fighters. Two Me 110s came in level from 9 o'clock. Their first pass was not pressed home closely as they passed underneath and turned to our rear. They were joined by two more Me 110s and lined up for another pass from 9 o'clock. This time they came in pairs. I looked out the right side of the aircraft as they came barrelling in and wondered how we could possibly escape major damage with four of them pressing home the attack. The Luftwaffe pilots were bad shots. A crew check after their pass revealed only two nicks in one of the props. The tail gunner reported one of the Me 110s was trailing smoke indicating at least one of them had been hit.

'Only a minute or so passed when two Me 109s were coming in from 1 o'clock high. They came in head-on and passed under the right wing as they attacked. We were now a sitting duck and knew they would continue the attack until we were shot down. We had watched this drama played out too many times not to know what the outcome would be. The lone cripple always lost. Crews that were lucky had enough time to bail out before the fatal blow was delivered. The unlucky crews went down with the plane as it blew up or went into its final spin. Our pilot contacted our own fighter escort and requested assistance. It was our lucky day. The Me 109s were still in their descending turn below us as two P-47s came out of nowhere and attacked them. Above us were two other P-47s flying an 'S' pattern back and forth to stay down near our speed. We were passed from one escorting fighter group to another. They covered us until we departed the enemy coast. Two P-38s joined us about half-way across the North Sea. They stayed with us until we saw the English coast. We were about 40 minutes behind everyone else as we landed. There was so little fuel in the tanks that it was almost impossible to measure it. Everyone had given us up for lost. We owed our lives to the courageous fighter pilots who stayed with us that day. We were the lucky ones. They arrived in time and from then on our lives were largely in their hands. You will never find ten more grateful crew members than we were on that cold winter afternoon.'[14]

'About six 109s came in on our squadron and we were quite busy for a few minutes' recalled Sergeant John D. Kettman of Chicago, Illinois, waist gunner on the crew of Lieutenant Harry L. Cornell from McKeesport, Pennsylvania, in the 305th Bomb Group. "One went by me smoking. Darwin Gidel the top turret gunner or George Meyer the bombardier must have hit him. I got in a burst at him. From then on they were with us all the way to the target and part way out. The group behind us got three 109s in just a few minutes. They got one B-17; we saw three chutes coming out. All our guns were going at once. We believed that our bombs fell short of our target, a ball bearing plant on the outskirts of the city. At the target the flak was accurate and heavy and there were rockets also. In fact they threw up everything but the kitchen sink! There were all kinds of fighters – theirs and ours. There were some great dogfights going on. We got back in a hurry due to a tail wind. Escort was good coming back.'[15]

At Deopham Green, two miles north of Attleborough in Norfolk, newsmen were waiting to interview crews in the 452nd Bomb Group. 'I saw smoke pouring up from the target. They hit it right on the nose,' recalled Staff Sergeant Zenas R. Cole the ball turret gunner on 2nd Lieutenant Stephen A. Gaal's crew. Gaal, born Flushing, New York, had boarded the *Queen Elizabeth* on 31 March 1944 the day his first son, Stephen Gaal Jr., was born and the crew decided to name their plane *Junior* for Gaal's son. (*Junior* would fail to return from the raid on Berlin on 19 May when all ten crew were taken into captivity). Staff Sergeant John G. Brown, right waist gunner of *Sunrise Serenade* claimed that, 'we really set Berlin on fire and it will almost take the entire Atlantic Ocean to put it out'. The Fortress was flown by 21-year-old pilot, 1st Lieutenant Francis Charles Smedley, born Winneta, Illinois. His mother, who lived alone in Oconto Falls, Wisconsin, dearly loved the Glenn Miller tune *Sunrise Serenade* so the crew agreed to affix the name to their plane.[16] Brown and seven crew members were taken prisoner after *Sunrise Serenade* was shot down on the mission to Metz on 1 May and broke in two, crashing near Nieuwermolen Castle at St. Ulriks-Kapelle, Brussels. Smedley was killed when his chute caught on the horizontal stabilizer. The left waist gunner evaded capture. Technical Sergeant Larry A. Zaccardi, radio operator on *The Reincarnation* aka *Shed House Mouse* retorted: 'Berlin will have a heck of a lot of rebuilding after this raid'.

Some groups on the 6 March raid experienced 'walls of bursting metal' and about nine B-17s received major flak damage. The 452nd lost *Flakstop* to fighters that killed Lieutenant Charles F. Wagner and four of his crew. Flak had claimed *Hell's Cargo* and John Buel the co-pilot. Nine crew members were taken prisoner. 'It was like a solid blanket' said 2nd Lieutenant Robert O. Lloyd, co-pilot of *Sleepy Time Gal'*. Staff Sergeant Andrew M. Vanover from Rush, Kentucky, the right waist gunner on *Tangerine,* told how he shot down a FW 190. 'I opened fire at him while he swooped down on us. Part of the engine blew off and fell towards earth. It had broken into five pieces before hitting the ground and the pilot never did manage to get out.' *Tangerine* had been named by the pilot, 2nd Lieutenant

Glenn T. "Tay" Butterworth Jr. of La Grange, Illinois who liked the popular song of the same name that was made famous by the Jimmy Dorsey Orchestra in 1942. Second Lieutenant Robert C. Schimmel, pilot of *Evanton Babe*, brought back his battered ship all alone to England from Berlin after it was hit by flak and then attacked by fighters, to crash land at Metfield airfield after he had ordered his entire crew to bail out over enemy territory when he thought it the only way they could survive. Second Lieutenant Walter J. Ziegele the bombardier, was killed when his 'chute failed. The navigator, 2nd Lieutenant Charles J. Mueller, who was from Chicago, Illinois recalled that upon their arrival in England, the scheduled airfield at Prestwick, Scotland had difficult weather conditions for landing, so they landed at an RAF airfield at Evanton Bay. The runway was short and not designed for bombers, so both tyres blew out due to the accelerated stop. While replacing the tyres, the RAF ground crew painted on the nose of the plane, a female figure and the name *Evanton Babe*.[17]

Staff Sergeant Robert Thornton the right waist gunner on *Jeanne* in the 94th Bomb Group in the Composite Group, which came under sustained fighter attack, later recalled: "The enemy opposition was extremely heavy. It was very unusual to see fighters in the flak field. They were in there this day. The sky was black from flak bursts. The Germans threw everything they had at us. We lost many planes. After 'bombs away' all you could hear on the headsets was "Let's get the hell out of here." We had no problems until about 1430 hours. We took a hit from flak and went into a dive, on fire. The hit was between the cockpit and the bomb bay. It was a very serious situation to say the least. We dropped approximately 5 to 6,000 ft, out of control. For some unknown reason the ship levelled off just long enough for the enemy fighters to pounce on us. Everyone was scrambling to get out except the co-pilot. He took a direct hit in the head from a 20mm. No head."

Lieutenant Charles Johnston, whose parachute was now riddled with holes, went to the escape hatch and attempted a partner escape with 2nd Lieutenant Robert E. Davenport his bombardier who like himself had been born in Philadelphia, Pennsylvania, but they never latched onto one another. Once the chute snapped open there was little hope for Johnston. He lost his grip and fell to his death.[18] Robert Thornton left the plane at approximately 17,500 ft. "The ship was an inferno. When my chute opened the loose harness hit me between the legs and I was knocked out. I regained consciousness just as I started through the clouds. I knew that I was hurt. My groin area was completely numb. My left leg was dangling. As I came through the clouds a Me 109 almost hit me. He was using the cloud cover to get to the formation. When he saw me, he banked around and throttled back. I thought that he was going to shoot me as I hung in the parachute. He came up alongside, took a good look, saluted and went back after the formation. Wow, what a scare. The wind at ground level was high; the ground was frozen and the field I landed in was ploughed. I was swinging and my left side took the brunt of the landing. My left ankle broke (both sockets), my left leg was immobile and needless to say, escape was impossible. I later found out that I was 13 kilometres from the border with Holland, near a small town named Lingen."[19]

The 'Snetterton Falcons' were positioned at the rear of the 45th Wing, behind the 388th and 452nd Bomb Groups and Lieutenant Stanley A. Peterson the 25-year-old navigator in the crew of *The Saint* from Truman, Minnesota had a bird's eye view of the panorama unfolding before him. As he said, 'You would have to see it to believe it.' He looked down the shadows the bomber contrails created on this clear day and estimated they were about 20 miles wide. To him, it was so symbolic of the approaching storm of defeat closing in on the Third Reich. Although the targets were in the suburbs of the capital, 'Big B' had been reached at last. Peterson looked down on the city and was surprised at how all this was possible. They flew past Tempelhof, past lakes and woods and then they began their bomb run. It was the only time he could remember that they continued to climb during the bomb run, as the anti-aircraft fire was extremely heavy. Peterson thought that this was a day neither the men of the 8th Air Force nor Hermann Göring and his leader would forget. Göring had promised the Berliners and especially Hitler that the American bombers would not appear over the capital city.

In the 388th Bomb Group formation Second Lieutenant Raymond R. Newark of Brooklyn, the bombardier on *Shack Rabbits* flown by 2nd Lieutenant Augustine B. Christiani, recalled the events of the day he would never forget. 'We got to Berlin and could see our checkpoints on the river. We were around 24,000 ft and ready. Suddenly, we were told to circle Berlin again. We had already survived the flak. We almost decided to abort. We made a very sharp turn out of the area and headed for the secondary target. We were scared. We did not want any more flying over Berlin. As soon as we relieved ourselves of our bomb load we headed back to base. We dodged some flak and there were no fighters. It seemed we were living under the wings of angels because other groups were getting picked up and strafed. When our lead navigator radioed that up ahead was the Zuider Zee and we could see it, we started a turn and began to relax; off came our oxygen masks and we started eating our Mars bars. All of a sudden, at about 2 o'clock high, I saw some specks in the distance. 'Here come the P-51s. It's about time,' I said. A few seconds later someone said, 'Hey they're flashing their lights at us'. Someone else said, 'they're not lights: they're shooting at us!' Sure enough they were the yellow-nosed kids from Abbeville.

'Those German pilots were terrific. They came through our group and we closed in as tight as we could possibly get. I shot at one that came across our nose from around 3 o'clock. I led him and saw him blow up. Then I ran my guns to another one which was coming in at 2 o'clock but I forgot to release my finger on the trigger and my guns froze. The formation at this time had really spread out and we wound up as 'tail-end Charlie'. All of a sudden I got hit in my left forearm by a 30-30, a 20-mm armour piercing incendiary (API) and another

30-30 simultaneously. (We knew they were firings APIs because we could see them going through the airplanes and exploding elsewhere instead of on impact. It was lucky for me because the API went right through my arm and exploded in the Nos.1 and 2 engines. One of the 30-30s bounced off my flak helmet and the other bounced off my flak suit. The impact of all three knocked me clear all the way back to the hatch underneath the pilot's seat.

'As I lay there looking up I could see that the plane was a blazing inferno. Salvatore Ciaccio the engineer was screaming in his top turret. He was on fire from head to foot. There was no way of saving that boy. I did not see 'Gus' [Christiani] or 'Clarry' Farrington, the co-pilot. I yelled to Lieutenant Leon Levy the navigator to get me an oxygen mask; I was starting to lose consciousness. Mine was knocked off by the impact and shredded. Luckily, the extra mask was lying near the escape hatch. He slapped it on me, plugged into the oxygen system and revived me. The next thing I know, I said 'Get my 'chute'. My chest pack was completely shredded. Luckily, the extra 'chute was available to be snapped on. Levy said, 'I'm going to pull the hatch door and get you out of here'. I said 'OK, providing you follow me'. He pulled the release and shoved me out at around 20,000 ft. As I left the door, suddenly it became quiet. I passed out momentarily. I revived and realised that I had to pull the ripcord on my parachute. I reached over and could not find my left arm, I thought, 'Oh my God; my arm's been blown off.' I pulled at my flight suit and there was my arm but it was dangling. I could do nothing with it so I picked it up and put the thumb in between my teeth so that it would remain there if and when I pulled the ripcord the impact wouldn't snap off my arm. I passed out again. The next time I revived I was face down and floating like a falling leaf. I was at about 2,000 ft and the ground was rushing up to me. I just did not have the strength to pull the ripcord. I said, 'God, give me the strength' and with one big yank I pulled the ripcord. The 'chute popped open and I bit my thumb so hard I killed all the nerves, permanently."

The Luftwaffe arrived to get Ray Newark the morning after his capture and drove him to an airfield where the 109s that shot his B-17 down were based. "A lot of captured Americans were there. So too was Hermann Göring himself! He was up on a stage in front of us and the whole squadron of Luftwaffe pilots. Over the loudspeaker he lauded us. 'Only the flyers are heroes in this war' he said. 'I salute you'. He broke out the champagne and passed round glasses. We all had to drink a toast with him. The irony of it all. He told us that the wounded would be sent to hospital and the others would be sent to a PoW camp. Christiani, Levy and Bill Kline and Bill Pope the two waist gunners were the only survivors from my crew. They were shipped off to PoW camps. I was put in a truck with four other fellers, on top of a bunch of dead bodies. In early June four of us left hospital on crutches and were moved to Dulag Luft and then PoW camp."[20]

The 388th Bomb Group was missing seven Fortresses. All ten men on *Shack Job* piloted by 2nd Lieutenant John W. McLaughlin, of Canton, Illinois, that was shot down by a fighter south of Bremen were taken prisoner. *Duchess of Dixie* piloted by 21-year-old 1st Lieutenant Clarence Asbury 'Clarry' Grindley Jr., was shot down by a fighter near the Dutch border and crashed at Schoeningsdorf, six miles west of Meppen, Germany. Second Lieutenant Eino V. Allanderwia the co-pilot of Indianapolis, Indiana who was wounded in action, died after his 'chute failed when he bailed out. The waist gunners, Staff Sergeants' Selmer Thompson and Bayne F. Tucker of Taylor, Texas also died. Thompson was born in Rangoon, Burma on 27 August 1911 and lived in Sanger, Fresno County, California. Staff Sergeant Donald E. Liebman the 20-year-old ball turret gunner of Davenport, Iowa who suffered a serious arm injury caused by a 20mm shell and later had the arm amputated, suffered a heart attack and died in a PoW hospital in Lingen on 2 April.

At Knettishall Harry Allert, *Blitzing Betsy*'s crew chief had waited in vain for the first-class buzz job over his tent that he had been promised by Lowell Watts but *Blitzing Betsy* had been severely damaged near Quakenbrück on the return journey by attacks from several FW190s. Though her gunners shot down two of the attackers, *Blitzing Betsy* was set on fire with hits to the #3 engine and to the oxygen bottles under the flight deck. Going into a spin she collided with Captain Paul E. Brown's B-17 flying above, detaching part of the left wing and knocking the ball turret off of that ship and peeling the roof away from her own flight deck. Staff Sergeant Edwin William Pfanner the 21-year-old ball turret gunner of Union City, New Jersey was fortunate to survive. Brown, of Joplin, Missouri, ordered the crew to bail out. It was the last order he ever gave. 1st Lieutenant John W. DuPrey the navigator who was from Minnesota and 2nd Lieutenant Holland T. Gill the bombardier from Livingson, California were blown out of the nose. Duprey was killed but Gill survived. Brown's aircraft commander, Captain George C. Job Jr., the 561st Bomb Squadron CO from New York State riding in the co-pilot's seat and 2nd Lieutenant Joseph P. Lechowski the co-pilot of Diakaum, Pennsylvania, who never got his chute on, were both killed. Staff Sergeant Walter Scott Reed the right waist gunner from Vian, Oklahoma, failed in an attempt to get the rear exit door open and died from lack of oxygen. Staff Sergeant William Angelo Marcario, the 22-year-old tail gunner from Brooklyn, New York and Tech Sergeants' Roy E. Joyce the engineer from Rockland, Massachusetts and John Basil Blatz the 26-year-old radio operator from Crystal City, Missouri, bailed out and were taken prisoner. Blatz died in a PoW hospital from injuries and severe burns on 18 March. Staff Sergeant Elbert P. Moyer the right waist gunner from Bethlehem, Pennsylvania, who must have passed out due to lack of oxygen, woke up still falling from the sky and opened his parachute just in time. He was taken in by a Dutch family but escape was impossible. He had been very badly burned when he opened the cockpit door to check on the pilots and fire shot out, badly burning his eyelids and his forehead and the wires in his electrically heated gloves heated up with the fire and melted to his hands. When he took them off the first layer of skin went with them. After capture and a few days being questioned Moyer was admitted to Frankfurt hospital. As well as receiving several skin grafts he had to have eyelids made for him.[21]

Emmett Murphy, Robert Kennedy, Edward Kelly and Tech Sergeant Ivan Nathan Finkle the 21-year-old radio operator had bailed out before *Blitzing Betsy* went into a spin and exploded. Tech Sergeant Joe Bryan Ramsey the 34-year-old flight engineer/top turret gunner from Timpson, Texas was pinned to the side of the fuselage with Staff Sergeant Raymond Hess the waist gunner pinned on top of him when the aircraft exploded. Ramsey was blown clear of the fuselage and though seriously injured was able to open his parachute but Hess was not wearing a parachute. Lowell Watts, who was just beginning to recover from the spin when the aircraft blew apart, was also blown clear of the aircraft. Staff Sergeant Robert M. Sweeney the 21-year-old ball turret gunner from Annapolis, Maryland, waist gunners' Staff Sergeants' Don Taylor (22) from Michigan, Ray Hess (21) from Wilmore, Pennsylvania and Staff Sergeant Harold Adrian Brassfield the 22-year-old tail gunner from Insull, Kentucky were found dead in or near the wreckage of their plane. Watts, Murphy, Taylor and Brassfield were on their 25th and final mission of their tour. Sadly, the day of the mission was Donald Taylor Junior's first birthday.

There was no sign of *Suzie-Sagtitz*. 'Monty' Givens' risqué-named B-17 had been hit at 1505 hours possibly by 28-year-old Hauptmann Hugo Frey of 7./JG 11 in his FW 109, who was killed after shooting down three more B-17s in the battle which took his score to 32; 25 of which were four engined bombers. Head-on attacks prevented Tom Foulds, the ball turret gunner of Detroit, Michigan from returning the attackers' fire. He had to be content with looking out for FW190s, which attacked from lower positions. The German fighters carried out such razor-sharp attacks that the bomber crews could see the faces of the enemy pilots as their aircraft "rolled" through the formation. "I felt a clear shock when our plane was hit" Foulds said. "In the second or third attack, I was wounded when 20mm rounds hit my turret and exploded, causing shrapnel to ricochet through the dome. Later it turned out that I had about 40 wounds in both legs and in my neck; most were small and shallow. My interphone stopped working and I could see that the two starboard engines were on fire so I opened the hatch and looked into the side hatch compartment. Sergeant Daniel Walstra the tail gunner was busy kicking open the side hatch and gestured me to follow and leave the plane. I put on my parachute and went to the escape hatch. Jim Geraghty the ball turret gunner came after me. When I passed Staff Sergeant Willard McGee the right waist gunner, he was still standing behind his machine gun and firing incessantly. It seemed he wasn't hurt."

Suzy-Sagtitz was in bad a bad way. Two engines were on fire and there was also fire in the fuselage; heavy clouds of smoke penetrated the cockpit. It was clear that the crew had to leave the plane, but not before Tech Sergeant Roy E. Kesanen the radio operator/top turret gunner of Mullen, Idaho had hit one of the attackers. (Other crew members confirmed that the fighter was going down).

Givens, who feared the fuel tanks would explode, signalled "abandon aircraft!" The crew reported one by one that they were going to jump. Jim Geraghty, who was from Yonkers, New York climbed out of the ball turret and parachuted to safety. Staff Sergeant Jack E. Karr the 23-year-old waist gunner, who could no longer reach the forward compartment because of the havoc, went out through one of the waist windows.[22] "Larry" McMillan, Kenneth Betts and Harry Teat all left through the front escape hatch. Givens activated the autopilot and was able to keep the plane horizontal for a while. Then, however, it began to climb and threatened to slip off. He quickly followed the others through the hatch, quickly pulled on the drawbar of his parachute, which then opened with a jerk. Looking around, he counted eight more parachutes, so all but one of the crew could have left the plane. He did not know then that the missing man was Willard McGee the 28-year-old waist gunner of Walnut Cove, Stokes County, North Carolina who had died at his guns. His body was found in the wreckage of *Suzie-Sagtitz* which crashed in flames near Darien in Holland. McGee left a widow, Nellie Virginia, who he had married on 4 September 1943. The cruel irony of fate meant that Willard's twin brother, who was a gunner in another Eighth Air Force group, had been killed just three days earlier. Givens and surviving crew were soon captured and taken to the town jail before being marched off into captivity.

Cloud banks had prevented attacks on Erkner and Klein Machnow and permitted just a few bombers to bomb Genshagen and the decision to abandon the attacks on the primary target was made too late for the B-17s to switch to radar bomb runs on the Friedrichstrasse station. Attacks on targets of opportunity were widespread and the loss of life was significant. The first American air raid on Berlin, which went down in the annals as 'Black Monday' had certainly flushed out the Luftwaffe, just as General 'Jimmy' Doolittle the 8th Air Force commander had hoped it would. The Fortress gunners and the fighter pilots claimed over 170 German fighters destroyed but the Americans had suffered record losses. The 1st Division had lost eighteen B-17s while the 2nd lost sixteen B-24s. The 3rd had lost 35 bombers; a loss rate of 10.2 percent. Eleven fighters also were lost. The Luftwaffe, some of whose pilots who flew five sorties that day, actually lost 64 fighters, including sixteen Bf 110 and Me 410 heavy fighters.

Thirty-six B-17s had set out from Thorpe Abbotts, led by Major Albert Max 'Bucky' Elton the 418th Bomb Squadron Operations Officer. 'Bucky's weight had, because of too many sleepless nights, come down to 103 lbs. Elton dreaded nightmares and went to sleep in the room with "Smokey" Stover, the medic to calm his nerves. After takeoff and assembly, six Forts returned leaving thirty to continue. At the controls of *The Nelson King* was Lieutenant Frank G. Lauro, who until joining the service had been the youngest member of the New York Stock Exchange. *The Nelson King* had been named in honour of radio operator Tech Sergeant Nelson King, an oversized farm boy from Kansas. On a previous mission to Bremen Nelson had lost fingers and parts of both hands when he exposed his skin to sub-zero temperatures in an effort to save ball turret gunner,

Sergeant Murray Schrier who had lost his oxygen mask. King had removed his gloves in order to tie the mask on the ball turret gunner. His bare hands had been in the cold for approximately twenty minutes. They were not frostbitten, they were frozen. King's numb fists had swollen to the size of grapefruits. Trying to bring feeling to them he hit the sides of the Fort, causing bits of frozen flesh to flake off like chunks of ice. 'I didn't see King's hands until we got down on the ground,' Lauro later said. 'Frostbite was no word for what happened to his hands. One of the flight surgeons looked at them and I looked at the 'doc' and what he must have been thinking wasn't pretty. King saved Schrier's life with those hands.' In a series of surgeries, all of King's fingers and thumbs were gradually amputated along with parts of both hands. The surgeons slit a portion of each hand between the bones of the middle and ring fingers to create claws. King spent a total of 22 months in the hospital before he returned home. The brave radioman was awarded the Silver Star for gallantry in action. Murray Schrier, who had worked in his father's hotel in New York before enlisting, recovered and resumed his position of top turret gunner on the crew.

Lauro had Captain Jack R. Swartout the 351st Squadron Operations Officer in the right hand seat. Regular co-pilot, 2nd Lieutenant Emanuel 'Joe' Greasamar, a lanky Ohio farm boy and part-time midget car racer, manned the tail guns, a position for which he was not trained. Swartout's reputation as one of the best lead pilots in the Group made him a natural to lead the Low Box of the 13th Combat Wing comprising the 95th, 100th and 390th Bomb Groups. The 1st and 3rd Bomb Divisions of B-17s had become detached from each other while flying through clouds over the English Channel. Losing sight of the 1st Bomb Division, the lead navigator of the 3rd Bomb Division had to do his own navigating. He made the necessary corrections for cross wind and was right where they were supposed to be, but without defensive fighter cover. Mission planners had massed all the defensive fighters over the lead elements of the 1st Bomb Division assuming that would be where the Luftwaffe would concentrate their fighter opposition. The 3rd Bomb Division and the unprotected 13th Combat Wing in particular, now paid the price, catching the full venom of the enemy fighter attacks. Captain Bob Shoens well remembers. 'It was a spectacular day, so clear it seemed we could almost see Berlin from over England. We took off on a gorgeous morning, climbing up along with the rising sun. Cloudless out over the North Sea and then, Europe laid out before us like a road map. *Our Gal' Sal'* was again part of 'Fireball Yellow', which flew lead and the group was going in with twenty planes – one short. Somewhere over eastern France we suddenly realised that we hadn't seen our fighter escort for several minutes. We had been without escort for about twenty minutes, which meant that a relay had not caught up with us. (The German fighters had engaged them somewhere behind us, knowing it would leave us without fighter escort.) The reason wasn't long in coming. Ahead of us, probably ten miles away, there appeared to be a swarm of bees – actually German fighters. Guesses ran to as much as 200.'

At high noon on reaching Haselüenne, a small German town 12 miles north east of Lingen the overwhelming numbers of enemy fighters, which in their first sweep, came head-on through the unlucky 13th Wing, 'bringing confusion abruptly'. 'They were coming right at us' Bob Shoens observed 'and in a few seconds were going through us. On that pass they shot down the entire high squadron of ten planes.'

Once he recovered from the initial shock, 'Bucky' Elton looked up and was stunned to see B-17s of the high squadron 'afire in formation, trailing long sheets of flame from their engines... As the fighters leaped in again others 'were in obvious trouble.' 'When an airplane went down' said Bob Shoens, 'you had to shut out the fact that it took men with it. On this raid it became most difficult because so many were lost. One loss in particular was an example of this. The crew from our own barracks were flying off the right wing of our airplane. Suddenly, during one of the fighter passes, their entire wing was on fire. In the next instant there was nothing there. The fighters made two more passes and when it was over *Our Gal' Sal'* was all alone. We saw another group ahead of us, so we caught up with it. The airplanes had an 'A' in a square on the tail so they were from the 94th. We flew on to Berlin with them and dropped our bombs. The flak was heavy but over Berlin the sky was black. The target was on the south-east side of the city. For reasons we couldn't figure out, the group we were with chose to turn to the left and go over Berlin. Since we were not part of the group we decided to turn to the right and get out of the flak. When we did that, a German battery of four guns started tracking. They fired about 40 rounds before we got out of range. None of them came close because of the evasive action we had taken. Higher up and ahead of us we saw another group so we climbed and caught up with it. It was also from our wing, having a 'J' in a square on its aircraft's tails (390th). We flew the rest of the way home with them without further incident. It was still a beautiful day and with a chance to relax we began to wonder what had happened to our group. It couldn't be that we were the only survivors of 'Fireball Yellow'.'

In thirty minutes the 13th Wing lost 24 B-17s and two more were damaged so badly that they were forced to land in Sweden. *Stark's Ark* in the 390th Bomb Group was shot down with the loss of Lieutenant Robert F. Starks' and two of his crew. The pilot, who was from Tallmadge, Ohio, was on his 25th mission. The 95th Bomb Group lost eight B-17s including *Situation Normal, Patches, She's My Gal' II* and *Berlin First* but worst hit was the 'Bloody' Hundredth, which lost 14 B-17s in the horrific battle over Germany. In the 349th Squadron, *Torchy 2, Going Jessies, Ronnie R* and two others took that squadron's total losses to five. In the 351st Squadron *Kinda Ruff* was hit the wing tanks by Oberleutnant Hans-Heinrich König of 3./JG 11 flying a Bf 109 and 1st Lieutenant Ed Handorf of Hammond, Indiana and seven of his crew were killed when the plane exploded. Only two gunners survived to be taken into captivity. Fighters set *Spirit of '44* on fire and the tail broke off before crashing at Aschenbehl Berg. Lieutenant Merril T. Rish of Creighton, Nebraska and three of his crew were killed.

In the 350th Squadron *Rubber Check* aka *Old Vibration* piloted by 1st Lieutenant Frank A. Granack of Hammond, Indiana was downed by flak. Eight crewmembers survived but the radio operator and the waist gunner were killed. Johnny Lautenschlager, who had indoctrinated John Gibbons on the Regensburg raid and eight of his crew on *Half and Half* did not reach the target. They were shot down during an attack by fighters near Haselüenne at about 1200 hours. Sergeant Johnny Stryjewski the radio operator gunner was killed and nine of the crew were taken into captivity. Six B-17s in the 418th Bomb Squadron including *Ronnie R, Snort Stuff,* piloted by 1st Lieutenant Samuel L. Barrick, who had to land in Sweden and *Terry and the Pirates* piloted by 23-year-old 1st Lieutenant William A. Terry of Cleveland, Ohio were missing. Terry's B-17 was attacked by fighters soon after turning northeast near the Dummer Lake. "Our plane was hard hit' recalled Lieutenant Robert P. Schremser the navigator of Trenton, New Jersey. "We must have lost our controls and we nosed over immediately into a spin. Firecrackers seemed to be exploding all over the nose area. I was hit in the arms and my face by fragments of a 20mm shell. The centrifugal force of the spin pinned me on top of my chute, which I finally managed to buckle on. I saw a hole break in the Plexiglas nose. Ralph Cotter sat there immobile but evidently was not hit. He had not put his chute on. After falling many thousands of feet, the wings came off and the fuselage twirled the rest of the way down. The centrifugal force let up. I headed for the hole in the nose. Cotter headed for the escape hatch without a chute. I dove out and drifted down an estimated 2,000 ft next to the ball turret gunner, James Bain, who had exited the tail in the same manner. Later, I learned that the tail had broken off and the control cables had snapped back, trapping the gunners. James Aitken the engineer who lost a leg below the calf to a 20mm shell was thrown out by Terry, co-pilot Bill Peterson or Cotter, just before the plane hit the ground. Bain and I were picked up immediately and loaded on a truck which had already picked up Aitken and some others. Prior to the pick-up, the bombs in our plane exploded as we were being captured. Germans and Americans fell face down in a ditch."[23] Terry, Peterson, Tech Sergeant Richard P. Howell, radio operator and Staff Sergeants' Charles C. Anthony and John R. Horn the waist gunners, Carl D. Hampton, tail gunner and Ralph Cotter, who had written to his mother the night before the raid, were dead.

The Nelson King, remarkably, remained airworthy – just – after a Focke Wulf 190 that failed to pull out of an attack on the Fort en route to Berlin while closing at 200 yards a second, tore off part of the B-17's vertical tailfin and rudder assembly. Lieutenant Frank Lauro and Captain Jack Swartout had to think fast as the B-17 slowed and dropped out of the formation. Lieutenant Emanuel E. Greasamar the co-pilot flying as one of the gunners, was knocked unconscious by the impact above his head. 'Joe' as he was better known, came to lying flat on his back looking up at the sky above. Thinking he was falling, he soon regained his senses and returned to manning his guns, unaware that a fighter had almost torn the Fortress in two. Having never had training, he just shot at everything until his guns got too hot to touch but the heated bullets continued to fire after he let go of the trigger.

Realizing the crippled bomber would never make it back to England alone Swartout decided to trail the formation to Berlin. He next dropped the bombs to reduce the weight, hoping to maintain as much airspeed as possible. Again, all hell broke loose. 'They just lined up tail to tail and started circling us like Indians used to make war on a lone covered wagon,' said Lauro. 'Occasionally one or two of them would peel off for a head-on attack. These were the worst of all.' A lone Bf 109 showed up from out of nowhere and fired several of its 20mm shells at the *King*. One of them exploded in the right side of the cockpit, wiping out the instrument panel, the hydraulics and the on-board radio communications and starting a fire.

'I'm hit, I'm hit,' Swartout yelled, as he thought he was wounded. It didn't take him long to realize he was merely covered in hot, red hydraulic fluid, although the butt of the shell did hit him in the chest severely enough to knock his breath out. Tech Sergeant Dewey Thompson the North Carolinian engineer came down from the top turret to assist, attempting to put a tourniquet on Swartout, who signalled that he was okay.

The *King* had two engines out, the number three gas' tank pierced and the oil cooler line damaged. The ball turret was covered in oil, making it impossible to see out. The top turret was soon put of commission by another hit. The cables to #4 engine were shredded and other systems were inoperative. The *King* could only maintain 140 mph. Anything more threatened further damage to the tail fin due to vibrations.

The *King* was a sitting duck for the German fighters. With the intercom out and a hole in the side of the pilot's cabin, the roar of the rushing air made it impossible to hear. Swartout looked at Lauro, tore off his headphones and motioned that he was taking control of the plane. The crew prepared to abandon ship, but Swartout had other plans. He ordered them to be ready to bail out but to hold steady until at least he made an attempt to fly home. With fighter pilot skills acquired in a P-47, he worked to evade the frontal attacks by the fighters. It took all of those skills to carry on the mission. With a good part of the oxygen system damaged, the gunners in the rear passed around oxygen bottles. Swartout guided the *King* toward Berlin, circumventing the flak and bombing runs, then intersected with the 390th Bomb Group that had just made its run.

Flying at a lower altitude, *Nelson King* was below the flak bursts, but three shells blasted through the wings and burst high above. Enemy fighters were still lining up to finish it off. Swartout guided the *King* under the higher 390th and up the formation's side away from trouble. As the other bombers stayed in their box for protection, Swartout dipped *Nelson King* and moved from side to side of the 390th to evade the attackers. He did this for a long time, doing everything possible to keep the damaged aircraft from the German fighters. It was then that a group of P-47s and P-51 Mustang fighters showed up, bringing a sense of relief to the beleaguered bomber's crew. The *Nelson King* made it safely back to England but the bomber was so shot up that patches of sky could be seen through the wings, tail, and fuselage, it was sent on to RAF Honington and the 9th Depot Repair Squadron there. Jack Swartout was awarded the Silver Star for bringing the *King* home and saving the lives of his fellow airmen, its crew suffering only two minor wounds.[24] Joe Greasamar wrote to his parents that night. "Boy oh boy, they about got us today. This is the closest we ever came to not coming back. We got our ship all shot up but we got home. We were one of the very few to get back.... We went to Berlin ... no wonder," he finished his letter.

Second Lieutenant Celesta B. 'Red' Harper in the 350th Squadron had "daringly evaded enemy fighters by putting *Buffalo Gal'* into an almost vertical dive to 5,000 ft at 270 mph". He and the ten other survivors in a ragged formation came limping home to Thorpe Abbotts at about 4 o'clock in the afternoon.

'When we got home we found that we were one of only five B-17s in the 351st Squadron to return to Thorpe Abbotts' recalled Bob Shoens (and *Nine Little Yanks and a Jerk* had to be salvaged). To say the least, we were upset, as was everyone on the base. Lieutenant Colonel Ollen 'Ollie' Turner, my squadron commander met us as we parked the airplane. He was in tears. It was hard to take but this was what we had been trained for.'

The acting CO, Lieutenant Colonel John M. Bennett Jr., who had been assigned to the 3rd Air Division in the summer of 1943 and, dissatisfied with a "desk job" had been granted active combat status, noted that every one of the 15 ships that came home fired red flares signifying wounded aboard. 'Just exactly 50% of our force, which entered Germany, had been shot down...' In less than two years the 100th Bomb Group was in action in Europe, it lost 229 Fortresses – 177 MIA and 52 from other operational losses. The 'Bloody Hundredth' became perhaps the most famous, albeit 'jinxed' group in the 8th. It was the worst hit group in the 3rd Division during the series of Berlin missions with 19 B-17s MIA on three raids on the German capital, on 3, 4 and 6 March.

As for the results of the 6 March raid, the majority of the bombs fell on a five-mile stretch of the suburbs, due mainly to overcast, creating huge fires and destroying the gas, power and telephone services. Oslo Radio, which was German controlled, regarded it 'as a catastrophe...' Even the Berlin News Agencies admitted that 'several hundred bombers had reached the city, despite intensive flak and unceasing fighter attacks.' Air Chief Marshal of the RAF Arthur Harris sent a message to his opposite number, General Carl 'Tooey' Spaatz: 'Heartiest congratulations on first US bombing of Berlin. It is more than a year since they were attacked in daylight but now they have no safety there day or night. All Germany learns the same lesson.'

The record loss of 69 bombers and a further 102 seriously damaged, meant that the survivors had lost many close buddies. At Knettishall the returning 388th Bomb Group were missing seven B-17s and 2nd Lieutenant Charles P. Wallace had to force land *A Good Ship and a Happy Ship* aka *Glory Girl* at Rinkaby airfield near Kristiansand in Sweden after losing the #4 engine to enemy action. His crew joined Sam Barrick's in internment. 'Goldie' Goldstein noted: 'All is quiet in the barracks. We heard late at night that the 8th Air Force suffered very heavy losses. I can only say how relieved I and the rest of the crew were. Our crew were so happy to be finished with our combat tour. I felt sorry for the men still flying but we had our share."

The Berlin raids cost the 8th scores of experienced crews and valuable aircraft to say nothing of the mental scars suffered by those who survived. 'Big-B' would be indelibly printed on their minds for days, months, even years, to come. Soon the nightmare for those who still had missions to fly would begin again. At one base a co-pilot, whose nerve was stretched ever since his crew had been shot down in his absence, had awoke during the night screaming having dreamt that he had been shot through the heart. The next night he dreamed that he went to Berlin by air. On 6 March he had gone to pieces. The flight surgeon told him not to fly. The co-pilot was in such a very bad nervous state that he had to be grounded permanently after that. Finally he had to be moved out of the crew hut. He was getting on everyone's nerves with his morbid conversation and moping attitude. He had not slept in a bed since his first big jolt, preferring to sit up all night in a chair or at the club.

Notes

1. In mid-June 1944 a ruling came down from 8th Air Force HQ that effective immediately, a tour would be 30 for lead crews and 35 for the all other crews. Existing Lead crews then had to fly a prorated 28 and the existing other regular crews had to fly 32. Crews assigned to the Group after that effective date had to do 30 and 35.
2. Correspondence with the author via Robert M. Foose. Appreciation is due to Ken Kline Jr. writing on the US Military Forum.
3. After being hit by flak and losing fuel *Hello Natural* Jack Parker the pilot turned towards Sweden and landed at Bulltofa airfield near Malmö and the crew was interned. They returned in July-September 1944.
4. *The War Lover* by John Hersey (Hamish Hamilton, London, 1959).
5. Ibid.
6. 'No-ball' was the code word for a V1 rocket site.
7. See *1944-03-06/06 B-24H 42-52226 Cripe Lake…- ZZAirwar*. While in Stalag Luft 1 Barth, Cripe handwrote a detailed account of his last mission in a book with blank pages that was provided by the YMCA. This became the basis of his autobiography *'Bittersweet Brutality'*.
8. Crockett returned to duty and on 25 April 1944 he and his crew were shot down over France. Nine men including Crockett were taken prisoner. One man evaded.
9. See *Liberator men of Old Buck*.
10. Sincere thanks to Oliver Clutton-Brock, Bruce Bolinger, Michael LeBlanc, Keith Howes and Brigitte D'Oultremont.
11. 42-52450.
12. It was Greiner's second claim of the day; he had shot down B-17G 42-38118 in the 91st Bomb Group, which was crash-landed southwest of Quakenbrück. Second Lieutenant

Benjamin J. Fourmy Jr. the pilot and 7 of his crew were captured. The bombardier and the radio operator were killed.

13. On 13 January 1943 Sergeant Thomas D. McMahon, the 18-year old ball turret gunner on B-17F 41-24471 *Four of a Kind* in the 306th Bomb Group was able to parachute safely after his B-17 was involved in a mid-air collision with B-17F 41-24498 in the 369 Bomb Squadron and broke in two just north of the target; the railway factories of Ateliers D'Hellemmes in Lille, France. The men were trapped in the tumbling halves, most finally either falling out or were able to claw their way into free air. Thom managed to evade capture until 24 April 1943 when he was captured at Brussels, Belgium. His pilot, Captain James A. Johnson and two of the crew were killed. 1st Lieutenant Jack A. Spaulding, returning to fly after an illness, and 5 of his crew on 41-24498 were killed. See *First Over Germany: A History of the 306th Bombardment Group* by Russell A. Strong (Hunter Publishing Co., 1982)

14. Correspondence with the author.

15. On the 24 March mission to Frankfurt Harry Cornell's crew was forced leave the formation after their B-17 was damaged by flak and fighters and bail out over Belgium. All ten crew were taken into captivity.

16. *452nd Bomb Group Plane Names Their Origins* by Jerry Penry.

17. Ibid. On 11 April 1944 on the Rostock mission Schimmel's crew on *Cow Town Boogie* were forced to land at Angelholm in Sweden after the #2 engine failed and they were interned.

18. Ken Kline Junior writing on the US Military Forum.

19. Lieutenant Charles Johnson and the co pilot died; 8 crew survived and were taken prisoner.

20. 2nd Lieutenant Clarence Darryl Farrington from Madison County, New York; Tech Sergeant Salvatore Ciaccio from Kings County NY; Sergeant John C. Griscom the 21-year-old tail gunner from Salem County, New Jersey; Staff Sergeant William Burtle Mayne the radio operator from Lackawanna County, Pennsylvania and Sergeant Rupert G. Smith the 29-year-old ball turret gunner From Tulsa County, Oklahoma were killed.

21. See *Dad's POW Story: Technical Sergeant Elbert Paul Moyer* (bonniemusser@yahoo.com.).

22. Senior Master Sergeant Jack Karr, who was born at Sharon, Pennsylvania on 7 September 1920, retired from the USAF in 1968 after WW2, Korean War and Viêtnam service. He was WIA three times during WW2.

23. Rona Simmons on the storiesbehindthestars.org/fold3 website.

24. In May, a new crew took over the *Nelson King* and was shot down on 24 May 1944, near Wittstock, Germany. The pilot, Lieutenant Emil J. Stiewert, bombardier 2nd Lieutenant Irving Jacobwitz and tail gunner Staff Sergeant Frank V. Kroczynski were KIA. The rest of the crew, who were on their 11th mission, were taken prisoner.

Chapter Four

The 'Big Friends' And 'Big B'

It had been a cold grey noon on 20 February 1944 when Slick Chick *a B-24H Liberator piloted by 1st Lieutenant 'Willie' Norris of Clearfield, Pennsylvania and co-pilot Owen Hassler of Wichita, Kansas, bomb bays loaded with flight bags and sacks of mail destined for Italy, sped across the runway at Mitchel Field, New York. After crawling lazily into the air, it headed south on the first leg of a half-way-round-the-world trip. The first course was to take the plane directly over the home of the navigator, 2nd Lieutenant Philip H. Meistrich and he heaved a sigh as he passed over his beloved Flatbush. As the B-24 passed over New York Harbour, swarming with its usual incoming and outgoing shipping, all eyes turned toward the 'Big City" for a last look. As* Slick Chick *touched Staten Island's shores they headed south, in stages, to West Palm Beach, Florida, the crew's jumping off point for the Southern Ferry Route and ultimately, to England. On the last leg of their journey, on Tuesday, 7 March the crew listened in on Radio Berlin. Meistrich heard the charming voice of 'Axis Sally' of whom later they were to hear a lot more. "She invited all Americans up to Stalag Luft, where the beds were soft and the sheets are clean and she'd be there. 'The food was also good,' she said. When she had finished, her friend, a renegade American newspaperman, speaking to his 'fellow Americans,' attacked the Plutocratic-Juder-Bolshevik President of the US. When this jerk was finished we switched to the BBC, where a charming female voice, sounding 'veddy-veddy' British, announced a programme of choice swing music, which was very enjoyable. All good things must come to an end and her programme did. Then the BBC reporter came through with a very depressing report about the 68 US bombers, which failed to return after a raid on Berlin. Gulp! And we were on our way to the Eighth Air Force. Yipe!*

From a story by Lieutenant Philip H. Meistrich.[1] Initially assigned to the 448th Bomb Group at Seething, in April his crew was re-assigned to the 735th Squadron, 453rd Bomb Group at Old Buckenham. Before returning to the States, the crew would complete 32 combat missions including D-Day.

'After interrogation' recalled Ernest Richardson in the 96th Bomb Group at Snetterton Heath, 'Steve' Condur, our top turret gunner, told us we were on pass and that we could take off immediately. I asked him where he was going and it wasn't long before we were waiting for a train to London. Dressing before we left, we kidded with the new crew that had taken Dickert's crew's place about being sure to hit the target etc. Take care of yourself and we would see them when we got back. When Condur and I arrived in London our first impression wasn't very nice, fog was floating around everything and it was quiet, blacked out and very gloomy. We ran into an Englishman and asked him how to get to the Red Cross Club. He gave us all kinds of directions ending with 'You can't miss it.' We couldn't make heads or tails out of what he said, but it made us laugh. Although we had a common language and it was our bond, we found that it was a barrier. We didn't understand it when they said 'keep your pecker up'. It meant keep your spirits up. 'Knock him up' meant to wake him up in the morning. When we did find the Red Cross Club it was full, so we just curled up and slept in chairs we found in the lobby.

'Tuesday, 7 March was bright and clear, so we were sure where the bombers would be going. Now that they knew they could go to Berlin, they wouldn't spare the horses – or should I say planes? Around 9 o'clock the bombers started passing overhead. There wasn't much doubt in our minds as to where they might be going. We were happy not to be with them. Condur and I spent most of the morning trying to find enough to eat and a place to spend the night. I think we hit every restaurant in and around Piccadilly Circus. It had the largest Red Cross Club in England. Around Piccadilly, a person could acquire almost anything, black market or otherwise. American soldiers, the English said were over paid, so anyone who had anything to sell usually brought it there. This also included ladies of the evening. Condur and I looked it all over. A lot of it was kind of disgusting but we realized England had been at war a long time. We wondered what it was like before the war. Our two day pass went by real fast. Before we knew it we were on our way back to the base. The train was crowded so we had to stand. Looking out the window we saw places the Germans had bombed and were still bombing. Some of it looked rather recent. At other times we saw ruins from the '41 Blitz; places beyond repair. It wasn't a very nice sight. Later, as we moved away from London we saw some Spitfires zoom by. We also saw some B-26s forming for an afternoon raid. All in all, it wasn't the sort of things that would raise your spirits. It would be another two weeks before we would get another pass; a lot could happen in that time.'

At Rattlesden crews in the 447th Group had climbed out of their cots at 0345 hours and headed to the mess hall for a breakfast of hotcakes and sausage and mash. Briefing was at 0500. At briefings on all the American bases it was announced that the primary target was Berlin (PFF). The secondary was the VKF ball-bearing plant. Crews were briefed that 623 bombers would be flying the third raid on the German capital in a week but the weather was so bad that the mission was scrubbed. The cancellation came after the regular briefing and the radio operator's briefing given by Tech Sergeant Harley Tuck on Lieutenant Thomas W. Gilleran's crew. Tossing everything back, Tuck managed to get to bed again by 0645 and he slept until 1015. Scrubs gave many crews another day to live but on 22 April Gilleran's crew failed to return from the mission to Hamm when their B-17, *Dear M.O.M.*, took a direct flak hit moments after 'bombs away' and exploded. Incredibly all ten men survived and they were taken prisoner. The name *Dear M.O.M.* was chosen by the Gilleran crew as a tribute to their bombardier, Lieutenant Marion O. McGurer, who received a compound fracture of a leg by flak on 3 February on the mission to Wilhelmshaven and was removed from flight duty.

At Thorpe Abbotts Colonel John Bennett was not alone in thinking 'thank God we had a day off to lick our wounds.' The respite was short however. Alerted on Tuesday evening, by 10 o'clock Bennett knew that the target the next day was again Berlin. The 3rd Division would lead the 8th to Erkner, the 1st Division flying in the middle, with the 2nd again flying 'caboose', bringing up the rear with 164 Liberators. At the B-24 base at Horsham St. Faith near Norwich, after enjoying breakfast at the combat officers' mess, 458th Bomb Group crews walked to their briefing hut. "This establishment was one of the rare Quonset huts on our base' said navigator Lieutenant Jackson Granholm. 'It was full of hard seats, and, at one end, was a platform. On the end wall of the hut, at the back of the platform, was a large, composite map of north-western Europe, England included. The map was covered with a green curtain until combat briefing actually began. Mission briefing was typically directed, conducted, and orchestrated by Captain Charles Booth, Assistant Group Operations Officer. He was a good choice for the job. He was always smiling, happy, charming and erudite – even early on a God-awful foggy morning when everyone present was going out to look death in the face in the skies over Berlin. To listen to Booth you would think we had all assembled for a Sunday school picnic."[2] Booth had flown his first mission of the war, five days' earlier, in *Satan's Mate* as command pilot of the Group formation. Now he would make his second trip, on *Bomb-Ah-Dear*, the Deputy Lead Liberator with 1st Lieutenant Philip R. Clark's crew 'looking death in the face in the skies over Berlin'.

Although it was not the Hundredth's turn to lead the 13th Combat Wing, John Bennett received permission to fly lead. Since he was acting CO John Bennett felt that the least he could do would be to fly with 'his boys' when they badly needed encouragement but he had only crews enough to put up 15 B-17s. The 13th Combat Wing would be the second Wing into the target behind the 45th Combat Wing leading 8th Air Force. 'It would be difficult to describe the feelings everyone had' Bob Shoens recalled. 'Do we have to go through it all again? Doesn't anyone have sympathy for what happened? Why Berlin again so soon? Of course, it had to be. There was no time to get caught up in your emotions or self-pity. The war goes on, life goes on. So, the 100th went on.'[3]

The Luftwaffe now concentrated on the leading Wing and the 100th took over the lead. After dropping on the Erkner ball bearing plant it turned for home. "The flak over the target had been surprisingly light. The 15 ships had delivered the goods. The trip home was uneventful" Bennett later declared. Not quite. After the target one of his B-17s was shot down, either by flak or fighters or a combination of both.[4] Manning one of the 13 batteries in the old Hanse town of Magdeburg south of Berlin, Friedrich J. Kowalke, a Luftwaffenhelfer (schoolboy) who had joined the flak school on reaching his 16th birthday in February 1943 had the opportunity to track many approaching B-17 boxes with the four-metre-base optical rangefinder. He and his comrades knew that the bomber stream was on its withdrawal leg, moving from east to west. 'At first many B-17 boxes were seen" he wrote. "Later on, B-24 boxes appeared too, making up the rear. This armada avoided the flak zone of Magdeburg to some degree, flying a west-north-west course, well timed by repeated placing of marker bombs or corresponding flares. The B-17s were clearly visible against high cirrus overcast, flying outside of our flak battery range. Our time was well after 12 o'clock. The most northern flak batteries of Magdeburg had fired all their ammunition against the bomber stream whose penetration leg ran along the Midland Channel from west to east. Some 109s were seen making head-on attacks on one of the B-17 boxes. The last observation I made that day was a single B-17 circling to the ground defended by a P-38. It was making interrupted loops, thereby shooting some salvos of flares and spinning down at last. I have learned that this was the fate of *Holy Terror III*, a B-17 in the 100th Bomb Group."

Holy Terror III had been allocated to 2nd Lieutenant Norman L. Chapman in the High Squadron because *Katie,* the B-17 he had christened after his wife, was in repair and he had re-named his replacement aircraft *Katie's Boys.* After being hit about 15 miles east of Berlin and determined to drop his bombs on the target come what may, Chapman dropped down into the low group, feathered #1 engine and then un-feathered it near the Dummer Lake. Although straggling he continued with the formation to the IP where he was attacked by three enemy fighters but continued on to bomb the target at Erkner. *Katie's Boys* appeared to be under control when last seen but Chapman was unable to maintain formation and after ordering his crew to bail out, crash-landed in woods 6 miles south east of Jüterborg, 31 miles south of Berlin. All ten crew were taken prisoner.

Bob Shoens shared the all round relief after the mission. 'Nothing happened. It was a beautiful trip all the way in and all the way out. However, we had ringside seats of another bomb group taking a beating like we had two days earlier.' At interrogation, the 100th Bomb Group gunners claimed seven enemy fighters. Major Marvin Somerset 'Red' Bowman the 50-year-old Group Public Relations Officer and an Intelligence officer, wrote: 'Combat crews, on their return, found a double shot of Scotch waiting each man, a new medical policy, which proved one of the best ideas yet. Morale went up tremendously.'

Of the 414 B-17s and 209 B-24s that were dispatched to 'Big-B' that Wednesday morning, 320 Fortresses and 150 Liberators were believed to have flown effective sorties against the VFK plant at Erkner. Other B-24s were forced to attack Berlin City and other targets of opportunity to avoid a B-17 unit approaching the capital and 36 B-17s either dropped their loads on armament factories at Wildau close to Berlin or other targets of opportunity. Once again the price was high. The 'little friends' had come to the aid of their 'big friends', claiming 79 enemy aircraft destroyed (the Luftwaffe in fact lost 42 fighters, with three pilots killed, 26 missing and nine wounded) for 18 American fighters lost but the leading 3rd Bomb Division that encountered the fiercest fighter opposition, still lost 23 Fortresses. General Curtis E. LeMay the 3rd Division Commander singled out the 45th Combat Wing, which lost sixteen Fortresses, for special praise. 'The crews delivered a punishing blow today to the morale of all Germany. In successfully putting bombs on the enemy's capital and his vital plants they furthered the war effort more than any of us can adequately evaluate. At the present writing, the major part of the hurt to the 3rd Division forces fell on the gallant crews of the 96th, 388th and 452nd Bomb Groups. The spirit and fight these units displayed made it easier on the other wings who wanted to share the brunt of the battle with them. Convey to all officers and men who participated, my deep admiration for the courage and determination with which they pushed the air attack into the heart of the enemy's territory and blasted Berlin.'[5]

At Knettishall the 388th was missing five B-17s. *The Princess Pat* was downed over Celle by a fighter which killed the navigator and one of the waist gunners. Eight men bailed out and were taken prisoner. *Screamin' Red Ass* piloted by 2nd Lieutenant Allan O. Amman from New York State was brought down by a fighter and crashed near Magdeburg. Only one of the waist gunners on the ten man crew survived. *Return Engagement* was shot down by a fighter over Hannover and the B-17 flown by 1st Lieutenant William Lentz Jr. from High Point, North Carolina was involved in a mid-air collision with a Focke Wulf 190 and exploded over Celle. An enemy fighter set off an explosion in the radio room on *Jimmy Lee* piloted by 22-year-old 1st Lieutenant Leonard Travis 'Toby' Tobias from Montgomery County, Alabama. The Fortress went down 30 miles North East of Brunswick with the loss of the pilot, co-pilot, Walt Yurkurtat, navigator: 2nd Lieutenant Herb Gotha and bombardier, 2nd Lieutenant Alf Hano.

At Deopham Green the 452nd Bomb Group had lost five B-17s too. Fighters knocked out the No.3 engine on *Tangerine* piloted by "Tay" Butterworth and then shattered the cockpit, killing 2nd Lieutenant Orville Earl Robertson the 24-year-old bombardier from Los Angeles, California at his station. Butterworth crash landed his Fortress on the bank of the River Weser, close to centre of Nienburg and he and the eight members of his crew who had survived were taken prisoner.

At about 1253 hours Tech Sergeant Wilburn C. Rowden the radio operator on *Sleepy Time Gal'* observed their P-47 escort turning back and heading for home. "We're losing our escorts," he stated over the intercom. Second Lieutenant Theodore J. MacDonald the 20-year old pilot from Rochester, New York acknowledged Rowden's comment and advised the crew to watch for the P-51s that were supposed to pick-up escort duty. "There's our escort at twelve o'clock high," a voice soon announced over the intercom. The fighters initially appeared as distant specks but grew larger as they approached the bombers. From head on and in shallow dive, the fighters rapidly closed on the bomber formation. The bomber crews soon realized that the fighters were not escorts as waves of ten to 15 single and twin-engined fighters, flying wing abreast, opened up on the bombers with machine gun and 20mm cannon fire..." The bomber suddenly began to lose speed and altitude. The head-on attack made by the German fighters set fire to *Sleepy Time Gal*'s #2 engine. MacDonald cut the fuel supply and feathered the propeller on the burning engine. The second German fighter attack set fire to the #3 engine and bullets riddled the nose of the plane, wounding 'Willie' Rowden and Jacob Moskowitz the 21-year-old navigator from the Bronx and also shredded Rowden's parachute and the 'chute belonging to 2nd Lieutenant Anton L. Harris the bombardier, who was killed. The German fighter pilots saw the crippled bomber as an easy victory and formed up for a second pass which wounded Bill Valigura the 20-year-old ball turret gunner from Temple, Texas and Bob Allen the tail gunner. MacDonald decided to put *Sleepy Time Gal'* down on the ground after giving his parachute to Rowden and ordering everyone to bail out. Mearl Cline the engineer and Wendell Dowell and Chas Batdorf the waist gunners and 2nd Lieutenant John Thomas Godsey 25-year old co-pilot from Virginia, joined the exodus and all eight men landed safely. Godsey however, was murdered by German civilians.

Two Bf 109s had taken up positions off the wings of *Sleepy Time Gal'* and escorted her down. With the landing gear still up and the bomb bay fully loaded, MacDonald managed to land in a marsh outside of Nienburg, 25 km northwest of Wunstorf. He crawled out the cockpit window but was found by a German soldier who was on leave and was walking his dog. The German marched MacDonald to a small town nearby where he took him into a tavern and locked the door to protect him from some of the townspeople when it looked like he might suffer the same fate as Godsey. Then the German soldier and the tavern owner bought MacDonald a cold beer.

"At sundown a little guy in a green uniform, with one of those spiked helmets on his head, came along on a motor bike" MacDonald recalled. "He ordered me to climb in, and took me across the German countryside to a jail near a canal somewhere. I was still in a state of shock after that plane crash. I stayed in the jail overnight; the next day a woman cooked me some pig hocks and sauerkraut and mashed potatoes. It was the last good food I was to eat for a long, long time. The next night a truck took me to a camp outside Hanover. They made me hand over everything I had in my pockets, of course. I had a pair of rosary beads that had belonged to my mother. The Nazi picked them up, sneered, spat at them and threw them onto the ground. I went for him. It was a fight that didn't last long. I lost." Next day MacDonald was taken to the Hanover railroad station and, with a group of PoWs, herded aboard a train, bound for the interrogation camp at Oberursel. "We were pretty tense on that train. We sweated out a bombing raid. We were suspicious and tired and trying to remember that there might be spies planted among us. Name, rank, serial number that was all we wanted to remember. We were very edgy." At Essen the train stopped and some German officers boarded. "A guy in a Nazi uniform, with staff sergeant stripes, came walking down the aisle. I could see him from a distance. He looked vaguely familiar. All of a sudden I heard him shout: 'Anyone here from Rochester, New York?' What a shock it was. I looked again and was sure I recognized him. He came up to me and said: 'You're from Rochester, aren't you?' 'I said; 'No' and turned away as though I didn't know him."He said: 'I know you, MacDonald. His captor was Walter Hanemann. 'I used to live over Tommy Halpin's barber shop in Park Avenue' he said. "Does Rabin still run the delicatessen? Does Frank Snelgrove still have the Atlantic station at the corner of Park and Berkeley? How's George Huss – do you ever see him?" Understandably, MacDonald was shaken. He listened as Hanemann continued to bombard him with neighbourhood talk. "I learned that Hanemann, who got to be an airplane pilot and was a skywriter for a while, had left Rochester in the late 1930s to return to his native Germany via South America and he had joined the Luftwaffe. He had flown Stuka dive bombers on the Polish front and was now on a rest leave but was being used as an interrogator because of his intimate knowledge of the States. "Get smart, MacDonald," he said at one point. "We're going to win this war easily. Come on and join Hitler's air force like I did." Before the train ride was over Hanemann said: *I'll be back In Rochester before you will, kid.*[6]

Paper Doll aka *Hank From Dixie* piloted by 1st Lieutenant Henry L. Wilson from Tullahoma, Tennessee crashed southeast of Magdeburg with the navigator and bombardier dead. Nine men on *Invictus* whose pilot, 2nd Lieutenant Frank S. Stephans, of Tulsa, Oklahoma had studied poetry in college and had adopted the name from the famous poem by William E. Henley, were taken prisoner. Co-pilot, 2nd Lieutenant Bill Mary of Knoxville, Tennessee, was killed. Hit by enemy aircraft on return. *'Lounge Lizard'* aka *'Dixie Jane'* headed for Sweden, but 26-year-old Captain Durward L. Sorensen of Detroit, Michigan was forced to crash land on a German airfield south east of Magdeburg. Seven crewmembers were captured. The 25-year-old radio operator, Tech Sergeant Arvo Olavi Palmer of Herman, Michigan, was thrown clear in the crash but broke his neck. Bernard T. Holmes the 27-year-old ball turret gunner of Opheim, Montana and James Nagy the 20-year-old tail gunner of Buffalo, New York also died in the crash.

Returning crews put a brave face on things for the assembled press correspondents. 'We gave them hell', commented Sergeant 'Fred' G. Fuller, radio operator of the *The Hard Way*. 'It was excellent bombing all over and I saw fires burning madly away in every section.'[7]

'Those fires sure toasted Hitler's bun', Staff Sergeant Elmer A. Parsons, right waist gunner on *Lucky Lady* remarked. 'Our bombs fell directly on the factory and the entire area was covered. It was a good job well done. While flying away all we could see was black smoke spiralling up in the sky'. Staff Sergeant Roland Clark, ball turret gunner on *Dog Breath*, claimed that 'all those fires made Berlin a madhouse'. (While still in training in Pyote, Texas, the crew spent time at a local bar. Pilot Herman "Butch" Beuchat would often have trouble getting his co-pilot Everett Phillips out of bed the next morning. Once Beuchat tried to wake him and Phillips blew in his face. Beuchat replied "Man, you have dog breath" – and the nose art was born). "Visibility was extremely good and we blasted away a portion of 'Beer Hall Berlin'. The residents on Wilhelmstrasse are looking for new quarters today." Staff Sergeant 'Fred' B. Hern, right waist gunner on *Dog Breath* celebrated his birthday by probably destroying a FW 190. 'It was a swell present from the German Air Force', commented the happy Sergeant.

'God really created something when he made mother earth, but Boeing really created something too when they made the Flying Fortress', in the opinion of 25-year-old 1st Lieutenant Harold 'Happy Hal' Fulmer, pilot of *Mon Tête Rouge II* in the 452nd upon his return from Berlin. The Visalia, California pilot's wife, Alyce had slightly of reddish hair and some French ancestry, so he came up with the name 'Mon Tête Rouge', which translates to 'My Red Head'. Fulmer sacrificed his crew in order to prevent the loosening up of the formation that he was leading. Just north of the target, a flak burst hit the number three engine, puncturing the oil cooler. Fulmer tried to feather the propeller but the oil had leaked out. The engine started to vibrate the ship and caused the plane to lose speed. "At this time", recalled Fulmer, "FW 190s and Me 109s hit us." Fulmer had a choice to make, he could remain at the head of the squadron, slowing it up and scattering it, thereby placing it at the mercy of the German fighters or else he could peel off from the formation and fly through the Luftwaffe horde alone to an almost certain end. He chose the latter. 'I dived out of the formation' continues Fulmer, 'trying to make it appear as if I was out of control, so that the fighters wouldn't come after us. I aimed for the clouds below us.' In the dive, Fulmer's entire crew stayed at their positions even though the plane was tearing through space at an excessive speed, well above the safety limit, for the distance of 15,000 ft. The well constructed plane held up. He had hid in the clouds and then ice began to form on the wings. The de-icer system had been shot up by the flak, making it necessary to come out of the clouds occasionally to shake the ice off. It was while doing this that we spotted enemy fighters twice and luckily lost them in the clouds. *Mon Tête Rouge II* arrived home safely, landing at Deopham Green in good condition and with all lives saved. It was a testimony to a sound leader, an excellent pilot and a perfect Flying Fortress.[8]

Ernie Richardson was 'kind of glad' to be back to Snetterton Heath after leave in London. 'The base' he said 'looked good; it was our home'. We walked into our hut expecting to hear some weird tales of aerial combat from the new crew. Both days we were away was flying weather. What we walked into was supply picking up their personal belongings. My God! Not again, remembering the last time we saw the same scene.

'Yeah,' ventured 'Fletch' who had gotten back a couple of hours ahead of us. Jack Fletcher was our tail-gunner. 'They got shot down today. No one is quite sure just what happened to them. I heard both pilots were shot up and the engineer was trying to fly the plane. Everyone in the formation was trying to get away from them. They were all over the sky. Their plane finally pulled out of the formation and blew up, no one saw any chutes.'

The 'Snetterton Falcons' had lost six ships in all. *Pegasus* and Lieutenant Don Otto Kasch's crew were shot down by fighters and crashed at Lutten, four miles north east of Vechta. Kasch, who was from Blue Island, Illinois and Gene Schadler his navigator were killed and the eight other crewmembers were taken prisoner.[9] *Lace's Aces* aka *The Iron Ass* which had three engines shot out by enemy fighters crashed at Beledorf, seven miles north east of Helmstedt after George Pond's crew bailed out at 18,000 ft. *Myasam Dragon* piloted by Captain Norman C. Thomas from Birmingham, Alabama was last seen being escorted by ten fighters to an airfield near Steinhuder Lake and was believed to have crashed in that region, Nine crew were taken into captivity. Staff Sergeant Gerry G, Caris the ball turret gunner from Bluffton, Ohio went down with the ship after his parachute was damaged and he was killed. All ten men on *Seventh Son* flown by 1st Lieutenant Richard F. Lemanski were captured after they bailed out when the B-17 was shot down at 21,000 ft. Better known as 'Baby LeRoy', the youngest pilot in the group and possibly the entire 8th Air Force, Lemanski, of Worcester, Massachusetts, spent his 20th and 21st birthdays and 14 months as a PoW in Stalag Luft 1, Barth. 2nd Lieutenant 'Jim' M. Swendiman's B-17 was shot down by enemy fighters just before target and crashed 11 miles west of Celle with the loss of radio operator, Roland Stallings, a Texan born in Gladewater, and left waist gunner, Emmett M. Holton from Henryville, Indiana who died from anoxia. Another Texan, 2nd Lieutenant Clark Ross Jr. and his crew were shot down by flak and fighters and crashed Hohlbeck, near Loburg, west of Berlin. Seven men survived to be taken prisoner. The body of Bill Ewart the ball turret gunner from Los Angeles, California was not found until 21 March.

At Snetterton 'Willard Berg and 'Chris' Christiansen the waist gunners came in while supply was still there' said Ernie Richardson. 'No one was saying anything. We were standing around sort of dumbfounded. 'That's it, I quit. I've got two kids.' It was Berg. He'd often threatened to quit but we didn't pay any attention to him. That day, I was sure he was serious. By now we all had faith in him and hated the thought of him dropping out. Reliability is very important at 25,000 ft. (Our original navigator, whose favourite line was *'Ah don't wanta be the best navigator in the world – Ah just wanta be the ol'est'* had got us lost one night right over Spokane so shortly after that Gillespie had got himself another named Chester Schultz). 'My folks would never forgive me if I quit.' It was 'Fletch'. I thought the remark was uncalled for and told him so. I figured if I ever decided to quit, I wouldn't care much what anyone thought, you know, 'better a live coward than a dead hero.'

'A short time after this happened we were moved to the 339th Squadron. The 413th went into path finding – a plane that was equipped with radar so they could bomb through the clouds. (Never could figure how that could be done). At the 339th we met another crew. They had one member who was 19-years-old who always yelled 'I'm too young to die' every time they woke us for a raid. He was only saying what most of us thought. I was 22 at the time. We had more raids than they did so they couldn't scare us with wild tales of combat. They told us the crew we were replacing had been shot down a day or two before we moved in. We weren't crazy about taking over someone else's bed so soon. I for one thought it would have been better if they would have kept their mouths shut. We were all superstitious as hell and didn't need anything else to worry about. Our next raids were mixed, some to France as well as Germany. Berg made every one of them. We were glad he didn't quit.'[10]

'Dick' Ghere, a gunner on Lieutenant Charles R. 'Chuck' McKeny's crew in the 'Bungay Buckaroos' recalled that his pilot had wanted to ask Lieutenant Herbert F. Bohnet Junior to let the crew fly *Shif'lus Skonk!* but *The Princess* was ready to go and McKeny took it off one minute before time for last takeoff. Ghere had quite a time with the Consolidated turret. "It was comparatively new to me and 'breezy... b-r-r-r. 'Rich' disliked the nose also. It had a Norden sight. Anyway we caught the formation and headed for Berlin. Hit flak at Osnabrück and Hanover. As we neared the target we saw *Shif'lus Skonk!* leave the formation, losing altitude and going far to the right. Three 109s jumped them and in a few minutes *Shif'lus Skonk!* was flaming. Four 'chutes came out. The plane exploded and another chute came out and then another chute opened from the pieces after that. That was a great blow to our crew. Our very close friends were MIA.[11] We hit for home and about 45 minutes out of the target area; three 190s surprised us out of the sun. They bore in very close – VERY close, made one pass and knocked down Merriman on our right wing. No chutes seen. A third crew was lost; Clifton McFar never returned to base.'[12]

The 458th Bomb Group returned to Horsham St. Faith less one Liberator when the B-24H piloted by 24-year-old 2nd Lieutenant John D. Adamson of Ventura, California whose crew were on their first combat mission was hit just short of IP hit by flak near Hannover. "The oil pressure on No.4 engine began to drop" recalled John J. Berrio the co-pilot, from Waltham, Massachusetts. "Near Berlin the turbo on No.2 engine went out and we were forced to salvo our bomb load. As we were leaving the formation, I called navigator Jesse Lack and asked for a course back to England. He gave me a course. I heard him talk to Flight Officer Charles Daskam, bombardier. I called later while we were under attack, but they never answered.[13] Fighter protection was called for, but never came. The enemy fighters (Me 210s I believe) picked us up and made numerous attacks to our tail and waist. When the plane caught fire, Adamson told me to give the order to bail out. When I left the plane he was standing with his parachute on. The plane crashed about 200 feet from where I landed and there was one 'chute wrapped around the tail. According to Sergeant Henry Forbes the left waist gunner, Sergeant Billy Freeman the tail gunner was hit in the first attack."[14] Berrio and four crew safely bailed out before the Liberator crashed on the outskirts of Finsterwalde.

Captain 'Chuck' Booth on *Bomb-Ah-Dear* was badly wounded one hour from the target. Sergeant Walter C. Fifer the radio operator standing behind Booth recalled: 'When Captain Booth was hit he jumped about a foot into the air and my first thought was that his electric suit had shocked him by 'shorting out'. In fact, he had been struck by a piece of flak that took the tips off his right hand fingers and the top of the right knee before lodging in the back of his left leg. It was -40 degrees at our 25,000 ft altitude so the wounds did not bleed much. I called Lieutenant Sidney A. Moore the co-pilot up from the waist and we did what we could for the captain before Moore assumed the now-vacant co-pilot's seat. I was afraid that Booth's electric suit pants were so riddled that the wiring might short out so I disconnected them and turned up the heat in his jacket and gloves. I also wrapped blankets and a coat around his legs for warmth. Although I thought he would be laid up for a time, he bore his injuries like a man and even refused to let me administer any morphine.' Despite leaving the cockpit, Booth still insisted on carrying out his duties and continued to give advice and encouragement to the crew. His action earned the award of the Distinguished Service Cross, America's second highest award after the Medal of Honor.

Later that day, at Wendling, about 19 miles west of Horsham St. Faith, Tech Sergeant Cletus M. Jeffcoat the radio operator on *Flying Patch* in the 392nd Bomb Group piloted by 1st Lieutenant Edward F. Wittel, wrote these words in his diary: 'Went to Berlin today. What a raid. Every plane we had was up there that day. It was very clear and we could see our bombs hit the target. (I mean the Group.) We got a 20mm in the leading edge of our left wing. Thought that the end of our wing was coming off so we had to drop our bombs and as luck would have it, we hit a little town and blowed it all to hell. Berlin looked like it was a pretty nice city. We saw a few bombers and fighters go down, but we made it back OK. We were the second to land. Everyone was looking at our wing. We nearly always get hit, but thank God we have always returned. I had better knock on wood right now.'

'On Saturday, 4 March, American aircraft appeared for the first time in the vicinity of Berlin" wrote German diarist, 36-year-old Hans Georg von Studnitz, born in Potsdam in 1907 of old Silesian stock and a journalist in Berlin since 1930, now holding down a senior post in the German Foreign Office Press and Information Section. "The American communiqué speaks of an offensive sweep over the German capital. On Monday, 6 March came the first American daylight raid, carried out against the south-eastern and south-western suburbs and Königs Wusterhausen. After a break on the Tuesday, a heavier attack was made on Wednesday against the outskirts of the city. The sirens usually go off at about 1.00 pm for these American attacks. In contrast to the British night raids, which usually last about 45 minutes, the American daylight raids go on for two or three hours. Whereas the British prefer to attack on dark nights and in bad weather, the Americans like daylight and a clear sky. Both Monday and Wednesday were beautiful days, without a cloud in the sky. The British drop their bombs quickly and at random – 'carpet-bombing' is their speciality – while the Americans prefer to take their time and make two or three trial runs over the target before releasing their bombs. It is now 12:40 and the alarm has just sounded. We have just spent two hours in the shelters. The main target was the eastern sector of the city. A sojourn in the Adlon Hotel air raid shelter is the very reverse of pleasant; the air is foul and the place overcrowded.'[15]

At Rattlesden on Thursday, 9 March the day began at 0330 hours for the 447th Bomb Group. 'Those beds were so warm' said Doyle Shields, navigator on Lieutenant 'Hamp' Morrison's crew 'it was a jolt to hit the cold floor, as was the cold air between the huts and the latrines. After fresh eggs at breakfast we were in the briefing room at 0550 hours. After Colonel Hunter Harris had made his opening remarks we learned it was 'Big B' again. Our weatherman prepared us for a 10/10ths undercast at the target, the Brandenburg Gate at the centre of Berlin. The intervalometers were set for maximum distance between bombs. We were to start releasing our 500 lb GP bombs, incendiaries and leaflets at the edge of the city to be sure that we hit 'the Gate'. When one man asked if this was indiscriminate bombing, he was ignored. This was one of the very few times we could have been accused of indiscriminate bombing.'

The Luftwaffe was notable for its absence, licking its wounds after the sustained American offensive of the past few days and six of the B-17s that were lost were victims of flak so thick that Berlin was covered by a black cloud from the bursts. A seventh Fortress, *Silver Dollar* in the 384th Bomb Group flown by 2nd Lieutenant Merlin H. Reed had its tail knocked off by a falling bomb from a B-17 in the High Group. Reed and seven crew members, including 39-year-old Military Occupation Specialty 612 – Staff Sergeant Emmett F. Hardy flying in the tail turret, were killed. Staff Sergeants' Arthur John 'Ozzie' Osepchook the ball turret gunner and John James Plotz the right waist gunner were taken prisoner. After ditching in the sea off the Dutch coast eight of the crew on *Piccadilly Ann*, a B-17 in the 447th Bomb Group flown by Lieutenant Herschel A. McGuire and a crew in the 447th Bomb Group captained by 1st Lieutenant Joseph E. Jurnecka of Berwyn, Illinois were rescued with the aid of airborne lifeboats dropped by RAF Hudsons on 279 Squadron. With the help of two Walrus amphibians two more Hudsons also picked up the two survivors on B-24 *Little Joe* piloted by 2nd Lieutenant Herman J. Meek in the 453rd Bomb Group. Unfortunately, only one man survived the ordeal.[16]

After 2nd Lieutenant Dean S. Flemming of Skowhegan, Maine piloting *Hi Mack* had dropped his bombs on the target, a steady headwind encountered over Germany caused him anxiety. Over the English Channel it became apparent that there would not be enough gas to make it back to Rattlesden, perhaps not enough to make it across the Channel. Flemming, 23 and his 25-year-old co-pilot, 2nd Lieutenant Edward J. Stull of Waterloo and Chester Streets, Devon, Pennsylvania, decided to cut two of the four engines in an effort to cross the water. Continuing on two engines they crossed the English coastline and headed for Horham, the first airfield they saw. The gas indicator when they were over the airfield registered zero but the two engines were still running. The control tower told the anxious members *Hi Mack*'s crew that it would be impossible to land immediately since a plane was taking off at that moment. Then the two remaining engines quit. At this time *Hi Mack* was very low over the runway. Flemming banked *Hi Mack* in an effort to turn and come back on another runway but he was too low. The only alternative was to make a dead stick landing in the freshly ploughed field. With wheels down *Hi Mack* settled into the soft earth, skidded across typical English hedgerow ditches and jolted to a stop. Flemming collapsed under the strain and was given first aid treatment by the waiting ambulance attendants. As the 24-year-old tail gunner, Staff Sergeant Leslie E. Orr of Bedford, Indiana said; "Lieutenant Flemming's skill really saved our lives. We hadn't had time to get into crash positions."[17]

In the co-pilot's seat of a 'Fightin' Bitin' Squadron B-17 in the 306th Bomb Group at Thurleigh in Bedfordshire, weaving its way through the intense and accurate flak barrage much in the manner of a broken field runner sat 2nd Lieutenant Robert C. Fife, Jr., of Newark, New Jersey. The crew had dropped the bombs and were turning off the target, their traffic pattern leading them over the heart of the 'Big B'. Running into an especially heavy concentration of flak, the pilot, 1st Lieutenant 'Frank' A. Warner, of Linden, New Jersey, asked Fife to hand him his flak helmet from under the seat. Fife, who had been dividing his time between watching the instrument panel and the flak bursts, was unaccustomed to the darkness of the interior of the plane. While reaching for the helmet his fingers touched what he thought was its strap and he pulled. It stuck slightly; so he pulled sharply. It came out and he found himself holding the red handle of a parachute rip-cord. At this instant, the ship was hit by flak and Fife realized his mishap had left his pilot without a 'chute. He didn't tell Warner what had happened, because he was having enough trouble with the flak and fighters.

'When I saw the 'chute open, I had the hell scared out of me', said Fife. 'I climbed out of my seat and stood by ready to aid in case of trouble. I couldn't call for an extra 'chute because there weren't any. As soon as we got out of the flak I leaned down and switched my 'chute for the opened one.' Fife then leaned back and prayed that nothing would happen. It was a long jump to make without a 'chute. He didn't tell Warner what had happened until they were well over the

Channel on the way home. Fife grinned, 'It was a hell of a place to be without a parachute.'

A total of 339 B-17s effectively bombed Berlin. The 165 B-24s dispatched were prevented from bombing the Heinkel 177 factory at Brandenburg because of 10/10ths cloud and instead bombed three secondary targets in the Brunswick, Hanover and Nienburg areas. 'Above the dense overcast the weather was clear and not too cold', wrote Wallace Patterson, Lieutenant Al Sanders' bombardier. 'We were carrying fifty 100 lb incendiaries. Over Hanover we ran into the worst flak any of us has ever seen. It was very accurate and I heard a big piece hit the ship. Directly in front of us, *Baby Shoes* flown by 2nd Lieutenant Everett Musselman took a hit on his No.2 engine and eventually fell out of formation." Last seen crossing the coast with one engine feathered *Baby Shoes* crashed North or Arendonk in Belgium. Musselman, who came from Terre Haute, Indiana, and seven crew were taken prisoner. Sergeant James T. Brown, the right waist gunner from Dallas, Texas evaded.

'We were late getting to the target' said Wallace Patterson "and then stayed around for hours it seemed, dodging flak and waiting for the Pathfinder to drop its flares. It never did and eventually we headed for home. All the way back until we reached Holland, planes were dropping their bombs. We got rid of ours and dodged flak all the way to the enemy coast. We landed awfully hard and 'Al' told me when we parked that we had had to feather two engines to keep enough gas' to land with the other two. We barely made it to the hardstand. There was a flak hole six inches from my feet but didn't come in. Next day was a stand-down so 'Bill' Trunnell and I decided on the spur of the moment to take off for London. While there we got a dog – a 'Chow puppy'- a bitch, which the boys named 'G.P.' (General Purpose).'

Just after 'bombs away' *Banshee III* in the 44th 'Flying Eightballs' Bomb Group at Shipdham in Norfolk was hit by four bursts of flak and one of the engines was destroyed. One of the flak bursts had torn off at the knee, the left leg of the pilot, 1st Lieutenant Kenneth G. Jewell and it struck him in his face. A bluff, plain-speaking man from Bedford, Pennsylvania with Indian blood coursing through his veins, he also had a reputation for run-ins with authority stretching back to his training days in Tucson, Arizona. Having trained to fly the B-17, Jewell was told he would be flying the B-24 Liberator. 'I refused to fly them' he wrote. That he changed his mind was due only to the threat of a court martial!

Lieutenant Harold L. Koontz, the co-pilot, who was on his first mission, was dragged unconscious from the flight deck. It seemed that he could not stand the sight of blood and he had vomited into his oxygen mask and passed out. Lieutenant Arthur Sakowski the navigator had told Jewell to get out of his seat and he would patch him up but when he tried to get up he found that he could not. Sakowski, an ex-football player and very strong, picked him up and laid him on the deck. He cut the trouser-leg off and it was a mess. Only the bicep muscle of Jewell's left leg was there. Sakowski had nothing to splint it so he put sulphur on it and gave Jewell two shots of morphine and then tore the bottom of the seat from the parachute to get the jungle knife. He then began to saw and hack at the remains of Jewell's leg but the blade was too dull. The next time Jewell awakened the co-pilot was in his seat and the Liberator was over the English Channel. Jewell put the B-24 under control and passed out. When he awoke they were above the balloon barrage in Norwich. When they saw Shipdham airfield it was around 1730 hours – five hours after Jewell had been hit. Someone shot red flares and the two pilots got *Banshee III* down and the B-24 buried its nose in the earth near the runway.

"We landed successfully, with nose high" said Jewell "and I passed out. The next thing I knew, someone said, 'I'll get him'' and I was picked up. The pain was terrible and I struck the person in the face. I was laid on a stretcher and demanded to see the damaged *Banshee* before I got in the ambulance. I remember being wheeled into the operating room and the last words I heard were, 'We'll save you Jewell." He did not come round until; the following afternoon. 'My sides hurt so bad that I forgot about the leg. My bladder had not emptied itself in thirty hours. I filled three urinal ducts. I threw back the sheets and I had no left leg! I got furious, flung myself out of bed, tore off the bandages and started bleeding again. I could not accept the fact. I was young, had a good career, a beautiful wife and here I was to be a helpless cripple all my life." Incredibly however, he was flying again less than a year after his terrible injuries. Fitted out with an artificial leg, he resumed flying duties in February 1945.

For his selfless heroism during that shattering mission to Berlin Jewell received America's second highest gallantry award, the Distinguished Service Cross. Brigadier General Leon W. Johnson, who presented Jewell with his DSC as he lay, recovering in hospital, apologised to Jewell. "He had personally recommended the Medal of Honor and could not understand the mix-up.'

In the 388th Bomb Group Bernard Dopko's crew finally ran out of luck on 9 March. The crew of *Little Willie* filled in with the 96th Bomb Group from Snetterton Heath when one of their B-17s in the low squadron aborted. Shortly after 'bombs away' the #2 engine was hit by flak which ruptured an oil line and set the engine on fire. The prop would not feather and the fire spread in the wing. All ten crew bailed out before *Little Willie* crashed near Forsterei Protze, 12 miles north-east of Oranienburg. Back at Knettishall 'BJ' Keirsted's crew who shared their hut with Dopko's crew did not have the heart to raid their possessions like they had done three days' earlier. Eight men on Dopko's crew were by now on their way to PoW camps. Sergeant Richard R. Herzberg the right waist gunner, who was from Katona, New York and Staff Sergeant Edward C. Naber the tail gunner of Chicago, Illinois escaped with two other PoWs and made it to a British tank outfit.

At Thorpe Abbotts on the 9th, 'Red' Bowman wrote: 'Berlin again. Only nine planes out this time and no losses. Results only fair. Thirteen new crews have arrived.' Unable to attack the primary target, due to 'a blanket of 10/10th's cloud,' the Hundredth bombed the city by radar. Luckily, 'the Luftwaffe failed to appear. According to the experts at a critique at Framlingham on the 10th the Hundredth did right well in the Berlin raids. Distinguished itself in fact.' On the 13th Generals' Carl "Tooey" Spaatz, Jimmy Doolittle, Curtis LeMay and August W. Kissner arrived at Thorpe Abbotts, it was assumed 'to boost morale after Berlin.' The official reason was to carry out a tour of inspection and to decorate personnel including Colonel Bennett, who was awarded the Silver Star for 'superb judgment and gallantry' for the Erkner raid.' After dinner in the officers mess Doolittle was confronted by a red-haired young second lieutenant who appeared the worse for drink who poked his finger in the general's chest and said 'You think we don't know what you're here for? Still prodding Doolittle he continued: 'Well, let me tell you we do; you're here to improve our morale and if there's anything goin' to ruin our morale it's havin' a bunch of generals around here trying to fix it. Spaatz was furious but Doolittle calmed him and no action was taken.

On Wednesday, 22 March a force of 688 B-17s and B-24s led by H2X-equipped bombers that were to raid the Berlin area again. Twenty-one year-old Lieutenant Herman C. 'Mitch' Mitchell's crew in the 'Travelling Circus' were flying their fifth mission this day in *Sweater Gal'*. The pin-up on the nose had previously been unclad and she had the risqué title of *Buck-Fifty Job* before orders were received to cover her up and change the name! Charles E. Clague Jr, the 21-year-old bombardier, who had been yanked out of college near Cleveland in 1943 and inducted into the Air Corps, said that they were on oxygen for six hours and the temperature was 45° below. He added that it was 'the most screwed up mission he hoped to be on. The tail turret was out, there were oil leaks in three engines, five electric suits were out and the 52 100 lb M-47 incendiary bombs would not release electrically. To cap it all, en route to the target the navigator, 23-year-old 2nd Lieutenant Howard 'Howie' W. Mesnard developed anoxia. Anoxia if left unchecked results in death. At altitude oxygen mask hoses were prone to ice up simply from breathing. If not monitored, chunks of ice could form and completely block the flow of oxygen.' Clague quickly cleared the obstruction before he became a victim of hypoxia himself.

This was John Kettman's 17th mission on Lieutenant Harry Cornell's crew in the 305th Bomb Group at Chelveston, five miles east of Wellingborough in Northamptonshire and his second trip to the 'big town'. 'We went by way of the North Sea going in and out through Germany and Holland. I flew in the ball turret the first hour and a half. Our escort picked us up around Denmark. We didn't see one enemy fighter all the way. Over the target there were all kinds of flak, all of it a little off to our right. We caught more flak on the way home. It was a long ride as usual. Just before the IP Lieutenant Eldred F. Whipple turned back and headed for Sweden. We prayed that he made it. Harry Hawkins, the ball turret gunner, who lived in my barracks, was on the crew. One of their engines was out. Whipple's crew failed to reach Sweden, crashing east of Oldenburg, and the pilot and four of his crew were killed. Five men including Hawkins who was from Lebanon, Indiana, survived to be taken prisoner.

The 452nd, led by their new Commanding Officer, Lieutenant Colonel Marvin F. Stalder, hit a target in Berlin. The Group diarist declared that: 'Our group hit hard and returned safely. This is a world's championship boxing match and the 8th Air Force has its opponents against the ropes, throwing dangerous punches into his most vital nerve centre. Nothing can save them, not even the final bell. Weather to the target was undercast. When the target was reached, undercast was 8/10ths. 'I think we did a pretty good job. There were breaks in the clouds and I could see the city through it. I don't think there was a hellava lot left of the target." 'Hitler must have moved a long time ago to new quarters', commented Staff Sergeant Robert A. Lalumiere, ball turret gunner on *Sunrise Serenade*.[18] Flight Officer James B. Williams, bombardier on *The Round Tripper* said: 'We saw the target through a break in the clouds and let our bombs go down. They really hit and we could see black smoke starting to pour up into the sky. They'll hang up the sign, 'Out of Order' on the door to the target. That is, if the door is still left standing.' Staff Sergeant Jimmie C. Campbell, tail gunner on *The Round Tripper* claimed that 'the sky was filled with our fighters. They looked like a flock of blackbirds'. (24 hours' earlier six men on *The Round Tripper* had made it back from Berlin with their bombardier dead and minus three men who bailed out and were taken prisoner).[19] 'We did a terrific amount of damage' exclaimed 2nd Lieutenant J. A. Kelly, bombardier on *Lady Satan*. 'Berlin is a city in flames tonight. Flak over the target was intense but not one of our planes was damaged seriously. Everyone returned safely to Deopham Green. Enemy fighter opposition was extremely weak, in fact, not one fighter was seen near any of the formations. This is a sure sign that our aerial blows are weakening enemy fighter strength considerably. Fighter escort was excellent, those P-47s, P-51s and P-38s just covered us up like a blanket, from top to bottom."

'I saw two FW 190s try to get into the formation but two P-47s chased them away', recalled 2nd Lieutenant Frank L. Houston, co-pilot from Montana on *The Punched Fowl*, so named by its original pilot James H. "Jimmie" Vallee. The nose art consisted of two ducks somewhat resembling the cartoon characters of 'Donald' and 'Daisy Duck'. The female duck is looking away with her tail feathers all ruffled, while the male duck is standing with a grin and a halo over his head. (Supposedly this name was a reference to having obtained sex). 'This was a good mission. Our pilots handled themselves well and the crew contributed toward the destruction of Berlin. Moderate flak was experienced by the group all the way back from the target.'

Seven B-17s and five Liberators failed to return from the Berlin raid and 8/10ths to 10/10ths-cloud cover prevented attacks on the aircraft factories at Basdorf and Oranienburg, so Targets of Opportunity were attacked instead. Altogether, the 8th Air Force dropped 4,800 tons of high explosive on Berlin in five raids during March 1944. Forty per cent were M-17 incendiaries, dropped in aim-able clusters which resulted in better accuracy. By the end of March the 8th Air Force was receiving another new fire bomb, the M-76, known as the 'Block Buster'.

'With the coming of the American daylight raids a new type of bombing came into being, 'carpet' or saturation bombing" recalled Private Norman Norris RAOC,[20] who had been taken prisoner in August 1941 and had marched to his first PoW camp at Neukölln in Berlin before being moved to Zernsdorf where work consisted of relaying the railway track in and around Berlin. "The first American 1,000 bomber raid on Berlin was, indeed, a fantastic sight, coming over in broad daylight; the sky seemed full of planes, in an unending stream they flew across the city dropping 'carpets' of bombs which just wiped out anything within the area. With the night and day bombing the city began to be pounded into destruction. Gun sites, factories, houses, everything began to slide into a heap of rubble. The fires started during the day only pin-pointed the city for the raiders at night. Just to pile on the agony, the Americans rolled a 'carpet' right to the perimeter of our camp. This caused great consternation amongst the local population (including us) and that evening numbers of civilians came round to vent their anger on us. Luckily it was only in words and in the slanging match that ensued, we more than held our own. Unfortunately, for us, the bombing was giving us extra work; apart from our normal work of laying the railway track, sections that were bombed also had to be repaired.

'We always left for work at 0630 hours. This meant a march to the station and then by railway wagon to the scene of construction or destruction. One member of the local population was always making complaints about us. He owned a large timber yard just up the road from our camp and as we marched daily to the station, would make disparaging remarks about our parentage. We had our own back on him later on; incendiaries from an American bomber burnt his timber yard to the ground.'

Notes

1. *The 2nd Air Division Journal, Vol.25, No.4 December 1986.*
2. *The Day We Bombed Switzerland* by Jackson Granholm (Airlife Publishing, 2000).
3. *Century Bombers: The Story of the Bloody Hundredth* by Richard Le Strange (assisted by James R. Brown) 100th BG Memorial Museum 1989).
4. According to research by Andreas Trotz this victory could be attributed to Feldwebel Werner Rubel of 6./JG 53 which operated in the Jüterborg sector this day.
5. Five B-17s in the 1st Division and 9 B-24s in the 2nd Bomb Division also failed to return.
6. On Armistice Day, 11 November 1948 MacDonald, who had received the DFC for his heroism, stopped in Bob Byrel's candy shop at 623 Park Avenue in Rochester to buy a box of candy. All of a sudden the door opened and in walked Walter Hanemann! "He said: 'Hello there, MacDonald, How's everything? I didn't get back to Rochester before you did, but I'm not far behind you.' *Democrat and Chronicle*, Sunday, April 12 1959.
7. Fuller; Clyde Rasmussen, flight engineer/top turret gunner; Dick Hoffer, radio operator and tail gunner, Mike Lamere were killed on 20 April 1944 when *The Hard Way* was

ditched just outside Calais harbour. The pilot, Joe Thomas and the five other men on the crew were picked up alive by an Air Sea Rescue RAF Walrus on 278 Squadron within an hour.

8. *Mon Tete Rouge II* and 2nd Lieutenant Lawrence Downy Jr and his crew were lost on 4 December 1944.

9. On the mission to Villacoublay on 5 February *'Kasch's Kids'* had turned back due to mechanical problems. The crew bailed out before the B-17F crashed at Dymchurch, Kent. On 10 February *Pegasus* was badly shot up by fighters and flak and pilot Robert H. Dickert ordered the crew to bail out but he was able to nurse the plane back to England after four took to their parachutes and the radio operator lay dead on the floor. When on 6 March Kasch taxied for takeoff in another B-17, the brakes failed and the bomber ran into a parked truck.

10. On 11 April 1944 on the mission to Rostock Sherman Gillespie's crew force landed at Bulltofta in Sweden and all ten men were interned.

11. Bohnet, of Brooklyn, New York, who had married Millie Keith on 2 June 1943 in Clovis, New Mexico; 2nd Lieutenants' Charles Zimmer also from Brooklyn, Robert E. Gilbreath from Fort Payne, Alabama and Herschel H. Carter from Blytheville, Arkansas and Staff Sergeants' Arden Cook and Raymond J. Schultz from St. Louis, Missouri were taken prisoner. Staff Sergeants' Robert R. Collings from Mercer, Missouri and Jerry Teetsel from Allentown, Pennsylvania and Tech Sergeants' Allan R. Martin from Turtle Creek, Pennsylvania and Gail R, Van Patten of Chicago, Illinois were killed. *The Princess* was shot down with another crew on 8 April 1944.

12. All 10 crew on B-24H 41-29292 piloted by Lieutenant James A. Merriman were KIA, as were all the crew on B-24J 42-100231 piloted by 1st Lieutenant Clifton C. McFar.

13. Jesse H. Lack of Brooklyn, New York and Charles Daskam (22) of Cresco, Indiana were KIA.

14. Sergeant Billy L. Freeman of Humphreys, Oklahoma was KIA.

15. *While Berlin Burns: The Diary of Hans Georg von Studnitz, 1943-1945* Frontline Books, 2001).

16. The complete story about the operation is detailed in *Dinghy Drop: 279 Squadron At War 1941-1946* by Tom Docherty (Pen & Sword Aviation, 2007).

17. Adapted from the report by the Public Relations Office at Rattlesden.

18. On 1 May when *Sunrise Serenade* was shot down on the mission to Metz, Lalumiere was replaced by Staff Sergeant James E. Gallagher who was one of 8 men taken prisoner.

19. *The Round Tripper* and 2nd Lieutenant Frank Brogan's crew went MIA on 29 May 1944.

20. Royal Army Ordnance Corps.

Chapter Five

Whom The Gods Love Die Young

Herodotus (c484-425 BC)

'We got up at 0130 for target study. The target was Berlin!' …We'd make seven trips to Berlin and they were all nasty.

Sergeant Carlyle J. Hanson, engineer-top turret gunner in 'Fred' Heiser's crew on *Poltergeist* aka *Vagabond* in the 385th Bomb Group, Saturday, 29 April 1944. Heiser's co-pilot, 24-year-old 1st Lieutenant Robert W. James, born New York City and 25-year-old 1st Lieutenant Terence S. Hall, navigator, born Gerritsen Beach, NY flew a second tour on Mosquitoes with the 653rd Bomb Squadron, 25th Bomb Group at RAF Watton, Norfolk and were killed on landing at RAF Shepherds Grove after a local training flight on 9 April 1945.

Benjamin Smith Jr., the radio-operator-gunner on Lieutenant Anthony 'Chick' Cecchini's crew in the 'Hell's Angels' Group at Molesworth looked up and down the row of bunks. There were many cigarettes glowing in the dark and not much sleeping going on. It was the night of Monday 17/Tuesday 18 April 1944 and 'Chick's Crew' had been waiting to fly their first mission since arriving in England in the bitter cold spring of March 1944. Their pilot weighed over 200 lbs and had been a policeman in New York State. Italian to the core, he was red-haired and looked like a big Irish cop. He wore a perpetual grin and was quite a womaniser. Ben Smith was one of two southerners on the crew and came from Georgia. He was never referred to as anything but 'Snuffy' or 'Houn' Dawg'. He doubted seriously if anyone knew his real name. New crews were given the most vulnerable places in the formation and had a way of disappearing after a few missions but though this callous treatment was heartily resented, after 'winning their spurs' new crews were as bad as the rest. In the early hours of 18 April the door flew open and their cheery CQ named 'Fluke' entered, switched on the lights and started calling off the crews who were to fly on the day's mission. He yelled, 'Cecchini's crew!' Ben Smith's heart sank. He felt like a condemned man. 'We donned our flying coveralls, heated suits and boots and headed to the mess-hall down the road where the cooks were putting on a mission breakfast. 'The chefs were very solicitous seemingly jovial. We could have pancakes, eggs sunny-side up, or any way we wanted them. Sort of like, 'It's your last meal – you can have what you want.' To me it seemed a somewhat macabre occasion and

I found their jollity very disquieting and out of place. I could eat none of the breakfast anyway.

'All of the crews, officers and non-commissioned officers were briefed together. The radio operators were also given a separate briefing at which time they received a canvas packet with coded data in it called a 'flimsy.' In the main briefing hall the target remained covered until the Intelligence Officer came in. He was a dapper individual, sporting a moustache and quite hearty in manner – for a good reason; he didn't have to go. These Intelligence Officers were non-flying personnel with some useful information and a lot more that was useless. His first move was to peel back the cover from the map, which act was always met with a loud groan from the assembled crews. They were a lively bunch and time had to be allowed for them to get over the initial shock, sound off and cuss a little while. After a time they subsided and he began. We could see that the red lines pinned on the map went deep into Germany. The target was hardly a milk-run: it was Berlin!'[1]

The 8th Air Force would dispatch 776 heavy bombers to hit aircraft industries, targets of opportunity and airfields including targets at Annahof, Brandenburg, Rathenow and the Heinkel plant at Oranienburg in the suburbs of Berlin, which was the target for 35 B-17s of the 'Hell's Angels' Group, plus two PFF B-17s from the 482nd Group. The secondary target, if PFF bombing was required, was the Friedrichstrasse Bahnhof, the centre of the mainline and underground railway system in the centre of the city. There was no last resort target.

'We were told we could expect heavy fighter opposition' wrote Ben Smith, 'with flak at the target described as 'intense.' In other words, the target was heavily defended. We could see from the diagram that we were flying 'tail-end-Charlie' in the high squadron. There would be a lead squadron and a high squadron.

'Briefing over, we got up and started out. We climbed into trucks and headed out for the hardstands where the Fort's were parked. The ground crews swarmed over our B-17 getting it ready. The armourers were arming the bombs in the bomb bay. It was still pitch dark. We put our machine guns into their casings and attached the gun belts. When this was done, we went to the dispersal tent and lay down on the canvas cots that were there for that purpose. We tried to log a little sack time before 'Start Engines.' The signal for this was a red flare from the control tower. These quiet moments in the dispersal tent were always the worst part of the mission for me. I was always inflicted with an unbearable sadness at this time. I can still hear the clanking coughs of the aircraft engines as they struggled manfully in the damp mist and then caught up. We were on board and soon taxiing out in trail until we reached the end of the runway. Every 30 seconds a Fort would gun its engines and hurtle down the runway into the black darkness. Finally, it was our time. We always sweated take-off as we were heavily laden with gas' and bombs.

Spirit of Wanette aborted when the oxygen feeder line to the ball turret broke and *Ain't Misbehavin* returned after one hour with a leak in the oil line that caused the No.4 propeller governor to run away. 'We climbed through the mist on a certain heading until we reached a predetermined altitude' wrote Ben Smith. At 10,000 ft 'Chick' raised a gloved hand to the intercom switch at his throat and told us to go on oxygen. Thereafter, we had periodic oxygen checks with each position checking in. We learned the value of this on a later mission when the ball turret gunner did not check in. We pulled him out of the turret unconscious and almost dead. His hose had become disconnected.

'During all this time there was complete radio silence, as the German interceptor stations were monitoring constantly. Looking back, I doubt if we ever fooled them. The planners would go to extreme lengths to conceal the mounting of a mission but I doubt if they could conceal something of that magnitude. I imagine the Germans had ample notice from their own agents in England of every mission we flew. I don't remember their ever being asleep when I visited Germany.'

Weak enemy aircraft opposition was encountered. For the most part, crews in the 303rd Bomb Group reported seeing two to four only. *The Road Back* piloted by 1st Lieutenant Lloyd L. Holdcroft who was on his 29th mission and the original crewmen who were on the last of their 25 mission combat tour was last seen just before making a turn after the target. Two engines were hit by flak and the propellers were allowed to windmill. At one point a Bf 109 pilot flew alongside, looked the Fortress over, saluted and flew off. *The Road Back* flew for ninety minutes before crash landing near Soltau, 65 km north of Hanover. All the crew survived and *The Road Back* was set on fire to prevent it falling into enemy hands. The crew divided into three groups to attempt to avoid being captured but their evasion attempts proved unsuccessful.

The Luftwaffe generally forsook the 1st Bomb Division and concentrated on the luckless 3rd Division instead. The enemy fighter pilots were aided by the weather which forced the Division to split and in the resulting confusion the escort became disoriented. The leading 4th Wing flew on in thick cloud which topped 30,000 ft near the IP but the groups following were forced to turn back and bomb targets en route. When the Fortresses finally pierced the cloud front, only the two 94th combat boxes and another box in the 385th remained. Both groups were alone and on the wrong heading and were also without fighter cover. At 1300 hours in the Havel area, north-west of 'Big B' a strong force of Bf 109s led by 27-year-old Major Friedrich-Karl "Tutti" Müller, Gruppenkommandeur, IV. Gruppe of Jagdgeschwader 3 "Udet" a 130 victory ace made 'pack' attacks on the unprotected Fortresses for over half an hour and claimed 43 B-17s destroyed. Three of these were claimed by Major Müller.[2] Fourteen B-17s were shot down – three PFF B-17s in the 96th Bomb Group leading the 94th and 447th Bomb Groups, eight B-17s in the 94th Bomb Group and three B-17s in the 390th Bomb Group. A fourth B-17 in the latter group was so badly damaged that it had to head for Switzerland where the crew was interned.

April 1944 saw the high-water mark of the 8th, the most sustained period of operations yet mounted. It was a record month with the highest expenditure

Captain Robert J. Shoens, pilot of *Our Gal' Sal'* in the 100th Bomb Group at Thorpe Abbotts in Norfolk.

Colonel Harold W. Bowman commanding the 401st Bomb Group at Deenethorpe, Northamptonshire, June 1943-5 December 1944.

The 'Worry Wart' crew in the 388th Bomb Group at Knettishall, February 1944. Back row (left to right) Lieutenants' Phil 'Bloodhound' Brejansky, navigator- B. J. Keirsted, pilot; Cliff 'Ace' Conklin, co-pilot; Kent 'Cap' Keith, bombardier. Front row (left to right) Staff Sergeants' Ed Kozacek top turret gunner and E. V. 'Pete' Lewelling, waist gunner; Tech Sergeants' Jack C. Kings, waist gunner and Larry 'Goldie' Goldstein, radio-operator; S/Sgt Robert Miller, tail gunner. (*Larry Goldstein*)

1st Lt Bill Owen and Lt Marshall Thixton of the 482nd Bomb Group; the first pilot and bombardier over Berlin, 4 March 1944. (*Marshall J. Thixton family*)

Colonel Gilger, 95th Bomb Group CO congratulating Lieutenant Colonel Mumford on the successful Berlin raid, 4 March 1944.

1st Lt Montgomery 'Monty' D. Givens in the 100th Bomb Group.

Master Sergeant (1st Grade) Harry Allert, *Blitzing Betsy*'s crew chief in the 388th Bomb Group at Knettishall.

2nd Lt Eugene H. Whalen, born Davenport, Iowa, pilot of B-17G 42-31595 *Flying Jenny* in the 457th Bomb Group who was KIA after a Me 410 that did not pull out in time crashed into his aircraft in the high box and the combined wreckage fell on 2nd Lieutenant Roy E. Graves' B-17 in the low box. All three fell to earth. Only the tail gunner on Graves' aircraft survived from the two Fortresses.

B-17G 42-31227 *Dottie Jane* in the 447th Bomb Group, which 1st Lt Arthur R. Socolofsky of Chicago nursed back to Rattlesden on 6 March 1944 following a direct flak hit under the floor of the radio room on the raid on Berlin. The radio operator vanished into thin air 5 miles above Germany. (*USAF via Chris French*)

B-24J 42-7586 *God Bless Our Ship* in the 445th Bomb Group on the Karwar Marshes 25 miles NW of Berlin after being badly damaged by flak on the mission to 'Big-B' on 6 March 1944. 1st Lt George H. Lymburn and his tail gunner Sgt Francesco Cittadino were aboard, the other crew members having bailed out over Berlin.

2nd Lt Charles A. Melton's crew on B-24 *Paddlefoot* in the 458th Bomb Group at Horsham St. Faith. Standing: U/I ground crewman; John Krpan; Charles Melton; Charles Weinum; Seldon King, Kneeling: U/I ground crewman; George Bahner; William Webster; Joseph Tomich; Vernon Goring; Robert Maher; Glenn R. Matson. (via Patrick Cook)

306th Bomb Group enroute to Berlin on 6 March 1944. The cloud of smoke on the right is all that remained after a B-17 had suffered an almost direct hit from a heavy flak shell. On the ground is the gigantic V 500 fire decoy site, 15 miles to the north-east of Berlin. In the bottom right-hand corner is the 'East-West' axis; a boulevard which is a distinctive aerial feature of Berlin.

B-17G 42-31919 *Evanton Babe* in the 452nd Bomb Group crash landed at Metfield airfield, Suffolk at the end of the mission to Berlin on 6 March 1944.

Lieutenant Ralph G. Cotter, 100th Bomb Group, who was KIA on 6 March 1944.

Colonel John M. Bennett, acting CO, 100th Bomb Group.

Captain Charles 'Chuck' Booth (far left), Assistant Group Operations Officer, 458th Bomb Group at Horsham St. Faith who was awarded the Distinguished Service Cross for his actions on the Berlin raid, 8 March 1944.

1st Lt Kenneth G. Jewell and the crew of *Banshee III* in the 44th 'Flying Eightballs' Bomb Group at Shipdham in Norfolk.

The burning VKF ball bearing plant at Erkner on the southern suburbs of Berlin from a departing B-24 on 8 March 1944.

B-24J Liberator 42-100353, 703rd Bomb Squadron, 445th Bomb Group, that crash landed in a field near Metfield, Norfolk on 8 March 1944.

B-17G 42-37781 *Silver Dollar* in the 384th Bomb Group, which on 9 March was hit over Berlin by a bomb from the 'High Group' that knocked off the tail section, killing 39-year-old S/Sgt Emmet F. Hardy in the tail turret before the Fortress crashed at Marienfeld, near Berlin. One of the waist gunners and the ball turret gunner, who were captured, escaped and returned were the only survivors on 1st Lt Merlin H. Reed's crew.

Flight Officer Bernard Michael Dopko's crew in the 388th Bomb Group that went MIA on the Berlin raid on 9 March 1944.

1st Lt Edward F. Wittel's crew on B-24H 41-29131 *Flying Patch* in the 392nd Bomb Group, 31 May 1944. Front Row: Sgt D. A. Roti, tail gunner. Middle Row: L-R: 1/Lt Edward F. Wittel; T/Sgt Cletus M. Jeffcoat, radio operator; S/Sgt Richard F. Williams, waist gunner; S/Sgt Phillip M. Lancaster, ball turret gunner; S/Sgt Bertrand J. Prost, waist gunner. Back Row, L-R: 2/Lt Warren R. Marsters, co-pilot; T/Sgt Vernon P. Cannada, engineer; 2/Lt John C. Zuk, bombardier; 2/Lt John F. Karl, navigator; M/Sgt Hubert H. Lee, crew chief. (Wittel)

A 384th Bomb Group B-17G releasing incendiaries over Berlin on 22 March 1944.

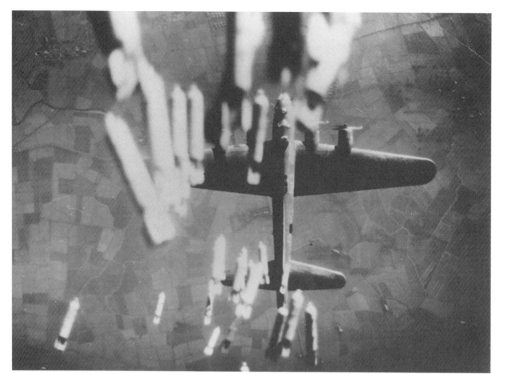

Strike camera photo of B-17 42-6099 *Ruth L* flown by 2nd Lt Nathan L. Young of the 96th Bomb Group about to be brought down at "Bombs Away" over Oranienburg on 22 March 1944. *Ruth L* crashed at Falkenhoehe, two miles NE of Falkensee, due east of Berlin. All ten crew were killed.

Debriefing.

A 452nd Bomb Group B-17G over Berlin Tempelhof on 29 April 1944.

On 8 May 1944 B-17G 42-38133 *Reluctant Dragon* in the 96th Bomb Group was nursed home by 2nd Lt Jerry T. Musser (far right) with 2nd Lt John C. Flanyak, the bombardier, from Chicago, Illinois and Tech Sgt Leon H. Sweatt, the top turret gunner and engineer who doubled as co-pilot. Musser was shot down on the Brüx mission on 12 May 1944 flying B-17G 42-31718 and taken prisoner. *Reluctant Dragon* went MIA on the Berlin raid on 30 November 1944. (*USAF*)

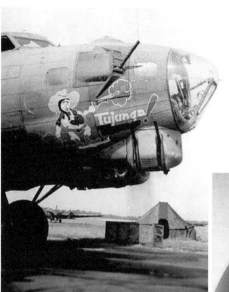

B-17G 42-97087 *Tujunga!* that Lieutenant Robert D. Lane's crew in the 457th Bomb Group flew on their final mission on 12 May 1944.

B-17G 42-31723 *Sparky* in the 100th Bomb Group piloted by Lt John Perry Keys, which barely made it back to Thorpe Abbotts on 19 May 1944 after a 20 mm shell blew a large section of the tail fin away.

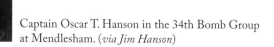

Captain Oscar T. Hanson in the 34th Bomb Group at Mendlesham. (*via Jim Hanson*)

B-17G 42-31367 *Chow Hound* of 91st Bomb Group over Berlin on 8 March 1944.

Lt. W.J. TOCZKO   Lt. E.H. PATTERSON   Lt. K.W. VERHAGEN (NAV) Lt. Doug REID (BOMB)

T. H. DODD   SSGT WEB BROWN   SSGT   SERRADELL   SSGT   HIGGS   SSGT G. EDGAR (RADIO OP)
ENGINEER   (WAIST GUNNER)   (WAIST GUNNER)   (TAIL GUNNER)   KIA 21 JUNE 44 (BERLIN)
KIA 21 JUNE 44 (BERLIN)   8th AF 2nd Air Div 389th BG 566th Sqdn. 1944   SSGT HOLCOMB
                                                                              (NOSE GUNNER)

Crew of B-24H 42-52579 *Fightin' Sam II* in the 389th Bomb Group at Hethel, Norfolk, who were shot down on the Berlin mission, on 21 June 1944.

B-24J 42-50466 *Ford's Folly* in the 392nd Bomb Group at Wendling, Norfolk, which was shot down at Allendorf on 11 September 1944. Only two men on 1st Lieutenant Charles R. Rudd's crew survived.

Staff Sergeant Harvey George Hoganson, the right waist gunner on *Ford's Folly* who was KIA on 11 September 1944.

Tech Sergeant 'Peedro' Maynard, the 20-year-old engineer/ upper turret gunner on *Ford's Folly* who was KIA on 11 September 1944.

B-17G 42-107003 *Bouncin' Baby* in the 710th Bomb Squadron, 447th Bomb Group at Leiston on 5 November 1944 which returned from Merseburg badly damaged on 2 November when it was hit by flak and lost the #4 engine. The '*Baby*' was able to maintain altitude on 2½ engines and made it to Leiston whereupon landing the prop on the #4 engine broke loose and landed mid-ship! On 21 February 1945 whilst having an engine test by the crew chief Curtiss Crossman at its hardstand at 0400 hours *Bouncin' Baby* jumped its chocks and crashed into a 4,000-gallon fuel truck and flying incendiaries caused *Bouncin' Baby* and *Big Shorty* to catch fire and explode; 6 other aircraft were damaged, 3 of which were written off. Two firemen were injured but amazingly there was no loss of life. The *Baby* had by this time, flown 80 missions. (*via Chris French*)

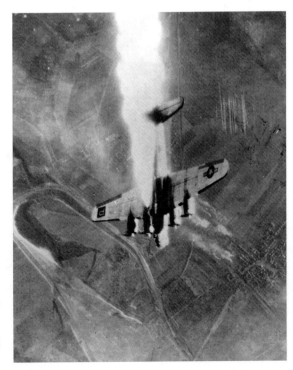

B-17G 43-37877 in the 487th Bomb Group piloted by 1st Lt Lloyd W. Kersten on fire and going down near Merseburg at 1314 GMT, 30 November 1944. Only the navigator and the bombardier survived from the 9-man crew. (*USAF*)

Staff Sergeant Hayward F. Deese Jr., engineer/left waist gunner, in Lt George M. Durgin's crew on B-17G 43-38241 *Ulpy* in the 493rd Bomb Group at Debach, Suffolk. (*Deese*)

Captain Vernon Gayle Alexander in the 34th Bomb Group.

Captain Oscar T. Hanson's crew on 21 August 1944 at Mendlesham. Back row: Lt Don Topping, navigator; Lt Lindsey Lipscomb, bombardier; Captain Oscar Hanson. Front row: Staff Sergeants' Paul Shull, flight engineer; Roy Alsbury, waist gunner (who flew some of the missions on the crew); Joe Burton, tail gunner; Sidney Brown, waist gunner, Lawrence Layton, waist gunner and George Simpson, radio operator. Lt Roy Keirn. co-pilot was absent that day. (*via Jim Hanson*)

Lt Robert E. Des Lauriers in the 34th Bomb Group at Mendlesham on the day he and their crew completed 35 missions proudly wearing his 15-mission crush that he was given by Oscar Hanson. (*via Jim Hanson*)

Lt Gordon Weir, navigator in the 493rd Bomb Group at Debach examines the remains of B-17G 43-38227 *Ramp Happy Pappy* at Woodbridge a few days after Captain Ellis M. Woodward landed the badly shot up Fortress on 12 September 1944 at the emergency airfield after suffering flak damage at Magdeburg. (*Gordon W. Weir*)

B-17G 44-6315 *Fearless Fosdick* in the 486th Bomb Group at Lavenham. L-R: Jim Bethavos (mechanic); Staff Sergeant Ralph Spiller (crew chief); Corporal Jim Pugh (mechanic). (*Edward Spiller/Brenda Jo Gallagher, daughter of Robert Browne*).

2nd Lt Jesse L. Wofford's EM crew in the 100th Bomb Group. Front to back: Raymond R. Uhler, ball turret gunner; Algie L. Davenport, top turret gunner, Joseph R. Urice, tail gunner: Carl E. Lindstrom, armourer; Norman F. Bowman, waist gunner and Reuben Laskow, radio operator.

Crew of B-17G 43-37993 *Mah Ideel* in the 324th Bomb Squadron, 91st Bomb Group. Standing: Raymond Kuenzler, tail gunner; Albert Nosse, ball turret gunner; Luther Hutton Jr., radio operator; Leon Schweda, flight engineer. Kneeling: Weldon Brubaker, pilot, Bill Uphoff, co-pilot, Harry Jensen, bombardier, Samuel Halpert, navigator.

Birmingham Jewell in the 379th Bomb Group at Kimbolton in Cambridgeshire, which had flown its 100th mission on 10 November, and was due to set an 8th Air Force record of 128 missions on 3 February 1945.

B-17s of the 452nd Bomb Group over Berlin on 22 March 1944.

The Französischer Dom in Luisenstadt, Berlin with the destroyed Theater am Gendarmenmarkt and Komödie. (left) on fire on 3 February 1945, when just over 1,000 B-17s aiming for Tempelhof dropped 2,267 tons of bombs over 'Big B', causing a city fire spreading eastwards, driven by the wind, over the south of Friedrichstadt and the northwest of neighbouring Luisenstadt. The fire lasted for four days until it had burnt everything combustible in its range to ashes.

10. Lieutenant Colonel Marvin Dell Lord, 91st Bomb Group operations officer who was KIA on 3 February 1945 flying as Command Pilot for the raid on Berlin.

B-17G 43-38594 *Lady Be Good* in the 457th Bomb Group force landed near Langemark, Belgium after being attacked by Me 262s on the Berlin mission on 18 March 1945. The Fortress was recovered and returned to the USA in June 1945.

2nd Lieutenant David Elmer Vermeer, pilot of B-17G 43-38607 *Lady Jane II* in the 401st Bomb Group who was KIA on the 18 March 1945 raid on Berlin.

B-24M 44-50537 *Second Chance II* in the 328th Bomb Squadron, 93rd Bomb Group approaching the bomb run over Zossen on 15 March 1945.

Zossen, target for 372 B-24s of the 2nd Air Division on 15 March 1945.

in men and machines. A total of 361 American heavy bombers were lost over Europe. On Saturday, 29 April 679 Fortresses and B-24 Liberator crews from eight B-17 and four B-24 combat wings arranged into three forces were awakened early for briefings for Berlin once again. The MPI or Main Point of Impact was again the Friedrichstrasse Bahnhof. 8th AF estimates put the Luftwaffe defence of the capital at 350 Fighters with opposition characterised as "fierce". To ensure continuous escort for all units while over enemy territory fighter support was provided by 814 P-38 Lightnings, P-47 Thunderbolts and P-51s in 16 groups of 8th Fighter Command, four groups from Ninth Fighter Command and two RAF Mustang squadrons.

'At long last, Berlin' Lieutenant Wallace Patterson in the 448th Bomb Group at Seething noted: 'first, second and last resort target; the Friedrichstrasse station right smack in the centre of town. The Forts were to hit with 1,000 lb GPs and we to follow with incendiaries.'

In the 44th 'Flying Eightballs' Bomb Group, 2nd Lieutenant Charles D. Peretti's Liberator crew would fly their third mission. His navigator, 21-year-old 1st Lieutenant John W. McClane, born Biltmore, North Carolina, recalled: 'Our first two missions had not been too rough and we were a little too complacent. After stumbling through the blackout to the breakfast that Saturday morning, the usual question was on everyone's lips, 'Where are we going today?' Was it going to be a 'milk run' over the coast of France or a deep penetration to the heart of Germany? As we filed into the large Nissen hut used for briefing, the men gathered together, as crews, sitting facing a stage with a huge map of Western Europe above it. However this map was securely covered with dark draw curtains. Suddenly the command, 'Attention' was sounded. In unison, all snapped to their feet and in walked the Commanding Officer, Colonel John H. Gibson and his staff. The briefing officer stepped forward with a long pointer and the map curtains were quickly drawn open. At this movement we all knew our target for the day. The ribbons pinned to the map led straight to the heart of Hitler's Germany, the 'Big B' – Berlin. The howl and commotion could have been heard a block away. Everyone settled down and the briefing officers proceeded to detail the crews' objectives. The predicted weather, the expected fighter opposition and flak concentrations were outlined. The stage was set; the battle would soon begin. Hundreds of men would be either killed, wounded, or missing this day but nothing could stop the mission once it had been set in motion. The engines were started and we mounted the plane. The moment of truth was at hand. There was no option but to go and only God knew who would return.'

The 2nd Bomb Division, flying 30 minutes behind schedule, bringing up the rear of the bomber stream, met sixty to eighty enemy fighters northeast of Hanover. These fighters attacked for ten minutes and then, after reforming, attacked for another twenty minutes as the B-24s neared Berlin. They finally broke off after the formation made its final turn to the target. After leaving Celle airspace the only protection afforded the B-24s was a solitary Mustang group, which was forced to retire just after the Liberators completed their bombing run. At the IP *Play Boy* in the 466th Bomb Group piloted by 25-year-old 2nd Lieutenant Franklynn V. Cotner, born Ohio, received a direct hit from an 88, which knocked out the No.3 engine. Cotner completed the bomb run but *Play Boy* was attacked by fighters after the target and went down over Holland. Twenty-two year-old Staff Sergeant Robert Illoe Falk, flying his first mission on the crew as waist gunner, was killed instantly by a shot through the head. Two of the crew evaded until they were liberated. Cotner was sent to Stalag Luft III.

'Mitch' Mitchell's crew on *Sweater Gal'* were in flak from the time they hit Berlin until 30 minutes later without letup and they ran into several fighters on the way home. A few minutes after leaving the target, the B-24 was 'really' rocked by a burst of flak nearby and was pitched up violently and over on one wing and then it nosed down and swung wildly back the other way. "The bail-out alarm bell rang loudly" recalled Charles Clague "and 'Mitch's insistent voice came over the Intercom, 'Bail Out! Bail Out!' The violent aircraft contortions may have lasted five or ten seconds – it certainly seemed much longer! While it lasted there was little chance that any crewmember could have successfully exited the craft. From my seated position, I had only to lean back and pull the red handle that would jettison the nose doors. I reached, may have even touched the handle but at that moment the plane seemed to calmly slide back to straight and normal flight." Very calmly the crew answered in order with their OKs although it had been a very close call. Mitchell's crew completed their combat tour just after D-Day, 6 June 1944. All except three of his crew returned to the States and received a 30-day leave. One became a briefing officer and Mitchell remained in England where he and the radioman delivered much needed fuel to the troops in France and Germany. 'Mitch's drinking brought on by combat stress ultimately led to alcoholism when he returned to the USA and he died aged 46 in 1969.

'Over the Channel" wrote Lieutenant Albert B. Saunders, a B-24 pilot in the 448th Bomb Group, "we decided that our oxygen wouldn't last and elected to continue to the target and then hit the deck if need be. We caught flak in Holland, over the Dummer Lake area; then for thirty minutes before the IP we ran into the most accurate, intense and long-lasting barrage anyone has ever encountered. Most flak alerts last only a minute or so. We figured we flew over Brunswick, Osnabrück and Hanover, all hotly defended towns. They threw every colour and every type they had at us. We were thirty minutes late at the target and from then on we were without fighter support. We saw plainly the target, the Olympic Stadium and the Tiergarten and most of the city. Their flak was not so intense but was of heavier calibre than on the way in and they also threw a lot of rockets at us. Lovell caught a piece that came through the nose turret and was stopped by the bulletproof glass. The bombing was good, what we could see of it."

After leaving, Saunders' crew saw two new crews in the 715th in trouble. Second Lieutenant Orland T. Howard from Billings, Nebraska was flying *Gypsy Queen* aka *Big Bad Wolf* with a feathered engine and 2nd Lieutenant John W.

Cathey had one engine smoking. Howard left the formation over Berlin after flak knocked out three engines and disabled the nose turret on the bomb run. Howard was determined to see if he could make the return trip, but began losing altitude rapidly. The bomb bay doors were cranked open by hand as they were damaged and when the crew reached Denmark they bailed out over the island of Bornholm. Tech Sergeant Harry J. Ambrosini the 24-year-old top turret gunner of Fresno, California who had been a farm hand when he enlisted in the Army Air Corps on 8 October 1941 was killed after his parachute failed to open.[3] Flight Officer Tom Verran the co-pilot and Staff Sergeants' Stanley E. Jones, nose gunner and Harold W. Nininger, left waist gunner were captured. The others were picked up by the Danish Resistance who got them to Sweden.

On Cathey's crew Sergeant Jack Arluck perished in the crash but the rest of the crew bailed out safely. German guards shot and killed Flight Officer Carl Carlson the bombardier when he refused to pack his parachute. 'Cathey's crew were our roommates' wrote Al Saunders ruefully; 'three of them married, one with a baby on the way. On the way back we left our group and went as low as possible to save the little oxygen we had left. We caught the same flak area because the goddamn lead navigator apparently didn't know where he was going. Near Holland we saw the first bandits. At first they circled stragglers and then one stood on its nose and dived on a B-17. It twisted around and headed back toward Germany. Next they went toward a B-24, which was also on the deck. I saw five individual attacks on the ship and clearly saw the 20mm stuff bursting around it. It disappeared into the clouds. Then Lovell called out "fighters at 12 o'clock". I looked and knew form my lessons that from the formations they were flying they must be bandits. There were six of them, all flying abreast and all painted white. Then they lined up stem to stern and came at the 448th formation we had left and shot down four B-24s, making six in all. One B-24 shot up in the air, turned on its back and dove down toward the ground. Another caught fire and spun in. We saw five chutes open.[4] Another went off, apparently under control but no chutes came out.[5] Then our fighters whom 'Al' called showed up and we were okay from then on except for some light flak. We were out of oxygen and nearly out of gas'. We landed with 50 gallons of gas' in one main tank and the other bone dry. We had started with 2,700 gallons. A great many ships ditched in the Channel because of lack of gas'. We had quite a lot of holes in the ship. The 715th was now quite short on crews, what with losses and leaves and my next one would be 12B for me. I hoped that it would be a short one."

Because the winds were both stronger and more northerly than predicted, the bombers were considerably behind schedule. As a result, the B-24s had no fighter escort from just west of Berlin on the way in, through the target area and for more than 200 miles on the withdrawal. German fighters harassed the B-24s all the way to the coast. The P-47s could not engage as they were running low on fuel. North of Hanover at about 1104, fifty German fighters in double line abreast attacked the 392nd Bomb Group formation. The crew captained by

27-year old 2nd Lieutenant Gerald E. 'Buck' Rogers' from Salinas, California had been the last to take off from Wendling, in *Double Trouble*, which was a replacement for *The Bad Penny*, their usual aircraft, which was grounded for repairs. Flying a different aircraft was always considered a bad omen and *Double Trouble* was already falling back due to engine problems when the fighters scored a direct hit on the nose with a 20mm shell, demolishing the nose turret and sending a line of bullets along the centre section. The B-24 caught fire and the bailout bell was soon sounded. Eight survivors were captured almost immediately. 'Fred' Kane the bombardier was found dead in the wreckage. 'Buck' Rogers' body was not found until 1947 when it was discovered in a forest some distance from the crash site with his parachute still intact. He had left a widow, Ruby and a son, Ronald G. Rogers.

Next to go down was the B-24 piloted by 28-year old 2nd Lieutenant Leo E. Ofenstein from Washington D.C., which was hit by a fighter whose shells lifted the bomber up to about 15 ft. It rolled over, came down and hit the left wing of the B-24J piloted by 2nd Lieutenant William T. 'Kamy' Kamenitsy of Youngstown, Ohio knocking off about ten feet of the wing and the entire left aileron. The co-pilot, 2nd Lieutenant George E. Graham Jr. immediately salvoed the bombs while Kamenitsy fought to keep the B-24 under control but he finally had to make a high speed crash landing. During the rollout there was a dirt farm road crossing their path that took out the nose gear and stood the Liberator on its nose. Kamenitsy's navigator, 2nd Lieutenant John J. Caufield from Chicago, Illinois; bombardier, 2nd Lieutenant Gene A. Miller from Omaha, Nebraska and radio operator, Staff Sergeant Joseph R. Trivison of Cleveland, Ohio were killed. The seven survivors were eventually taken to an air raid shelter in Hanover. Ofenstein, who left a widow, Lucile, and four crewmembers were killed. Fighters that attacked the B-24J piloted by 2nd Lieutenant Robert R. Bishop from El Reno, Oklahoma badly shot up the right elevator and the Liberator spiralled down into a horse pasture killing all ten crew. About an hour after the impact, a bomb exploded in the wreckage, destroying much of what remained of the Liberator.

Two more 392nd Bomb Group crews also went down. *El Lobo* piloted by 2nd Lieutenant 'Bert' W. Wyatt, which was one of four crews chosen to fly with the 44th 'Flying Eightballs' crashed in a forest near the small town of Dinklage about 230 miles due west of Berlin. All ten men were killed. The B-24 piloted by 2nd Lieutenant Fred C. Shere was hit by flak just after 'bombs away' and one engine had to be feathered. A short time later, three German fighters came through the formation, knocking out two B-24s above Shere's Liberator and causing another engine to windmill. The crew shot one fighter down, another abandoned the attack and the third, which caused the fatal damage, attacked from below and to the left. No longer able to stay with the formation, Shere headed toward England alone, steadily losing altitude until finally, he ordered the crew to bail out. On landing they were surrounded by people from a nearby village. A young boy acting as interpreter asked if they wanted to go to Berlin. He was told, 'Hell, no, we just came from there.' Immediately the civilians shook a few pitch forks at them. Tail gunner Sergeant Marvin O. Morris, one of the seven survivors on the crew, spent about two months in a German hospital where the downed German pilot came to visit him. He had been hit during their gun battle and the two men compared war wounds.

Axis Grinder piloted by 1st Lieutenant Floyd Slipp was hit by flak about 75 miles from Berlin and 15 Bf 109s raked the Liberator with 20mm shells. Slipp salvoed his bombs, feathered the #3 engine and left the formation. Soon after, two Bf 109s spotted them and attacked. Slipp dived for the cloud cover below and flew so low across Holland that German soldiers in a windmill shot at them with rifles. *Axis Grinder* crossed the English Channel just above the water and Slipp had to gain altitude to get over the English cliffs. The crew landed at Wendling at 1316 hours.

The crew of *Ready Willing and Able*, piloted by 2nd Lieutenant Bernard Fryman crashed near the base killing all the crew. Second Lieutenant Reed at the controls of *Alfred II* which had been badly damaged over Berlin, made a sharp turn out of the formation and jettisoned his bombs and reached England where at about 1320,eight men bailed out and landed near Beccles, Suffolk; another jumped out moments later and landed near Ingham, Norfolk. Reed then set the automatic pilot and bailed out but he was believed to have hit the B-24 while exiting and was unable to open his parachute. *Alfred II* flew on for several miles before it finally crashed and burned near Walcott on the Norfolk coast at 1329.

It was not until the surviving Liberators reached the Dummer Lake on the homeward journey that P-47 Thunderbolt escorts reappeared but most of the P-51s that were supposed to replace the P-47s had mechanical problems and turned back at 1116 without ever finding the Liberators. German ground controllers, seized upon the time lapse and directed over 100 fighters to the Hanover area to intercept.

One of three Liberators that ditched in the sea on return from Berlin was flown by 22-year-old Oklahoman, 1st Lieutenant Alfred H. Locke. His PFF ship in the 'Sky Scorpions' at Hethel just outside Norwich had led the 466th Bomb Group to 'Big-B'. Five of the 12 man crew were killed in action and when combat damage knocked out an engine and caused a fuel leak Locke was forced to put the B-24 down on the sea off Great Yarmouth. Locke and eight of his crew were rescued by a Royal Navy motor launch but two of his men died soon after. Nine men were saved from a B-24 in the 453rd Bomb Group which ditched 39 miles off Orfordness. All ten crew were picked up from another 44th Bomb Group B-24 that was ditched.

'Germany announced the raid as soon as we hit the IP, eighteen minutes at least from the target' recalled Lieutenant Milton P. Rudd, radio operator on Captain William L. Gibbons' crew in the 457th Bomb Group formation, which was more famously known as 'The Fireball Outfit'. 'There was little flak going in but plenty over the target. Their aiming point seemed to be in the lower boxes and we were in the higher box so we didn't get touched. The mission was planned for PFF but we could see the target quite clearly. Plans seemed to change at the last minute and we made a 360 degree turn near Berlin and went in thirty minutes late. We dropped three 1,000 lb demolition bombs and six 500 lb incendiaries which hit near a river bridge in the centre of the capital. Each plane dropped three tons right on the target. The place must really have taken a beating: three divisions of ten wings bombed different sections and I saw only one plane go down, right over the target. It was in flames and broke up after a direct hit from flak.'

The 4th Combat Wing veered to the south after radar equipment in one of the Pathfinder aircraft failed completely and it worked only sporadically in the other. Off course and unescorted, they were hit hard for over thirty minutes in the Brunswick area by an extremely determined and aggressive force of about 125 FW 190s and Bf 109s that wreaked havoc among the unprotected formation, damaging several Fortresses in the 385th and 447th Bomb Groups in twenty minutes. The 385th Bomb Group was flying its 100th mission this day. Technical Sergeant Clarence L. Mossman, the left waist gunner on the *Worry Bird* flown by 28-year-old Cleveland, Ohio pilot, Lieutenant Richard A. Spencer recalled: 'We were flying a tight formation and all the squadrons seemed to be in their right positions when the German fighters attacked. We did evasive action to help us from head-on attacks. We first spotted about 200 fighters about 12 o'clock high and in a few minutes they attacked us head-on, coming down out of the sun in waves of 40 and 60 at a time and doing barrel rolls right through the formations. They made three passes. Our left and also our right wingman went down. We had a lot of flak damage on our aircraft and also damage to our wing from 20mm shells fired by Me 109s that came down through our formation. All of the crew came through the mission without being wounded or killed.'

Lieutenant Paul E. Suckow's B-17 crew in the 452nd Group had to ditch. Richard Walsh, the engineer-top turret gunner had suggested that they name their B-17, *Section 8*, which was heartily agreed upon. Walsh even managed to get an eightball painted on the plane. A Section 8 was a discharge based on an assessment of being psychologically unfit or possessing character traits which made one unfit for duty. The crew figured they were crazy to get in a plane and fly over Germany.[6]

'As we hit our IP' relates Walsh 'we could see up ahead, the great big wall of flak. I looked down on this country where so much trouble came from. From five miles up it looked like any other place in the world but you can't mistake the winding Rhine River that passes through the heart of Germany. To the right I could see the big park that we were briefed to help locate the target.

'Bomb bay doors coming open,' the bombardier said.

'I checked the doors and relay. 'Doors open and all clear below.

'Roger' says he.

'Then it happened.

'We weren't getting any flak until then, that is, direct flak, but now they were on us and we were hit, or should I say, blasted out of position and the Nos.1 and 3 engines were out. No.1 feathered OK but No.3 did not. None of the crew was hit but the ship was a sieve. We had a hole big enough to drive a jeep through in the left wing. The fuel transfer pump worked overtime 'till the last. By now we had lost 8,000 ft and were completely alone. Our speed was approximately 120 mph; dangerously close to stalling speed, if the ship was not flown perfectly. Several things happened that required fast action and skill and through all this not one of us was panicky but we were scared. All guns and ammo' were thrown overboard, also all of the armour we could loosen. The ball turret was dropped. That in itself was a great help because of its weight and wind resistance.

'Well up to now things weren't too bad. We were alive anyhow. We then had a new worry; Gas'! The gunners and bombardier stripped the ship expertly because of some past experience. Now it was just a matter of time. The radioman was in contact with ASR and we were fixed. With a few parting bursts of flak we left the Dutch coast and started across the Channel. Altitude about 5,000. We passed B-26s of the 9th Air Force going in and two P-47s saluted us and hung around for a while. We were in constant touch with the horizon when I looked at the gas' gauge, which read '30 gallons' for each engine. Then I remembered what the books said a long way back; 'Don't use all the gas' and then crash land'. Do it while the engines are turning.

'This was it. We had to prepare to ditch. The pilots pulled their safety belts on and the rest of the crew took their places for the ditching procedure. We started down to the smooth green water (it looked like it anyhow). At about 500 ft the two remaining engines 'conked out' so we had to dead-stick on the water. She skipped twice before mushing in completely underwater and then she bobbed to the surface like a cork. We scrambled out and counted heads. All present with no casualties. Both dinghies inflated OK and we got in and pushed away.'

'We were floating in the Channel for about an hour and a half when the shore patrol picked us up' reflected the ball turret gunner, Pfc George Pruitt of Ardmore, Oklahoma. On Pearl Harbor Day Pruiit had been working in Wyoming and was headed back home when his bus stopped at a hole-in-the-wall diner in Denver, Colorado for lunch. 'We heard the news broadcast announce the attack' he recalled. 'The next day, I joined the Army Air Corps. My brother joined on the same day, but neither of us knew it.

'I'd never been so glad to see a boat in all my life. We were given a ditching citation and we immediately became members of the 'Gold Fish Club'.' The crew's final mission occurred on D-Day.

All told the 452nd lost three B-17s this day. *Rugged But Right* flown by 2nd Lieutenant George O. Haakenson was hit by flak and fell behind before it was shot down by a fighter. All ten crew bailed out and were taken into captivity. The *Karen B* (which was named by the original pilot, Paul Skinner in January

1944, in honour of his six-year-old daughter, Karen Barbara Skinner) was hit by flak over Berlin. With #2 engine badly damaged, 2nd Lieutenant 'Hal' J. Nelson, who was from Iowa City, nursed *Karen B* homeward but when two more engines malfunctioned, he ordered the crew to bail out while he still had some control. But the crew was still aboard when he crash landed at 1330 hours at Het Vellert, five kilometres south of Ruurlo in Holland.

The B-24H piloted by 23-year-old 1st Lieutenant William Frantz Moore from Atlanta, Georgia in the 467th Bomb Group was hit by flak shortly after the target and ran low on fuel over Holland. The order to bail out was given before the doomed Liberator crashed on a farm at the Elspeterweg in Uddel, killing 19-year-old Gemmigje Mulder. Major Robert Louis Salzarulo the 25-year old CO of the 788th Bomb Squadron of Richmond, Indiana riding in the co-pilot's seat and 2nd Lieutenants' Edgar J. Powell the 24-year old co-pilot riding in the tail turret and Edward Verbosky the 28-year-old bombardier; Staff Sergeant Henry Hayes Allen, ball turret gunner and Staff Sergeant Werner George Braun the left waist gunner from Coldwater, Ohio were taken prisoner. Tech Sergeant Clinton Loftin Watts, the 26-year old engineer/top turret gunner landed safely but tore his upper right thigh muscle and had to be treated at the Luftwaffe hospital in Amsterdam before being sent to a PoW camp.

Bill Moore was reunited with Lieutenant John Lewis Low Jr., the 25-year old Group Bombardier by the Dutch Resistance. Moore successfully evaded for about six months and Low evaded for 296 days in enemy-occupied Holland until he was liberated on 29 April 1945. On 1 October the Germans had raided the safe location used by the Dutch Resistance where Moore's fellow evaders were in hiding. Sergeant David L. Smith, the right waist gunner on B-24 *Tell Me More* in the 466th Bomb Group, which had crash landed virtually intact near Apeldoorn on 29 April, had joined this group on 15 May.[7] Tech Sergeant George P. Paulk of Barton, Florida and Sergeant Floyd E. Ragsdale from Honea Path, South Carolina, the radio operator and the tail gunner respectively on the *Karen B*, had joined the group on or around 10 August. Sergeant Robert W. Zercher the ball turret gunner of York, Pennsylvania, who had also been taken in by the Dutch Resistance, was apprehended while in hiding. On 2 October he (along with RAF Flight Sergeant Ken Ingram) and six members of the Resistance were shot in cold blood in the back garden of the headquarters of the Sicherheitsdienst (Security Service of the Reichsführer-SS, or SD) in Apeldoorn.[8]

Bill Moore was unable to hide with his fellow evaders and was arrested and imprisoned at the King William III barracks in Apeldoorn. He refused to reveal the whereabouts of the evaders and Staff Sergeant James Reese Anslow the 20-year old radio operator, Captain Franklin Dent Coslettt the 29-year-old navigator and John Low were able to escape. Coslett evaded capture for over seven months but was apprehended on Christmas Eve while in hiding near Assen in the province of Drenthe. He was sentenced to death for 'terrorism and espionage' but survived and was liberated by the Allies on 13 April 1945.

Sergeant Walter Thomas Kilgore the 25-year-old right waist gunner evaded capture and on 8 May 1945 he was finally liberated by Allied forces. James Anslow was liberated in Meyac, France in mid-July 1945. On 28 November an attempt was made by the Resistance to liberate the prisoners held at the King William III barracks. This failed and two of the three Resistance fighters involved were killed. On 2 December Bill Moore was murdered in cold blood at the barracks and twenty of the Resistance fighters were executed by members of the Sicherheitsdienst (SD).[9]

When John McClane had landed at Shipdham at 1730 hours after the Berlin mission he was so pleased to be back that he bent over and kissed the ground. 'I had been in the air 8 hours and 15 minutes. Now I knew why we were told that if we flew 25 missions at an average of four losses per mission we had a 100 percent chance of being shot down. According to *Stars and Stripes*, our ETO newspaper this was the heaviest daylight assault in history on any one target. This was one of the worst days ever for the 8th Air Force.'

The first words Lieutenant Richard Spencer uttered to the *St. Louis Globe Democrat* reporter as he stepped from his battered B-17 at Great Ashfield were: 'The fighters were so thick and so close to us today that I feel sure that if I had a .45 calibre automatic up there with me I could have picked off a Jerry myself. Rows of ten and twelve Me 109s weaved through our formation in head on, do-or-die attacks in a seemingly endless stream. And a lot of them died, my gunners alone getting six of them, but they took a lot of Forts with them too. I've never seen the sky filled with so much confusion – exploding planes, flying debris, white and brown parachutes, bursting flak, exploding shells – it was fantastic but horribly real to us up there."

"The first sign that we had of fighters was when the whole attacking force hit us at once" stated 2nd Lieutenant Donald R. McNeeley, his 24 year-old co pilot from Toledo, Ohio. "Sixty Messerschmitts and Focke-Wulfs suddenly loomed up dead in front of us, and for a moment I sat there amazed as they seemed to come from nowhere. Glancing to the left of the ship I saw another formation of sixty Jerries heading in. I thought for a moment that I was seeing things, but when they started to blaze away at us I knew that it was not a nightmare."

"The two Ohioans at the controls put their Fort through violent evasive action, making themselves as difficult as possible to hit" championed the *St. Louis Globe Democrat* reporter who was understandably anxious to headline the feats of the aerial gunners. "At the same time the gunners had a hard time sighting their targets from the rocking, rolling positions, but they are claiming six destroyed" he added. "The bombardier, 2nd Lieutenant Daniel F. Carl, Aliquippa, Pennsylvania got the first attacker, the beginning of the end for six Me 109s, in the first wave to hit the formation. The 33-year-old right waist gunner, Staff Sergeant Lloyd K. Jutler from Springvale, Maine got the second fighter in the second attacking wave. Claims for numbers 3 and 4 were made by the 20-year-old ball turret gunner, Staff Sergeant Marvin D. Baird, Hutchinson, Kansas, Technical Sergeant Gabriel V. Kushner, 30, of Duquense, Pennsylvania, was the next to score a kill. Fighter number six was claimed by the 21-year-old left waist gunner Staff Sergeant Clarence Mossman Jr., from Brussels, Illinois."

'This undoubtedly was the worst day in my life to date' said Carlyle J. Hanson. "After turning on the IP about 150 enemy fighters struck at us. They made three passes at us, knocking down seven out of our group. Humour for the day was when 'Jerry' was coming in like a swarm of bees. Julius King the left waist gunner hollers out, 'Flak at 3 o'clock!' We had been flying through accurate and heavy flak for half an hour. We didn't even get over Berlin, as the weather was too bad. It would have been twice as bad if we had have tried it. We dropped our bombs on Brandenburg about thirty miles southwest of 'Big B'. I think we ploughed up a field. Fred and Bob James kept the plane going after No.1 engine was knocked out and another was smoking. We got a little flak on the way home. One waist gunner was hit in the head by flak but wasn't too serious. A 20mm shell hit No.1 engine. Flak flew all over the plane (it looked like a sieve), knocking out the radio compass. I had my flak suit off and parachute on once and really thought I would be using it. One of the fellows in our barracks went down and it was his first mission. This was Fred and Tony's 13th mission [Anthony J. Ardzinski, the 21-year-old tail gunner born in Poland in April 1923] and my 14th. Now we sweated out Bob James' twelfth. It couldn't be any rougher. God answered my prayers for sure.'[10]

Starting at 1417 hours the B-17s of the 447th began landing back at Rattlesden. Air and ground crews had gathered in front of the control tower to watch the ships return, the omnipresent meat wagons drawn up at the far end of the runway. As the formation came around over fields of beet and barley, those with wounded shot Red-Red flares and the bombers began to form a traffic pattern. There was a shout from the tower the more experienced men began to count. They were stunned! Where were *Lady Lilian; Gum Chum; Solid Sender; Spare Parts; Rowdy Rebel; Bloated Body* and *Mississippi Lady* and the other four? They checked again and again but it was true; the Group was missing 11 Forts![11] One by one the wounded and the dying[12] were respectfully placed in the backs of the meat wagons for the attention of the flight surgeon. One tail gunner had lost both hands but was alive, others with chest wounds and fractures and shock caused by deadly cannon shells awaited the mortician and their maker.

At interrogation, gloomy, wide-eyed men congregated around the edges of the debriefing tables filled with exhausted crews. On the other side of the room Scotch was available. It was to help spill their guts but many didn't need it – they had their reasons. Instead men mostly ate cakes and drank hot coffee served by the Red Cross. From about 1100 to 1200 hours and without any fighter support from around 1030 to 1200 hours remorseless pack attacks of 125 fighters and upwards had assailed the luckless Group like demonic, death dealing destroyers, their guns spitting destruction in every direction. Crews spoke of the fearless

German pilots, who made co-ordinated attacks of six or more at a time, with pairs attacking simultaneously from both sides and from above; but mostly they came from the nose. "They came in from 12 o'clock high … from 3 o'clock and 4 o'clock low" pilots added excitedly, gesturing with both hands, palms down to demonstrate the manoeuvres of the Forts. As the remaining B-17s reached the target they encountered heavy flak and the last of the eleven aircraft were lost. The crews on *Due Back* captained by 2nd Lieutenant Carl J. Blom, from Portland, Maine and *Mississippi Lady* piloted by 2nd Lieutenant Edgar P. Farrell, from Atlanta, Georgia – had flown their first – and last – missions. Both lost four men killed and 6 taken prisoner. 'Hot News' was wired to headquarters for immediate action.[13] At supper there were 110 empty mess hall seats, perhaps a few more, but Lieutenant Dean S. Flemming's crew, having had to ditch *Wolf Pack* on the way home, were rescued and returned later. Depressingly, the losses took the 447th's monthly total to 22 aircraft. Replacements slept none too soundly in dead men's beds that night.

Opposition, by an estimated 350 fighters, was fierce. A total of 38 Fortresses and 25 Liberators including one that crashed with its bomb load into the Volkswagen factory near Fallersleben were lost and three P-38 Lightnings and ten Mustangs were shot down. A 458th Bomb Group Liberator piloted by 2nd Lieutenant Dale R. Morris, whose crew had only arrived at Horsham St. Faith the previous Sunday, was attacked by FW 190s at 1104 hours in vicinity of Celle seconds before bombs away. One engine was knocked out and the B-24 fell out of formation in "an easy spin" but Morris recovered control and made it to Sweden. Sixty-four of the bombers claimed 73 enemy fighters destroyed while American fighters claimed 22 for thirteen lost from the 814 dispatched.

The bloody carnage had a resounding effect that was felt on all the bases and the bad memories would live with everyone until the day they died. At Rougham, John Moser's co-pilot, Leo C. Riley in *Kismet* in the 94th Bomb Group wrote: 'Things are pretty sad around Nissen 91 today. We started on a raid to the heart of Berlin and had to turn back over Amsterdam. Second Lieutenant Kenneth L. Chisum and the crew of *Passionate Witch* stood by but took off at the last minute and have not been heard from since.' (Flak damage caused crew to bail out at Herzberg, the *Witch* flying on for another 100 miles, crashing at Hassenberg, 9 miles East of Coburg). 'There is no way to explain our feelings when men we knew and loved as brothers go down. Of course, there is a chance for them. There is always a chance, except for a direct hit and explosion. (Nine men survived and were taken into captivity but the right waist gunner, Sergeant Gene C. Powell of Rossville, Indiana was killed when his 'chute failed). I never knew before how many times a day one could find time to pray, if one will try.'

Bombing was described as "fair" but the Friedrichstrasse section of Berlin the railway station escaped major damage. The U-bahn and S-bahn only ceased operations on 23 and 25 April 1945 respectively due to shortage of electricity. In just under 38 minutes 679 B-17s and B-24s had plastered Berlin and Brandenburg,

Magdeburg and targets of opportunity dropping 1,271 tons of bombs in 8/10ths cover. Sergeant Milton P. Rudd, ball turret gunner on Lieutenant Marsden W. Mattatall's crew in the 457th Bomb Group said he could not see how the city could be standing that night. That evening in Berlin Ursula von Kardorff, a 33-year-old journalist working for the *Deutsche Allgemeine Zeitung* managed to attend a performance of Shakespeare's *The Winter's Tale* only hours after enduring the heavy American raid. To reach the theatre she had to clamber over rubble, 'past blood-spattered people with green-tinged faces' but she felt almost physically lifted out of her present existence and transported into a dream world.[14]

Notes

1. See *Chick's Crew: A Tale of the Eighth Air Force* by Ben Smith Jr. (Rose Printing Co, Inc. 1978, 1983 and 2006).

2. On 6 March, IV, Gruppe, led by Müller, claimed the destruction of seven B-17s, four B-17 Herausschüsse (separation shots – a severely damaged heavy bomber forced to separate from its combat box and which the Luftwaffe counted as an aerial victory) and a P-51 Mustang for the loss of one Bf 109G-6 damaged. In this encounter, Müller was credited with the destruction of two B-17 bombers. Müller was killed in a landing accident at Salzwedel on 29 May 1944 when his Bf 109G-6 stalled on landing approach at low altitude.

3. airforce.togetherweserved.com.

4. *Chubby Champ* piloted by Lieutenant James G. Clark Holyoke, Massachusetts who was KIA along with four of his crew after the B-24 was hit by flak and by fighters in rear fuselage. Five men survived to be taken into captivity.

5. *Miss Happ* and Lieutenant Max E. Turpin's crew and *Sweet Sioux* and 2nd Lieutenant William M. Rogers' crew were both lost each with one killed and nine taken into captivity. *Sad Sack* flown by 2nd Lieutenant William F. Ponge from Hollis, New York who was killed went down with five other men KIA and three taken prisoner.

6. *452nd Bomb Group Plane Names Their Origins* by Jerry Penry.

7. He was recaptured in January 1945 and sent to Stalag Luft I.

8. 'Hal' Nelson: co-pilot, Chas Ramlow; bombardier; Phil Cavanaugh, flight engineer/top turret gunner, Mike Dencavage and waist gunner, Vic Ryczko also evaded.

9. See *Aircrew Remembered* and *One Way Ticket to Berlin: A Day in The life of the Mighty Eighth* by John Meurs; Aviation Safety Network; The American Air Museum and the 467th BG (H) Association.

10. On 27 August 1944 *Poltergeist* was ditched in the North Sea after a mid-air collision with another 550th Squadron aircraft (43-38270) on return from Merseburg. 2nd Lieutenant Otho J. Quick the pilot and six others on the crew came home but the bombardier, James H. Shaver and top turret gunner, Edward F. Myers were taken prisoner after they had bailed out. 43-38270 was later transferred to the 390th Bomb Group. Ironically, on 21 November it was lost in another mid air collision and crashed at Pyremont, France. Eight of Jim Webb's crew died.

11. Of 33 B-17s that took off, four aborted. Of the 18 that returned, 16 received battle damage.

12. 38 men were KIA; 62 men became PoW.

13. I highly recommend *My Private War: Liberated Body, Captive Mind: A World War II PoW's Story* by Norman Bussel (Pegasus Books LLC (New York 2008). Norm, just 19-years-old, was one of six men on Farrell's crew who were taken prisoner. Four others were KIA.

14. *Diary of a Nightmare: Berlin 1942-1945 by Ursula von Kardorff*, Ewan Butler (translator). (Rupert Hart-Davies 1965).

Chapter Six

Four Miles High

...the most impressive sight was our glimpse of Berlin. As we passed by, we all vocally pitied the poor devils who drew it as their target for the day.

Captain Harry H. Crosby, a navigator in the 100th Bomb Group and a veteran of many of the 'Bloody Hundredth's more harrowing missions.

In East Anglia on Thursday, 4 May 1944 the sun shone only faintly here and there. Bad weather fronts over the continent halted deep-penetration missions like the one to Berlin, Brunswick and targets in central Germany when cirrus clouds between 13,000 and 23,000 ft forced 591 B-17s and B-24s to abandon the mission over the Low Countries. At a chilly Thorpe Abbotts Major 'Red' Bowman studied the day's reports with a practiced eye. A consummate New Englander, born at Somerville, Massachusetts on 30 December 1895, the son of a New Hampshire Congregational minister, between the wars 'Red' was news editor of the *Boston Sunday Advertiser*. He noted that the Hundredth's citation for the first bombing of Berlin 'bounced' at 8th Air Force Headquarters. A legend in his own time, able to recite volumes of Shakespeare and Milton, Bowman never hesitated to heap contempt on writers if he felt they needed it. 'Somebody doesn't like us, maybe' he wrote. 'The 390th and 96th have both been cited – God knows why. Both have screwed up enough missions to get plenty of recognition, but hardly of that sort.'

On Friday 5 May the 'Bloody Hundredth' was scheduled for Berlin but the operation by the 8th Air Force was cancelled just before briefing and a practice mission flown instead. Two days later, on Sunday, 7 May, Berlin was on the mission list once again and this time it would go ahead as planned. When he was awakened at about 0300 hours, 1st Lieutenant Joseph P. Wroblewski, pilot of *Shady Lady II* in the 351st Bomb Group at Polebrook already had a good feeling as to where they were going. 'I began to sweat this one out. If any one of us had our own way we would have all gone back to bed.' Born in Sunderland, Massachusetts on 4 April 1918, Joe's Fortress was one of 330 B-17s in the 1st Bomb Division that joined with 270 more Forts in the 3rd Bomb Division that were aimed at 'Big-B' Another force of 322 Liberators meanwhile, were dispatched to Münster and Osnabrück. This, the eighth raid by the 8th Air Force on Berlin was the first time that over 900 heavy bombers were dispatched in one day.

Just as it was leaving England at 0713, *Cap'n Crow*, Lieutenant Ralph W. Wright's B-17 in the 'Bloody Hundredth' dived out of formation after flares, stored in the top turret compartment suddenly began to ignite. Wright immediately ordered the crew to abandon the aircraft but was then overcome by the smoke and fumes, as was the co-pilot, 2nd Lieutenant 'Jack' Raper. After attempting to beat out the flames with a box lid, Tech Sergeant Alden 'Pat' Madsen, engineer/top turret gunner passed a parachute to Lieutenant Wright and bailed out of the tail hatch, as the waist hatch was blocked by one of the gunners whose 'chute had opened outside. *Cap'n Crow* crashed into a wooded area at Herringfleet Hall near Lowestoft where it exploded, killing the pilots and 2nd Lieutenants' Rich Curran, the navigator and Carl A. Herrmann the bombardier and waist gunner, Sergeant Randy Moore. At the same time two of the bombs flew out of the wreckage and went through a wall into the hall but fortunately did not explode. The five dead were buried at Madingley Cemetery, Cambridge. Although painfully burned, Madsen soon returned to duty. Radio operator, Bob Montonado; ball turret gunner, John Pontzious; waist gunner, Jack Willburn and tail gunner, Alf Bridges also returned to duty.

Just over 1,246 tons of bombs were dropped on 'Big-B'. The Luftwaffe chose not to oppose the American formations in any strength and eight B-17s only were lost to enemy action while no fighter claims were made by bomber crew gunners. Four Fortresses were damaged beyond economical repair and were written off later while a further 265 Fort's were damaged.

Despite the demands made on the maintenance crews in East Anglia 500 Fortresses were on the Battle Order the next day, Monday, 8 May for a follow up raid on Berlin. At Snetterton Heath when the Briefing Officer slowly pulled back the curtain to show the target for the day and the route in and back loud groans arouse from the group – such as: *Not Again; We Were There Yesterday. BERLIN! – two days in a row*! The crew of 1st Lieutenant Harold Lee Niswonger, the 23-year-old pilot of *The Chief* who was from Las Vegas, Nevada that had barely made it back the day before with a badly damaged plane, were just as loud with their groans and remarks as the rest. 'Suffice it to say that no one was very happy about the prospect of going back to Berlin – let alone flying a mission over Germany' said 2nd Lieutenant Thomas L. Thomas, the 26-year-old navigator of Chicago, Illinois. 'In spite of all the 'bitching' you can be sure that the mission went as planned.'

The main focus of the attack was effectively carried out on the Wilhelmstrasse bahnhof in the Mitte and Kreuzberg (Friedrichshain-Kreuzberg district) by 386 B-17s in the 1st and 3rd Bomb Divisions and 67 Forts hit the Brandenburg district, Brunswick and two other secondary targets. When the 96th, 388th and 452nd Bomb Groups lost touch with their Divisional formation and joined the 307 Liberators heading for Brunswick, devoid of escorting fighters, the three 45th Combat Wing groups came under a mass frontal attack by FW 190s in the Nienburg area. In the 388th Bomb Group *Nasty Nellie's* #3 engine and wing were set on fire and six men bailed out before it crashed at Hustedt 19 miles southeast of Bremen. *Little Joe Jr.* crashed 15 miles east of Hoya, Germany after five men had bailed out and *Peg Of My Heart* aka *Sweet Adeline* crashed in the Channel off Ste-Suveeur-le-Vicomte, 19 miles south of Cherbourg. Five men on the crew were killed and the five others were taken prisoner. The left wing on *Kickapoo Joy Juice* in the 452nd Group was set on fire and crashed east of Runingen, 2 miles south of Brunswick after all ten crew members had bailed out. Returning to Deopham Green another of the Group's B-17s crashed into a truck on the base, killing the driver. But it was the 'Snetterton Falcons' formation leading the wing formation that suffered the most. Between thirty and fifty enemy fighters in their initial wave and a second wave ten minutes' later shot down eleven B-17s in the formation. Eight men on *Laura Jane* piloted by 2nd Lieutenant Frank L. King Jr., of El Dorado, Arkansas were taken prisoner after bailing out. Bill Reade the navigator from Atlanta, Georgia, was killed when he was hit by a 20mm shell and Bill Lloyd the tail gunner died at his guns. All ten crewmembers on *Smilin' Thru* piloted by Flight Officer Leo T. Green of Socerast, Ohio bailed out and were taken prisoner after being shot down by fighters. Bob Blevins the waist gunner on *Reluctant Dragon* piloted by 2nd Lieutenant Jerry T. Musser from Coral Gables, Florida was killed at his guns and six crewmen who bailed out were taken prisoner. Musser wrestled with the controls to right the B-17 after a 10,000 ft dive, assisted by Tech Sergeant Leon H. Sweatt, the top turret gunner and engineer, from Divine, Texas who doubled as co-pilot and they and John Flayak the bombardier returned safely.

Leutnant Leopold Münster, Staffelführer, Jagdgeschwader 3 "Udet", whose claims stood at 95 victories, was killed in a collision with *The Chief*. Harold Niswonger and Tech Sergeant Bob Morrison the 20-year-old radio operator, who was hit in the stomach when the radio room was struck by a 20 mm shell, died on the aircraft. Niswonger and Tech Sergeant John R. Caum the 20-year-old tail gunner from Erial, Camden County, New Jersey had gone back to help Morrison put on his parachute and help him bail out. As he was sitting at the navigator's desk entering this information in his log, Tom Thomas heard that dreaded cry of 'Fighters at 11 o'clock high.' As he turned his head to look, he heard a loud explosion and found himself on top of the escape hatch at the front of the plane. Since he kept his chest parachute there he decided that it would be wise to put it on – which he did. He then tried to crawl to his position at the navigator's machine guns. However, his right arm was numb and useless as well as bleeding and he was also bleeding from his right chest. He had been hit in the right arm by a 20 mm cannon shell and across the chest by machine gun bullets from FW 190s. The cannon shell had gone through his right arm and exploded at the bulkhead just below the co-pilot's position occupied by 25-year old 2nd Lieutenant Roderick Bruce Steele of Portland, Cumberland County, Maine – wounding him in the legs. There were two more loud explosions and he heard Harold Niswonger say that the No.3 engine had been hit and that they were on fire.

Thomas was still trying to get to his guns when *The Chief* was hit again by three to six more FW 190s. The right wing was hit again and the ball-turret was blown away. Just by luck Staff Sergeant Edwin H. Marsh the 21-year old top turret gunner of Denham Springs, Livingston, Louisiana had just crawled out of it to get more ammunition. At this point Niswonger rang the 'Bail Out' bell and told them to get out as soon as possible. Flight Officer Tom Fitzgerald the 22-year-old bombardier of Asbury Park, Monmouth County, New Jersey dumped the bomb load and then jumped from the front escape hatch, delaying opening his parachute and watching for other members of his crew bailing out. Before they were all out he witnessed his B-17 blowing up with a great big ball of fire. John Caum bailed out but was probably beaten and killed by German civilians when he hit the ground. Tom Thomas and Staff Sergeant 'Al' Grick the 22-year-old ball turret gunner of Dickson City, Lackawanna County, Pennsylvania were taken by truck to the town of Verden where they met other members of their crew including the two waist gunners, Staff Sergeants' Robert R. Robinson (20) of Wisconsin Rapids, Wood County, Wisconsin and 22-year old Dale J. Johnson of Washta, Cherokee County, Iowa and they were immediately put in jail.

Eight of the eleven B-24 Liberators that failed to return were from the 453rd Bomb Group at Old Buckenham.[1] The third highest single loss of the day was five B-17s lost in the 306th Bomb Group. Thirty planes had taken off from Thurleigh but five of the low group aborted when they were unable to maintain formation. At 0959 hours 2nd Lieutenant Darvin A. Smith dropped behind before returning later then dropped back again and the B-17 was never seen again. His Fortress crashed at Steenwijk in Holland. All the crew were killed. At 1042 hours in bad weather in the vicinity of Wittstock northwest of Berlin there was a collision when the B-17 flown by 2nd Lieutenant Dick Lambert was bounced hard by propwash, probably from a group ahead and came down on *Four Leaf Clover* flown by 2nd Lieutenant Edwin H. Jacobs that lost its tail section in the collision and hit the right wing of 1st Lieutenant Edwin C. Schlecht's B-17 and all three B-17s went down. All ten men on Jacobs' crew and seven on Lambert's were killed. The top turret gunner was the only survivor on Schlecht's B-17. A fifth B-17 that had difficulty staying with the formation and dropped down into a group flying below and was last seen at 'bombs away' over Berlin. 2nd Lieutenant Louis F. Matichka was later reported to have ditched the B-17 in Swedish waters off Vallo. All ten crew were picked up and interned.

A total of 896 tons of bombs were released over Brunswick by 288 Liberators for the loss of eleven B-24s, of which eight were from the 453rd Bomb Group at Old Buckenham. A total of 892 tons of bombs were dropped on 'Big-B' by 386 B-17s of the 1st and 3rd Bomb Divisions and the Brandenburg district received an additional 42 tons dropped by 17 B-17s. The Berlin correspondent of the *Scandinavian Telegraph Bureau* was convinced that 'the city was doomed'. He wrote of 'houses in ruins, or reduced to piles of rubble, of bomb craters in the streets, of houses with their fronts shaved off and of curb stones having been hurled hundreds of yards.' The Stockholm *Morgon Tidningen* reported 'thousands of people had been killed...while many fires had broken out, particularly in the western part of the city.'

Crews who still needed missions to complete their tour must have been relieved to find over the next few days that the red yarns on the briefing maps converged mainly at airfield and marshalling yard targets in France, Belgium and Luxembourg. Berlin seemed to be off the menu, which was a relief, especially for those whose next mission meant completion of a tour and home. On 9 May 823 bombers attacked transportation targets. On 11 May, 973 bombers bombed marshalling yards in Germany and the Low Countries. Next day the 8th Air Force was assigned oil targets at Brüx, Böhlen, Leipzig, Merseburg, Lützkendorf and Zeitz, while a smaller force was to attack the Focke Wulf 190 repair depot at Zwickau. Over 880 bombers, escorted by 735 fighters would fly a common course in trail to the Thüringen area where the bomb divisions would peel off and attack five targets: the big Leuna plant at Merseburg, 18 miles west of Leipzig; Lützkendorf and Bohlen in the same general area; Zeitz, 25 miles southwest of Leipzig; and Brüx, 42 miles northwest of Prague. This was the first time that the 8th had been assigned a target in Czechoslovakia although Brüx had been bombed before by the 15th Air Force. Now it was the turn of the Fortress crews of the 3rd Bomb Division.

One by one the B-17s took off and completed their complicated group and wing assembly patterns. Manningtree was the final assembly point and crews carried on over the Channel in a bomber stream. The bombers crossed the enemy coast between Dunkirk and Ostend near the French-Belgian border. The 94th Bomb Group missed their rendezvous with the fighter escort and all hell broke loose. At the target flak was moderate, which at least gave crews a respite from the fighters.

In the 452nd Bomb Group formation everything seemed to be going smoothly for Lieutenant Fred Whitlinger's crew on *Smokey Liz*. Her pilot was from Pittsburgh known as the "smokey" city. His wife's name was Dorothy Elizabeth. The crew figured that naming the plane *Smokey Dottie* didn't sound too good, so they had chosen *Smokey Liz* instead. Fifteen minutes from the IP" recalled Ralph Reese the left waist gunner 'we saw some 'planes on our wing go down in flames. To our delight, they were enemy planes being shot down by our P-47 fighter escorts. We saw one P-47 shoot down three enemy planes but the flak was very heavy over the target and beyond. We saw one B-17 shot down and I saw ten 'chutes open and glide towards the ground. The group behind us [100th] was attacked by Bf 109s, who stayed out of range and were able to reach our planes. We lost 14 ships out of our group.

Ralph Munn peered out from the close confines of his ball turret below *Lucky Lady* and watched the flak. 'As usual, the enemy was reluctant to attack until our escorts made the turn for home base. We had considerable action, mostly high level attacks down through the squadron, until just short of the target.' The crew did not see another fighter until they reached eastern Belgium when two 109s pulled up close on their right wing. Almost out of fuel and too damaged to make it back to the Channel Dick Noble called everyone to hold fire and prepare to bail out. Within a matter of minutes all the crew evacuated the not so *Lucky Lady* before it pancaked in on a hillside at Namur.[2] Altogether, the Luftwaffe shot down 46 bombers and ten fighters on 12 May for the loss of almost 150 fighters.

On 19 May Lieutenant Robert D. Lane's crew in the 457th Bomb Group at Glatton (Conington) had one more mission to fly, which would make them the first crew in the 'Fireball Outfit' to complete their tour and it would be on *Tujunga!* – the same B-17 that they had brought overseas in January. They could only pray that last mission would be anywhere except Berlin. "We got up at 4 am and went to briefing "hoping for a milk run" said Sergeant Winfred 'Bob' Kincaid, one of Lane's waist gunners 'but the target for our 25th and final mission was 'Big-B' – a heck of a way to spend our last mission!" The battle order for Berlin, the primary target, with Kiel as the secondary target in case 'Big B' was socked in, totalled 588 B-17s of the 1st and 3rd Bomb Divisions. A raid on Brunswick would be flown by 300 Liberators in the 2nd Bomb Division.

While Bob Lane's crew could only curse their luck at drawing Berlin as their final mission, for some others on this day of all days it was their first! 1st Lieutenant Theodore R. 'Bud' Beiser and 2nd Lieutenant Richard R. Johnson his 22-year-old co-pilot in the 427th Squadron in the 303rd Bomb Group had only one mission under their belts and learned that their squadron would lead the group. They would fly #5. New crews had a bad habit of quickly disappearing without trace and Dick Johnson probably thought he would never live to complete a tour of 32 combat missions. The son of migrant farm workers and sharecroppers, by living in abandoned houses, barns and tents during the Great Depression, his family managed to survive while putting Dick and his brother through eight elementary schools in six states. After high school Dick had hitchhiked from Southern Illinois to Norfolk, Virginia to work in a defence plant. He joined the Army Air Force after getting a draft notice in 1942 and with only a high school diploma had managed to pass all the requirements to become a pilot of a Flying Fortress.

"Our Group Commander, Colonel Kermit D. Stevens was leading this mission, flying with Lieutenant Berton A. Bordelon of our squadron. Each B-17 was loaded with twenty-seven hundred gallons of gas' and 12 x 500 lb bombs'. At 6 lbs per gallon, the weight of fuel for each plane was 16,200 lbs and bombs weighed 12,000 lbs, for a total of over 14 tons. The B-17G carried over 5,000 rounds of ammunition for its 13 machine guns. The weight of these .50 calibre machine guns, plus oil for the engines and oxygen for the crew, often brought the takeoff weight of these aircraft to over 65,000 lbs. Empty, they weighed about 35,000.

"Our route north over the English Channel was hampered by dense and persistent vapour trails of the preceding groups. Our cloud ceiling at take off was 2,000 ft, which altered our forming up a bit. However we departed the English coast with eighteen aircraft plus two radar ships from another group. Soon, the lead ship of the low squadron aborted due to a supercharger problem. Our route to Berlin took us up the English Channel past Hamburg and across the Jutland peninsula to a south-easterly heading. This took us about midway between Hamburg and Kiel. Our escorting fighters were P-38 Lightnings and a few P-51 Mustangs. Their fuel range would not allow them to escort us all the way to Berlin and they dropped off just past Hamburg. Fortunately, we saw no enemy fighters close enough to identify and so our main problem was flak.

"As we approached the target, the flak was unbelievable. It was as if someone had painted a thin black line across the sky and it was exactly at our altitude of 26,000 ft. As we approached Berlin, clouds covered over half the earth below us, which made the target difficult to see. Many of our aircraft dropped 'Chaff'. This helped only during cloudy weather, as the German anti-aircraft gunners' preferred visual sighting. Their 'final aimer' usually aimed for the left wing root of the lead plane. These 88 mm cannons were all on turntables and all six guns turned in unison. The gunners were so good that they could fire a burst of six, every three seconds or so. While the aim was done from a control site, all six guns pointed parallel to each other and did not converge on the target. This allowed a wider pattern of bursts, which could cover an entire group of airplanes.'[3]

"We had a great deal of flak over Berlin' wrote 2nd Lieutenant John E. Borg the flight engineer/top turret gunner on Captain John P. Watson's crew on *Mairzy Doats* that carried 42 67 lb M-47 incendiaries. "The sky was black with anti-aircraft fire" wrote Dick Johnson. "Of the 19 aircraft from our group, one[4] was shot down by flak, three received major damage, eleven suffered less severe damage and only four B-17s came back unscathed. Our aircraft had several flak holes in the leading edges and a few in the sides and was listed as 'major damage' due to the fact that during the bomb drop, we were forced out of position by a neighbouring B-17. This put us directly behind the lead plane, so that when he dropped his bombs, his 'Sky Marker' bomb enveloped our plane with a white acid fog and flying home was difficult due to the milky looking windshield. Due to 6/10th cloud cover over Berlin our bombing results were not very good. We felt let down, feeling that our effort was largely wasted after facing such battle conditions. Total flight time over 8 hours; three hours and a half over enemy territory. We reported 'Hot News' of a German naval convoy in the Hamburg Fjord on the way in, but couldn't see it on the way out, because of the ruined plexiglas."[5]

"Johnny Watson really brought us through today" says John Borg. "He picked the right patch to avoid the fire from the ground. They could see us today. It was maximum effort, which means every Fort that could fly, was in the air. On the way to the target, a B-17 on my left had an engine lifted right out by the flak.

The plane put her nose down and went in to a dive. One 'chute came out but the plane blew up at about 10,000 ft and we were at 25,000 ft at the time. Yes, it's surprising to see all the things and to see another ship and crew blown up in front of your eyes. Whoever said 'war was hell' knew what he said. We were in the air for about 9½ hours.'

A total of 321 effective sorties were flown by the Fortresses in the 1st Bomb Division that dropped 683 tons of bombs on Berlin. Forty-nine B-17s bombed the secondary target at Kiel. Only one of the 175 B-17s in the Third Division failed to get its bombs away over the Reich capital and had bombed a target of opportunity instead. The remaining Fortresses had released just over 392 tons of bombs on 'Big-B' for the loss of eight B-17s missing in action.[6] One of these was *Little Joe* in the 388th Bomb Group, which Lieutenant W. T. White ditched 30 miles north of Great Yarmouth on return with all ten crew being rescued by a minesweeper nearby. At the start of the mission *Patty Jo* flown by Lieutenant Donald G. Salles in the same group was involved in a mid-air collision during assembly with *Rosalie Ann II* in the 452nd Bomb Group flown by Lieutenant William C. Gaither, which crash landed at New Buckenham, Norfolk after the collision in which two of his crew died. *Patty Jo* was landed at RAF Watton, Norfolk and took no further part in the bombing war, though following repairs she was later used as a transport Hack by the 361st Fighter Group while based at Chièvres in Belgium.

At the target the crew of 1st Lieutenant Ralph Delmore Horne Jr., a New Yorker from Brooklyn, who were on their 20th mission, were one of three B-17 crews in the Bloody Hundredth that were shot down. 'We were hit by FW 190s from 12 o'clock high' recalled the co-pilot, 1st Lieutenant John M. McGrath of White Plains, New York. "The numbers 3 and 4 engines were hit and lost all power. We tried to feather the two props but to no avail. That's why we looked like we were in no serious trouble. As we dropped out of formation we were attacked from the rear. The tail section was severely damaged. How Joe Staron the tail gunner escaped with a scratch is a miracle. As I glanced out my side window the FW 190 was overtaking us and was no more than 20 yards off our right wing. He must have been wounded; no sane pilot would come that close and slow. He continued slowly to pass us and continued in a slow left turn in front of us where the bombardier and navigator finished him. We were losing altitude fast and our navigator said with our rate of decent we would never reach the Channel, but we might reach Sweden. We opted for Sweden but never made it.'[7] All crew members except the two pilots gathered in the radio room and the plane was ditched in the Smaalandsfarvandet, 8 kilometres SSE of Glænønear. Two dinghies were launched before the plane sank and after an hour of rowing all of them safely reached the coast of southern Zealand. The crew split up into two teams and they were picked up in Nyrup by the Germans the next day.

Sparky piloted by 26-year-old Lieutenant John Perry Keys barely made it back after a 20mm shell blew a large section of the tail fin away. Keys had left his home town of Elizabethton, Tennessee shortly after the United States entered World War II. *Sparky* was repaired and was later lost on the 29 July 1944 Merseburg mission, or 'Murdersburg' as crews called it. John Keys' crew had flown 25 missions over enemy territory when they took off in *Varga Venus* on 8 August 1944. They never returned. *Varga Venus* was hit by flak in the #2 engine 90 seconds before unloading over an occupied area near Perigny in the Calvados about thirty miles southwest of Caen. Only Sergeant Gilbert Arnold Borba the 21-year-old waist gunner of Salinas, California survived after bailing out of the aircraft and he was taken prisoner of war. 2nd Lieutenant Elton Dickens, the bombardier, of Spokane, Washington also bailed out but died later that day from a leg wound.[8]

'We had been hit with light to mild flak over the target so we thought we had a good flight" recalled Sergeant Clarence F. Cherry, left waist gunner on *Alice From Dallas II* aka *Rogers' Raiders* piloted by 2nd Lieutenant Julian P. 'Buck' Rogers. "On our way back over Denmark we were flying low squadron and 'tail-end Charlie' position when we were attacked by fighters. They made about six passes at our position before my gun was completely blown out and I was wounded in the head. They removed me to the radio room for aid and began to throw out equipment to lighten the ship. Already, two engines were gone. Finally, Rogers told our crew to prepare to ditch in the sea. We made a rough landing. They threw me out of the top window in the radio room and I came out on the wing and started to float away from our sinking Fortress. They pulled me into the life raft. It was shot with cannon holes. We were close to two islands off Denmark. We could hear the small engines on the boats in the harbour. Julian said to us, 'Row out to sea.' We were not going to be PoWs. I don't know how far we rowed. Later on a Fortress came low and made a fix on our position. Forty hours' later an RAF ASR plane came over us and dropped a smoke flare on the water for wind drift. They dropped a wooden boat which had three parachutes attached to it. It dropped very close to us in the sea. We climbed aboard and started towards England. We ran into two Danish fishing boats and they interned us on their boat. They were going to take us back to Denmark as PoWs, but the British flying above us told them to stay put or be sunk. An ASR launch was on its way for us. We were taken to Great Yarmouth Hospital. All of my crew was saved. I stayed in hospital for a few days and then went back to flying and completed my tour.'[9]

As the 'Bloody Hundredth' headed for home over the Baltic a formation of about 25 enemy fighters were spotted flying parallel to their course, flying out of range and gradually pulling ahead, getting into position for an attack. They were broken up by a pair of Mustangs, who, diving into the formation, scattered the fighters into the path of the Fortresses. In the ensuing 15 minutes the Luftwaffe lost ten FW 190s while three B-17s in the 100th Bomb Group were shot down. The last ship in the Group, piloted by 2nd Lieutenant Martin D. Rupert of Farrell, Pennsylvania, lost two engines in the first attack and then a fire started in the forward compartment while all the gunners continued to fire at their attackers. Rupert gave the order to bail out after the Fortress went down under control circling to the right. Just six chutes were seen but only 2nd Lieutenant Lynn H. Barbour the bombardier of LaFayette, Indiana survived. He was rescued by a Danish fishing boat and was taken prisoner.

The 1st Bomb Division had dropped 683 tons of bombs on Berlin for the loss of seven B-17s missing in action and 49 Forts had attacked the secondary target at Kiel without loss. The 2nd Bomb Division had dropped just over 700 tons of HE on Brunswick for the loss of a dozen B-24s, of which nine in the 492nd Bomb Group were shot down, which took the total losses for the day to 28.

'It was nice to have another Berlin mission under my belt" wrote 1st Lieutenant 'Ed' Miller in the 'Hell's Angels' Group, adding, "Hopefully it will be my last'. (Miller would complete his tour of 32 missions which included ten to Berlin, with 14 missions as a 1st pilot). 'It wasn't as bad as it might have been" said 1st Lieutenant Robert H. Halpin, pilot of *Special Delivery*. "We had loads of our own fighters and didn't see any Germans. The flak was rough over the city but they only hit one Fort.' (On 29 May Halpin completed his 29th and final mission of his tour, 19 of them as a lead crew tail gunner/observer). Staff Sergeant Edgar B. Hart, ball turret gunner on *Wallaroo MK II* who had been to Berlin five times, was not impressed by 'Big B's defences. 'I've been there before and it didn't seem any thicker. I've seen a lot worse in other places' he said.

Before reaching the target 'The Fireball Outfit' was attacked in force by Bf 109s and FW 190s and *Liberty Run* aka *Pocahontas* piloted by Lieutenant Philip H. Birong of Buchanan, Michigan had two engines set on fire. The B-17 left the formation and began a spiral toward the ground. The radio operator, Staff Sergeant Norman Musial spilled his parachute in the plane and, in spite of urgings from the other crewmen, would not jump with the folded parachute in his arms. He stayed with the plane and died when *Liberty Run* crashed near Koenighorst, 19 miles northwest of Berlin. The rest of the crew were taken prisoner.

Lieutenant 'Bob' Lane's crew on *Tujunga*, who had been hoping for a 'milk run' for their final mission went over the North Sea and passed into Germany south of Kiel. 'We had beautiful escort by P-51s' said Sergeant Bob Kincaid 'but as we reached the outskirts of Berlin we ran into a lot of flak. There was only scattered cloud and I had a good view of the city. We passed over the main part of town and dropped our 42 100 lb incendiaries.' *Tujunga!* had no trouble on the way back from either fighters or flak and over the North Sea Lane dropped down and was at deck level by the time they hit the coast of England. 'As we came back to the field we started shooting off flares' recorded Kincaid. 'We had about 60 of them and used them up in the three flare guns. The tower was shooting flares, our ground crew was shooting double green flares and the whole damn field was down at the flight line to see us come in. We were the first in our Group to finish 25. The pilot buzzed the field and the tower, chased everyone down ladders from the tower. We were doing over 200 mph in old *Tujunga!* as we came across the field at zero altitude with the props seeming to be cutting the grass. It was like a 4th of July celebration. At interrogation they gave us all the 'spiritus stimuli' (whiskey) we wanted. The Red Cross gave us all the candy, cigarettes and doughnuts we wanted too. Boy! What a reception! And so ended our combat tour. A total of 193 hours and 55 minutes combat time for an average of around seven hours and 45 minutes per mission.'[10]

Commenting on the mission at the interrogation at Podington, 2nd Lieutenant Jack Pearl, a B-17 pilot in the 92nd Bomb Group said, with rueful good nature: 'I've put in four missions since I joined the Group and every one of them's been Berlin. So tomorrow, sure as hell, it'll be a milk run to France and I won't be on it.' It was a milk run – the target was Orly airfield south of Paris – and a last minute change put the young pilot on it. It cost him his life.

Thirty-six planes were scheduled to take-off, in groups of 12 each, starting at 0655 hours. The high group was successfully airborne from Runway 23 through a cold and patchy fog and at 0711 hours, the lead group began taking off. Pearl's ship was the seventh in his group. Speeding down the runway its tail wheel unlocked during roll off and the B-17 veered off the runway. Pearl attempted to get corrected and pulled back onto the runway, but just as it began to get airborne, the bomber struck part of a concrete wall and then crashed just beyond the edge of the runway. An ambulance left the control tower and started around the perimeter track towards the scene. Due to the fog and the position of the aircraft deep in the woods, they had not located it at the time of the second crash. Directed there, the ambulance arrived at the time of the first explosion suffering slight damage from flying particles. The ambulance picked up the five survivors of the next B-17 in line, piloted by 2nd Lieutenant William W. Seitz that had begun its run, but stopped approximately halfway down the runway, apparently having seen the red warning flares fired by the take-off controller and heard the radio order from control tower to stop take-off. Seitz turned his plane around and started back up the runway. The following ship in line, piloted by 1st Lieutenant James E. Wiggins did not stop its run. Presumably Wiggins could not see the flares through the low hanging fog and when he did see Seitz's Fortress it was far too late. The aircraft collided head-on and burst into flames. Five crew members managed to escape from each plane – all being near the rear – before the first of five terrific explosions began about three minutes after the collision. Each B-17 carried a bomb load of 6 X 1,000 lb GP bombs. The final explosion was Pearl's ship. All the crew were killed. Romeo Bellevance the line chief and Harry Collis, his assistant, were asleep in a Quonset hut on the line when the crash occurred and when the .50 machine gun bullets started going off, Bellevance woke Collis just as a large fragment came through the wall and took his pillow with it. The runway so badly damaged as to require a platoon of the 831st Engineering Battalion (Aviation) for three nights, in addition to the work of 45 Air Ministry employees in the daytime, to restore the defective concrete sections, and to resurface with tarmac.[11]

On Wednesday, 24 May 616 B-17s in the 1st and 3rd Bomb Divisions were dispatched to bomb 'Big-B' again. After take-off from Thorpe Abbotts the 'Bloody Hundredth' had difficulty forming up with the Wing and when the B-17s started across the North Sea they were badly strung out and behind the rest. They entered enemy territory in this same condition and the low squadron was badly strung out and behind by several hundred feet. 2nd Lieutenant Francis 'Frank' J. Malooly, born Chicago, the pilot of *Powerhouse* recalled that the mission, his 27th, was 'a complete disaster from beginning to end. We were 'meat on the table' for the Luftwaffe and were soon attacked by a large group of enemy fighters. They decimated the low squadron. What was left of our Group finally caught up with the other B-17s and I have no idea if with our proper Wing. We proceeded to Berlin and dropped our bombs. While still in heavy flak over Berlin I noticed the lead plane lose altitude and starting a right turn which was the wrong way. I called on the radio but getting no response I told the Group that he was going down and to reform on me. This action by the leader (instead of properly aborting his lead position and letting me take the lead) again got us off by ourselves. We were attempting to get the Group back into position when we were jumped from behind by a group of FW 190s. They were firing 20mm shells into us with predictable results." Twenty-three year-old 2nd Lieutenant Lindley L. Williamson piloting *Big Stoop* on Malooly's left wing stayed 'till the bitter end' when both B-17s caught fire and all ten men on Malooly's crew and all except the radio operator on Williamson's crew bailed out.'

The 'B' Group lead with the command pilot Major Maurice J. Fitzgerald aboard was piloted by Captain James R. Geary, who had completed a tour with the 390th Bomb Group and had then been assigned to the Hundredth. As they approached the Hamburg area they were attacked by several FW 190s and were 'hit by a shower of lead,' which knocked part of the interphone system out and damaged the oxygen lines. A 'flak chunk' also 'lodged in the bombsight, chest high.' Staff Sergeant Jack W. Domenig the left waist gunner had caught a flak fragment in the forehead and Staff Sergeant John E. Trout, the right waist man, had administered a bandage. Then fighters at 1 o'clock level attacked and all the forward guns started working. Flak had knocked out the manual controls and Geary put the ship on AFCE. They were all by themselves and the sky was swarming with FW 190s.

1st Lieutenant Edwin Stern Jr., the bombardier heard a yell of 'Help! Radio room!' over the intercom. 'A couple of 20mm's had made a lace curtain of the radio room. Trout's face was covered with blood and Tech Sergeant Lou Paltrineri the radio man was holding his leg, yelling 'Take care of him first!' "After I wiped the blood away, I found that Trout had been hit on the bridge of his nose. I stuck a sulphur bandage on and he held it in place…There were small 20mm fragments peppered over Paltrineri's thigh, but he was all right. I was out of breath and feeling faint.

'Back in the waist the noise was unbearable. The engines were beating themselves to death and the chatter of the guns was deafening. The gun-smoke in the ship was heavy and the smell of burnt powder was nauseating. After many passes, No.3 engine had been set on fire. The situation was like some fantastic nightmare.

'Engineer Francis Acker and Paltrineri were fighting the fire, which had spread to the bomb bay. Their efforts were useless. I was busy with our chums outside. The ball turret was jarring the floor with its incessant firing. The noise grew louder, the smoke thicker. I was going to vomit. I never did.

'Trout and Paltrineri came out of the radio room with their chutes on. 'Pilot says Jump!' Paltrineri yelled. They kicked out the waist door and left, with Jack Domenig following. Carl Schuster was still in the ball firing. He poked his head out and said: 'OK if I come out now?'

'Hell yes,' I replied. 'Get your butt out that door.'

'He went. The plane was thick with smoke and the engines were beating on my eardrums. I hurtled through the door.

'The slipstream caught me and bounced me around for about five seconds. Then it was smooth, like hanging in space. There was no sense of falling. It was cold and quiet… deathly quiet. We had bailed out at over 20,000 ft. I saw three open 'chutes and that old query of 'will this thing open' raced through my mind. I pulled hard on the ripcord and thought I had run into a Mack truck. The shock of the 'chute opening tore my chest muscles and groin. I was laughing hysterically like a madman in a second-rate thriller and couldn't stop. I tore off my oxygen mask and took a deep breath of cold, fresh air. I felt better and looked down. 'I seemed to be coming down right on top of a Luftwaffe base…' All ten men including 1st Lieutenant Arthur J. Harris flying as Formation Officer in the tail landed safely and were taken prisoner.[12]

The de-briefing at Thorpe Abbotts was 'a gloomy affair indeed'. The 'Bloody Hundredth' had suffered badly, losing nine Fortresses from the day's total loss of 33. It became clear that the Hundredth, 'split by the weather and contrails,' had been 'opposed by 200 enemy aircraft…In return, the gunners claimed 11 fighters, four of which were knocked out by Staff Sergeant William P. McNally, the tail gunner on 1st Lieutenant James B. Noble's crew, 'as they came in, Indian file on Regal Eagle's tail.'[13]

Lou Paltrineri had landed in trees and was immediately captured by German troops. After three days of interrogation he was sent to a hospital for treatment to his wounds. After two weeks there he was sent to Stalag Luft IV. Treva Paltrineri gave birth to their first child ten days later, just after receiving the telegram saying that her husband was missing in action.

Over the target cloud and thick contrails caused the 381st Bomb Group to lose contact with other groups in the 1st Wing and paid the price. A fighter shot off the left wing and the #1 engine of Return Ticket piloted by 2nd Lieutenant Carl M. Dasso of Rock Island, Illinois and the B-17 crashed near Gratze, 19 miles northeast of Berlin with the loss of the pilot and four crew members. The navigator and three of the gunners were taken prisoner. *Spam Can* piloted by 26-year-old 2nd Lieutenant Walter K. Higgins was attacked by a FW 190 and pieces immediately flew off the bomber, followed by explosion north of Berlin, the aircraft crashing five miles south of Rostock with the loss of six crew. Four men were taken prisoner. Higgins left a wife, Mary. His hometown was Seattle, Washington. *Avengress* was attacked by Bf 109s that knocked out the #3 engine and set the wing on fire and crashed at Wilmersdorf, four miles east of Bernau with the loss of the 36-year old pilot, 1st Lieutenant Carl A. Gardon from Meriden, Connecticut and his bombardier, Bill Moseley of Camden, Arkansas. The seven remaining crewmembers were taken prisoner. The B-17G flown by 23-year old 1st Lieutenant Clarence W. Ezzell of Sepulyn, Oklahoma was hit in the #1 engine during a fighter attack and then the aircraft exploded, crashing between Melchow and Biesenthal, 18 miles North of Berlin. Harm Beninga the ball turret gunner of Marietta, Minnesota and Carl Schaaf the 21-year old tail gunner of Lincoln, Nebraska were killed. The seven other crew members survived and were taken prisoner.

Carolina Queen was involved in a mid air collision with the B-17 piloted by 1st Lieutenant Clarence Dale Wainwright Jr. of East Pembroke, Massachusetts and crashed at Gratze, 17 miles northeast of Berlin with only two survivors. Badly wounded, Clarry Wainwright bailed out but died later of his wounds. All the crew on *Carolina Queen* led by 25-year-old 1st Lieutenant John A. Wardencki of Linden, New Jersey were killed. On return to Ridgewell on 8 April 2nd Lieutenant Leslie Bond had belly landed the *Queen* after a bag containing the tools needed to cut the ball turret loose before they could make a wheels-up landing was lowered into the radio room from a liaison aircraft piloted by Major Conway S. Hall, operations officer flying above them.

The raid on 24 May registered a total of 464 effective sorties flown and just over 1,081 tons of bombs dropped on Berlin. This was the last raid of the month to 'Big B', whereupon missions to marshalling yards and airfields in France and the Low Countries once again became the order of the day. Towards the end of the month these were extended to these types of targets in Germany. Then, on the 28th a record force of 1,341 bombers was directed against mostly oil plants in the Reich with marshalling yards as targets of opportunity in the event of bad weather over the seven primary targets. The raids were heavily contested by 300 Luftwaffe fighters and the 1st and 3rd Bomb Divisions lost 26 B-17s and three B-24s in the 2nd Bomb Division failed to return from the attack on Merseburg-Leuna. Three B-24s in the 3rd Bomb Division were lost attacking Lützkendorf. *Mike the Spirit of LSU*, one of two losses in the 486th Bomb Group, was named after LSU's mascot 'Mike the Tiger', as its regular pilot, 26-year old Lieutenant Alfred M. L. Sanders from Baton Rouge, was a former track star at the Louisiana State University. 'Smokey Al', as he was more familiarly known, and his left waist gunner, Sergeant Autley B. Smith, a fellow Louisiana State University

Alumni, were among five men on the crew who were taken in by the Belgian Underground and hidden until liberation in September 1944 by the American Army. The five other members on the crew were taken prisoner.[14]

In the first week of June, D-Day came and went with the Allied Air Forces providing massive aerial support to the land and sea operations. Among those flying his first mission that momentous day was 1st Lieutenant Oscar Thorvald Hanson, a 24-year-old pilot in the 34th Bomb Group at Mendlesham in Suffolk. Born, Benidji, Minnesota, he had begun his military flying career as a flight instructor with the RCAF in 1941 and at the base canteen had met Clara, his future wife who had grown up in High River, Canada. A year later he transferred to Perrin Field, Texas as a flight instructor and at the end of 1943 he was assigned to the 34th Bomb Group which was converting to the B-24 Liberator. In April 1944 the Group left for England and Oscar said his goodbyes to his parents, seven siblings and his pregnant wife and their two young boys, Eric and Jerry.

D-Day was only a few hours old when on 7 June Oscar was piloting one of 26 B-24s on the mission to Tours, France. Returning over eastern England at dusk, Ju 88 and Me 410 intruders of III./NKG 51 *Edelweiss* at Chartres, France that had followed the 34th Bomb Group back, shot down four B-24s in the landing circuit in a matter of minutes. Fifteen crewmembers were killed and at least eight others wounded. *Wilson* crashed into an equipment store about 150 yards from the Cholchester family's farmhouse killing eight of the nine-man crew. In the flare from the explosion, Mr. Cholchester and his son Roy saw a parachute and went out to try to find the parachutist. 'We met him in the orchard' recalled Roy Cholchester 'and were greeted with 'I'm hit; I'm hit' and so he was. Edwin J. Irwin the 38-year old tail gunner from Rapid City, South Dakota had cannon shell wounds diagonally across his back and more in his thigh. My father, with First World War experience, dressed his wounds from the first aid kit I fetched from his parachute, which was draped over our stockyard hedge. There was bedlam on the airfield and about three hours passed before he could be collected by the ambulance and taken to the base hospital, where he spent a month before he was discharged home. I picked up the parachute D-ring only about 100 yards from where Edwin landed, so he was very lucky the parachute opened in time, as the B-24 was only about 1,500 ft when hit passed over our farm in flames.' Irwin was the only survivor on 21-year-old 2nd Lieutenant Hazen Dale Eastman's 9-man crew.

Sweet Sioux aka *Picadilly "Tilly"* crashed off base near Wethering Stell killing three crew members and destroying three thatched cottages. The pilot, 27-year-old 1st Lieutenant Wilmer J. Dreher of New Baden, Illinois and seven other survivors managed to parachute out. A farmer in a barn at the crash site who was with a calving cow, lost a buttock when the B-24 exploded.[15] *Scotty* aka *Glamour Girl* crashed at Nedging in Suffolk. First Lieutenant Stanley McMillan Brain the 25-year-old pilot from Minneapolis, Minnesota and six crew members bailed out. As the pilot exited the aircraft he noted that Staff Sergeant Stuart Stygall the 25-year old radio operator was dead and found that Sergeant Chester Frank Nowakowski the 22-year-old tail gunner of Detroit, Michigan had bailed out, but his 'chute must have failed to open as he was found dead on the ground. The body of Staff Sergeant Ernest Ashman Tipton the 21-year-old ball turret gunner from Burrton, Kansas, who was at first listed missing in action, was found at harvest time on 2 August in a field of wheat.[16]

Hells Belle, piloted by Lieutenant Bob Simpson barely averted falling victim to the German fighters and successfully diverted to Little Walden airfield nearby.[17] Staff Sergeant Don Fillman, engineer on *The Belle of the Brawl* was getting into position to call out the indicated airspeed and saw two B-24s in the approach ahead. "Someone said 'Look at that!" He was looking out the co-pilot's window and at a quick glance I saw the ground, a lot of very black smoke. Soon I saw two tracer shells that came very close to us. They were very bright and they hit the bomber on our left in the #3 engine and fuselage. Later I found out that it was Oscar Hanson's plane, *Cookie's Wailing Wall* which peeled off to the left." Staff Sergeant Sidney C. Brown the 23-year-old waist gunner from Darian, Connecticut had just remarked about the beautiful moon, seconds before they were hit. The waist gunners had the insides of their weapons already laid out on the deck, when the B-24 was hit several times. "When we were hit" recalled Staff Sergeant Paul A. Shull the 24-year-old engineer from Kansas City, Missouri, "we had peeled off next in line to land and were probably only about 200 ft in altitude. Hanson pulled the plane up and gave it maximum power to gain altitude. Even 500 ft was dangerous, because parachutes might not have time to open." The No.3 engine caught fire and a fire also started in the bomb bay. One of the pilots opened the bomb bay doors and the fire started to go out. After they feathered No.3 engine, they climbed to an altitude of 1,500 ft, so the crew could bail out. Sidney Brown recalled, "Our tail gunner, Joe Burton, couldn't find his parachute, which was under some equipment. Finding it in the darkness, I helped Joe get it on. He said that he thought it was on backwards, but I told him to get out before they blew up!" They both went out through the aerial camera hatch into the darkness. Brown's parachute opened seconds before he hit the ground hard. His knees came up and hit him in the face. A civilian armed with a shotgun found him. Finding a loaded shotgun pointed at his face, Brown quickly indentified him as an American, and the civilian helped him back to base.

All of the crew bailed out, except for Hanson and Shull, who recalled: "Hanson skilfully manoeuvred the plane, as every ground light was out, as they thought it was a paratrooper attack in all the confusion. After he ordered the crew to bail out, I grabbed a fire extinguisher and put the rest of the fire in the bomb bay out. Then I checked everything and reported that the electrical and hydraulic systems were out. He thought he could still get the plane down. I went down below and kicked the nose gear out and locked it down and then hand cranked the main landing gears down, only to find that the right gear had been shot ¾ inches through by a 20mm shell. Hanson could see a darkened airfield in the moonlight, so with no hydraulic or electrical systems, and no flaps, we came down. He set the plane down at 120 mph, holding the right wing up as long as possible and then, as the plane settled, we spun around out onto a grassy area. The impact was a severe jolt and I was tossed around like a rag doll, hitting bulkheads. I ended up with bruises all over."

Sliding to a stop, Shull cut the fuel valves and ignition switches and went out through the top hatch. He then noticed Hanson was still in the cockpit. He went back and found that his seat belt and parachute harness were tangled up. After helping his pilot out of the cockpit, they both slid down the wing onto the ground and ran clear before the bomber blew up. Some Red Cross workers came out and gave them some cups of hot chocolate to calm them down. Shull recalled, "We both broke into a cold sweat and our nerves seemed to collapse, as we were badly shaken up. Neither of us could hold the cups steady as we both shook uncontrollably. We slopped at least half the cups, trying to drink. It was well after midnight when they transported us to our base, five miles away. We spent most of the remainder of the night finding the rest of our crew. Some of them were pretty badly injured. We saw our ball turret gunner with broken ribs that had punctured his lung. Another one of the crew had a broken foot. The rest had sprains and bruises. After that crash, two of our crewmembers were replaced because of their injuries. We had crashed our B-24 at Eye airfield, where the 490th Bomb Group was based."

When the crew went to look at their ship the next day they counted 14 holes from 20mm cannon. It was peppered with shrapnel and it was miraculous that no one was hit. The nose gunner broke his leg when he landed. 1st Lieutenant Roy C. Keirn the 26-year-old co-pilot of McKeesport, Pennsylvania jumped without his leg straps fastened and came very near to falling out of his chute. Sergeant Joe N. Burton, the 23-year-old tail gunner's chute failed to open so he fed it out with his hands. Sergeant George H. Simpson the 27-year-old radio operator of Wabash, Indiana pulled four times on the wrong handle before finding the ripcord and Lieutenant Lindsay Lipscomb the 22-year-old bombardier of Conroe, Texas landed right on his home field and was immediately surrounded by GIs who thought he was a German paratrooper. '*Don't click them bolts at me, Ah'm from Texas!*' he said!

It was not until mid-summer's day, Wednesday 21 June when secret plans called for an aerial assault on Berlin by three air forces, which promised to be the greatest in history. One thousand bombers from Italy were scheduled to fly north to 'Big-B', while 900 RAF Lancaster bombers were to follow the 8th Air Force to the centre of Berlin for their first daylight raid into Germany.

Crews with tired minds and aching bodies slumbering fitfully in Nissen and Quonset huts scattered throughout East Anglia like dormitory towns had no inkling of what was in the wind and would remain in that state until all was revealed to them at briefing. Around midnight, like harbingers of doom, the Charge of Quarters unceremoniously turned on the lights to shock the men awake. A living nightmare in the crucible of war was about to begin once more.

Notes

1. One of the losses occurred when the pilot of one B-24 collided with another while under fighter attack and went down with the combined loss of 15 men KIA and six being taken prisoner after they bailed out. Only two men survived on *Gypsy Queen* and six men were KIA on *Pug*. Two of the gunners were killed on *Lucky Penny* and the eight others survived to be taken prisoner. The ball turret gunner and one of the waist gunners on *Choo Choo Baby* that crashed at Ovelgoone were KIA. On the two other B-24s that FTR, 14 men were KIA and six taken prisoner.

2. Dick Noble evaded capture but was killed in August in attempt to get to the Allied lines. Co-pilot, Daniel G. Viafore and radio operator: Robert Atkins evaded capture. Navigator, Richard D. Laule; bombardier: Bruce W. Clago, flight engineer/top turret gunner; Lloyd A. Martin; Ralph Munn: waist gunners' George V. Brush and Vernon L. Moody and tail gunner, Leon H. Davies were taken prisoner.

3. Correspondence with the author.

4. Shortly after "Bombs Away" *Sky Duster*, in the No.3 position in the high squadron being flown by 20-year-old 1st Lieutenant Ernest L. Roth of Los Angeles was hit on the nose by flak and it blew off the #3 engine and the B-17 exploded. Only four parachutes were seen to emerge from the stricken aircraft, which crashed at Pichelsberg, near Berlin. Roth and four of his crew were killed. Five crewmen were captured but 2nd Lieutenant George John Beys the 28-year-old navigator of Chehalis, Washington had suffered a fractured skull, a broken leg and internal injuries. He died in a Berlin hospital about two hours after capture. He left a widow, Lillian.

5. Ibid.

6. From the 95th Bomb Group at Horham came a ninth loss, *Smilin' Sandy Sanchez* (named after a tail gunner) that was force landed at Akesholm in Sweden. Captain William S. Waltman and his nine crew members were interned.

7. Correspondence with the author.

8. Thanks are due to John Keys' niece, Judy L. Jones.

9. Correspondence with the author.

10. *Tujunga!* went MIA with another crew on the Munich mission on 31 July 1944.

11. See *The Route as Briefed* by John S Sloan (Argus Press, Cleveland, Ohio 1946).

12. On 20 February 1944 1st Lieutenant Arthur J. Harris' crew were forced to land *Half & Half* (42-39792) in Sweden where they were interned for a short time.

13. On 28 July Noble's crew on 'Island F for Fox', a PFF ship on loan from the 95th Bomb Group was shot down over Dillenberg on the raid on Merseburg. Sergeant McNally and Staff Sergeant Arthur L. Roberts the right waist gunner were killed. The rest of Noble's crew and Captain Floyd H. Mason, the 349th Bomb Squadron Operations Officer and Command pilot on the mission were taken prisoner.

14. See 1st Lieutenant Alfred M. L. Sanders' story on the Air Forces Escape and Evasion Society website.

15. I am most grateful to Jim Hanson for sending me the late Roy Colchester's account (see: *'A Landscape And General History Of The Parish Of Mendlesham From The Stone Age To The Present'*). Jim also adds: "Jack Blackham (former 34th Bomb Group flight engineer) who flew that mission" recalls Jim "stayed in the Air Force and was a Luke AFB when they were training German pilots on the F-104. He recalled that one of them heard that Jack had been in the 34th Bomb Group and after a brief conversation, he mentioned that he had been one of the night fighter pilots who took part in that mission. He said that afterwards they called the 34th the "Red Devils from Mendlesham" because of the large red sections on the tails of their B-24s. The German night-fighter pilots who would claim

shoot-downs that night were Feldwebel Beier and Oberfeldwebel Trenke of NKG/51. Nine B-24s and 61 crewmen were lost for two Me 410s and four crewmembers.

16. On 16 January 1945 1st Lieutenant Brain died in the crash of B-24J 42-50691 in the 2123 Base Unit 19 miles SE of Harlingen, Texas, unable to bail out after mechanical problems forced abandonment of the aircraft.

17. *Hells Belle* was involved in a mid-air collision with B-24 42-51190 *Ann* on 19 July 1944. All 10 crew captained by 2nd Lieutenant Donald H. DeMatio on *Hells Belle* were killed and 9 men on 2nd Lieutenant John W. Little's crew died with only the co-pilot surviving.

Chapter Seven

Return From Rattlesden

Seven pairs of tired eyes look up at the Charge of Quarters. He began to read, 'Lieutenant Voorhees and Lieutenant Altman's crews; briefing will be in 45 minutes. They had but four hours' sleep and they put on their clothes while more asleep than awake.

'How much gas' today, CQ?'

'Well sir, the Tokyo's are topped off.'

A long sigh arose from the whole barracks and then one voice made of seven said, 'Big B' I'm sure as hell!

'On our way to breakfast the half-haze, half-fog morning mist practically concealed the men just ahead of us. The mess hall looked cheerful and warm after the cold of the early English morning. Faces equally as tired as my own looked up from the tables. Only here fresh eggs were served; nowhere else in England could one obtain them. This was a special treat for us before our mission.

'We gulped down our breakfast and coffee and then we rushed to the trucks waiting outside to take us to the briefing room. Little red glowing coals all around told us that we were not alone. The cigarettes were the only lights in the trucks. The bumps on the way to the briefing room woke even the sleepiest of us.'

Raid On Berlin by 2nd Lieutenant Leebert W. 'Mac' McFarland, co-pilot on 2nd Lieutenant Herbert S. 'Skipper' Altman's crew on *Bouncin' Baby* in the 447th Bomb Group at Rattlesden, 21 June 1944.[1]

Early on Wednesday 21 June crews in the 447th Bomb Group shuffled anxiously on benches lined up in rows inside a huge Nissen hut that was the briefing room. There was an aisle between the two rows for the projection machine. A screen was hanging before the map. Concealed behind the screen was their target for the day. They were all seated when Colonel Hunter Harris Jr., the Group Commanding Officer came in. Someone yelled, 'Attention!' And everyone stood until he reached the front of the room. 'Please be seated. Let's get this target today; and we won't have to go back.' He took his chair and the briefing got under way. Altogether too slowly the screen was raised and the map was exposed. Coloured pieces of yarn charted our curves in and out of Germany. The red yarn showed the route in; it went up over Holland and then to Berlin – the 'Big B'. The blue yarn indicated the route home through northern France. Pieces of transparent plastic outlined in red covering sections of the map represented flak gun positions. The large areas were for many flak guns, the smaller ones for fewer guns. There was a noticeably large piece over Berlin. It indicated a concentration of anti-aircraft guns in and around that city.

At Thorpe Abbotts the sense of the dramatic made Major 'Red' Bowman's early morning briefing sessions into real productions. On 21 June the 100th Bomb Group Intelligence Officer in charge of briefing flight crews before missions surpassed himself. 'Red' slowly turned the curtain so it opened in England and tentatively revealed the route and destination. Crews whistled as they followed the red yarn zigzagging into Germany and then curving towards Russia. Bowman continued to draw the curtain aside so slowly and theatrically that the whistlers ran out of breath before he got to the remote target. A formation, code-named 'Frantic' consisting of 163 Fortresses of the Thirteenth and 45th Combat Wings would fly the route to bomb the Ruhland-Schwarzheide Benzol plant 50 miles south of Berlin and then fly on to Russia, escorted by 72 P-38 Lightnings, 38 P-47 Thunderbolts and 57 Mustangs. After the attack, the supporting P-51s would be relieved 50 miles southeast of Poznan, Poland by 65 other P-51s which would accompany the B-17s to the USSR. To further confuse the defences, Berlin would be attacked from two different directions. The first force would fly over the North Sea and enter Mecklenburg west of Stettin, follow the River Oder and turn left to attack 'Big B' from the east. At the same time the second force would arrive in the Hanover area and fly north-west on to Berlin. 'Red' Bowman considered that he was 'fortunate enough' to get an assignment to go along as S-2 Officer. Interested in seeing what the air war was like, by now he had flown four missions and the Russian shuttle would earn him the Air Medal.

As well as their oil target an additional thirteen B-17s in the 100th were included in the second force mission to bomb the aero-engine plant at Basdorf to the north of Berlin. A total of 1,071 B-17s and B-24s consisting of 496 B-17s of the 1st Bomb Division escorted by 267 P-38s, P-47s and P-51s and 207 B-17s of the 3rd Bomb Division with an escort of 280 P-38s, P-47s and P-51s would make attacks on Basdorf and Berlin. In the 2nd Bomb Division 368 Liberators escorted by 411 P-38s, P-47s and P-51s would attack targets in the Berlin area with Genshagen, Marienfelde and Niederschönweide and Berlin the primaries. The 4th Combat Wing and a Composite from the 3rd Division would lead the 8th with the 1st Bomb Division next in line, then the 2nd Bomb Division with the rest of the 3rd bringing up the rear. After bombing, the bombers were to return to England.

'The rumour was that the British were going on this trip in daylight in retaliation for the buzz bombs that were hitting London every day and they would be at 14,000 ft' recalled 2nd Lieutenant Dick Johnson in the 303rd Bomb Group at Molesworth. 'We were all elated, knowing that the Germans would be after them instead of us. We figured that our part of the mission would surely be a 'milk run'. These rumours didn't last very long and the mission went along just like any other large mission.'[2]

Though these two operations were scrubbed and only the 8th would attack, thus reducing the effort by more than half before takeoff, the operation remained the largest to date. In all, 1,234 bombers and 1,170 fighters (including five groups in the 9th Air Force) were being launched.

At Old Buckenham 27-year-old 1st Lieutenant Melvin Harry Williams of Cope, Colorado and his crew were not scheduled to fly but they wanted to make thirty missions before the quota for going home was raised again, so they went. It was their 28th mission. Williams' crew were assigned a war-weary B-24H named *Archibald* which had been patched up using so many scavenged parts that it flew poorly and its engines were so lacking in power that it had trouble holding formation right from the time it left England. Staff Sergeant 'Dush' Vukelich, the right waist gunner, was a 20-year-old Serbian kid, the son of hard-working immigrants, Theodore and Milica Amelia "Mildred" Vanjnovich from the south side of Pittsburgh, who ran his own dice game at thirteen, ran numbers for the local gangsters and played water polo and basketball. The south side was a neighbourhood where just about everyone, including most of the males in the Vukelich family, worked in the steel mill. In 1942 'Dush' had a high school diploma, a good head for maths and a chance at college. He enlisted as soon as he turned 18, figuring that the AAC offered a more glamorous life than that of a foot-soldier.[3]

At Attlebridge (Weston Longville) in Norfolk, 24-year-old Lieutenant Robert Dean Johnson's crew in the 466th Bomb Group waited to fly their thirteenth mission. Johnson, of Toledo, Ohio and his crew had made the journey to England after picking up a brand new B-24H Liberator named *Madame Shoo Shoo* in Topeka, Kansas, which was almost immediately assigned to another group on their arrival in theatre. Their replacement B-24H would later take the name, *Penthouse for Ten*. 'Briefing started at 0130" recalled 23-year-old Tech Sergeant Stephen Fecho the engineer-gunner. Born in Mahanoy, Pennsylvania, Fecho had lived in Brooklyn, New York before enlistment in October 1942. "The lieutenant pulled back the curtain and showed us the target. There were a lot of 'oohs,' 'ahs' and 'wows' for our target was aircraft installations just outside of Berlin. Our secondary target was a large railroad station inside of Berlin, in case we couldn't bomb the primary target visually. We all hoped we could get the primary target, as there was too much flak in Berlin. The lieutenant briefed us on the route, flak batteries and target. We were told where to go in case we had to bail out. South of Berlin, try to get to Czechoslovakia. North of Berlin, head for the northern parts and get a Swedish boat to Sweden.'

At Rattlesden the trucks had waited for the crews outside the briefing room. Drivers were yelling 'Low numbers here!' or, 'High here'. *Bouncin' Baby* was a high number, so 2nd Lieutenant Herbert S. Altman, a New Yorker, and his crew piled their equipment on the 'High here' truck. "On the way out to our planes" said 2nd Lieutenant Leebert W. 'Mac' McFarland, the co-pilot, who was from Florida, "I heard a quiet voice say, 'What a hellova way to make a living!' We could feel, rather than see, the smiles all around us."[4] Lieutenant Lowell F. Simmons in the 708th Bomb Squadron had captained a crew at MacDill Field, Florida during training in the spring of 1943 and this was the combat orientation mission. He would take the co-pilot's seat beside 2nd Lieutenant Gerald L. Carter, a Texan from Phillips, named for the dominant employer, the Phillips Petroleum Company, by a vote of the people.

"At Molesworth after briefing was over the Catholic chaplain had told the Catholic boys to stay awhile and when the others had left, we all knelt and said a prayer" wrote Dick Johnson. "We then went to our lockers; got our A-3 bag and 'chute, were given a bar of candy and some gum and got a truck to take us to our plane. We were not flying *Buzz Blonde*, our usual ship, due to extensive damage incurred on the Hamburg raid when our plane had returned with 260-odd flak holes. We got to *Miss Lace* at 0230. The weather was pretty bad. There was light drizzle; the clouds were heavy and only 200 ft above the ground. We were hoping they would scrub this mission. I checked my guns. Everything in the airplane was in good condition. We had 8 x 500 lb M17 incendiary clusters and two 500 lb incendiaries aboard. When going to Berlin each B-17 carried 2,700 gallons of gasoline and five tons of bombs. Gasoline weighs 6 lbs per gallon, giving a takeoff weight of 65,000 lbs. An empty B-17 weighs about 36,000 lbs.

"The 303rd was sending up 42 airplanes for the mission; eighteen being in our low group. We were to fly right wing of the slot position in the high right section, almost the last to take off, so we didn't start our engines until take-off time, 0445. The Group sent the B-17s off at 25-second intervals. We took off at 0505 and headed into the overcast and broke through at about 1,300 ft. The sky above was clear. The clouds were visible above us except out in the distance. The morning sun was just breaking through. Below us as far as the eye could see, lay thick dark clouds. When we were about 15 minutes out, we loaded our guns and test fired. They were all working OK. We headed for our forming area on the coast, east of Norwich to form at 11,000 ft and were glad as we wouldn't have to put on our oxygen masks. We assembled in position on the lead group and departed in combat wing formation. After filling out my forms and seeing that everything on the ship was okay, I went into the top turret. I hooked up my mike and headset, also my heated suit as it was starting to get a little cold. The free air temperature gauge showed -10C. I got my flak suit and put on one piece on each side of me and sat on the other. After forming for two hours, we started to head out for our target at 0645. The sun was pretty high now. We headed due east over the North Sea."[5]

'All the way over the North Sea until we hit Germany the clouds were thick and heavy, but snowy white' wrote Tech Sergeant Stephen Fecho, engineer on *Madam Shoo-Shoo*. "Nowhere was there an opening so we could see the water. The trip from England to Germany was made in a slow climb, so when we hit the German coast we were at 20,000 ft I had put on my oxygen mask at 14,000 ft. We entered Germany at Cuxhaven and headed southeast. No sooner have we hit the coast, than we were greeted by flak. It was heavy and off to the right a little, so we went around it. All along the way they threw flak at us, but most of it was too far to the right or left, although a few came pretty close. Our route was plotted so as to not go over any flak batteries whenever possible and the lead navigator did a good job in following the route. From the coast to about Magdeburg, the weather was clear, except for a few scattered clouds. The towns of Hamburg, Bremen and Brunswick had smoke screens over them. We turned east of Magdeburg. There were clouds in that direction but they were broken in many places.

'When we were southeast of Berlin, we turned north and about 12 miles south of Berlin, we turned west. The clouds covered our primary target, so we headed north into Berlin. Flak was coming up on all sides of us while we were on our bomb run. We opened the bomb bay doors at 0955; below us I could see the city. The bombardier yelled 'Bombs Away' at 1008. We then made a sharp turn to the left, as there was quite a bit of flak ahead of us. They started to track us and then we were among it. It was bursting below, at our level and above us just right off our wing tips. I'd watch them burst and then duck my head between my guns. I wasn't as scared as I used to be of flak. There were bombers as far as I could see. There were supposed to be 1,500 targets in and around Berlin.

'Someone called over the interphone and said 'three Messerschmitt 109s at 8 o'clock low'. I swung my turret in that direction. They were pulling away, but they came in for another attack. They came within 600 yards of us; I shot a few bursts at them but they were too low for my turret. The waist and tail gunners also got a few bursts at them. I didn't hit them, but it made them pull away. They tried a third attack; then out of nowhere came five P-51s. The last I saw of the Me 109s was when they dove into a cloud bank with the P-51s hot on their tail. I had been so engrossed in watching the enemy fighters that I had completely forgotten about the flak, which was still bursting pretty heavily and accurately around us.

'We finally got out of their range. In the distance, in all directions, they were shooting it up at other formations. On our way to Berlin we were escorted by P-47s. Over the target we had P-51s and now on our way back we were being escorted by P-38s. We headed northeast from our own target. The flak came up all the way to the German coast but we stayed pretty well clear of it. We didn't see any more fighters; we saw quite a few bombers heading for Sweden. They were probably pretty damaged from all the flak. We seemed to have got ten through it without any damage.'[6]

'Our sortie would take 8 hours and 18 minutes from takeoff to landing' recalled Dick Johnson. "We passed by Hamburg, still burning big and black from our raid the day before. At 0924 hours the sirens began to sound in Berlin. 'The weather over the target was fairly open and the city could be seen. We assumed that visual bombing would be the order, so our group began to take interval. We were to drop our bombs 'in train'. Soon after the IP and opening bomb bay doors, the order came for PFF bombing, so our group pulled back into wing formation. Bombs were away at 1016 from 25,900 ft.

'In the target area the flak appeared to be from at least two flak batteries. It was moderate, but very accurate, being continuously pointed. One three gun battery was firing directly at our squadron. About a quarter mile to our left I noticed a triple burst and every three seconds there was another, only closer. Beiser was flying the plane during this bomb run and I could see burst after burst getting closer and closer, tracking our speed to perfection. Finally, a burst of three came just off the left wing tip and I could hear bits of metal strike our plane. I gritted my teeth, knowing that the next burst would be dead centre on our aircraft. I had noticed that the bursts were showing elongated patterns, meaning that we were almost beyond their range and that final burst never came, as the German gunners moved their sights to another group following us. This was the most fear that I had encountered in combat, because I had time to think about it.

'Most of the time we were so busy that we didn't have time for fear. Usually, after we got into formation and headed for the enemy coast, the anticipation and fear would build until the first burst of flak was seen. I then settled down into a grim attention to duty and thought very little of it unless it got really rough.

'We had observed flak at five other places before Berlin which was all black in colour. Over Berlin the flak was mostly black from their regular 88 mm flak guns, but we also encountered white bursts from larger guns. Most large cities in Germany were defended by some fixed guns of larger calibre. Some were 105 mm and some were 128 mm, which we sometimes referred to as 155 mm for some reason. The German gunners sometimes signalled their fighter planes by using different coloured bursts. Occasionally the German fighters would fly into their own flak bursts in the frenzy of battle, trying to press home an attack on a bomber.

'We had thrown out a lot of 'Chaff' to disrupt the German radar which they used when firing through clouds. Today the 'Chaff' seemed to do a little good, as most bursts of flak were low, as evidenced by the loss of most of our low squadron. Three of our planes were shot down over the target. One was the leader of our 427th Squadron and his number 4 and 5 planes. First Lieutenant Charles R. Allen's plane received a direct flak hit just after 'bombs away' and fell out of formation to the left. Three men were coming out of the main fuselage door. It then went into a steep dive with the radio operator-gunner [Staff Sergeant John H. Reed] still inside [and crashed at Schielowsee, Germany]. All the others were made prisoners of war. The plane flown by 1st Lieutenant Henry G. Way went down about the same time Allen's plane was hit. [When last seen, Way's plane appeared to be under control with no feathered engines. Two parachutes were spotted opening]. Way and his co-pilot [2nd Lieutenant Warren G. Raese] were killed as were three others of his crew. Four survived to be taken prisoner."[7]

Mairzy Doats in the 358th Bomb Squadron captained by 2nd Lieutenant Thomas H. Morningstar was not flying with its Squadron on the bomb run and since he was the lowest and farthest to the rear he was not observed leaving the formation before 'bombs away'. Morningstar dropped his bombs early due to a bomb rack malfunction before crashing near Techin. The crew survived, being listed as prisoners of war. Allen's wingman, 1st Lieutenant Chester N. Oranges, was carrying bombs with long delay fuses. He survived the mission, returning home with the rest of the group and completing his combat tour the following day.

Flak was continuous, intense, and extremely accurate in the target area and 33 B-17s in the 'Hell's Angels' Group sustained flak damage. *Heller's Angel* in the 359th Squadron, flying as the 41st Combat Wing 'B' lead Group lead had its flares ignited that caused a fire in the waist.[8] The bomb run was continued with the high and low Groups bombing on the lead Group. Lieutenant Colonel Lewis E. Lyle was awarded the Silver Star for his mission leadership. Friendly fighters did not accompany the Fortresses until ten minutes after the target. Two aircraft had engine problems. *Ain't Misbehavin* flown by 1st Lieutenant Russell W. Meier bombed the rail yards at Westerhever and completed his 25-mission tour and *Jigger Rooche* captained by Lieutenant Wilford T. Means bombed an airfield at Parchim. He would complete his 30-mission tour and sign up for a second tour as a lead crew bombardier only to be removed from crew when it was changed from ten to nine men.

'In our 41st Wing formation of two groups and one high squadron" continues Dick Johnson "our high squadron had only three planes with minor damage and none with major damage. Our lead group, which was at the middle altitude, had nine aircraft with major damage and eight with minor damage. The low group, in which I was flying, had two aircraft with major damage and eleven with minor damage. We were lucky. We had been over enemy territory for two hours and thirty minutes but our plane was listed as 'minor damage', since we only had a few holes to be repaired. Remarkable!"[9]

The bombing, which lasted only thirty minutes, covered the whole city, from aircraft factories in the north to railway centres in the south. The government buildings around Wilhelmstrasse were also hit. Some 2,000 tons of bombs were dropped on the targets. When the sirens sounded again at 1113 hours the whole city was covered with smoke, which the sun could not penetrate. Over 6,000 people were killed and almost 20,000 were injured. Despite the intense fighter cover, the Luftwaffe managed to make a few attacks on the Berlin force. Near the capital Me 410s swooped on the rear of the 1st Division formation and made several attacks on the B-17s.

"Mac" McFarland finally heard 'Bombs Away'"- the sweetest words in the English language" over *Bouncin' Baby's* interphone. "The bomb bay doors were quickly closed and prayers were quietly said to help us to leave the flak area safely. Bursts covered the sky in all directions. Our right wing was raised and lowered by a too-near explosion."There was a terrible explosion and the *Baby* raised her nose above the horizon. McFarland could smell the smoke from the flak shell, even through his mask. Looking down in the nose he saw Lieutenant Jay W. Ames the bombardier in the arms of the navigator, 2nd Lieutenant 'Ted' Hocking and he wasn't moving! On 31 July 1943 during his pre-flight schooling at Santa Ana, California, Ames had married his fiancée, Julia Kathryn Helmheckel. Hocking tenderly laid Ames on the floor and got his oxygen connected again. Hocking doctored a dirty cut in Ames leg. A piece of flak half an inch by three-quarters of an inch by three and a quarter inches had torn through his upper left thigh and knocked him unconscious. McFarland felt tears running down his cheeks. He didn't try to hold them back. Ted Hocking pressed the morphine tube against Ames' leg and injected it. All at once he moved. He was alive! McFarland gave thanks to God. Now his tears were for joy! The leg was bandaged and he asked for his mike to be connected. There was a wonderful voice that said, 'Well, I have a medal you guys haven't, I've got the Purple Heart.' "Good old Ames" said MacFarlane "he relieved the tension."

Coming home, flak was reported over many German cities – "just to let us know' wrote "Mac" McFarland. 'We didn't care today for we had dropped our bombs on target. Soon the navigator reported, 'We'll leave the coast in twenty minutes. The Channel was under us again. Permission was asked to leave the formation and it was granted. As we left the group, the throttles were pushed forward to get Ames to the flight surgeon sooner. The navigator's course was true and soon the field was below us. As we landed, Jones, the top turret gunner, fired red flares to tell the tower we had a wounded man aboard. The ambulance could be seen going to the end of the runway to pick him up.

'We cut our engines near the ambulance and the flight surgeon came aboard. He congratulated Ted on his good first aid work as he examined the wounded leg. As a stretcher was taking him away, Ames asked for his flak. A queer sort of souvenir, but we understood. We promised to bring it to the hospital 'unless you get back before tomorrow.'

'The engines were started again and we taxied to our hardstand where we were met by the ground crew. The other planes flew over the field before landing. Eyes strained to count them. A truck carried us to the briefing room for interrogation. The Intelligence officer asked us many questions in order to get a complete report. The number of fighters, methods of attack, amount of flak, accurate or inaccurate, all of these interested him. One crew reported some barges on the Dutch Canals. That 'Hot News' was wired to headquarters for immediate action.'[10]

A total of 935 heavy bombers attacked motor industries and targets of opportunity in and near Berlin, Genshagen, Basdorf, Rangsdorf, Trebbin, Belzig, Potsdam, Stendal, and surrounding areas. Nineteen bombers, including just one B-17 in the 447th, were lost. It was the plane flown by Gerald Carter and Lowell Simmons which had been shot down by flak. Nine of the crew survived and were taken prisoner. Tragically Simmons' chute fouled on the aircraft when he jumped and he went down with the ship. His original crew would go on to complete their tour, flying 35 missions with several first pilots. Herb Altman's crew continued flying missions while Ames was recovering. On 11 July they took off for a mission to the marshalling yards at Munich in *Piccadilly Ann II*. They were hit by flak that caused the crew to feather the No.3 propeller and put down at Dübendorf in Switzerland where they were interned. 'Mac' McFarland and Frank Hocking later escaped to England. Lieutenant Jay Ames meanwhile, returned to flying status and flew his next mission on 27 August. As luck would have it the target was Berlin but there was a recall and the mission was scrubbed. He completed his missions in November 1944 and was later reunited with his wife in California.[11]

At debriefings there was always a gripe sheet that is later printed and given to headquarters. On this mission the sheet was a little longer than usual, as Dick Johnson recalled: "Apart from the technical 'gripes' three gripes were about the need for more passes or space between missions. I hadn't had a pass for eleven missions in three months. 'One gripe was for short supply of ammunition and six gripes for not enough sleep. Why do we have such early missions? Why couldn't we have them a little later so we can get more sleep? In answer to this latest question: 'The target should be encountered as early in the day as possible before afternoon cumulus clouds obscure too much of the area.' There were two complaints about the sandwiches that we carried on a mission ('more meat or peanut butter instead of jelly'). Today our liquor allowance after missions was absent and there were three complaints about that. We needed whiskey, especially after a Berlin raid. Our crew flew this mission with a plane whose guns hadn't been cleaned and Beiser complained about that. I suspect that the harried ground crews were very busy repairing airplanes from our mission to Hamburg yesterday.'[12]

The 'Frantic' force meanwhile, had flown the northern route to Germany, climbing northeast to a point above the Frisian Islands, then heading due east as though to southern Denmark. 'We penetrated the German coast between Flensburg and Bremen" wrote 'Harry' H. Crosby. "Of course, although we were miles from it, Bremen threw flak and smoke screens all over the place. From the German coast on, the wisecracks subsided. Gunners scoured the skies for fighters. If they were friendly we relaxed. By now we were on oxygen and in our heated clothing. With all those wires, if you turn around twice in the same direction you feel as though an octopus has you. There is a maze of intercom cords, oxygen tubes, electric heating lines and parachute harness all tangled about you. Every 15 minutes or so I gave a position report: 'There's Kiel off to the left. We're in the middle of the enemy twin-engine belt. Keep your eyes peeled.' Or: 'There's Brandenburg. We're 15 minutes from the IP. Some P-51s are due. Watch for them.' Occasionally, the bombardier requested an oxygen check and each crew member called in to let us know he was okay. During the trip to the target, the most impressive sight was our glimpse of Berlin. As we passed by, we all vocally pitied the poor devils that drew it as their target for the day. There was the usual cloud of flak to wade through and there's no rougher job. We saw a few B-24s go down as their turn came.'

The 389th 'Sky Scorpions', the last Group in the Liberator formation, in 'Purple Heart Corner', lost six B-24s. Lieutenant Edward H. Patterson's crew were assigned *Fightin' Sam II* and flew in the low squadron in the last element, truly 'tail-end Charlie'. Staff Sergeant Charles Holcomb Jr. the 19-year-old slightly built nose gunner born in Sandusky, Ohio and raised in Helena, who was on his 17th mission, remembered it as "the first day of summer, a hot day in Berlin but cold thousands of feet in the air." Just south of Berlin the Me 210s and Me 410s came down through the formation firing their cannon. The B-24 flown by Lieutenant James L. Kissling of Uniontown, Ohio and *Fightin' Sam II* were damaged during the first pass.[13] Patterson had to drop back as Lieutenant Wilfred J. Toczko his 22-year-old co-pilot from Detroit, Michigan feathered #4 which had been hit and caught fire. The decision was made to drop their bombs on Berlin although they were being attacked by FW 190s and Bf 109s and took quite a beating. Engine power to #2 was dropping off as Lieutenant 'Doug' Reid the bombardier from Jamaica, New York sighted the target, the Daimler-Benz factory at Genshagen, who opened the doors and salvoed the bombs. About this time it seemed that every ack-ack gun in Berlin was sighted in on the lone B-24 and *Fightin' Sam II* shuddered after being hit in the left wing, which caught fire. "Flak took two engines out" said Charles Holcomb; "eight of us bailed out and were taken prisoner." The navigator, 2nd Lieutenant Kenneth W. Verhagen from Green Bay, Wisconsin landed safely by parachute and was taken into captivity but the engineer, Tech Sergeant Harrison J. Dodd Jr. of Millburn, New Jersey, who was wounded in the face and head and was pushed out of the bomb bay by Wilfred Toczko after clipping on his chest pack, fell to his death when his 'chute never fully opened. Toczko jumped and after waiting to clear the Liberator pulled his ripcord before he descended over Johannistal airfield whence he became a target for small arms fire but the bullets only succeeded in holing his canopy. Shaken, he landed 50 ft or so from the burning wreckage of *Fightin' Sam II*.

The oxygen bottle connected to the ball turret had caught fire, trapping Sergeant George M. Edgar the radio operator from Zion, Illinois, inside. He was found dead in the ball turret. Holcomb's captors later confiscated his matchbook in which he carried a small photo of Carol, his high school sweetheart and future wife pictured with his young niece, Sandra, who also went by name "Cookie" but he was allowed to keep the photo. A Russian prisoner in the camp made a cigarette case out of aircraft aluminium for Holcomb, who liked to smoke 'Lucky Strikes'. The Russian PoW fashioned a heart atop the cigarette case and carved a circle into the heart. Inside the circle, he carefully fitted the photo of Carol for Holcomb, who was a 'Kriegie' for 11½ months before being forced to walk hundreds of miles in the brutal winter as part of the infamous "Black March."[14]

In the rear of the B-24, Staff Sergeant 'Don' Serradell, the right waist gunner from Antioch, California, heard the bail-out bell as flames raced through the waist section. He noticed Staff Sergeant Web Brown the left waist gunner of Macon, Missouri leave the plane but the tail turret gunner, Staff Sergeant John E. Higgs of Normal, Illinois, was not coming out of his turret. Higgs' parachute was on fire and Serradell sprayed the area with a fire extinguisher but the 'chute could not be used so he pulled Higgs from the turret, strapped a spare chest 'chute to his harness and shoved him out of the camera hatch. During all of this activity, Serradell discovered that he had been without oxygen, lost his gloves and had been hit in the left leg by shrapnel. After leaving the plane he had a free fall and when he pulled his ripcord he was over an area which was burning and bombs were still exploding. The heat from the fires caused severe oscillation and he landed on the roof of a house with such force that he broke through the tiles. After jumping off the roof and being beaten by civilians until rescued by an officer, he was taken to the Luftwaffe hospital where he was reunited with Toczko, Brown and Higgs. Toczko finished the war in Stalag Luft III but he never saw Patterson again.

Within a matter of minutes *Nuff Sed* piloted by 21-year-old Lieutenant Robert J. McAulliffe of Philadelphia, Pennsylvania was set on fire in the forward fuselage and he and five of his crew were killed. Lieutenant George J. Schukar's Liberator was hit by flak and finished off by a fighter. The bomber disintegrated into several sections before seven of the crew managed to escape. The navigator and left waist gunner died on the aircraft. Second Lieutenant Albert P. O'Steen's B-24 was hit by fighters and became separated from the Group. It meandered on towards the southwest in the direction of Magdeburg where it finally went out of control and dived towards the ground. Seven crewmembers survived but O'Steen, who was severely injured, had to be helped out but his parachute failed to open and he died in captivity. The tail gunner and the bombardier were killed on the aircraft. Lieutenant Willis B. Core's B-24 was shot down on a second attack by fighters and crashed at Uklei in Holland with the loss of all except Tech Sergeant Thomas C. Jarbeaux the radio operator of Corpus Christi, Texas. *The Magic Carpet* captained by Lieutenant Carl E. Hartquist, from Cortland, New York was set on fire in the bomb bay. 2nd Lieutenant Charles M. Preis the bombardier, of St. Louis, Missouri who tried to put it out and Staff Sergeants' Donald D. Jerred the ball turret gunner who had been born in Tempo, Arizona and Francis Fite, the tail gunner of Huhommald, Tennessee, were killed when fighters made a second pass on the doomed Liberator, which crashed near Gross-Beeren.

In the 453rd formation *Archibald* came under attack by nine Ju 88s before reaching the target. "A Ju 88 is a twin engine fighter and fires 20mm explosive shells" Mel Williams said later. "One shell knocked a large hole in No. 1 prop dome. We immediately lost all oil in that engine and had no control over engine or propeller. Another shell entered cockpit at right side of instrument panel and came across my co-pilot Robert Hagan's lap, through the back of my seat and exploded against the left wall of the radio compartment. It opened up the wall so that we could see the fuel tanks in the wings. It set fire to the wall covering." A shell fragment hit Technical Sergeant Charles Burton, the 26-year-old radio operator of Saginaw, Michigan, in the forehead. "It just laid it open to the bone the complete width of his head" said Williams. Burton was left for dead until Staff Sergeant John V. Pool the ball turret gunner of Ellisville, Mississippi crawled forward to save him. Staff Sergeant Leroy Steingraber the 20-year-old nose turret gunner of Rivergrove, Illinois was momentarily trapped in his disabled turret for a time. Miraculously, all ten crew bailed out safely. They were captured on the outskirts of Berlin. Ten months of increasingly harsh prison camp life followed, including a brutal winter march to the west beyond the reach of the advancing Russians. After he was freed 'Dush' Vukelich felt cheated; cheated out of nearly a year of his life. He was ahead of the game but for most of his life he would work in deep tunnel construction jobs.

Sixteen Fortresses in the 3rd Bomb Division and 19 Liberators in the 2nd Bomb Division went missing in action on the Genshagen (Berlin) mission and 216 B-17s and 150 Liberators suffered damage. Nine B-17s were lost on the Basdorf mission including a B-17 in the 452nd Bomb Group that got caught up in a prop wash just after 'bombs away' and was involved in mid-air collision with *Borrowed Time* before crashing at Rheinberg, east of the target. (*Borrowed Time,* which the 22-year-old ball turret gunner, Staff Sergeant John F. McCallum Jr. christened after going to see a movie of the same name in his home town of Anderson, South Carolina just before the US entered the war,[15] would make it to Poltava where it was destroyed by enemy aircraft.). Twelve Liberators landed or crashed in Sweden. In the 466th Bomb Group *Lovely Lady's Avenger* piloted by 1st Lieutenant Leo LaDean Mower of Fountain Green, Utah was landed at Bulltofta where the brakes failed and it slid over a hill. The eight crew members were safe and interned for some months. (The bombardier, William Hoopes, was not scheduled to fly the mission and one of the gunners, Harry Melin, had turned up with an injured hand and unable to fire his guns. It was too late to find a replacement gunner). *Dual Sack*, which was flak damaged, was the seventh B-24 in the 448th Bomb Group to land in the neutral country and one of four from Seething that landed there on 20 and 21 June.

Stephen Fecho on Lieutenant Bob Johnson's crew in the 466th Bomb Group recalled: 'We passed the east of Hamburg and headed straight into the peninsula beneath Denmark. We turned east and passed over the German coast at 1125, near the town of Heide. We were at 23,000 ft now and when we were about twenty minutes out we started to let down slowly. The clouds below us were thick and heavy, but broken in some places. I took off my oxygen mask at 15,000 ft. The time was 1230 and we were nearing the English coast. When we hit the English coast at 1245 I got down from my turret. There was a break in the clouds so the formation circled around it, letting down and then going through it. We broke through at 500 ft. We were ninth to peel off and we made a perfect landing.

We hit the ground at 1310. Two planes were still on the runway ahead of us and another close behind us. We taxied to our revetment and breathed a sigh of relief when the props stopped. We looked the plane over and she was undamaged. We took a truck back to the lockers and changed our clothes and then we went to operations briefing room for interrogation. We had some coffee and sandwiches and also a double shot of Scotch whiskey. We learned we had lost one plane from our group and he headed for Sweden. It was now about 1445 so we grabbed a truck and headed for our hut and then we hit the good old sack.'[16]

A newspaper report said later: 'Though anti-aircraft opposition was extremely heavy, the Luftwaffe failed to react strongly. About 60 Me 410s and 109s, Ju 88s and FW 190s took part in an attack on one Liberator squadron and fifty Ju 88s dived on a Fortress wing. The two attacks were not concentrated and the enemy aircraft were soon driven off. Other formations reported that they saw no enemy fighters. In an attempt to beat off the attack, the Germans spread a smoke screen over the city. The bombers were able to see their targets, however and pin point attacks were carried out. As the aircraft left, great clouds of smoke were coming up.'

Of the 163 B-17s that were given the Ruhland synthetic-oil plant south of Berlin en route to the Ukraine, 123 B-17s bombed the primary target, 21 bombed Elsteriverda and a lone B-17 bombed Riesa due to a bomb rack malfunction. Fifty miles southeast of Brest Litovsk twenty to thirty Luftwaffe fighters attacked the force. In the resulting battle one P-51 and six German fighters were destroyed and one B-17 was lost to unknown causes. *BTO In The ETO* in the 452nd Bomb Group piloted by 2nd Lieutenant Louis R. Hernandez was shot down by an enemy fighter as Alfred R. Lea the 25-year-old navigator recalled. 'Those in command decided it would be good for the morale of the people in Warsaw if we went off course and flew far enough North to fly over Warsaw. It caused riots in the streets; the first Allied planes to fly over since their own did it in 1939! Unfortunately, it gave the Luftwaffe time to rise up against us. Near Swory and Biala Podlaska we were attacked by 15 109s." Despite 2nd Lieutenant Frank T. Sibbett, a valiant P-51 pilot in the 4th Fighter Group who went down defending *BTO in the ETO*, the B-17 was shot down. 'The Poles gave Sibbett a hero's burial and made a wooden cross marker with an emblem depicting wings and a propeller. Three of our crew were so badly wounded they could not escape the German forces and were taken prisoner. I and the other six (including Sergeant Robert Gilbert, a P-51 crew chief who was flying with us) evaded capture. We were picked up by Polish partisans of the 34th Regiment and served as infantrymen for 40 days, attacking German forces and pillaging Russians preying on Polish civilians. Our adventures were all under extremely adverse circumstances as the 34th was limited to rifles, machine-guns, pistols, grenades and plastic explosives. The Germans had unlimited resources and personnel but were unable to restrain our 200-300 man unit. Our opponents included the Gestapo, Wehrmacht and the Luftwaffe. At one time plans were being laid to take over a Luftwaffe base long enough for the seven of us to commandeer a Ju 88 and fly it to England! We had captive pilots' manuals to study but we called it off because it would have been too costly in partisans' lives for just seven of us to get away. The planes looked very tempting as we surveyed them from our hiding places in the adjacent forest!'[17]

All told, 144 B-17s landed in the USSR, 73 at Poltava and the rest at Mirgorod. The 64 remaining P-51s landed at Piryatin. During the night of 21/22 June the B-17s which earlier landed at Poltava were attacked for two hours by an estimated 75 German bombers led by aircraft dropping flares. They destroyed 47 B-17s and most of the remainder were severely damaged. Heavy damage was also suffered by stores of fuel and ammunition and 200,000 gallons of aviation fuel plus 253 gallons of aviation oil went up in flames.

The next American raid on Berlin did not take place until 6 August when 414 B-17s in the 1st Bomb Division were dispatched to bomb aircraft assembly plants at Brandenburg and Genshagen and at Stendal airfield. Another force consisting of 154 B-17s in the 3rd Bomb Division was sent to raid the Berlin Diesel Works and Nordholz airfield. Sixteen Forts failed to return from the two raids and no less than 209 suffered various damage. While most of the 8th Air Force was hitting Berlin, the 390th and 95th Bomb Groups escorted by 154 P-51s flew to Russia on the USAAF's 5th 'Frantic' shuttle mission, 75 B-17s bombing the Kannenberg aircraft factories at Gotenhafen (Gdynia) en route. On 7 August 55 B-17s and 29 P-51s flew a shuttle mission in accordance with a Soviet request on an oil refinery at Trzebina, Poland without loss and returned to bases in the USSR. On 12 August all aircraft flew to 15th Air Force bases in southern Italy. Next day 72 B-17s took off for England, bombing Francazal airfield, just south of Toulouse in France en route with their Mustang escorts, thus completing FRANTIC-5.

After D-Day one of the bloodiest ground battles had flared up in the Falaise Pocket in Normandy, where Generals Omar Bradley and George Patton managed to entrap thousands of German troops. To strengthen the Allied position, the 8th Air Force was called upon to bomb the areas where Germans were trying to break through. On 13 August 798 B-17s and 466 B-24s provided much-needed Battle Support, dropping just over 3,265 tons of bombs on enemy positions. Seven B-17s and five B-24s and 13 fighters were shot down. One of the B-24s that was lost to the heavy and accurate flak was *Passion Pit* in the 44th Bomb Group. Named after the basement bar of the Santa Rita hotel in Tucson, Arizona where the crew took their phase training, it was flown by 1st Lieutenant John L. Milliken, born Grand Chenier, Louisiana and a resident of Little Neck, New York. He and his crew were on their 31st and final mission. John McClane, navigator on 25-year-old 1st Lieutenant Charles Dominic Peretti's crew saw *Passion Pit* fall out of formation, followed by a massive explosion. "The Nos. 1 and 2 engines were torn from the wings and went tumbling through the sky with their props wind milling as they fell in a large linear arc. The wings, fuselage and tail were torn to shreds. The pieces of aluminium drifted and twisted while they were falling. With each turn the sun would reflect off their surfaces back into my eyes, as if they were mirrors. But the most spectacular sight was the fuel cells which had been torn from the wings. They did not explode their gasoline, but rather, they burned in huge orange tongues of flames streaming out behind the cells as they fell in a wavy fashion toward the earth." At the road junctions between Le Havre and Rouen the crew of *Passion Pit* fell into German-held territory and were taken prisoner but John Milliken slashed a hole in the canvas top truck taking them into captivity and he got clean away, finally reaching the British lines and freedom." Two thirds of McClane's thirty missions were as a lead navigator, the last two months as the 68th Squadron navigator. During that time over 1,000 holes were shot in his B-24, *Lili Marlene* with not one scratch on any crew member.

Raids on targets in France and Germany resumed on the 14th with just two bomber losses from 1,183 despatched. Next day, when just over 930 bombers attacked airfield targets in Germany and the Low Countries, flak and fighters shot down sixteen heavies. Worst hit was the 303rd Bomb Group at Molesworth which was the low box in a formation sent to bomb the airfield at Wiesbaden. The attack on the 'Hell's Angels' group which began ten minutes after the target by more than twenty FW 190s of 11/JG 300 was relentless. Five of the nine B-17s that were shot down in the space of just two minutes, 1145 to 1147 hours, were claimed by JG 300. *Fearless Fosdick,* the lead aircraft piloted by 27-year-old Captain Arnold S. Litman of New York and co-pilot, 26-year old 1st Lieutenant Larry Stein of Philadelphia, Pennsylvania had all four engines knocked out. No. 1 engine was set on fire and the propeller had to be feathered. No.2 engine was spraying oil and No.3 lost power. No.4 detonated. Second Lieutenant Larry M. Wolf of Dallas County, Texas, who was on his 13th mission, was hit in the back by shrapnel when a 20mm a shell exploded and he immediately lost consciousness. Despite efforts by Lieutenant Wayne Krouskup the navigator to revive him, the 21-year-old bombardier died within ten minutes. Litman crash-landed *Fosdick* near Wittlich, Germany. Seven of the eight survivors evaded capture and were returned to England on 3 September. Bill Truesdell the 19-year-old ball turret gunner from Minnesota, who was apprehended, twice escaped from prison and returned to England two days' later.

Bad Penny flown by 2nd Lieutenant Arthur L. Goss from Spokane, Washington pitched up and then exploded. All crew members bailed out or were blown free of the aircraft, which crashed at Seinsfeld. Second Lieutenant Lester E. Reuss The 21-year old navigator, landed near the village of Preist, but his 'chute tangled in a tree. A Nazi party officer and two civilians beat him to death with hammers.[18] The following day Patsy Rocco the radio operator was shot by a policeman during transport to Bitburg. The War Crimes Tribunal sentenced him to life imprisonment, but it was reduced to two years.

Helen Heaven aka *Hell in the Heavens* was attacked from behind by FW 190s and the pilot, 20-year old Second Lieutenant Sam Smith tried to fly evasive action but when the left wing caught fire he had to give the bailout order and after putting the B-17 on automatic pilot he bailed out. The co-pilot, 2nd Lieutenant E. Paul Boat flew the plane for another ten minutes before bailing out himself. The five enlisted men on the crew were found dead in the wreckage at Adenau, west of Koblenz. The officers were marched off into captivity. *Jigger Rooche* aka *Kraut Killer* exploded in flight killing 21-year-old First Lieutenant Henry C. Clark of Kingsport, Tennessee and five members of his crew. Three gunners who bailed out were taken prisoner. *Tiny Angel* flown by 26-year-old 1st Lieutenant Harry Cook of Kansas City, Missouri, who was killed along with waist gunner, Staff Sergeant Jesse Joyce, crashed at Bitburg. Six men including Bob Eaglehouse the 21-year-old ball turret gunner from Latrobe, Pennsylvania and John Smalley the tail gunner, who were both badly wounded, bailed out safely. Staff Sergeant Joe Slight the top turret gunner was shot dead whilst in the air. Smalley was later repatriated after his wounded leg was amputated. The right wing of *My Blond Baby* exploded and 2nd Lieutenant Ollie Lawson and seven of his crew bailed out and were taken prisoner. John Gard the navigator evaded for a time before being captured. John Draves the bombardier was killed after he bailed out when his parachute got caught on the aircraft. Nineteen men on the three other Forts that failed to return were taken prisoner, six were killed and three evaded. *Flying Bison* and *Little Tush* that made it back were only fit for salvage.

Next day, 16 August, 23 bombers from a total of 1,090 B-17s and B-24s dispatched were shot down attacking a range of targets in Germany. Of the ten losses in the 1st Bomb Division, six of the B-17s were from the 91st Bomb Group at Bassingbourn which were shot down by fighters in about thirty seconds on the mission to bomb the aircraft factories at Halle, Germany. Enemy aircraft riddled the fuselage of *Texas Chubby the J'Ville Jolter*, a spare, flying in the rear or "diamond" position, which exploded in mid air and crashed in the Forest of Mollenfelde in Germany. 1st Lieutenant Halstead Sherrill the pilot of Littletown, Pennsylvania and four crew members were killed and the four others were taken prisoner. *Lassie Come Home* was hit in the radio room which caught fire and the Fortress exploded, killing four men on the crew of 2nd Lieutenant Leonard F. Figle, who along with four of his crew was taken prisoner. *Boston Bombshell* was hit in the left wing which caught fire and the B-17 went into a spin before crashing just south of the road between Hermannrode and Marzhausen, Germany. The pilot, and his navigator, 2nd Lieutenant Hubert B. Carpenter were the only survivors.

Four other B-17s including one also piloted by Flight Officer Louis C. Marpil, which was savaged by fighters, failed to return to Bassingbourn. After finally getting the ailing bomber under control and levelling off at 14,000 feet Marpil went back into the fuselage to take stock of the damage and tend to Sergeant

Gerald J. Peters the radio operator, who had been hit in the ankle and had a gaping hole in his leg. Staff Sergeant Truely S. Ponder the ball turret gunner tried to get out of his turret but the body of Sergeant Clayton O. Tyson the waist gunner was lying on top of the hatch. Tyson had died instantly after being hit in the head and throat. Ponder saw that Sergeant Clem Pine, the tail gunner, who was wounded in the left thigh, had bailed out. (Pine, who like Ponder was on his second tour, was taken prisoner). Ponder gave Peters a morphine shot and filled his ankle wound with sulphur powder before returning to his turret.[19] Marpil nursed the lone Fortress back home and crash landed at Boreham, Essex. Too badly damaged to repair, it was later salvaged for parts.

At Knettishall crews in the 388th Bomb Group, who had flown the long, very tiring mission to Brüx, Czechoslovakia on 24 August, awoke in the early hours of the 25th hoping, praying, for a short run to France. Staff Sergeant Richard Lewis Bing of Rantoul, Illinois, the 19-year old radio operator on 2nd Lieutenant Leon Christer Sutton Junior's crew, had heard that Allied armies were on the outskirts of Paris and "just maybe, they needed some help" he hoped. "After Brüx, we needed a break. However, at briefing it was revealed that the target was another oil refinery, at Pölitz; 15 miles northwest of Stettin. And Intelligence estimated about 90 88mm flak guns. 'But German fighter planes haven't been seen in weeks" he added.

"We were assigned *Cutie on Duty*, a fairly new B-17G. She had eighteen bombing raids to her credit and a welcome change to the clunkers we had been flying. Overnight, her ground crew had patched 32 flak holes in her tender body and replaced a two-foot piece of metal blown away from her tail. "The young recuperate quickly," I thought. The enlisted men were the last to arrive at the revetment area. Sutton, who was from Norfolk, Virginia, was joined in the pilot's compartment by his co-pilot, Lieutenant Harlan Stacey Thompson, a 25-year-old happy-go-lucky character from Athol, Massachusetts. Before joining the crew, 'Tommy' was a B-26 pilot in the States. He had it made but chose to volunteer for combat. He had just recently become the favourite of the enlisted men. At his insistence, we had all been promoted staff sergeants. Until then, I must have been one of the few flying corporals in the ETO. Sutton, at 20 years of age, was young for a bomber pilot but I had seen lieutenant colonels in the 8th Air Force who were still in their twenties." Sutton, who was from Norfolk, Virginia, was the first member of the crew to fly a mission over Europe. On 4 August he went along as an observer on a raid on Hamburg. He was a changed man after that, becoming quiet and withdrawn.

'In *Cutie's* nose section 2nd Lieutenants' George E. Healy the 24-year-old navigator, from San Diego, California and Harold Fisher the 22-year-old bombardier, of Cotuit, Massachusetts, got ready for the day's mission. Married, Healy was a serious, no-nonsense type. He was quiet and knew his job. "Fish", our comic relief from Brooklyn, New York had washed out of pilot training but was rapidly becoming a good bombardier. He constantly reminded us of his Jewish heritage. "If we're ever shot down, remember, my name is *Fishetti*!" Staff Sergeant Walter "Midge" Midget the only other married man on the crew joined Sutton and 'Tommy' for *Cutie*'s pre-flight check. "When airborne, he manned the twin 50, in the top turret." In the radio room Dick Bing, better known as the "Chicago Gangster", busily tuned the liaison and command radio sets, checked the interphone communications and got the code books in order. "Joseph John Camarda, waist gunner, born Chicago, Illinois; ball turret gunner Emerson D. Coleman, of Winter Haven, Florida and tail gunner Fred Joseph Bernjus, born Greene, New York, helped the ground crew load the crates of ammunition aboard. They wouldn't load and check their .50 calibre machine-guns until we were over the English Channel.

"At 0805 hours *Cutie* and her crew waited patiently at the tail end of a long line of B-17s near the edge of the runway. It was still a grey, English morning and the ever-present fog threatened to scrub the mission. "Skies over the target area are clearing," advised tower control, "you should be taking off shortly." Pilots instinctively revved their engines. At 0820 hours the fog lifted briefly and a green flare pierced the murk. The mission was Go.' One by one 22 Forts of the 388th, which was flying lead and low groups in the 45th Combat Wing, roared down the runway and leapt skyward in search of their rendezvous with the 3rd Division over the Channel. One B-17 aborted for mechanical reasons. 'The sky cleared as we climbed steadily. A voice from Divisional Command said "Let's tighten up that formation; you're looking a little ragged." Hundreds of B-17s snuggled closer and got to know each other.

"I tuned into BBC in London. The announcer spoke of an Allied success. "The Paris radio announces that the French capital has been liberated, with the German commander ordering his men to cease fighting immediately." I quickly switched to intercom. "Hey it's official. They took Paris this morning."

"Whee" came the reply. From the crew's reaction you'd think the war was over.

'It was now 0830 hours. England's fog was far behind. Europe's sun was rising. It was going to be a bombardier's sky. From the radio room I could see the coast of Holland. *Cutie* purred along. "We climbed past the 10,000 ft level. The air was getting thin and the crew donned oxygen masks. Every air-mile the weather improved. It would be a beautiful day. German flak greeted us over Denmark. It was low and to the left (one score for the Briefing Officer). My mind began to wander. I thought of something totally unrelated to the mission. Before take off a rigger had said, "you guys better get back today 'cause Glenn Miller and his orchestra are gonna be here tonight for a concert. And according to one rumour, there would be 300 girls from Norwich and another 500 from London and Cambridge." One officer had said "confidentially, they have to find their own quarters and absolutely be off the base in three days!" Musically, Miller was my favourite but what about the rigger's rumours?

"Hey skipper, we gotta get back today," I said feebly on intercom.

"OK. Let's knock off the idle chatter" was the reply.

'Over the Baltic the 3rd Division swung right. Bomber Command broke radio silence. "10 minutes from IP." Silently, I prayed this was Germany's last remaining oil refinery. Pölitz was a son-of-a-bitch.

"We've passed the IP," called the Group Commander. "We're committed to target."

'In the nose, Fisher had the best view. He saw it first. "Oh my God! Look at that flak, its pattern, and they're right on us!" Within minutes we were right in the middle of it.

"I've seen three or four go down ahead of us," said a dejected voice.

"We're coming up on target," said Sutton. "Bombardier, you've got control; confirm!"

"Roger, I've got control. Bomb bay doors open."

"Thank God I couldn't see what was up front. Outside the radio window flak shells exploded in harmless looking black puffs. The rain of metal on *Cutie's* fuselage sounded like hail stones on a tin roof.

'Bang! *Cutie* took a hit in the right wing. She rolled a bit but held her course. Fragments of another shell ripped into the radio. The concussion knocked me down. From a prone position I surveyed the damage. The transmitter was smashed and three or four of the rudder cables severed. I scooped them up, matched their thickness and held on for dear life. My hands moved with each rudder manoeuvre by the pilot. Was I helping or not? What did I know about flying a plane?

'I heard, "Bombs Away!" *Cutie* rose as she discharged her cargo of death. She took another hit in the waist. Why didn't somebody say something? Another explosion rocked the ship. We fell out of formation. It was a mortal wound. *Cutie* groaned and plunged earthward out of control. In the cockpit Leon and Tommy fought to right her.

"Let's have an oxygen check," said Tommy, breaking the silence. All the crew members responded. No apparent injuries. Coleman didn't answer. "Get him out of the ball! Coleman, get out of that turret!"

"Okay," said Sutton, "here's the situation. We've got her on automatic pilot and have some manual control. Make preparations to abandon ship." (Hell, I had that in mind back on the runway.) *Cutie* swung north. The Baltic was clearly visible. The dark land mass of neutral Sweden loomed in the distance. (Come on girl, it was beautiful war over there!)

"Waist gunner to pilot: better keep her over land, skipper. We're trailing gas. Fire's hitting the tail section. Fish? Keep the bomb bay open. We can't get out back here."

'The order is definite: "This is 'Tommy' to crew. Get the hell out of this plane!"

"Midge" was the first to jump. I noticed a certain fear in his eyes but he didn't hesitate. Camarda was next. He straddled the bomb bay, dropped his GI shoes, brought his feet together and disappeared into space. I was up next. If my tough guy buddy can do it, so can I. Gulp! I hesitated. I looked towards the pilot's compartment. 'Tommy' was almost running towards the bomb bay. He had popped his 'chute and with his arms full of nylon I could see he wanted out in a hurry. Coleman and Bemjus crowded in behind. *Cutie*'s wing fire was rapidly becoming *Cutie*'s bomb bay fire. For some God-awful reason, the words of the Army Air Corps song came to mind. *"You live in fame or go down in flame 'cause nothing can stop the Army Air Corps."*

"Bullshit! Geronimo!"

Dick Bing landed safely but Sutton had gone down with the ship which crashed near Stettin. Healy's parachute failed to open. Dick Bing teamed up with Thompson and after evading capture for two hours their captors led them to the body of Midge' Midget. He had caught a bullet in the back of the head, almost execution style. His body was stripped of shoes, watch and wedding ring. A young teenager, waving a pistol, was boasting how he had killed the enemy. Bing and Thompson were ordered to carry 'Midge' to a clearing nearby and a truck carrying Camarda, Fisher and Coleman drove up. They joined Bing and Thompson and Bernjus and all six were escorted into captivity for the remainder of the war.[20]

Cutie was the only loss in the 388th although 19 out of the returning twenty Forts at Knettishall showed marked signs of minor flak damage. The oil campaign had claimed yet another victim while for the victors, the spoils. That night in a hangar at Knettishall the Glenn Miller Orchestra played to a packed house and tunes like *Moonlight Serenade, Chattanooga Choo Choo, A String of Pearls, Little Brown Jug* and *Tuxedo Junction,* for a brief interlude at least, dispelled thoughts of combat and war and death and replaced them with happier times back home.

On Monday, 11 September the 8th Air Force began their third 'Frantic' shuttle-bombing mission, as 75 B-17s of the 3rd Bomb Division with 64 Mustangs briefed to bomb an armament plant at Chemnitz and land at Russian bases. At the Fortress and Liberator bases in the 1st and 2nd Bomb Divisions the Battle Order had arrived late on Sunday night, at 2200 hours. In the 392nd Bomb Group at Wendling, Staff Sergeant Odell F. Dobson the 22-year-old left waist gunner on *Ford's Folly*, the first B-24H to be built by the Ford Motor Company of America, had remained on the base, taking it easy while the rest of the enlisted members on the crew captained by 1st Lieutenant Charles R. Rudd, a West Virginian, born Jan Lew, were away on a one day pass. 'Dobby' Dobson, who entered service at Charlotte, North Carolina in August 1942, was, at 6 feet 1½ inches was too tall for the ball turret – his first choice after 'washing out' of pilot training. *Ford's Folly* had flown more missions than other American bomber in the ETO – 79 raids in all – and had so many battle-damage repairs that it should have been written off, but when Rudd's Squadron CO told him that if he 'pushed her total up to 100 missions he and his crew could take her back to the States on a War Bonds Tour' Rudd had readily agreed.[21]

After pre-flight breakfast very early on Monday morning crews were briefed for another 'maximum effort'. Oil was still the main objective and 351 B-17s in the 1st Bomb Division were given the refineries at Merseburg and Lützkendorf and 396 Liberator crews in the 2nd Bomb Division, Misburg and Magdeburg and other targets including ordnance manufacturing depots in Magdeburg and at Hannover. At Wendling crews were told that they were part of a formation of 88 B-24s that were to hit the depot at Hannover but only 24 out of 48 B-24s were flyable as there had been no chance to carry out a flight test and guns and turrets were not checked. It was still very early when 'Dobby' Dobson went over to the flights to install his guns in *Ford's Folly*. Part of his duty was to check the nose-turret guns for Staff Sergeant Richard E. Modlin – born Spruce Creek, Pennsylvania – a 'washed out' navigator who acted for 2nd Lieutenant Jennings B. Dawson, – born Glen Ellyn, Illinois – the regular navigator, in the event of an emergency. 'Dobby' Dobson fixed Modlin's guns while he attended the navigators' briefing but did not bother to check the electrical circuit to the nose turret. Then, feeling tired, he took a blanket and went for a nap in a nearby wheat field while he waited for the rest of the crew to show up. It was mission thirteen. Choosing to defy superstition Tech Sergeant Clairborne Maynard, the 20-year-old upper turret gunner and engineer, born Durham, North Carolina and better known as 'Peedro' simply said: 'This is not Mission 13; it is Mission 12a.'

'No' cut in Tech Sergeant Roger E. Clapp Jr., the radio operator, born Spruce Creek, Pennsylvania; 'Don't kid yourself. We're taking off on Mission 13 and this is the one where we go down.'

On a superstitious impulse 'Dobby' Dobson slid through the 3 ft x 5 ft camera hatch back onto the ground, scrubbed his feet several times on the grass at the side of the runway and then climbed back into the Liberator.

A series of problems afflicted some of the .50 calibre machine guns. As *Ford's Folly* crossed the Belgian coast the electrical motor operating the tail turret manned by Staff Sergeant Robert K. Place – born Newport, Indiana -caught fire and burned out, putting the turret out of action. As the B-24 flew over the Ardennes, 'Dobby' knew they would soon be swinging north, heading up towards Hanover. As he stared out of his open gun position seated on an empty ammunition box he realised they were flying in one of the most vulnerable sections – lower left squadron, with only 'Tail-end Charlie' behind.

Suddenly, someone yelled 'Fighters!' For the first time since 28 May the Luftwaffe contested the bombers in force – over 500 fighters. The sky seemed black with Bf 109s. Place had stayed in the useless tail turret calling out enemy planes in a clear calm voice and tracked the planes manually with his turret – materially aiding other gunners ward off enemy fighters.

A 20mm shell hit 'Dobby's gun and exploded, peppering his chest with white-hot metal fragments and one piece striking him clean between his eyes, cutting his hard rubber goggle frame and entering his head right at the top of his nose. The force of the explosion knocked him down on the deck. Although he did not know it at the time, the shell had smashed both his legs. Everything went black. He could not see but was still aware of what was going on. Over his headphones he was conscious of 2nd Lieutenant William A. Spencer the bombardier, born Charlotte, North Carolina, telling Rudd that he should salvo the bombs to lighten the aircraft because by this time both engines on the right wing were out of action. No.3 was feathered while No.4 was wind milling and burning.

"Peedro" Maynard had half his head blown away when a shell hit his turret and exploded in the first fighter attack. Roger Clapp saw him slump forward and then slither out of his turret, down onto the floor below. He put 'Peedro's head in his lap and tried to put a bandage over a gaping hole in his skull, but he never spoke, or even opened his eyes.

After a while 'Dobby' Dobson was able to see out of his right eye. There was blood running out of wounds in his head and dripping on the severed half of his goggles dangling on his left cheek. He tried to raise himself up but did not get very far. Staff Sergeant Harvey George Hoganson, the right waist gunner who was from Illinois, was still firing but then he was hit and fell down on top of Dobson. Twice 'Hoggy' struggled back up and continued firing at the incoming fighters and then a 20mm shell hit him in the head and he fell and stayed down.

Dobson was sure that the bomber would explode any second. Struggling out of his flak suit, he clipped on his parachute and crawled to the camera hatch, which he managed to open. He prayed that if the B-24 exploded he would be blown clear. Still connected to the interphone, he heard Rudd say: 'Hang on boys. I'm going to hit the deck.' Rudd was last seen leaving the cockpit with 2nd Lieutenant Robert J. Benson the co-pilot – born Chapel Hill, North Carolina – and standing on the flight deck buckling his chute harness before the Liberator went into a spin.

As they started to descend Dobson guessed they were at around 27,000 ft. The bomber dived and then inexplicably, began to climb at an acute angle before it stalled, rolled over to the left and started spinning. If he were to get out at all that time was now. Before he left he had time to take one last look inside the aircraft. Back near the tail Robert Place had climbed out of his turret and was sitting with his back to a bulkhead; his oxygen mask was off and blood was streaming down his face. 'Hoggy' was lying where he had fallen, he eyes glazed. As 'Dobby' looked at him his buddy half-raised his hand for a second and then it fell back to his side. There was nothing that 'Dobby' could do to help. The next second the slipstream caught him and pulled him out of the doomed Liberator. Dobson and Roger Clapp were the only survivors on the crew and both were taken prisoner.[22]

The day's missions cost the 1st Bomb Division 13 B-17s, the 3rd Bomb Division 16 Forts and the 2nd Bomb Division ten B-24s for a total of 40 planes lost. Worst hit in the 3rd Bomb Division was the 100th Bomb Group with 11 Fortresses lost while in the 1st Bomb Division the 92nd Bomb Group was missing 12 Fortresses. *Canvas Back IV* in the 326th lead and high Squadron piloted by 1st Lieutenant John E. Glasco

Jr., born Decatur, Illinois and his co-pilot, Moses J. Lovenstein, born Romney, West Virginia was the first to go down, as Tech Sergeant Ernest M. Heidt the engineer-gunner, born Mount Vernon, New York later recalled. "We encountered heavy flak (88 mm) over the Rhine; very accurate except about 50 ft too high. Hell, one burst popped over my head and I figured it had to go through our plane to get there but apparently not or I would not be writing this now. No enemy fighters encountered on way to target. We had the ever-loving little brother fighter escort. We passed the IP...on bomb run...bomb bay doors open...at approximately 1 minute from 'bombs away' at 29,000 ft we took a direct hit on the left wingtip which blew off about 5 ft of the tip and part of the aileron. We immediately drifted toward the lead ship so Glasco dove; then we went into a flat spin and salvoed the bombs. We took a direct hit at the ball turret area. This blew radio operator Bob Heare and waist gunner Chester Hinds out of the plane. One chute was opened by concussion, or ripcord hooked onto something. I had pulled my oxygen hose and intercom chord off, dropped to the floor groping for my chest pack chute when I felt the terrific concussion against one leg that was against the bomb bay forward bulkhead. I actually looked and felt my leg to confirm it was still attached. Found chute, clipped it to harness and headed towards the forward escape hatch. Glasco was alone fighting the controls with his feet on the controls. I shouted at him – could I help? He shouted at me to "Get the Hell Out!" All I recall after that was Hunching over by the escape hatch and rolling out. (Always afraid of bailing out with bomb bay doors open as the door is right in alignment to cut you in half).

"In all this excitement I forgot to connect my mask to a portable walk around oxy bottle and I passed out from anoxia. When I regained consciousness I was falling feet first in a free fall. My chute harness had pulled loose from the slipstitching and was hanging over my head. I pulled one strap down to reach the ripcord, pulled it and the chute opened. It was very cold (I lost one of my gloves) and quiet with a slight sound of the wind. I then had an uncomfortable feeling as I attempted to steer the chute. One of the leg straps was unhooked and the other was carrying my weight with my left testicle. It hurt. I tried to dislodge it from this position until I got so weak I could hardly move. Then too, I could have accidentally unhooked the leg strap and gone into a real freefall. Even though it was quiet, the Germans were still firing their 88 mm guns at the rest of the formation. Some of the flak bursts seemed to send me back up in the air. I counted five other chutes, all higher than me. As we came closer to the ground small arms firing was evident by the pop and whistling. It seemed at least like ten minutes before I hit the ground. At about 50 ft the ground comes up damn fast. I hit the edge of an apple tree in an orchard. 'Alby' Knight the bombardier landed about 100 ft from me. I got out of my harness, ran over to him and here came the unwelcome committee consisting of five non-English speaking Germans with a pistol and two pitch forks who helped us for a few minutes until a soldier with a rifle showed up and took over."[23]

There was some relief at Podington when four crews returned or were accounted for the next day; having either landed or abandoned aircraft in France of Belgium.

At the 385th Bomb Group base at Great Ashfield in Suffolk on Wednesday, 4 October, William Y. Ligon Jr., the 21-year-old right waist gunner on *Dozy Doats* aka *Rio Tonto* flown by Lieutenant Everett L. 'Ike' Isaacson sat down to write a letter home after the crew returned from London on leave. Born in Dallas, Texas on 9 August 1922, in 1940 Ligon had graduated from Sunset High School where he was a member of the high school baseball team for two years. After leaving school he worked for the Walgreen Drugstores until he enlisted in the AAC in 1943 and trained as a bombardier and then Staff Sergeant gunner on B-17s. Ike's crew had been ordered to England in July 1944. All through training and in combat, Bill wrote a series of letters home to his 'folks' – to mum and dad, Minnie and William, brothers John R. and Jimmy, sisters Lucy and Anne and Mrs. Delia Ligon, his grandmother, all of Dallas.

"*Dear Folks:* he began. "*Just got back from London again. Same old place. The bombs have almost stopped and everybody is coming back to the town. All the trains are crowded with people coming back. But trains leaving aren't so crowded. Of course there's still danger and the government tells them not to come home hut that's like telling Americans not to travel in wartime. I hope you can read this. This English ink isn't so good and I can hardly read it myself...*"

It would be the last letter he would write.[24]

At Lavenham, home base for the 487th Bomb Group, on the evening of Thursday 5 October the yellow flag was flying at the 836th Squadron orderlies' office building which signalled an alert for a mission. Crews would always look for the yellow flag when returning to the barracks just as everyone else did. The barracks was one half of a Quonset hut on the southern edge of the field and a long way from everything else. Everyone including Robert H. Densmore, a 22-year-old co-pilot[25] expected that he would be taking a trip into the wild blue on the morrow. He was right. Densmore's mission on Friday, 6 October would be his 15th. At briefing it was announced that just over 1,270 bombers escorted by 784 fighters would be in the air over a range of targets throughout Germany. The 3rd Bomb Division force, which comprised 418 B-17s targeting Berlin, would split to bomb a munitions dump and two war components plants at Spandau and the munitions and tank plants at Tegel. After an engine fire during assembly, *Blind Date* in the 388th Bomb Group crash-landed at Holly Tree Farm, Walpole without injury to the crew.

At the IP near Nauen at 1206 hours the 29 crews in the 385th Bomb Group formation peeled off and as the High Group in the 4th Combat Wing bringing up the rear of the formation took its position for the bomb run but they were forced to fly about 1,000 ft below very high cloud which was hiding upwards of seventy Bf 109s and FW 190s of JG.4 and JG.300. In the first of two mass attacks the Gruppen hit the bomber formation from the rear and above and in quick succession shot down eleven Fortresses in the 385th Bomb Group and a B-17 in each of three other groups. In the 94th Bomb Group *Our Baby* and *The Filthy Hag* also went down and on the way home the B-17 piloted by Lieutenant

Carol E. Davis of Bradford, Pennsylvania, ditched in the English Channel with the loss of all ten crew. A fourth B-17 in the Rougham group ditched a mile off Lowestoft. Only two crew members survived and they were rescued. 'My first and as it turned out, my only trip to Berlin and it was no picnic" wrote Bob Densmore. 'What could be worse than a mission to Berlin?' he asked himself." But though the Lavenham group suffered some damage, none of its planes was lost. In stark contrast only one B-24 in the 2nd Bomb Division was lost and 127 were damaged from just over 400 Liberators that were detailed to bomb the Rhenania oil refinery at Hamburg, a munitions dump at Glinde and aircraft factories at Klockner and Wenzendorf.

Next day, Saturday the 7th, when more than 1,400 B-17s and B-24s escorted by 900 fighters set out to bomb synthetic oil plants at Leuna, Rothensee and Bückau at Merseburg and at Pölitz, Ruhland, Böhlen, Lützkendorf and Kassel/ Altenbauna, forty heavies were lost and no less than 234 Forts returned with damage mainly caused by flak. Two were damaged beyond repair. At Rougham, which was still smarting from the loss of five B-17s the day before, onlookers in the 94th Bomb Group were dismayed to see that nine Forts were missing from those that had set out for Böhlen. In the 333rd Squadron *Duchess* and two others and *The Spirit of Valley Forge* in the 410th Squadron were gone. Worst hit was the 331st Bomb Squadron with *A Little Behind* aka *Fortress Joker*, *Renovation*; *Tommy*, *Goon Girl* and *Belle of the Brawl II* failing to return to Rougham. After suffering combat damage inflicted by fighters and the co-pilot, navigator and tail gunner had bailed out, 1st Lieutenant Roy E. Kennedy had crash landed *Renovation* at Florennes/Juziane Air Depot (A-78) in Belgium.[26] This took the total number of men on the raid that were now on their journey into captivity to 35 and 32 had been killed in action.

For the second day running, the Liberator crews in the 2nd Bomb Division were spared the high losses suffered by the B-17 groups. From the force of 489 B-24s that set out to bomb six primary targets, four Liberators were lost, one damaged beyond repair and 183 damaged. Magdeburg and the Rothensee and Bückau oil refineries and the Altenbauna oil refinery and the Henschel armoured vehicle plant at Kassel and Clausthal, where the large railway station building and 70 other buildings were destroyed, were well hit. Targets of opportunity also had been bombed.

On 24 October an official telegram from the Office of J. A. Ulio The Adjutant General addressed to Mrs. Minnie R. Ligon at 409 South Polk Street in Dallas informed her that her son Bill Ligon Jr. had been reported missing in action over Germany since 6 October when eleven of Van's Valiants' B-17s were shot down with 31 men being taken prisoner and 61 KIA. In the 549th Squadron nine men on *Roger the Dodger* aka *Rebel* piloted by Lieutenant Bill Leverett with Lieutenant Colonel Richard H. Phillips in the co-pilot's seat and a photographer along to record the flight for posterity, bailed out safely. Staff Sergeant James P.

Davis the 25-year old waist gunner was killed on the aircraft. Staff Sergeant John L. Albers the 28-year old tail gunner's left arm was shattered by 20mm cannon shells but still managed to bail out. On the ground he was beaten and shot in the right arm by civilians. He was taken to a hospital near Perleberg, where his left arm was amputated the same evening. The next day he was transported to Neurrupin Prison Hospital, but he died of blood loss on the trip.

The 551st Squadron lost four B-17s including *West Virginian* with seven men killed. The 26-year old pilot, Captain Raymond C. Noiseau and 1st Lieutenant Metro James Marchyn the 23-year old navigator were taken prisoner. *Wee Willie Wilbur* crashed with no survivors on 21-year-old 2nd Lieutenant Bill Jens' crew.

The 548th Squadron lost six B-17s including the PFF ship, which crashed at Senke. It was flown by 24-year-old Captain Jack Gillem Wilbur Batty from Battle Creek, Michigan who had been in car sales in his civilian life. He and six of his crew, including Lieutenant William Gadsen Daniels the Mickey operator; 21-year-old top turret gunner, Tech Sergeant Michael Galicia (born Miguel Antonio Galicia in Guatemala City, Guatemala); and Captain Edwin R. Herron the co-pilot, were killed. (On 13 February Herron had at first been reported KIA when *Dragon Lady* was ditched in the Channel and he had received the DFC for helping save six of the crew by pulling them into a dinghy although his hands were badly burned). Captain Robert M. McGhee Jr., the 23-year-old bombardier/DR navigator, Staff Sergeant Casper Rene Dovall Fields, the 20-year-old waist gunner, who had been a farmer in civilian life, and the crew navigator, Lieutenant Joseph L. Jones, were taken prisoner. Batty left a widow and two daughters.[27] Three men on *Lamplight Lil* including the pilot, 1st Lieutenant Hyman Kaplan a 22-year old New Yorker, were killed. Six men bailed out before the Fortress crashed at Liepe. *Texas Bluebonnet* went down with eight men dead on 25-year old 1st Lieutenant Lucien C. Courcelle's crew. Staff Sergeant Marvin B. Wolverton the 27-year-old waist gunner, who was the only survivor, was taken prisoner. *Dozy Doats* had crashed at Brandenburg after four crew members had bailed out. 'Ike' Isaacson and co-pilot 2nd Lieutenant Filbert F. Dye; radio operator, Tech Sergeant Howard C. Ryan; tail gunner; Sergeant Joseph M. Mandarano, and Bill Ligon the right waist gunner would never see their homeland again. A letter dated 29 June 1945 was sent to Bill's mother by ball turret gunner Staff Sergeant Joseph M. Matuszak, one of four survivors on her son's crew.

Dear Mrs. Ligon,

I wish to express my deepest sympathy to you upon your son's failure to return from his duty.

I cannot ever forget his overwhelming energy and desire to do his best at all times. William was a man of refined character, a true soldier and a real gentleman. He never did fail, whether it was on the ground or in the air. He came through all his endeavors as a man of distinguished ability. In company his presence was ever prevailing. His upstanding ideals will not easily be forgotten. I looked up to him and valued his advice to the greatest extent. He did his job to the greatest perfection. I am proud to have served with your son.

On the sixth of October while we were on our target over Berlin, our airplane was attacked by German fighters (FW 190's and Me 109's). There were somewhere between 300 and 400 of them. We didn't have a chance. They let loose with all they had. Our bomb bay, radio room and waist were hit and caught on fire. William was still in the waist. He still was there when I bailed out. The airplane exploded in the air when the fire reached the gas tanks and oxygen system.

The Supreme Sacrifice was made for his men so that someday they would return and live as they once did. His sacrifice will live forever in the eyes of his fellowmen. He died in order to accomplish his duty to his country.[28]

Notes

1. *Raid On Berlin* by 2nd Lieutenant Leebert W. 'Mac' McFarland.
2. Correspondence with the author.
3. Letter by Dan Vukelich to the *Albuquerque Tribune*, April 15, 1992.
4. *Raid On Berlin* by 2nd Lieutenant Leebert W. 'Mac' McFarland.
5. Ibid.
6. Ibid.
7. Ibid.
8. Named after Captain William C. Heller who flew on two lead crew missions in this B-17 on 24 May and 12 June 1944, *'Heller's Angel* and 1st Lieutenant Arthur F. Chance and crew went MIA on the Merseburg raid on 21 November 1944.
9. Ibid.
10. *Raid On Berlin* by 2nd Lieutenant Leebert W. "Mac" McFarland.
11. *Raid On Berlin* by 2nd Lieutenant Leebert W. "Mac" McFarland.
12. Ibid.
13. On 7 July Kissling and his crew on B-24H *Polyana* were shot down by Leutnant Oskar Romm of IV.(Sturm)/JG 3. Kissling and six crew were taken prisoner. Three men were KIA.
14. 'Kriegies' was short for Kriegsgefangenen or prisoners of war as termed by the Germans.
15. *452nd Bomb Group Plane Names Their Origins* by Jerry Penry.
16. The crew went on to complete their 31-mission tour. Stephen Fecho died in Reading, Pennsylvania on 14 May 2007.
17. Correspondence with the author.
18. In June 1945 they were found guilty of murder by War Crimes Tribunal and were hanged. A home guardsman was sentenced to death but sentence was reduced to life at hard labour.
19. See *"Mary Ruth" Memories of Mobile... We Still Remember: Stories From the 91st Bomb Group* by Lowell L. Getz (2001).
20. Correspondence with the author.
21. *Aircrew: The Story of the Men Who Flew the Bombers* by Bruce Lewis (Leo Cooper, 1991).
22. From excerpts of 'Dobby' Dobson's report on the loss of his crew and aircraft in a memorandum letter, dated 5 April 1946, addressed to Chief, Casualty Branch, Adjutant Generals Office.
23. Correspondence with the author via Robert M. Foose. Aarne Karvonen, navigator, Chas Wild, ball turret gunner and Glenn Edwards, Flight engineer/top turret gunner were killed.

24. After their mother's death in 1980 Anne Ligon Morton became the custodian of her brother's letters. In 1983 she compiled them in a small book called *"Bill's Letters"* which are held in the 2nd Division Memorial Room, Norwich Central Library.

25. Bob Densmore had married Imogene Porterfield on Sunday, 1 December 1940, in Los Angeles. Both were 19 years old. They had met by chance in their senior year in high school. The following year their son Bobby was born. In October 1942 Densmore enlisted in the AAF. In February 1943 he was called for active duty. On 27 June Imogene's brother 'Chuck', a co-pilot in the 93rd Bomb Group at Hardwick had died instantly when *Hell's Express* flown by Lieutenant John Pryor crashed and hit a tree near Morton on the Marsh in Gloucestershire on the first leg of a trip to North Africa. The B-24 had been delayed at Hardwick for 18 hours due to a mechanical problem. It finally left for Portreath and flew on for 195 miles before all four engines apparently cut out. Of the 14 men, 9 crewmembers died instantly.

26. *Renovation* was condemned to oblivion after a ground accident on 14 April 1945 when the engines were being run-up at Rougham for the next day's mission and the brakes failed and the aircraft jumped over chocks, running over GMC Oil service truck and striking the left outer wing panel of 44-8415.

27. See *WikiTree Where genealogists collaborate.*

28. Bill was buried in the village cemetery at Buschow in Brandenburg but later disinterred by the American War Graves Registration personnel and moved to the American cemetery at Neuville-en-Condroz, Belgium. He was reburied in Dallas, Texas on 15 June 1949.

Chapter Eight

Bloody Magdeburg, Merciless Merseburg

The missions we flew were exhausting and frightening. One of the most frightening experiences was the Flak that we had to fly through, with almost no manoeuvrability. The words 'flak happy' were understood and experienced by most airmen. The flak would tear into our planes, making loud noises and causing many ships to crash or blow up, and because of this continual exposure most of us would jump at any noise, even the dropping of a soap dish. We would laugh at ourselves and kid each other, but this reaction remained with most of us for months after completing our missions. Nevertheless our morale was excellent – we felt proud of American and British efforts to destroy Nazi Germany, and we knew that we would win the war. We knew also that our people at home were backing us 100 per cent!

Staff Sergeant William C. Marshall 'Flaps' Brownlow, tail gunner on 2nd Lieutenant William W. 'Woody' Bowden's crew in the 861st Bomb Squadron, 493rd Bomb Group at Debach.

As a boy in western Massachusetts, Gordon W. Weir took little note of happenings elsewhere in the world that would affect his future. The *Greenfield Recorder-Gazette*, which his brother Bob and I delivered daily, had few headlines about Europe and even fewer about Asia. American concerns in the '30s were local, concerned more with making a living during the Depression years of widespread unemployment. Weir became aware that Hitler was seen as a threat to world peace on a visit to New Jersey. Newsboys ran through the evening streets waving the Newark papers and shouting, "Extra! Extra!" (Just like in the movies! he thought.) Hitler had become Chancellor, effectively Dictator of Germany. Weir's schoolboy friend Harry Frank and his family, who had come from Germany, as well as many other Americans, saw Hitler as the strong leader who would pull Germany out of its slump. "For the most part, few thoughts of what the world's troubles meant to our country rattled around in my adolescent head as I approached maturity after the family moved to Venice, a neighbourhood in Los Angeles. A close friend in the Venice High School who did think seriously about America in a troubled world was Robert Conrad. He was a likeable leader of our class, a bright student who would have his pick of colleges. When I asked Bob about his plans, he surprised me by saying that he was not going on to college. "A war is coming and we have to get ready for it." Bob urged me to go with him right after graduation to join the Navy. Well, as a youth who once got seasick on the Hudson River and who lacked Bob's vision, I let him go alone. Now in Hawaii, you'll find Conrad's name carved into the marble wall of the USS *Arizona* Memorial."[1]

In 1940 Weir went off to college: first Santa Monica Junior College, later the University of Southern California. Also he had several small jobs, later what he considered a major one: a blueprint runner at the Douglas Aircraft plant in Santa Monica. "I was on call to deliver prints to departments all over the plant. At that time we were building twin-engined, two-seat bombers for the British. I went to work at midnight, worked till 7:30, attended classes till 1:00, ate, studied, slept, then back to work and often put in two extra shifts on weekends. Of course, I was pleased with my pay check (65 cents an hour plus time-and-a-half on Saturdays and Sundays), but I was also proud to be part of a workforce arming America.

"At the outbreak of our war, as a youth of 19 years, I was not eligible for the draft. The draft age was soon lowered; indeed, enlistment at age 17 was urged. What were my options? Not the navy – all that water always swishing up and down. The army? Possibly, but an earthbound service. I looked upward. Years of whittling balsa wood into airplane models, reading the adventures of air aces in pulp magazines and following the exploits of real airmen, such as the explorers Charles Lindbergh and Richard Byrd, or the racers, such as Jimmy Doolittle in his bee-like GB flyer, had given me a romantic view of flying. Not until early 1943 did I and many college friends receive mimeographed pages notifying us to report to the Air Force Training Centre in Lincoln, Nebraska for "pre-aviation cadet basic training". To leave California was to say goodbye to my family at 703 Boccaccio Street: Mother, Dad, and brother, Donald. Also it was to say goodbye to many uncles, aunts, and cousins of the Weir clan in sunny California."

By the age of 21 Weir had graduated from AAF navigation school at the Hondo, Texas Army Air Field. He was soon assigned to Lieutenant Ellis M. 'Woody' Woodward's B-24 Liberator lead crew in the 493rd Bomb Group which had only recently been activated under the command of Colonel Elbert Helton and was the last 8th Air Force Group to become operational. At the end of April 1944 the Group received orders to take their B-24s to England, their final destination being Debach airfield in Suffolk about 5 miles to the southeast of Woodbridge by road. Only ten more miles south was the city of Ipswich. London was 60 miles further. On the morning of 6 June 1944, the war began for the 493rd Bomb Group. Weir envied those who flew the D-Day mission, but not too much. The group lost two planes and their crews in a mid-air collision over the Channel.

During the last week of July 1944, General Doolittle carried out the first stage of his plan to convert all five Liberator groups of the 3rd Bomb Division to the B-17. Between the end of August and mid-September the three B-24 groups of the 93rd Combat Wing – the 34th, 490th and 493rd Bomb Groups – also changed over to the B-17. The 493rd Bomb Group's conversion to Fortresses took place over one weekend with a quick flick through the 'handbook', a couple of briefings, and then straight into the 'practical'. "As for our feelings about the B-17 versus the B-24" wrote Gordon Weir "we admired whatever plane we were flying. The 24 could carry more bombs farther and faster and its front and rear power turrets meant that it was better armed than the '17. Nevertheless, we instantly liked our new Flying Fortress, amusingly named *Ramp Happy Pappy*. The pilots found it easier to fly and Marvin 'Mike' Wright the bombardier from Grand Rapids, Michigan and I liked it for the increased visibility from the nose – we could make ground checks more easily. We all believed that the '17 was a rugged plane and that certainly proved true. For a brief period the 493rd and other B-24 groups in the 3rd Bomb Division stood down – the war went on without us as we became familiar with our new machines. The transition went quickly, however, and the group was commended for it. Less than three weeks after receiving our Flying Fortress, we were riding it through the flak on our 15th mission."[2]

The 493rd Bomb Group flew their first B-17 mission on 8 September 1944 when the target was Mainz, Germany. Crews were surprised and pleased with their new aircraft, as Ellis Woodward recalled: "We'd had to physically wrestle the B-24 off the ground in order to avoid flying into some trees that were a couple of hundred yards past the end of the runway. Today, however, things were different. We were taking off on our first mission in a B-17, and we were using the short East-West runway. Where it intersected the North-South runway – about halfway down there was a hump about 2,100 feet from where we started – the B-17 jumped into the air. We simply kept a steady back pressure on the column and, lo and behold, the B-17 remained airborne. We could hardly believe it after all of the trouble we had getting the B-24s off the ground with three times as long a run. It was a real pleasure to be flying an airplane that seemed to want to fly."[3]

Three more missions followed in quick succession. Then, on 12th September – a day 'Helton's Hellcats' as they were known, would never forget – a total of 217 B-17s in the 3rd Bomb Division were given two targets in the old Hanse town of Magdeburg – the Brabag synthetic oil refinery at Rothensee and the ordnance depot at Friedrichstadt. Another 299 B-17s in the 1st Bomb Division were to attack oil targets at Ruhland and Brüx. And 241 B-24s in the 2nd Bomb Division were to attack three primary targets at Hemmingstedt, Kiel and Misburg.

In the briefing room at the 3rd Bomb Division bases the long red tape stretched to Magdeburg, a city defended by thirteen flak batteries each comprising six, later 8, 88 or 105mm guns, and two railway-mounted flak batteries comprising four 105 mm guns. "If we took out the munitions plant on the Elbe River" wrote Gordon Weir, "fewer shells might be thrown at us on future missions." Weir's crew led the Low 'C' Squadron in *Ramp Happy Pappy*, flown by 'Woody' Woodward and Bill Rawson. "The group – which dispatched 38 B-17s, two aircraft aborting, leaving 36 to bomb the target" – wrote Gordon Weir – "made the now-familiar entry into Europe over Egmond-aan-Zee and then along the edge of the northwest polder in the Zuider Zee of the Netherlands. Then zigging and zagging around known gun batteries, we followed a roundabout route into the heart of north-western Germany. The 493rd was to be the second group over the target. The skies were cloudless, a boon to the bombardiers aiming from above and to the AA gunners aiming from below. "All went well until we neared the IP, the Initial Point, and a ground feature over which the bomb run to the target would begin. We were then about 50 miles south-west of Berlin and I fancied that from my five-mile high seat in the sky, I could see Potsdam in the suburbs of the Nazi capital. At the turn over the IP, standard operating procedure was for each group to separate into three squadrons for the attack: the lead squadron goes in first, the high squadron then follows, and the low squadron heads in last. The group ahead of us had already shaken out into the bomb run, and our lead squadron was swinging toward the target. I heard 'Woody' wonder aloud, 'Why don't they turn?' because the high squadron, impeded by winds or other troubles, seemed late in bending toward Magdeburg. Meanwhile our squadron had to veer off so the high squadron's bombs would not fall on us. When we could finally make our turn, our new course took us into a violent headwind that slowed our approach to the target to an agonizing crawl.

"My job on the bomb run was to help 'Mike' Wright pick out the target, but he quickly identified the buildings near the river. Then for a while we had little to do but wait and watch. Up ahead the flak was fierce: 'So thick you could walk on it!' we'd wise crack after a mission – but not when we were flying into a blackening sky. The squadrons in front of us were being lashed by shrapnel. Suddenly, one of their B-17s burst into flames and then exploded; nothing was left but four thin black streaks as the burning engines plunged earthward.

"Off to the side another '17 was twisting down. I wondered how many men were struggling to get out, held back by the forces of the spin. Our turn came. Around us flashes of red blossomed into black columns of smoke, and our plane bounced in the turbulent air. Then I felt a sharp thump, meaning that it was punctured. Mike was bent over the bombsight taking aim at the munitions plant; the plane rose a bit as the bomb racks emptied. Instead of calling out 'bombs away!' Mike yelled, 'I'm hit!' and began clawing away at his clothes to reveal the wound in his chest. I saw the hole in the Plexiglas and nervously relayed Mike's words on the interphone."

Gordon Weir's message was drowned by an urgent call from Sergeant George Kenawell, firing the tail guns. 'Fighters! Fighters!' "Then the intercom went dead. Our plane shuddered from repeated hits. A Focke Wulf 190 flashed by over our left wing. Our plane nosed steeply down. I grabbed my parachute and tore open the escape hatch. What a long, chilling way down! Mike, too, was busy fastening his parachute. I was still on the intercom expecting the command to bail out when 'Woody' let us know that our precipitous descent of thousands of feet was because much of our oxygen supply had been shot out (at 30,000 ft an airman dies quickly from anoxia).

"Great strips of aluminium had been torn off our left wing. Engines were leaking oil – the plane vibrated: one more blow from the fighters would surely finish us off. Where were they? Yet all these happenings were but a minute of a lifetime. I returned to my desk to find out exactly where we were and to figure the heading to England. Could we get there? We learned that the elevators at the tail had been torn up. One of bounces on the bomb run had been from a shell that had ripped through the open bomb-bay, tearing out the rubber raft stowed above; so if we ditched in the sea, we'd have only our inflatable Mae Wests to keep us afloat. Flight engineer Joseph Vales, who manned the mid-upper turret, missed being severely wounded or even killed because on Woodward's orders, he had just come down to manually close the jammed bomb-bay doors; as he did so, a shell exploded in the gun sight. Staff Sergeant Blair Archer also had a narrow escape when the swivel of his ball turret was shattered by enemy action. Fragments of 20mm shells from the fighter cannons had cut other holes in the fuselage and splinters blasted from the plywood floor had cut Tech Sergeant Joseph Sutton the radioman-waist gunner in the face. Over the intercom he and 'Mike' Wright claimed their wounds were minor.[4] And there was more good news, because Kenawell had destroyed an attacking Me 109. The German fighters did not come back. Though at our lower flying level we were an easier target for anti-aircraft gunners, we escaped further harassment by flak. To lighten the load we tossed out all equipment we could spare, and the waist windows were chopped out to make for easier exits. But we were going on. I looked around: of the 11 other planes in our squadron, only one remained."[5]

Savaged by enemy fighter attacks, and in just nine minutes – 11:09 to 11:20 hours – at an altitude of 23,000 ft, nine B-17s in the 493rd were shot down in repeated Luftwaffe fighter attacks. Four of the Forts went down in flames and one exploded. "In the 860th Squadron, there were twin brothers, both of whom were pilots" wrote 'Woody' Woodward" and they liked to fly on the same missions. In addition, their preference was to fly in the same element, one flying in the No.2 position, and the other flying in the No.3 position. Being near to each other and being able to see each other apparently provided them with comfort and solace. However, there was always the possibility that this closeness in formation could turn from comfort into horror, and this day on this mission to Magdeburg, it did." 1st Lieutenant Edwin Bisaro, flying in the No.3 position in the Idahoan twin brothers' 'A' Squadron Lead suffered a direct hit in the gas tanks while over the target and the tanks burst into flames. "The flames above the wing appeared to be about 50 ft high and they stretched from wing tip to wing tip, which measured just over 103ft. The plane continued on course for a few seconds and then banked (tilted) into a slow turn to the left. Within a few seconds the plane went into a steep bank and within another few seconds, the plane exploded. When this happened, it reminded me of a firecracker. When you throw a firecracker and it explodes, all you can see is a little black powder accompanied by tiny pierces of paper floating to the ground. When this B-17 exploded, it fit the description of the exploding firecracker exactly. There were no distinguishing features in the aftermath of the explosion. You couldn't see wings or a tail, or engines, or wheels, or parachutes, or people – nothing. It was sickening to watch.

"After witnessing the explosion we dropped our bombs, cleared the flak area over the target, breathed a sigh of relief and turned left and headed for home. But our relief was to be short-lived. Over the intercom came the dreaded word, "fighters." When this alarm was sounded by one of our gunners, we were leading a flight of twelve B-17s. Within 60 seconds, we could feel some of the hits from 20mm cannon shells ripping through the airplane. And within 90 seconds of the warning, we looked around and found that there was no one left in our squadron except us and our deputy lead – our right wingman. All ten B-17s had disappeared, each with nine crewmen aboard. What a catastrophe! Arithmetically, that amounted to a loss of one human being per second."[6]

Captain Wesley Evert Carter's ship in the 860th Squadron was hit directly in the bomb-bay and Carter and four of his crew were killed. The navigator, bombardier, flight engineer/top turret gunner, ball turret gunner and Major Bob Colligan the on-board observer, bailed out and were taken prisoner. 1st Lieutenant Alfred L. Goodman's crew in the 861st Squadron was lost too. 1st Lieutenant Gavin D. Brown in the 862nd Bomb Squadron only just managed to make it home with four wounded crewmen. His aircraft was so badly shot up it had to be salvaged.

The fighter escort arrived just after 'bombs away' but after the bomb run, Focke Wulf 190s hit the formation from the rear. "On the first pass they shot down four B-17s in the 863rd Squadron" said Staff Sergeant Hayward F. Deese Jr., the 24-year-old engineer/left waist gunner on Lieutenant George M. Durgin's crew, who were leading the high element in *Ulpy*. "They came after us and the two wing crews that were left and shot us up with 20mm cannon and 13mm MG." The B-17 piloted by 22-year-old 2nd Lieutenant James Paul Kittleson from Greybull, Big Horn County, Wyoming went down and he and three of his crew were taken into captivity. The five others on the crew were killed. 1st Lieutenant Charles W. Spencer and three of his crew died; five crewmembers being taken into captivity. Frank Deese got three pieces of 20mm in his back and Don Gray, the right waist gunner, had a 20mm explode in his face and 13mm slugs in each leg. "I was standing on two flak jackets and when I picked them up to return them after the mission there was a hole about 8 inches in diameter under them and a lot of 20mm shrapnel right where I had been standing. The flak jackets were in shreds, but they surely saved my legs and my life. Durgin called me to look at the left elevator damage, but I knew what was wrong because I had put a burst of 50 cal' through it, shooting at a Me 109. We landed at Brussels [as did Lieutenant Rodney L. Crick's crew in the same squadron]. Gray, Ray H. Higginbotham Jr., tail gunner and me were put in the Canadian 1st Army Field Hospital. Gray died that night. When we flew back to Debach the next day we were the only crew out of twelve from the 863rd Squadron to make it back and we were two men short." Higginbotham was so badly wounded that he never flew again. Frank Deese was patched up and he finished his tour of 35 missions on Durgin's crew.

On 1st Lieutenant Edwin F. Cookerham's B-17, which crashed at Hillerge, North of Gottingen, the only casualty was Staff Sergeant Jim Bartholomew the tail gunner. The B-17 flown by 28-year-old 2nd Lieutenant John Harry Oates crashed at Semmenstedt, south of Brunswick. Oates and the 19-year-old tail gunner, Sergeant Lee Laverne Garrigues were killed. The B-17 piloted by 22-year-old 2nd Lieutenant George William Owen whose crew were on their 13th mission, was shot down over Wackersleben and crashed at Üplingen. Owen and three crew members were killed. 1st Lieutenant Albert L. Tucker and his crew, who were also on their 13th mission, were shot down with Sergeant Floyd Ford, the radio operator the only survivor. Staff Sergeant Edward J. Borowy was now the sole surviving original crew member. He had been taken off the crew when the ball turrets were removed from the B-24s (on the B-17s the nose gunner went into the ball turret). That night, sleeping, or rather lying awake, would be Borowy's loneliest night in the Army, for apart from his old crew who shared his Quonset, the other crew in the hut had also gone down. Even though he had only 21 missions, when his new crew finished their 35 missions, on 30 January 1945 Borowy went with them to Southampton and they all sailed home together!

"Our prospects for completing the journey home looked awfully dim" wrote Ellis Woodward. "Just when we assumed the end was at hand, for reasons unknown to us, the German fighters broke off and dove down and away from our squadron. We couldn't understand why since we were "sitting ducks". This allowed us to limp back [with Captain William C. Holman flying off their right wing in the deputy lead position] to land at Woodbridge and return another day.'Their faithful B-17 would not. "Our oil-stained, flak-lacerated *Ramp Happy Pappy* was happy no more" wrote Gordon Weir "and the remains were for the scrap pile. But we owed much to the sturdiness of the B-17 – if similar damage had been done to us flying a thin-winged B-24, we'd have fallen. The 493rd never again suffered a downing of planes like that on 12 September" wrote Gordon Weir "but commonly, one or two planes failed to return from a mission."[7]

"The Magdeburg mission produced a fear that lingered with us for the rest of our tour of thirty lead crew missions" wrote Ellis Woodward. "When arriving at my bunk I fell into it and didn't get out of it for about 17 or 18 hours. I didn't want to talk with anyone about anything but rather just wanted to be left alone with my thoughts. The lasting effect that the mission had upon our crew was to deprive us of ever feeling 100% happy again. It produced a fear that lingered with us for the rest of our tour of thirty lead crew missions. On the last 15 missions the crew members, including myself, entered a trancelike state, while staring into and flying through the flak bursts. We didn't emerge from this self-hypnosis until the bombardier announced, 'Bombs Away!' This meant we could turn away from the target and head home."[8]

In the 1st Bomb Division the hardest hit was the 306th Bomb Group at Thurleigh where at briefing crews had been alarmed to see that the red yarn on the wall map stretching across Northern Germany to Ruhland wound its way around the northern edge of the Berlin flak coverage, southward a short distance to the target and then, in an almost straight line, stretch westward towards England. If the route did not flush out the Luftwaffe then nothing would. Sergeant Joseph M. Hoffman, engineer top turret gunner on 2nd Lieutenant Leon A. Risk's crew recalled: "Our lead navigator took us too close to Berlin and we got the works." The turn north of 'Big-B' attracted heavy flak, that shot the Fortresses out of formation and caused them to fan out. Three or four jet-propelled aircraft made their appearance and they were soon followed by Focke Wulf 190s 25 abreast who in the space of 5 or 6 minutes accounted for seven Forts in the 306th Bomb Group formation until P-51 Mustangs arrived on the scene.

"Enemy fighters in one wave wiped out the lead ship and wing man" said Joe Hoffman. "The second wave wiped out the rest of the box. They attacked from 6 o'clock and at the same level with firepower that was hard to match. My crew was flying High Element and we had a ring side seat. We never made the bomb run. The German fighters just kept coming, wave after wave. The final wave came in for the kill on the High Element. We took 20mm fire in the radio room; the rudder cable was almost cut through and so we had to go onto autopilot until it was repaired using wire from the bomb racks. Also, No.3 engine had taken a direct hit in the oil tank; the #2 engine propeller pitch line was hit and the #4 engine was losing power from lack of fuel but we were able to keep it going by taking the fuel from the dead engines and transferring it to the #1 and 4 engines. When the last wave of fighters came in we returned fire and they peeled off and went down. One fighter flew a close formation with us, so close that we could not fire because if we hit him and he exploded we would have been in trouble. We waited. In one split second we dropped and he raised and I fired in the side of the FW 190 and got a direct hit on the pilot. His head went back against the headrest and blood was coming from around his oxygen mask. The fighter rolled off on its left wing, went down and exploded about 1,000 yards below us. A P-47 picked us up and stayed with us until we were back over friendly territory. We crossed the English Channel at about 500 ft. We had lost our radio and could not identify ourselves and British anti-aircraft guns fired on us and only stopped when I fired a Red-Red flare."[9]

The furious fighter attack was over almost before it began and few got good shots but Hoffman got credit for the FW 190.[10]

"On 26 September, two weeks after losing most of our squadron", wrote Gordon Weir "replacement crews filled the emptied slots and we were again leading a formation into north-western Germany to destroy a tank factory at Bremen. The battle at Magdeburg was much on my mind and because of this, the Bremen mission, number 16 in our count, was a most difficult one for me and perhaps for the others in the crew. I was petrified as we headed into the thick flak over the target, and exhausted by the time we rolled into the hard stand at Debach. After Bremen I was in better command of myself and at least masked my fears. Fortunately my duties as a navigator kept me totally absorbed during much of our flights. 'Mike' Wright also faced the Bremen mission with foreboding, and as an extra precaution rounded up extra flak vests. This 20th-century armour consisted of metal plates sewn into heavy cloth; each vest weighed a hefty 20 lb but it did offer some protection against shrapnel. Mike lined our compartment with them. I appreciated the extra shielding, but 'Woody' and Bill found the added weight forward made the plane more difficult to fly. Our squadron's bombing on this mission was not good. A strong tailwind made for hurried aiming and our bombs fell far from the tank factory, probably farther from the target than on any mission before or after. Months later, after many more grim ventures over Germany, Mike and I were wryly amused when the Bremen mission was cited among the missions in which we earned the DFC for displaying 'courage', 'technical skill' and 'devotion to duty' in a 'devastating' attack 'destroying vital enemy installations'."[11]

During September 1944 German oil production had plummeted to only 7,000 tons and draconian measures were called for. Reich minister Albert Speer was given 7,000 engineers from the army and an unlimited amount of slave labour, to reconstruct the synthetic oil-producing plants. Hundreds of additional flak guns were erected around the Hydriesfestungen – as the plants became known – and workers, who now came under the direct supervision of the SS, built deep shelters in which to take cover during air raids. On 28 September 445 B-17s of the 1st Bomb Division were sent to Magdeburg to bomb the Rothensee oil refinery but the raid was a failure. Most of the bomber crews dropped their bombs on Magdeburg itself and a few hit targets of opportunity, 23 B-17s were lost and 126 Forts were damaged.

2nd Lieutenant Hank Wetherhold, pilot of *Miss Dee Day* in the 305th Bomb Group at Chelveston, whose crew was on their 11th mission, summed up the thoughts of many when he said: "This was a mission that we wished never would have happened. Over the target our #4 gas line in the right wing was hit by flak and our #4 engine was leaking fuel. The left wing had a large hole in it and we had a slow oxygen leak. Dale Reckley the radio operator was hit by flak while throwing out "chaff". He was knocked against the other side of the fuselage and his right arm was almost torn off. With his oxygen mask on, while using his left arm, he groped his way back to the intercom and finally called for help. Leonard Melvin, the bombardier, responded to his call and upon finding him, Reckley said, "I sure look good on that radio room wall don't I?" There were parts of his arm, (bone, flesh and blood) splattered over the right side and rear area of the radio room, with blood all over the floor. Melvin took care of him with the waist gunner, James Downing, assisting him. A tourniquet was placed on his arm.

Morphine, as well as sulphanilamide was given to Reckley and he was treated for shock. They rigged up a couple of electrically heated suits, threw jackets over him to keep him warm and used an Aldis (heat) lamp to keep warmth at his feet. There was a 5 inch by 3 inch flak hole in the fuselage by the radio room table. We also lost our intercom. There was damage to the nose of the plane where the bombardier and navigator were stationed and there was a hole in the chin turret and a couple of holes in the nose fuselage. Pieces of flak hit Mason Dear the navigator's suit and it saved him from being wounded. It also put holes in his map and log book.

"We were more than three hours flying time away from our home base and Melvin stayed with Reckley during the entire trip. Upon arrival at Chelveston, Reckley was given plasma in the "meat wagon". As he regained consciousness, he said, "It was like turning the lights on!" Reckley's Mae West, his parachute harness and his clothing were cut from his body and that he stayed undressed for a long time. He was told that a pool of blood had hardened from the cold on the radio room floor and had to be chipped off. After his wounds were addressed, Reckley was transferred to a hospital and then shipped home where his total time in the hospital was 13 months between England and the States."[12]

A further 342 B-17s of the 3rd Bomb Division were dispatched to Leuna, 3 miles to the south of Merseburg for a strike on the vast I.G. Farbenindustrie's synthetic oil refinery which was rated the number one priority target and estimated to be producing 10 per cent of all Germany's synthetic oil and a third of the enemy's ammonia and other chemicals. Just over 300 Forts got their bombs on target. Most of the 262 B-24s whose target was the Henschel armoured vehicle works at Kassel hit the primary with over 700 tons of bombs with only one Liberator lost.

German oil producing plants quickly demonstrated a remarkable ability to regain full production quotas and between bombing raids were able to produce 19,000 tons during October and in November, 39,000 tons. On 5 October, 1st Lieutenant Arthur A. Bisaro, who had recently returned from home leave in Kellogg, Idaho after the death of his twin brother, prepared for the mission to an airfield near Münster. Lieutenant William A. Johnson filled in as co-pilot. New pilots usually flew the co-pilot seat alongside an experienced pilot and then he would be able to indoctrinate his own crew on his second mission. "We took off just before dawn and as we climbed to our assembly altitude, we flew straight into sunlight" recalled Johnson. "It was a beautiful day and finally, I was going to be part of the war! The climb and the assembly were routine and I soon found out that I needn't have worried about trying to remember a co-pilot's duties. Everything worked out well because I merely did whatever became necessary on my side of the cockpit. I had the responsibility to monitor 3rd Bomb Division radio frequency so I could relay any Division messages to the pilot.

"As we left the coast of England, we continued to climb until we reached our assigned bombing altitude, then we levelled off. As we turned to the southeast, we could see the coast of Holland and the Zuider Zee. We could also see many other groups of planes both ahead and behind us. All were headed east toward Germany. Our 'little friends' were dodging in and out and crossing and re-crossing our path, but they also matched our progress to the east. We flew all the way to the target without seeing any flak bursts. I was quite disappointed at this, because I wanted to be able to tell my crew back in England what it felt like to be shot at.

"We dropped our bombs when the rest of our group did. Then off to our right wing I spied about eight or nine flak bursts. I was about to ask the pilot if that was all there was to it, when I felt a jarring jolt to the plane. Looking in the direction the jolt seemed to come from, I saw that an 88mm shell had gone completely through our #1 engine without exploding. Dense black smoke came from the nacelle. I helped the pilot feather the #1 engine and trim the plane for 3-engined flight. By this time we had dropped out of our formation and had so reduced speed that we were being tracked by the flak battery. Again we were hit by an unexploded shell that had its fuse set for a higher altitude. This time the shell went completely through our right wing between the #3 and #4 engines. The #4 engine went dead and the #3 engine began to smoke fiercely. I feathered the #4 propeller. The hole in the wing allowed a steady stream of 100 octane gasoline to spew out like the stream from a fire hose. By this time, I was sure that we were doomed."[13] Rudi Guerrero, the 19-year-old tail gunner and Dan Adams the bombardier who bailed out over Holland were captured and sent to a PoW camp. Johnson, Bisaro and the five others on the crew returned to duty.

"It was on the Merseburg mission that we soon found out that the Germans were really guarding their oil with walls of thick flak" said Wayne E. Cose, the 20-year-old top turret gunner-engineer on David 'Moon' Mullen's crew in the 486th at Sudbury. On their first mission, to Bremen on 26 September, the relatively few puffs of flak had not seemed to be close enough to register but Cose had not realised the 'punch behind those puffs'. On his second mission, to Mainz on 27 September, when a B-17 disappeared in front of him with a single direct flak hit he too took back his thought, 'Is this all there is to it?' "Wow, nine men and a plane gone in one puff – those Germans are out to get us! Now the bursts were getting closer and closer. The thin aluminium skin was really taking a beating. In fact it was beginning to look like a sieve. There were huge holes in the wings where the flak pierced the self- sealing gas tanks. Nos. 2 and 3 engines were completely knocked out and No 2 was feathered to cut down wind resistance. Bob Atkinson, one of the waist gunners, was busy in the waist compartment mending severed control cables with electrical heating suit cords. Mullen told us to get ready to bail out. Salvatore 'Sal' Muscarella got out of his ball turret OK. We enlisted men in the back grabbed our chest pack parachutes, hooked them to our harnesses and stood by the waist compartment door, awaiting the actual bail-out order. Even though none of us had parachuted before, the possibility didn't look that bad now, considering the condition of the plane. We waited for what seemed like quite a while when 'Moon' called to say we seemed to be holding altitude pretty well and we might ride it out for a while. He told us to throw out anything that had any weight which we could do without. We proceeded to throw out most of the guns and ammunition, extra flying suits, flak aprons and ripped non-essential radio equipment off the walls. We limped on and on this way. We hoped German fighters wouldn't jump us. Kolker was doing a bang-up job of navigating. 'Moon' and co-pilot Larry Iverson coaxed more out of the B-17 than the Boeing engineers ever planned or believed possible. We gradually lost altitude, but they actually brought our riddled plane over the continent and the English Channel to Sudbury. The ground crew later commented there were about 300 holes in the plane.'[14]

On Saturday, 7 October crews in the 3rd Bomb Division were awakened early for Merseburg again. At Rattlesden in the 447th Bomb Group Lieutenant Alan S. Cook, co pilot on the Lead Crew in the 711th Squadron captained by Ernst 'Bob' Rohde thought that they were virtually a virgin when it came to real air war though this would be their 12th mission. "We had acquired that well-known Air Force disease of over-confidence. For me, it was to be an especially exciting day. My fiancée, Patricia Yulle of Southall, a London suburb, was scheduled to travel from the big city to quarters I had found for her in Ipswich, less than an hour's travel by train and bus from Rattlesden. I had every expectation of getting home from our day's work in plenty of time to meet her late afternoon train. That's how cocky I had become and I think the rest of the crew shared my high level of confidence that we were near invincible. As we sat through briefing I don't recall that our Intelligence Officers gave us any special insights into how dangerous our target of the day, the Leuna synthetic oil refinery at Merseburg, truly was."

Cook's confidence might have sagged had they once again been allocated *Umbriago*, a 'beat up' and 'ugly looking' old model B-17F named for Jimmy Durante's mythical sidekick whom he sang about in the song of the same name, but they were down to fly *Skylark*. "A misfit and a mongrel from the day of its origin, *Umbriago*'s name was painted on its shiny Alcoa surface, only that surface was hardly shiny; it was a dirty camouflage burnt umber colour. She was an ugly duckling, bowlegged, with a pronounced curvature of her vertical stabilizer. But once in the air, her ungraceful form trimmed up to fly as in a pilot's dream."

"This particular Saturday was a clear day at Debach" wrote Gordon Weir "and 'Helton's Hellcats' set out for the continent without a PFF leader to Merseburg at Leuna. "Crews had another word for their target. To them it was 'Mercilessburg': the most fearsome target in Europe. The oil refinery and chemical complex was vital to the Nazi war effort and surrounded by more guns and more heavy guns than Berlin. These guns were grouped in large batteries, were aimed by radar, and fired in unison to batter the sky with clouds of shrapnel. The 8th had lost many planes over this target and the 493rd had already been cut up there."

"The weather turned a bit gloomy as we penetrated the German heartland on our route to the Leipzig area" recalled Alan S. Cook on *Skylark*, "sneaking just south of the flak guns at Munster and Bielefeld, and avoiding the heavy concentration of anti-aircraft firepower at Kassel. It wasn't until long after, on our return to Rattlesden, that we learned that German fighters had been tailing the Group just as we turned at the IP onto the bomb run, now spread out and completely helpless in our commitment to the target that Lieutenant Harwood's ship, *TNT Katie*, had been picked off."

Robert I. Harwood's 20-year-old navigator, 2nd Lieutenant Karl W. Wendel of Livingston, New Jersey wrote: *Position, Merseburg, Germany. Time 1230 hours. Altitude, 28,000 ft. Magnetic heading, 170 degrees.* "The flak, which had been stalking us across the sky, closed in. Someone sang over the interphone that the flak was thick enough to land on." The group leader was shot down and Wendel, who had flown his first mission, to Berlin, only the day before, found himself momentarily in the position of lead navigator. "*Katie* was going great until the first direct hit. Half the oxygen system went out and there was a scramble to connect the oxygen masks to another supply. Corporal George Bulgarelli the ball-turret gunner screamed for help. He could not breathe." Corporal Sam Manipella the radio operator from Brooklyn, New York, helped him.

Staff Sergeant Russell W. Tolle the top turret gunner of Kansas City, Missouri came on the interphone. 'Engineer to pilot, gas leaking like Hell from the wing tanks!'

"There was a violent shudder and yaw' Karl Wendel said "and then Richard Roberts the waist-gunner reported, 'There's a hole big enough to drive a jeep through back here!'

"The very heavy flak kept tracking us. Number three engine was out and number two's propeller was out of control and wind milling frantically. Oil flowed like venomous bleeding. I could see it congealing. *Katie* dropped from formation and we began throwing all loose equipment overboard to lighten the ship. On two engines we could not maintain our altitude."

Flight Officer Art Skarsten, the bombardier of Altadena, California salvoed the bomb load over the suburbs as the formation pulled away and proceeded to the alternate target because clouds obscured Merseburg.

'Navigator to pilot' said Wendel on interphone. 'Course two-nine-zero; heading to nearest safety is 290 degrees, if we can make it. 'Roger', returned Harwood above the noise of the engines and flak as *Katie* turned on the new course. "The navigation plan was to head west to a 'dead reckoned' position near Eisenach, then to change course to 240 degrees to cut south of 'Flak Valley' (the Ruhr) and to fly into southern France. This plan was the best possible since the wind was from 040 degrees at 50 knots (a strong tail wind) according to the division report at the last control point. Our B-17 dropped like a stone. Number four engine was hit and caught fire. Out of all this the prosaic sound of a ringing bell added to the confusion and excitement."

'Are we bailing?' Wendel asked, but Harwood, who was from Providence, Rhode Island and 2nd Lieutenant James E. Kelley the co-pilot from Henderson,

North Carolina did not reply. Wendel heard Corporal Ronald D. Fleming 'the lonesome kid in the tail-gun position' from Chula Vista, California repeatedly ask 'are we baling out?''

'Bail Out! Bail Out!' Wendel ordered as he watched Art Skarsten beckon to him and then slip out the navigator's hatch. Slowly, Wendel unfastened the connections to his oxygen mask and electric suit so he could jump the diminishing 22,000 ft. The parachute pack was hooked properly. Wendel's mind clicked. 'Must un-strap and take my watch from the 'Gee Box'. Dropping from the navigator's hatch as he usually did when they landed he was surprised to find that his feet did not strike the ground as he left the aircraft.[15]

As the crew of *Skylark* made a sweeping turn at the IP onto the bomb run Alan Cook was stunned by the sight ahead – "a solid black cloud of flak bursts, the number and precision of which we had never before encountered. This flak exactly bracketed the course we were about to fly. We could only look at each other in stunned silence. We had heard the expression, "flak so thick you could walk on it," and here it was, only more so! When I describe the flak over Leuna as a cloud, I don't mean just a wall of smoke; it was a box, the length, width and depth of our route to the "bombs away" point. The Leuna gunners were economical: they didn't waste any ammo above or below or outside the pattern through which our Third Air Division had to fly.

"Navigator John Stockham was hit in the knee by a piece of flak; no one else was wounded, but when I felt a thump on my thigh, I looked down to find a still warm piece of shrapnel on my lap. We had taken critical blasts in both numbers two and four engines. At least, if we had to lose two engines, they were not on one side of the ship. #4 was hit directly in the planetary gear system leaving it impossible to feather. Its drag was thus a serious detriment to efficient flying and the resulting vibration from the wind-milling prop as a cause of concern. #2 engine suffered strikes in its gas lines, its main oil tank and its accessories section. Fortunately we were able to feather it due to Bob's quick action before the limited oil supply for that purpose drained away. When Gordon Serrott the bombardier tried to close the bomb bay doors, after first jettisoning our load and giving first aid to John, he discovered the door motor controls had been shot out. Thus it was up to our aerial engineer, Walter Hemhauser of Avenel, New Jersey to climb down from his top-turret perch to laboriously hand-crank the doors shut. We were forced to crash land *Skylark* at Eindhoven and leave it there. This would be the worst mission we had to experience throughout our tour of thirty. Back at base our generous Ground Executive Officer gave us all a couple of days off and I had a joyous reunion with Pat at Ipswich that same evening."

Gordon Weir in the 493rd formation couldn't believe his luck when, well into Germany and after dodging some flak, a radio message turned them around. "Because we'd been under fire, we were credited with a combat mission, even though we had had not flown through the maelstrom of steel waiting for us at Merseburg. Five weeks later, on Thursday, 2 November, no recall message came and on the wing of a Pathfinder we were flying through the storm of steel over Merseburg."[16]

Crews had been warned that German fuel and replacement pilots were in such short supply that Reichsmarschall Hermann Goering was massing his fighters to strike a telling blow on a single mission. All they needed was an opportunity and a slice of good fortune. On 2 November when 1,174 B-17s and B-24s were despatched principally to bomb four oil targets, I. Jagdkorps sent up 490 fighters against the 683 B-17s in the 1st and 3rd Bomb Divisions that were to hit the Leuna synthetic oil plant at Merseburg yet again, and two smaller formations of B-24s and B-17s, the refineries at Castrop/Rauxel and Sterkrade respectively. As usual the box barrage at Merseburg was heavy around the target and a number of bombers were badly damaged. After the target the 35 Fortresses in the 91st Bomb Group formation blindly followed Captain James L. Griffin's Lead aircraft after it had inexplicably left the protection of the main bomber stream. Sturmjäger pilots engaged the luckless group and in short order shot down in flames *Man O' War II; Cannon Ball II; Miss Slip Stream; Gal' of My Dreams; White Cargo; My Baby II; Bomber Dear; Winged Victory; Pard; Sherries Cherries; Cheri; Jub-Jub-Bird* and *USA The Hard Way* for a total of thirteen B-17s missing, 49 men killed and 68 taken prisoner.[17]

The 35 B-17s in the 457th Bomb Group formation, blown 35 miles off course and away from the target by a 50-knot wind flew on alone and sought the secondary target at Bernberg. At 1248 hours the 'Fireballs' had still not joined the rest of the Divisional bomber stream when they came under attack from about 40 German fighters. Attacks were made on the low squadron from 6 to 8 o'clock low. The American gunners opened up on the Bf 109s and FW190s and some fighters did go down but one by one the 'Fireballs' fell out of formation and hurtled down. *Lady Margaret* had its fin severed by the wing of a passing FW190 and several other hits sent it down in flames. It exploded shortly afterwards with only two men bailing out in time. *Prop Wash* followed her down and another seven B-17s including *Paper Doll* and *Delores* exploded or crashed. Nine others were badly damaged and *Lady Luck* was only fit for scrap. Only the timely intervention by Mustangs saved the group from total annihilation. In all, the 1st Division lost 27 B-17s (including one shot down on the Sterkrade mission) out of a grand total for the day of 39 B-17s and one B-24.[18]

The 3rd Bomb Division's loss of a dozen B-17s included six Forts in the 447th and three in the 493rd Bomb Group. In the Rattlesden Group 2nd Lieutenant Emile E. Tetrault was forced to ditch *Bonnie Baby* in the Channel, all nine crew being picked up. After 'bombs away' the #3 prop of Lieutenant Raymond L. Hayes' B-17 cut 2nd Lieutenant Charles J. Moses' plane in half at the radio room and it went down with eight killed and the tail gunner, Sergeant Robert B. Humphreys taken prisoner.[19] Hayes' crew managed to keep control and force landed in Holland. They returned safely to Rattlesden. The lead ship piloted by Captain William A. Reynolds and Major Wilbur C. Allen (who had accomplished 75 missions in various theatres) took a devastating direct hit and exploded. Pieces of the PFF ship drifted back through the formation. Reynolds and Allen and three crewmembers were killed. Five men were taken prisoner. *Tailwind* piloted by Lieutenant Robert E. Johnson Jr. went down with one crewmember KIA and eight men taken prisoner. Four of 2nd Lieutenant Roy A. Wing's crew on *Quien Sabe* (Spanish for 'who knows'), which was hit by flak and enemy fighters that combined to knock it down, were killed and five taken prisoner. Lieutenant James R. Hight's crew on '*Virginia Lee II*' landed safely in France. Lieutenant Clifford W. Harmon's B-17 and *Blonde Bomber II* piloted by Lieutenant Donald L. McDermott were badly damaged and limped back over the Channel to land at Woodbridge airfield.[20]

Concussion from a flak explosion about 150 ft to the left of *Bouncin' Baby*, which was being flown by Lieutenant John H. Lovett, knocked out the #4 engine and the B-17 dropped several thousand feet as the pilots and the engineer battled to straighten up and determine the damage. "Surprisingly, there was no fire" recalled Frank Frison the bombardier. "Oxygen, instruments and controls were operational but there was extensive vibration. As we levelled out on course to England (two or three minutes) neither the squadron nor the group were in sight. Power was reduced and airspeed cut to 120 mph to reduce vibration. The #4 propeller could not be and was wind milling and the shaft was red hot. The bomb bay doors were warped a foot on front and even with reduced vibration they and the landing gear shook down. The gear could be raised mechanically but not the bomb bay doors. To say that we were tense was an understatement but we were possibly in a controlled state of panic as we watched for fighters. Lady Luck must have joined with God in providing an 'uneventful return to an available field in England. A P-47, a P-51 and a P-38 checked their status as they cruised along. *Bouncin' Baby* was able to maintain altitude on 2½ engines. As a precaution the ASR was contacted as they approached the coast but fortunately they made it to Leiston in Suffolk. Upon landing the #4 prop broke loose and landed mid-ship. Oil dripped on the radio operator as he closed his log!'

Bob Rhode's crew experienced a repetition of events of October 7th "including the same fears and anxieties, but fortunately, no physical wounds" said Alan Cook. "Number 1 engine was hit and on fire. We dropped our bombs and fell out of formation slipping and skidding to put out the fire, which we did, thanks to Bob's skills. #3 engine had also been hit in its gas and oil lines but we were able to draw full power on it. That was a good thing. We had been having trouble with a runaway supercharger on #4, and were not able to get full force from it. Thanks to the new USAAF policy of reducing the amount of feathering oil in each engine to reduce weight, we were unable to feather the beast. Its vibration was so great it shook the engine into pieces; broke the crank-shaft and the prop fell off as we landed. The navigator-bombardier compartment suffered a lot of flak damage but both John and Gordon escaped unharmed. The entire mid-section of the airplane from the top turret back to the waist guns was full of holes and Frank Wisniewski wound up with a splinter of plexiglas from his ball turret in one hand. Again we had been lucky; no injuries."

"The 493rd was attacked by six Me 163s almost immediately after we dropped our bombs", recalled Lieutenant John O. Ramsey, navigator in Captain Bernard L. Iwanciow's B-17 flying in the 'tail end Charlie' position in the final three-plane element in the low squadron. "Two of them made passes at our squadron, one at a time, from the rear, our top turret and tail turret gunners got in good shots at them as they came in at 6 o'clock. One of them exploded about 400 yards behind us. Only a great pilot like Bernard Iwanciow could hold a bomber in the 'tail end Charlie' position all the way to the target and back like he did at Merseburg. We were in intense flak for 18 minutes and heavy flak for thirty minutes. Somewhere in there, a Me 163 went straight up ahead of us at about 500 mph. He then went to our right wing (3 o'clock), turned, and went high to 12 o'clock and then on around to 9 o'clock. He apparently thought we were going to fall behind and be separated from the Group. You can bet that was farthest from our minds. He must have decided that we were not about to become easy prey and he turned directly away from us at 7 o'clock. Staff Sergeant Phil Eannarino, the tail gunner and Tech Sergeant Gordon A. Nelsen, flight engineer-top turret gunner, were both putting a lot of lead at him. Phil's gun turret jammed. We saw Nelsen's tracers hit the Me 163 and it exploded. Nelsen was later awarded a cluster to the Air Medal for the first Me 163 downed by a bomber gunner – and apparently, one of the only two destroyed by bombers during the entire war."

Lieutenant Colonel George B. Whitlock, the 863rd Bomb Squadron CO at Debach, was flying as Command Pilot in the leading 34th Bomb Group formation, on the B-17G flown by Captain Vernon Gayle Alexander, who was on his 19th mission. A native of Kentucky, he had once named his B-24 *Kentucky Kloudhopper*. On 7 December 1941 Gayle (as he preferred to be known) was at the University of Kentucky and out on a date who told him that Pearl Harbor had been attacked. 'Where the hell is Pearl Harbor' he had asked her. His older brother was already in the Air Corps and Gayle was already in possession of a Private Pilot's Licence which he had gained aged 15 when he would rent a Piper Cub for $3 an hour, the 3$ being donated by his grandmother. He enlisted an air cadet December 18th 1941 and got his wings on 9 October 1942. After leaving the target and before the Rally Point Alexander's B-17 received a direct flak hit between the #2 engine and the fuselage. Whitlock, from the co-pilot's seat instructed members of the crew to bail out, whilst he held the aircraft level. He died when the aircraft crashed.[21] 'The whole plane disintegrated' Alexander said. "The next thing I knew, I was falling head-first at 28,000 ft."

Captain Henry B. Skeen, pilot of *Milk Run*, who was flying his first mission, which he later described as "an absolutely terrifying trip," saw his leader's plane beside them blow up. "Whitlock's left wing was on fire as well as the section from the radio compartment to the tail. The left elevator had been shot away and the aircraft dropped off to the left, under control. After losing altitude slowly for almost a minute, it went into a steep dive and passed through the undercast out of sight. No chutes were seen."

Gayle Alexander, shot in the leg, recalled passing out as he parachuted down into a field to be greeted by a group of farmers with shotguns. He was convinced that the arrival of an army truck with two soldiers saved his life. They stripped him of his flying suit and watch – but gave him back his toothbrush – and he was then marched for hours in stockinged feet and freezing weather until arriving at a train station. He arrived with his escort at a small town following a harrowing train journey and was immediately put into solitary confinement – standard practice – for probably a week. Whitlock and Second Lieutenant Robert B. Waggoner riding in the tail turret were killed on the aircraft. Tech Sergeant Howard Claydon the engineer of Lansing, Michigan got caught on a door handle trying to exit the aircraft and died when the aircraft crashed at Sömmerda near Leipzig. Lieutenant Joeseph C. Saleski the bombardier made it out of the aircraft but navigator Donald Schulman believed that he was attacked by German civilians who stabbed him with pitchforks, puncturing his lung. Saleski was admitted to hospital and died of his wounds two days later. Alexander and five of his crew were sent to Dulag Luft for a further spell of solitary before being questioned. Alexander's interrogator, a major, offered him a drink and a cigarette both of which he declined and then recited the American's service record in full, even to details of his final raid. Alexander was then given new clothes and sent on a further traumatic train journey to Stalag Luft III at Sagan with Harry Graves his co-pilot and Lieutenant Schulman. They were given no food or water for three days. Staff Sergeants' Harry Froese the right waist gunner and Salvatore Sciame and Tech Sergeant Charles Mills were sent to prison camps too.

A few minutes after the loss of the lead ship, while leaving the target area, *Straighten Up and Fly Right* piloted by 2nd Lieutenant Robert I. Prochwit Jr. of Ogden, Utah was hit by flak that caused the #2 engine to begin smoking badly. The ship fell behind the rest of the formation and peeled off to one side under control. It crashed at Pogau. Sergeant Dick Stones the ball turret gunner of Cuyahoga Falls, Ohio was taken prisoner, the other eight men aboard evading with help from the Dutch Underground. They were hidden until May 1945.

"As we struggled alone at a pace less than ideal on the equivalent of 2½ engines" concluded Alan Cook, we were the object of two separate passes by enemy fighters, but again our luck held – they were poor shots. Finally we were picked up by a most welcome P-51 pilot who swept ahead of us for flak and escorted us to allied territory. That plane was piloted by 21-year-old Major Richard A. Peterson of Alexander, Minnesota of the 357th Fighter Group. In addition to his protective action, Peterson kept our spirits up by his cheerful wise-cracks over the radio. Other than sweating out whether or not we might hit Lieutenant Rosenblum's wreck of an airplane on the runway, our return to Rattlesden was relatively uneventful".

Lucky Stehley Boy had been hit by three enemy anti-aircraft shells. Second Lieutenant Jerome Rosemblum's navigator, Lieutenant Robert E. Femoyer, who two days' earlier had celebrated his 23rd birthday, was severely injured in his back and side but had refused morphine and asked to be propped up at his desk to enable him to still use his faculties to guide the Fortress home safely. He died shortly after landing back at Rattlesden. Femoyer was posthumously awarded the Medal of Honor; the only 447th Bomb Group man to receive it and one of only fourteen in the entire 8th US Air Force.[22] At the post mission interrogation Alan Cook took advantage of a buddy's gift of his two shots of whiskey in addition to his own rations! "Our Group Intelligence Officers had much to note and write about on that ugly day of November 2nd."[23]

Next day the report in the *Stars and Stripes* headlined "*Luftwaffe Up, Loses 130 Planes*" referred to the "not-so-down-and-out Luftwaffe (that) showed itself in strength yesterday" without saying how many bombers had been destroyed. In his November report the 493rd Bomb Group flak officer stated that, including the two B-17s lost, 81% of the Group on the 2 November mission suffered flak damage. The bomb groups were stood down for two days following the raid. On the 5th the 91st put up a full complement of 36 B-17s on a mission to Frankfurt. On Wednesday the 8th bad weather dogged the mission to Merseburg and caused the recall of the 3rd Bomb Division force. The three squadrons in the 'Fireball Outfit' that were dispatched had difficulty in assembling. With just four B-17s in formation, it was decided to proceed to the first Control Point, where it was believed the weather would improve but the other aircraft were unable to assemble and 457th was then recalled. The low squadron, having a full complement of aircraft, flew on in a futile attempt to bomb with another group until they too returned to Glatton. At 18,000 ft in thick haze over the Channel, *Bad Time Inc. II* collided with *Arf n' Arf* piloted by 20-year-old Lieutenant Amet Lee Furr from Vesderburg, Indiana. This hybrid B-17, that had been rebuilt from two B-17s that were salvaged after a taxiing accident, broke into two pieces; the olive drab front-half and the unpainted aluminium aft section going into steep glides and disappearing beneath the waves. *Bad Time, Inc. II* circled the scene hoping to spot any survivors but none were seen so the pilot turned for home and made an emergency landing in England. Only the 267 B-17s in the 1st Bomb Division tried to reach 'the dreaded city' though this time just two Fortresses were lost to enemy action. While the next thirteen days saw missions going 'here, there and everywhere', crews sensed that trips to Merseburg were not yet over and that the respite, though welcome, would be all to brief.

On 21 November 1st Lieutenant Bob Welty, the 21-year-old co-pilot on Joe Tarr's crew on *How Was It? Well?* in the 603rd Squadron, 398th Bomb Group met 2nd Lieutenant Robert T. Gaynor, Charlie Howell's bombardier on *Fuddy Duddy* coming out of the early briefing at Nuthampstead. Gaynor's face seemed flushed.

"Where are we going?" Welty asked him.

"You've been there before," Gaynor said.

Welty didn't have to ask again. He knew it was Merseburg – dreaded Merseburg.[24]

The crew on *Zoomeriago* in the 603rd Squadron captained by Lieutenant Frederick C. Wismer of Lansing, Michigan had visited Merseburg twice before. 'To say the least, shivers always ran up and down our spines when we saw this mission on the map" wrote Tech Sergeant Herman L. Hager, the radio operator from New Orleans, Louisiana, who had 19 missions under his belt. "Like Schweinfurt and others, this was one mission on which you could count your blessings if you returned unharmed.'

Of the 421 Forts in the 1st Division that were dispatched to the Leuna plant, fourteen were lost with 205 returning badly damaged. Hardest hit was the 398th Bomb Group and the 603rd Squadron bore the brunt of the losses. "Where are the rest?" Colonel Frank P. Hunter, the 36-year-old Group CO asked 1st Lieutenant Warren L. Johnson, leader of the three-ship "squadron" that returned to Nuthampstead, more than eight hours after takeoff. "There are no 'rest'," answered Johnson, as he identified his two wingmen, Ernie Spitzer and Harold Spangler, the trio certain that they were the only survivors from the 37 Fortresses that Hunter and Chaplain James Duvall, standing at the end of the runway, had begun waving off at 0751 hours.

Due to engine problems *Fuddy Duddy* was the last of thirteen B-17s in the 603rd Squadron to take off, at 0850.[25] Charlie Howell did not find his position in the lead element until well over the North Sea. Assembly and flight to the target had been as briefed but, as the three squadrons started to take interval prior to the IP, dense and persistent contrails and a heavy layer of cirrus cloud were encountered. The 398th climbed through the cloud layers to 30,000 feet but the squadrons became separated in the process. The 602nd and 603rd Bomb Squadrons dropped their bombs on secondary targets using PFF while the 601st bombed targets of opportunity. Shortly after the target, the 603rd Squadron began moving back into a defensive formation for the return home. About ten minutes after leaving the target, at an altitude of 29,000 feet, the 603rd was still flying alone. Suddenly, ten Focke Wulf 190s shot out from the clouds and made a frontal attack on the squadron.

'We received a direct hit in our left wing' wrote Herman Hager. "The great amount of smoke seemed to fill up the entire aircraft. We didn't seem to be able to maintain the speed nor the altitude needed to stay with the formation so Fred Wismer left his position and tried to hang on at "Purple Heart Corner".

'Moments passed which seemed like hours. We hung on for dear life, at least hoping to make France. However, our luck ran out and six fighters took us on for a sure kill. We requested fighter support but not soon enough I suppose. It was 1157 hours and *Zoomeriago* seemed to be burning everywhere. The magnesium alloy skin was actually on fire. I looked back towards the tail to see that Dave

Levy the tail gunner had bailed out. I left my position only to find the ball turret gunner, John Butler, without electric power to position the turret so he could get out. I immediately started hand-cranking so he could exit and, after a brief signal of thanks, he lost no time in baling out. Marvin Clarke, the waist gunner, had released the emergency handle on the waist door and insisted I go first. By this time the ship was flat spinning. I sat at the threshold of the door and rolled into space. After pulling my ripcord the only other figure to come out of the waist must have been Marvin Clarke. His 'chute blossomed at approximately a quarter of a mile away at about 23,000 ft. There was 10/10ths cloud cover so the earth was not visible. I found out later that the tops of the clouds were at about 10,000 ft and the base at about 600 ft."

Hager enjoyed only the briefest of freedom before being captured in the Leipzig area by an SS trooper on a motor cycle. Later, he was marched through a throng of about 300 irate villagers and had a tooth knocked out by a rifle butt after turning to look at a Me 109. He was taken to a jail in Erfurt run by Gestapo before being sent to Dulag Luft for interrogation. He subsequently became 'a guest of the German government' at Stalag Luft IVA, Keifheyde, in Pomerania.[26] Fred Wisner and six of the other crew members were taken prisoner also. Marvin Clarke was the crew's only fatality and may have been murdered by local civilians.

All told, five B-17s – all from the 603rd Squadron – were shot down by two waves of five or six FW 190 fighter-bombers in JG 26 that were almost overlapping in the split second exchanges. Lieutenant Ken Hastings the 22-year-old pilot of *Nutty Huzzy*, the High Squadron lead (PFF) ship that was shot down and crashed at Nesbgach, near Eisenbach was found dead in the wreckage. His 23-year-old co-pilot, Kenneth Lightner Buzza and the rest of the crew survived and they were taken prisoner. Howell, Gaynor and five others on the crew of *Fuddy Duddy* were killed. The radio operator and the two waist gunners were taken prisoner. *Witka Tanke Ton* (*Bird that lays the big eggs* in the Lakota Sioux language) was lost with Lieutenant Paul H. Rich Jr. of Franconia, New Hampshire and six of his crew dead. Only the bombardier and the radio operator survived to be taken prisoner.[27] Six more B-17s including three in the 603rd had force landed on the continent. Tarr's crew made it back to England but had to land *How Was It? Well?* at another base. 'Lord Haw Haw' announced on German propaganda radio: "We got them all" while reminding his listeners that the bombers that were shot down carried a 'Triangle W' on their tails. But the 'Abbeville Boys' claim that they shot down the entire squadron was not quite true, but almost.[28]

With the number of Merseburg missions being flown during the month of November it is likely that on occasion many combat crews probably guessed where they were headed, even before the actual 'target for today' was revealed at the early morning briefing the following day. By checking out the refuelling details from ground crews on the line, the old hands could work out relatively accurately whether they were in for a 'milk run' or worse, a long tiring trip to

Berlin, or even Merseburg once again. On Saturday, 25 November 766 Fortress crews in the 1st and 3rd Bomb Divisions escorted by an escort of 800 P-51 Mustangs had to fight their way through to the dreaded city where they dropped over 1,400 tons of bombs on the Leuna plant for a cost of eight B-17s lost and almost 200 more damaged. Then, during the late hours of Wednesday 29 November the teletype machines on the bases went into overdrive once again when HQ 1st Division received orders for an attack the following day on the synthetic plants at Zeitz and Böhlen with Merseburg 20 miles to the north as their secondary target. At the Third Division bases too, orders were received for a strike at Merseburg by 539 B-17s. At the 2nd Bomb Division bases, 291 B-24s were on the Battle Order for two marshalling yard targets.

Call it fate or intuition but an agitated Captain Oscar Hanson had a premonition that fateful Wednesday evening. When he entered the officers club at Mendlesham Hanson tossed his 50-mission 'crush' cap that he had bought at Perrin Field, Texas to Lieutenant Robert E. Des Lauriers, a co-pilot in the 391st Squadron who shared the same officers' hut on Blue House Lane with Hanson and the other officers on the two crews. Born in Waukegan, Illinois on 29 February 1924, Des Lauriers had been raised in Los Angeles. Following his graduation from Huntington Park High in 1941 the family moved to the north shore of Oahu, 11 miles from Pearl Harbor where he worked for Hawaiian Construction as a carpenter on military projects. The family arrived just two months prior to the Japanese attack on 7 December when the 17-year-old was working at Wheeler Field and watched the bombing of Pearl Harbor from his family's front yard. Nine months later Bob returned to Los Angeles to join the Army Air Corps. While waiting to be accepted he worked for Western Pipe & Steel Ship Building Co. as a designer-draftsman on pressure tanks and liberty ships. In February 1942 he was inducted into the Army and began flight training. He always surprised himself by being calm just after wake-up for a big mission. 'We confronted the cold, the fog, the mist. We especially felt the cold. Asleep, awake, on the ground, in the air, we were always cold,' he said. After briefing Des Lauriers remembered a fellow crew member saying, 'I hope we get Hitler today.'

Des Lauriers and his pilot, Dean Hansen had their bunks across and next to Oscar. Dean was from St. Paul, Minnesota so, Oscar being from Bemidji, Minnesota, they became friends. 'I had never seen him that upset, as it wasn't in his nature' said Des Lauriers. "Oscar always seemed on the upswing". Hanson's promotion to captain was well earned. He was one of the better pilots in the 34th Bomb Group and always had very high regards for the enlisted men in his crew. Oscar's crew became a lead crew in July and as a lead pilot, he instructed the replacement pilots in his squadron to fly missions, and most of them survived. "Maybe the stress of all the missions had built up in him" said Des Lauriers, but later in the hut, I tried to give it back to him as it had gone on most of his combat missions. It fitted me better than my own cap, so I took it with me on the mission the next day."[29]

During the early morning briefing at Mendlesham on 30 November the 36 assembled B-17 crews in the 34th Bomb Group learned that their primary targets were Merseburg/Leuna and Lützkendorf and their targets of opportunity, should the primaries be clouded over, were Weisenfels and Zeitz. Captain Hanson would lead the low squadron in *Chesty-V.*

Second Lieutenant Bob Browne, co-pilot of *Fearless Fosdick*,[30] in the 487th Bomb Group at Lavenham piloted by 1st Lieutenant Donald L. Church, sat at the briefing given by the CO, Colonel Robert Taylor III and along with everyone else was startled to see that the target was all the way to Merseburg. 'The veteran pilot seated at my right turned to me and said, "Serves us right, I guess, for goofing that last raid five days ago". He was referring to the 25 November mission to the same target, when one of the poorest displays of 8th Air Force "precision bombing" resulted in such minor damage that Germany's hottest target – the synthetic oil refinery at Merseburg – was in full production again, only 12 hours later!'

Both the 1st and 3rd Bomb Divisions flew the route as briefed to Osnabrück but the leading 1st Division formation flew on instead of turning for Zeitz. The 3rd Division wings were five to 15 miles south of the briefed route. The error placed them within range of 90 flak batteries at Zeitz and the Fortresses were subjected to an intense and accurate barrage. A strong headwind reduced their speed and aided the German defences.

'Our escorts followed us to a point approximately 20 miles northwest of Merseburg' recalled Bob Browne. "As we turned onto a southeast course at this point, it had become apparent where our target was. It was 18 miles straight ahead. The sky was so full of ugly black explosions that none of the blue sky could be seen through it! We were later informed that this was the largest concentration of artillery ever known in the history of warfare! Also, that the Germans even had women and children pulling lanyards while men aimed and reloaded. As the forward bomber groups ten miles ahead penetrated the flak area, I could see a veritable curtain of Forts streaming earthward in flames.' Browne watched the terrible sight ahead of him and knew that he would be in the middle of it in less than three minutes. 'An almost hopeless feeling welled up inside of me. It occurred to me that only God could see me through it safely. In desperation I silently bargained with God, "Lord, if you'll bring me through this alive, I'll serve you for the rest of my life." This hasty communication brought much relief from the almost unbearable anxiety.

'Now, our bomb group was at the IP, the point where the ten-mile run began in meticulous sighting and correcting for target alignment. Flak now was bursting all around us. Several bursts exploded right in front of the nose. More bursts right on top of the right wing. Another group burst straight ahead. Black puffs were everywhere. Forts were going down all around us. The colonel had already lost his right wing man. Didn't even see him go. There were two giant white balls of smoke about a mile ahead, showing where two Forts' gasoline tanks had exploded, probably taking other Forts with them. They were still falling. Even through the oxygen masks you could smell cordite. Enemy fighters were waiting outside the flak corridor, not daring to follow us through the seemingly impenetrable barrier of flying steel.[31]

"Bombs Away!" There was the usual upsurge of the craft, bringing instinctive reflexes for forward control wheel, as the 6,000 lbs of bombs dropped free. What an awesome sight, as thousands of 500 lb bombs fell in train simultaneously! Now the formation was in a steep bank to the right. The colonel's voice could be heard over the airwaves, "Let's get out of here!"[32]

Just after "bombs away" *Chesty-V* in the 34th Bomb Group piloted by Captain Oscar Hanson, took a direct flak hit in the No.2 engine, causing a major fire so intense that the co-pilot who had acquired Hanson's '50-mission crush' cap flying behind him in the low squadron felt the heat from his wing for a second as he swung past his plane, sliding violently under the formation, losing 2,000 to 3,000 ft of altitude. Hanson and co-pilot 1st Lieutenant Roy C. Keirn died on impact when thrown from the aircraft as it broke apart over Bad Kosen. Minutes after five members of the crew bailed out at 27,000 ft, the left wing broke off, sending the bomber into a dive over Bad Kosen. Fifteen-year-old Karl-Heinze Giesecke and his friend, standing in the street saw part of the wing and two of the engines plunge into a garden about 150 metres away and they ran for safety into the cellar of the next house. Later they inspected the nose with its pin-up in a 'seductive sitting posture'. They had never seen anything like it before. In Nazi Germany, it was forbidden! Giesecke saw two farmers collect two dead bodies and remove them on a horse and cart. His cousin, who was driving on a nearby road stopped as members of the Volkssturm[33] were busy recovering another body. One of the Volkssturm holding papers in his hand said something like, "Again an American with a German surname." Hansen was a popular German surname then as even in Bad Kosen there was a shop owned by someone named 'Hansen'."

The tail gunner, Staff Sergeant Joe Burton; 1st Lieutenant Lindsey Lipscomb, bombardier; Staff Sergeant Paul Shull, engineer/top turret gunner; 1st Lieutenant Donald G. Topping the 22-year-old navigator and waist gunner Staff Sergeant Sidney C. Brown, survived the parachute jump out of the flaming aircraft and remained 'Kriegies' in Germany until liberation. Shull, who was locked in a shed with another crew member for a while would later find this to have been his only good fortune of the day. Later they were marched out under guard and shown the bodies of Tech Sergeant George H. Simpson the radio operator and Staff Sergeant Lawrence D. Layton the 20-year-old ball turret gunner. *Chesty-V* was the only one out of the 36 B-17s from the 34th Bomb Group that was lost. Oscar Hanson's premonition had come true. Don Topping said, "About a week before the Merseburg mission, Oscar had a bad dream about going down in flames. It had bothered him enough that he talked about it to me and Lindsey."[34]

"Oscar's cap was under my seat" recalled Bob Des Lauriers. "When we returned to the base shot full of holes [about 80 % of the B-17s in the low squadron suffered major flak damage and his B-17 came home with about 240 flak holes] I noticed a flak hole just inches from his cap which Oscar had written his name on the inside band. If he hadn't tossed me the cap, it would have gone down in his bomber! I decided it must be lucky, so it went along with me on all of my 33 missions."[35]

"The flight back" recalled Bob Browne "was relatively uneventful. What a relief to park old *Fearless Fosdick*. But I dreaded to inspect the old bird for battle damage. Staff Sergeant Ralph Spiller the crew chief was always so obviously distressed when the Fort's skin was even scratched. How much more if she looked like the sieve I expected? As I left the forward escape door I could hear ambulances as they raced to pick up wounded and dead from other aircraft. Sergeant Spiller was already at the nose of *Fearless Fosdick*, looking her all over. As I approached him, I could hear him muttering something. As he turned to me, I finally heard what he was saying. "I can't believe it," he muttered over and over. It was the sergeant's way of expressing the fact that he could not find a single scratch on *Fearless*. The old Fort sat there all shiny and spotless, as though she had never left the pad that day! The 8th and 9th Air Forces had just lost 29 bombers altogether on this bleak day and it would take about two weeks before the 487th could repair enough aircraft for another mission but Merseburg had suffered its greatest damage, too and no doubt this helped considerably to bring the terrible conflict to an end.'

Berliners meanwhile, had suffered relatively few raids by the US 8th Air Force, engaged as it was in the strategic bombing of Germany but after supper on Monday, 4 December 451 experienced B-17 crews and new replacements at the 1st and 3rd Bomb Division bases were alerted for a mission the next day. They were not to know – yet – that they would be making PFF attacks on munitions and tank plants at Berlin/Tegel and 129 B-24 crews in the 2nd Bomb Division were to bomb the marshalling yard at Münster. Just over 400 Fortresses attacked Tegel and 114 B-24s bombed the marshalling yard at Münster. Fifteen escorting fighter groups met an estimated 285-300 fighters and claimed 90 destroyed. Lieutenant Charles Joseph Wagoner, pilot of a B-17 in the 729th Squadron, 452nd formation struggled back towards England on one engine but over Lohnerfeld the Fortress was hit by Major Karl Borris of 1./JG 26 and crashed at Talgewilsten, west of Lingen with the loss of eight crew. Joe Norocos the radio operator was the only man on the crew to survive.

On 16 December, using the appalling weather conditions to his advantage, Field Marshal Gerd von Rundstedt and his panzer formations attacked American positions in the forests of the Ardennes on the Franco-Belgian border and opened up a salient or 'bulge' in the Allied lines. In England the Allied air forces were grounded by fog and it was not until 23 December that the heavies could offer bomber support in what became known as the 'Battle of the Bulge.' On Christmas Eve a record 2,034 8th Air Force bombers and 500 RAF and 9th Air Force bombers, took part in the largest single strike flown by the Allied Air

Forces in World War Two, against German airfields and lines of communication leading to the 'Bulge'. The 1st Division made a direct tactical assault on airfields in the Frankfurt area and on lines of communication immediately behind the German 'bulge'. Crews were told that their route was planned on purpose to go over the ground troops' positions for morale purposes. It was a memorable day, one that crews would never forget. Gordon Weir on Ellis Woodward's crew in the 493rd Bomb Group was moved to write: "Christmas 1944 we lifted off at dawn. Hitler was initiating his last attack, the Battle of the Bulge, and a week of foul weather had protected the advancing Germans. Skies had finally cleared the day before, and an immense armada of more than 2,000 aircraft had harried the Nazis. This holiday it was our crew's turn. The heavens were still moist. At fighting altitude our planes left long, thick and lasting contrails. We created the clouds we had to fly back through. On the flanks of the bomber stream we could see many dogfights. The Luftwaffe fighters tried to come in at us, but our P-51s kept them away. The 493rd was to zero in on a railroad tunnel near Arweiler, south of Bonn in south-western Germany. This was a strange mission to be assigned to a heavy bomb group – such small targets were usually taken out by low- flying, twin-engined medium bombers or by swift, bomb-carrying fighters. The purpose of the attack was to cut off the rail transport feeding the German troops guarding lines south of the Battle of the Bulge. We accomplished little, because our bombs did not fall at the mouth of the tunnel.

Joe L. Nathan, the navigator on Al Saunders' B-24 crew in the 448th at Seething, who on his first mission, late in November had felt "pretty damn important toggling 7,000 lbs on the German bastards' was on one of the last bombers leaving the English coast as the first groups were bombing the Bulge. "We were eating up all the prop wash in the sky that was just a sea of it. It was a short mission and should have been an easy one but the Jerries had guns all over the front and were throwing up very accurate flak at us all the way to the target and back. For the first time on a mission I had a completely visual run. After I had toggled the bombs Bob Wallace looked down at Germany and hollered, 'Merry Christmas you bastards'. I saw red flashes spring up and thought that it was the muzzle flash of the flak guns until I saw black smoke roll out from each of the flashes and I realised that it was our bombs striking. What little we hadn't hit was plastered by the squadron behind us. When we turned to the Rally Point there was nothing but smoke. Christmas couldn't have been a happy one for the Germans with 2,000 bombers dropping about 6,000 lbs apiece all over a wide sector of the front."

As usual, Gordon Weir was kept busy charting his crew's path, but while not unmindful of his personal safety with fighters off to the side and flak ahead, his thoughts kept drifting back to Debach. "The past few weeks we and our hut-mates had been stockpiling food and fuel, purloined, appropriated and liberated from mess-hall supplies. Added to the locker were special treats from home. Eggs were bought on the black market at a bargaining price of thruppence [1p] or ten cigarettes each. The raid on the Inverness distillery gave us a beverage to drink and booty to trade. All this economic activity was aimed at producing a party of holiday cheer beneath the curved, corrugated iron of our Nissen hut. My darker musings were that if we got shot down or were forced to land elsewhere than Debach, Captain David L. 'Doc' Conger and his crew and a few lucky guests would get to lap up all the goodies we'd long been scrounging for Christmas Day. As it turned out, we got back safely and on time. I for one enjoyed the hut party, especially the fancy eggnog concocted by Frank Littleton. However, I couldn't have partaken of the joy of that evening if I'd known that at the same time my brother Bob was laying on the straw of a Belgian farmhouse with his head cut open by Nazi shrapnel."[36]

Overall, the Christmas Eve raids were effective and severely hampered von Rundstedt's lines of communication. The cost in aircraft though, was high. One of the casualties was Brigadier General Fred Castle, commander of the 4th Wing, who was leading the 3rd Division on his 30th mission in a 487th Bomb Group Fortress. All went well until over Belgium, about 35 miles from Liège, his right outboard engine burst into flame and the propeller had to be feathered. The deputy lead ship took over and Castle dropped down to 20,000 ft. But at this height the aircraft began vibrating badly and he was forced to take it down another 3,000 ft before levelling out. The Fortress was now down to 180 mph indicated air speed and being pursued by seven Bf 109s. They attacked and wounded the tail gunner and left the radar navigator nursing bad wounds in his neck and shoulders. Castle could not carry out an evasive manoeuvres with the full bomb load still aboard and he could not salvo them for fear of hitting Allied troops on the ground. Successive attacks by the fighters put another two engines out of action and the B-17 lost altitude. As Castle fought the controls in a vain effort to keep the stricken bomber level he ordered the crew to bail out. Part of the crew bailed out and then the bomber was hit in the fuel tanks and oxygen systems, which set the aircraft on fire. Castle attempted to land the flaming bomber in an open field near the Allied lines bur nearing the ground it went into a spin and exploded on impact. Brigadier General Castle was posthumously awarded the Medal of Honor – the highest ranking officer in the 8th Air Force to receive the award.

Many bombers crashed during their return over England as drizzle and overcast played havoc with landing patterns. Tired crews put down where they could at any of the bases like Mendlesham and Thorpe Abbotts, due to the weather. Along with all the 8th Air Force bombers, a squadron of RAF Halifax's also set down that night at Mendlesham, bringing it up to 125 aircraft! Only 150 aircraft were available for another strike on 26 December. Next day the wintry conditions were responsible for a succession of crashes during early morning takeoffs. On 30 December the 8th again attacked lines of communication and on the final day of the year the 1st Bomb Division kept up the attacks while 3rd Division crews returned to oil production centres. This time they were assigned

Hamburg. The bombardier on *Queen Mary* in the 95th Bomb Group at Horham, Staff Sergeant Jasper Clyde Crowley, born Greenbank, West Virginia, was flying his 33rd combat mission. 'There was another togglier in my squadron, Sergeant Bates. It was his turn to fly but he had gotten himself grounded because of a cold. I had a bit of a stuffy head myself but I was told that if I flew the mission my flight officer said he would see if he could get my tour of duty ended and send me home. This sounded like a good deal. When I went to briefing and learned that the target was to be Hamburg my spirits dropped. I snapped on my 'chute before take-off, something I rarely ever did.

'The day was a very cold and clear one. At the target area the flak was heavy. We started our bomb run. I opened the bomb bay doors after arming the bombs. When we reached the target I dropped the bombs. Sergeant Herman Finklestein the radio operator, who could see into the bomb bay, called me on interphone and said one bomb was hung in the rack. I tried again to unload the bomb but it wouldn't go so I asked Lieutenant Chas O'Reilly the pilot to jettison racks and all. He did this and as soon as Finklestein announced the bay was clear I closed the doors. With a combined sigh of relief everyone seemed to be chatting at the same time. But not for long. Sergeant Finklestein saw an enemy aircraft approaching. Our gunners fired but he got through and near enough to hit us with at least one 20mm shell. The ship was on fire. The pilot gave the order to abandon. Since I already had my chest pack on I probably was the first to get out. I kicked out the escape hatch and was gone. Four others managed to get out before the plane disintegrated.[37] The rest of my tour overseas was spent in two Stalag Lufts.'

On December 31st Roland L. Douglas, the 19-year-old replacement tail gunner on Lieutenant Clifton M. Williams crew on *Kramp's Tramps* in the 'Bloody Hundredth' was actually relieved when at briefing it was announced that that the mission was Hamburg. "On my first mission with *Brown's Clowns* on 4 August when we bombed this target it wasn't too rough so I figured it wouldn't be too bad on my 26th mission. The only difference was that on 4 August there were 170 anti aircraft guns in the target area and now there were 490 reported."

The Hundredth was supposed to fly in above Heligoland Island but instead they came in below and had to turn directly into the wind to reach the IP. Heligoland was the secondary target and even though crews knew that the two islands were well defended they were wishing that they could drop their bombs there. Finally, the Group reached the IP, turned on their rack switches, opened the bomb bay doors and started down the bomb run. At this point crews usually cut off their heated suits because the nervous energy was enough to keep them warm even though it was 50° below zero. The turn onto the bomb run was to the right and the Group was on the outside which caused it to lag behind a little but finally they were able to get back into position. The target could be seen from the IP even though it took about ten minutes to reach it. A group hit an airfield off to the right and groups in front were getting shot at and the Hundredth knew that they would soon be in the thick of it. No-one spoke. They were all just hoping and praying that they would come through without any trouble. Finally, the 100th got back into the flak which was so close crews could hear the shells as they burst. At 1133 hours the lead ship dropped his smoke bombs, the signal for all of the wing ships to drop their bombs.

Fools Rush In piloted by 25-year-old Lieutenant Floyd E. Henderson took a direct hit by a shell from a German 88 while on the bomb run. Twenty 250 lb bombs were salvoed before the Fortress nosed down sharply and crashed into *Kramp's Tramps*. 'When the other plane's wing cut us in two the tail was pointed almost into the bomb bay of this plane" recalled Roland Douglas. "After the collision the tail section stabilised, oscillating slowly in an upright position and tilted slightly on the door side of our plane. I salvoed the tail door but I didn't think I could get out so I crawled past the tail wheel to the waist door which was open, stood with my back braced against the side, put on my parachute, cleared my ears and looked out and saw a man on the ground wearing a flying helmet staring up at me. I stepped out and pulled my ripcord immediately. My shroud lines went past my face and then my feet touched the ground so lightly that I didn't break the thin ice on the navigation canal where I landed. After I got my chute off I tried to jump across it and landed in the middle and broke through and got wet to the waist. The man I had seen from the air grabbed me and kissed me on both cheeks. It turned out he was a Polish forced labourer. One of his group produced a knife and proceeded to cut my alpaca flying pants off."[38]

Only two other men on Williams' crew bailed out and they were taken prisoner along with Douglas. Six men on *Fools Rush In* died. Floyd Henderson left a widow, the former Violet Thomsen of Illinois. Ten other B-17 losses took the 'Bloody Hundredth's' total to 12; half that lost to flak (10) and fighters (14) by the 3rd Division as a whole.

January 1945 marked the 8th's third year of operations and it seemed as if the end of the war was in sight. The Ardennes breakthrough was on the verge of failure and Germany had no reserves left. In the east the Red Army prepared for the great winter offensive which would see the capture of Warsaw and Craców and see the Soviets cross the German border. But there were signs that the Luftwaffe at least, was far from defeated – on 1 January the 8th Air Force encountered enemy fighters in some strength during raids on the tank factory at Kassel, an oil refinery at Magdeburg and marshalling yards at Dillenburg. The Magdeburg force came under heavy fighter attack while the Kassel force was badly hit by flak. Next day the bombers once again pounded lines of communication and raids of this nature continued for several days until the position in the Ardennes gradually swung in the Allies' favour.

On 5 January the severe wintry winter over England was responsible for several fatal accidents during take-off for a mission to Frankfurt. A period of fine weather, beginning on 6 January, enabled the heavies to fly missions in support of the ground troops once more. Mostly they were against lines of communication, airfields and marshalling yards. Hitler's last chance now lay in his so-called 'wonder weapons' – the V1s and V2s. At Debach, one dismally wet afternoon, Gordon Weir was splashing along toward the mess hall behind two airmen unknown to him and he could not help but overhear part of their loud talk: 'We had to abort and come back over Germany alone. We thought about the rockets falling on London and decided to teach the Germans a lesson, so on every little village we passed over, we flipped a bomb smack in the middle of it!' Something to think about! War is brutal and brutalizing. If it went on long enough, we'd all be brutes. Our final 16 missions were against well-defended targets in Germany. Nine times we disrupted the rail network; three times we burned oil installations; three times we blasted armament factories; once we aided our ground troops with a carpet bombing attack."[39]

It was not surprising that when New Year came some in the 8th Air Force like Gordon Weir, who still had three missions to go for a ticket home, saw no reason to celebrate. "On the second day of the year we had turned in from liberated France to bomb the rail yard at Bad Kreuznach, near Mainz. At this point, the supercharger on an inboard engine failed, and we flew into south-western Germany with only three engines. If this had been one of our earliest missions perhaps we'd have turned back, but by now the crew was with 'Woody' in his determination to go on and get it over with. Eight days later we attacked the heavily gunned rail yards at Cologne in *Ole Rambler*, the 13th, an unlucky number, gave us lucky number 30. We completed our tour by coming back safely from wrecking the rail yard at Bischofsheim, north-east of Frankfurt; that day after briefing, I tossed down my shot of whiskey. Conger's crew tallied their thirtieth the next day and in our shared hut that evening, the 14th, we truly celebrated 1945.

"But was it, after all, worth it? The material and manpower given to making airplanes, the immense operational facilities, the months of training to convert a man from the street into an airman, and all the young men that we left out there in the empty air? Did the 8th Air Force strategy and tactics shorten the war? One thing is certain, and that is that future air battles would be different: the bomber armadas of World War II with their parade of squadrons in neatly stacked Vs were as obsolete as the Macedonian phalanx.

"German production of fighter aircraft actually increased through 1944 into 1945, largely because the manufacturing plants were so well dispersed that it was beyond our power to damage them seriously. Therefore, some post-war surveys concluded that our bombing offensive was a failure. But our bombing was just good enough that the Luftwaffe fighters had to keep rising to attack us, and then they were mostly destroyed by our P-51s and P-47s. So in fact the Luftwaffe suffered a shortage of pilots rather than a lack of planes; and thanks to our efforts at such places as Misburg and Merseburg they ran out of fuel before they ran out of pilots. Thus we gained mastery of the skies, and from D-Day on our troops knew that their enemy was earthbound.

"Military heroism is perhaps mostly a matter of getting used to combat as a way of life, to carrying on in a normal way in an abnormal environment. In our B-24s and B-17s we had no way of warding off the shrapnel fired at us – we had to sit there and take it. Some men of the 493rd could not function in combat and so they were sent home. What were the limits of personal endurance? What if all the missions had been like the one to Magdeburg? We could not know our breaking point. And yet I like to think that if our crew had been ordered to fly a 50-mission tour, as did many bomber crews in the 15th Air Force out of Italy, we'd have done so with no more than the usual number of expletive- punctuated complaints.

In 1944-45 I didn't indulge in philosophical speculations on the turn-in from the IP; as we floated through the flak in our aluminium foxhole, I was trying to climb up into my helmet. Nevertheless, the lesson learned from combat is that there is a lot of luck, chance, and fortune in life. I've been lucky."[40]

On 5 February Gordon Weir was back in the USA eating a meal of milk and apple pie standing at a counter in the swirl of humanity in the palatial Grand Central Station of New York City. The next two weeks he was home at 703 Boccaccio Street in Venice, California.[41]

Notes

1. Correspondence with the author, 13 January 1998.
2. Ibid.
3. *Flying School:Combat Hell* by Ellis M. Woodward (American Library Press Inc, 1998).
4. The other waist gunner was George Spinney.
5. Ibid.
6. *Flying School:Combat Hell* by Ellis M. Woodward (American Library Press Inc, 1998).
7. Ibid.
8. *Flying School:Combat Hell* by Ellis M. Woodward (American Library Press Inc, 1998).
9. Correspondence with the author via Robert M. Foose, 12 December 1982.
10. Group losses totalled 8 when on the return a badly damaged B-17 which crossed the Channel on one engine lost their last engine on final approach to Manston, crash landed, hit a tree, crossed a ditch and knocked down a searchlight tower. Two crew members were killed. *First Over Germany: A History of the 306th Bombardment Group* by Russell A. Strong (Hunter Publishing Company, 1982).
11. Ibid.
12. I am indebted to Brian Francis for this story which he made available from the *WWII Memoirs of Henry K. Wetherhold 1943-1945* (unpublished).
13. Correspondence with the author.
14. Correspondence with the author.
15. Correspondence with the author. See *Home By Christmas? The Story of US 8th/15th Air Force Airmen at War* by Martin W. Bowman (PSL 1987). Bob Harwood, Jim Kelley, Karl Wendell, Russell Tolle, Sam Manipella, Dick Roberts and Ron Fleming bailed out and like Karl Wendel, became prisoners of war. Art Skarsten and George Bulgarelli were KIA.
16. Ibid.
17. Major Griffin was killed on 15 May 1944, one week after VE Day, while performing low level rolls in a P-47 over Bassingbourn airfield.
18. Of 305 German fighters that engaged the 8th Air Force formations, 133 were lost, 73 fighter pilots were killed and 32 sustained injuries. American losses were 16 fighters.

19. Moses had been forced to ditch 42-97794 in the Channel on 12 May 1944 when the target was the Zwickau oil installations. Attacked by fighters en route to the target knocking out the No.4 engine but the prop could not be feathered. On return more fighter attacks knocked out the radio. Aircraft was making a descent towards the Channel at 145-150 mph and losing about 250 ft altitude per minute. When about 5 miles north-east of Dunkirk at about 2,000-3,000 ft, a direct flak burst came through the left side near the upper turret and set the plane on fire. Moses gave the bailout order but as soon as one man had bailed out (and subsequently taken prisoner) the fire was extinguished. 2 men were killed. The 7 survivors were picked up safely by 2 RAF Air Sea Rescue Walrus aircraft at 1700 hours.

20. This B-17 is generally credited with a career spanning 75 combat missions.

21. His widow Byra Louise remarried John Hadley Hemmingway, the son of Ernest Hemmingway in 1949.

22. The name *Lucky Stehley Boy* is likely to have come about some time after Pilot John Sollars flew the ship for the first of 19 missions, 1 April 1944. Apparently his father was a dentist, and his dentistry partner was Mr. Stehley. (Correspondence with Chris French).

23. *The Story of Umbriago*, written in 1998 by Alan Cook.

24. Dave Welty interview with Bob Welty, 28 November 1997, *Recollections of the Mission to Merseburg 21 November 1944*.

25. B-17 43-37825/J was forced to abort the mission over the sea.

26. *Castles In The Air; The Story of the B-17 Flying Fortress crews of the US 8th Air Force* by Martin W. Bowman (PSL, 1984).

27. Colonel Frank P. Hunter, who had flown *Witka Tanke Ton* from Rapid City AAB to England was KIA on 23 January 1945.

28. See *398th Bomb Group Remembrances* by Allen Ostrom (1989). The 492 B-17s in the 3rd Division that attacked communication targets in Germany lost seven Forts and from the 366 Liberators that raided oil refineries at Hamburg/Rhenania, four B-24s were missing.

29. Extracted from an article called, *The Cap* in the *Tri County Canary* newspaper supplement.

30. Cartoonist Al Capp initially conceived of 'Fearless Fosdick' as a parody of Chester Gould's comic strip detective *Dick Tracy*. But the bumbling parody was so popular that Capp used him again and again and he became an integral part of the "Li'l Abner" strip for decades.

31. 43-37877 piloted by 1st Lieutenant Lloyd W. Kersten, co-pilot; Lieutenant Henry Gerland, Tech Sergeants' Arnold Shegal, top turret gunner and John Eberhart, radio operator: Staff Sergeants' Everett Morrison, ball turret gunner; Joe Miller, waist gunner and Maurice Sullivan, tail gunner (7 KIA). Lieutenants' Jim Hyland Jr., navigator and Warren Richhart, bombardier were taken prisoner.

32. Correspondence with the author.

33. Nazi national militia.

34. Oscar's third son Dwight was born just three days after he was killed.

35. Extract from *"The Cap"* in the *"Tri County Canary"* newspaper supplement. Des Lauriers and Oscar Hanson's nephew Jim Hanson became good friends and when Des Lauriers passed away, his family sent Jim the cap, as he wanted him to have it along with his wings because of their friendship.

36. Ibid.

37. Navigator, Ellsworth Quinnell; Flight engineer/top turret gunner, Len Vandal; waist gunner, Joe Heichel and tail gunner, Gordon Bonenberger were the others taken into captivity. Chas O'Reilly and co-pilot Chas Cohen; radio operator, Herman Finklestein and ball turret gunner, Walt Exley were killed.

38. Correspondence with the author via Robert M. Foose.

39. Ibid.

40. Ibid.

41. Gordon Weir died October 5th 2011, just four days short of his 89th birthday.

Chapter Nine

A Battle Zone At Last

I met Earl Sheen just once and that was inside the nose of a '17 on the pre-cold morning of February 3rd, 1945. We were on our way to Berlin, my 35th mission. He was the togglier and I the navigator on the #2 ship alongside the squadron lead ship leading the entire wing. All went well until over the target at 'bombs away'. A burst of flak demolished the lead ship, breaking it in half at the waist. Then we lost the #3 ship. We were the only ship left in the lead element. I didn't know that the hose between my mask and the oxygen regulator had been severed by flak. When I failed to respond to a call from the pilot, Sheen turned around and saw me slumped on the floor. Thirty seconds without oxygen at our altitude and you are gone. I'll never know how long I was out but he managed to revive me by hooking me up to one of those walk around oxygen bottles. We didn't talk much about it afterward.

A Real Good War by Sam Halpert who flew the required 35 missions in the 324th Bomb Squadron between 9 September 1944 and Saturday 3rd February 1945 culminating in an 8 hour 50 minute mission to Berlin on *Mah Ideel.*

In February-March 1945 the 8th Air Force crews would mount the last heavy bomber raids on the Reich capital. Marshal Grigori Zhukov's Red Army was within only 35 miles of Berlin and the capital was jammed with refugees fleeing from the advancing Russians. On Friday night, 2 February, in their 12 man barracks in the 418th Squadron area directly across the narrow asphalt roadway from the Orderly Room hut at Thorpe Abbotts, 2nd Lieutenant Jesse L. Wofford's six enlisted crewmembers as usual, tuned their 120 volt AC radio that one of the crew had brought over from the States, to the American Armed Forces broadcast. On every late night broadcast, the station disc jockey would play the 'Les' Brown record arrangement of *Sentimental Journey* with vocalist Doris Day. Later in the year the DJ said that he didn't intend to play that record anymore and that remark was followed by a sound that seemed to be a breaking crash of a vinyl record. He had obviously been requested to play the song far too many times. At lights out, Algie L. Davenport the 21-year-old engineer/ top turret gunner, from Rossville, Georgia, always took it upon himself to turn the radio off after all were sacked in. He must have been a very patient person since he occupied a top bunk and had to make an extra effort to do that chore. There were three double-stacked wooden bunks on both of the long sides of their crew's half of the hut that they shared with another crew in the other half. They would share the hut with this crew for only two nights before they went down on the New Year's Eve mission to Hamburg. They had not even had time to get to know their names or what crew they were on. About dark on the 31st, a sergeant entered the hut, gathered each of the downed individual's clothes and personal items, stuffed them into the heavy removable cloth mattress cover, gathered them all and left without ever saying one word.

In the middle of the room stood a British "slow but sure" small metal coal burning stove about 3ft high called a "Turtle". Davenport and Carl E. Lindstrom, the 27-year-old armourer, who had a daughter at home in Minneapolis, Minnesota, were the only married members on the EM crew. 'Moanin' Norman F. Bowman, the 20-year-old waist gunner was from Minneapolis also. The two Minneapolis gunners taught several others to play cribbage during barracks time. Reuben Laskow, the 22-year-old radio operator was from Middle Village, Long Island, New York. Raymond R. Uhler the ball turret gunner was from Wooster, Ohio. Joe Urice, the 20-year-old tail gunner of Taft, Texas realized that they were to fly a mission because the small red, green and yellow box at the O.R. was showing green. There were strict black-out requirements on the base at night, so the box was semi-concealed by being enclosed in the three-sided entry way of the hut at about eye level. Joe could always see the box clearly from his lower bunk; it was the first thing he looked at any time he woke during the night so that he might check to see if it had changed. It rarely did, but if it did change it seemed always to go from a no-mission red to a mission-on green.[1]

At Bassingbourn, a RAF pre-war base in distant Cambridgeshire, in a barracks in the 324th Squadron area, some of Weldon Brubaker's crew on *Mah Ideel* were having problems sleeping. Harry Jensen the bombardier was up in his bunk writing a letter home. Sam Halpert was trying to pick up Radio Bremen through the static on the little radio with its cracked case of yellow brown Bakelite. All he could make out was Radio Antwerp before someone played *Don't Fence Me In* with a polka beat on a tiny accordion. Finally, he tuned in to Radio Hamburg with Jack Teagarden fading in and out with *Muskrat Ramble*. Halpert hit the sack and tried to read a book of stories by a writer called Ring Lardner, but he couldn't stay with it. The announcer came on the radio rattling off something in rapid fire German. 'Turn that shit off' Harry Jensen said.

Sam Halpert didn't know when he nodded off but the next thing he knew was someone switching the light rapidly on and off and saying in a flat voice, 'OK let's go; breakfast is at three, briefing at four'. It was the CQ orderly room GI, who they called 'The Hangman'. Halpert awoke in what seemed like half a minute. It was the 'Hangman' again with his flashlight burning into his eyes. 'Breakfast at three; briefing at four. Come on, move it, we're late.'[2]

The routine that Saturday early morning was the same at all the bases. At Debach the Charge of Quarters charged into the hut occupied by the enlisted members on *Miss Green Bay*, turned on the light and said, 'Okay men, maximum effort today. Everybody awake? Get up!' When he went to bed knowing what was coming at 3 am Jack Rude, the 20-year-old nose gunner from Herrin, Illinois on the crew led by Lieutenant Harry B. 'Bud' Harris Junior from Pennsylvania got little sleep and was awake at 3 am when the CQ opened the door. "This day was different than most days when our CQ would take his flashlight, walk from bunk to bunk and politely wake up only the crew members who were flying that day, always being careful not to wake up the wrong person. The CQ's job was tough. Some people were not very nice when they first woke up, but the CQ had to be tough because he did not want to hear later that someone was late, "Because the CQ didn't wake me up." I don't know how a person got the job of waking up flight crews, but we always had the same person, and he knew most of the guy's name and which bunk they slept in. We never had a problem in our hut, but I heard stories of CQs who, instead of getting a thank you, had a boot or something thrown at them. But on this maximum effort day, Anderson Kelley, our waist gunner from Massachusetts, who slept above me, jumped down, put his foot into my back, and said, "Rise and shine Rude. This may be the most exciting day of your life."

"George W. Tedder our radio operator from Florida chimed in with, "Yeah. It may be the last day of your life.'"

Someone else said, "So what. We wouldn't have to wake up at the North Pole anymore."

"Just a very few minutes later, someone said, "I hear the trucks coming. Let's go."

"As the door opened it was spitting a little snow, and I still remember thinking, "Wow, what a way to start the day!"[3]

At Thorpe Abbotts the morning was as cold as it always seemed to be in the winter in Diss and that chill carried over into half of each of the enlisted men's huts. At night men always left their little turtle iron stove burning coal and that helped take the chill off the night. It was probably about 3:30 am when the CQ came in with his flashlight and woke them. They quickly crawled out of their zippered sleeping sacks, which were simple closed sacks made from unlined GI khaki wool blankets with an opening at one end sufficient for one's head to protrude. They then quickly pulled on their two-piece 'long handles', their flying coveralls and shoes for the walking trip to the enlisted chow hall. Of course, the officers had a separate dining room and quarters so the enlisted men didn't see them until joining them later at the briefing hut. After a good breakfast of coffee, fresh eggs and biscuits smeared with orange marmalade, the crews went to the 100th Bomb Group's large briefing hall where the mission of the day was to be announced. Following the staged entrance of the CO and his briefing staff, all of whom proceeded down the centre aisle from the rear, some brief opening remarks were made by the Group Commander, Colonel 'Tom' Jeffrey. Then a curtain was pulled back revealing a huge wall map of Europe. They saw the target route to and out of Berlin. The routes were clearly emphasized by a coloured, pinned ribbon and as usual the return flight was different with it being slightly to the north of the entry route. Jesse Wofford's crew normally flew a different B-17 on every mission. This one would be no different. Wofford, 22-years old and from Jackson, Mississippi, would pilot *White Cargo* on what was to be his crew's most difficult mission.

At Bassingbourn Sam Halpert ate his breakfast in a hurry. 'KPs heaped the powdered eggs, burnt toast, vaselined sausages, bacon and grits on to my tray. I drowned it all with gobs of ketchup and wolfed the eggs down with perhaps four cups of scalding black coffee. I pushed the sausages and most of the grits aside when I recalled the previous mission's jumbo 15 second farts. The bombardier took my grits and sausages and washed them down with the canned grapefruit juice that he called battery acid. Neither of us had much to say through breakfast nor on their way to briefing.

'The hut was filling rapidly with crew members. Most were heavy smokers and they were chain smoking now. Some of the boys chomped on one inch cigar butts, trying to look tough. The place smelt like a dirty ashtray, with a thick layer of smoke hovering like cumulus under the low arched ceiling. The crews greeted each other with smacks on the back and punches on the arm, everyone wearing their own idea of uniform for comfort and warmth. It's was almost like a motorcycle gang. The noise built to such a level that if I wanted to talk to anyone, I would have to shout to be heard over all the chatter but I didn't want to talk to anyone there.

'On a wall where the bottom of a map had been torn off were scrawled letters as crude as a ransom note. Although rubbed away in spots, I could make them out. It said: *'Beware The Handwriting On The Wall – Fog; Fire; Flak; Fighters; Fear; Frost; Flames; Fatigue; Fucking Up; Focke-Wulfs; Foul Weather and this above all – The Five Fickle Fingers of Fate.'*

'Colonel Henry W. Terry bounded up on the platform and the commotion stopped abruptly as a hang-up on the phone. He nodded for the sheet over the map to be removed. The red cord zigged and zagged at different points and wound up at the red blotch near the upper right corner of the map – 'Big-B'. The droning undertone of moans and muttered curses died down when Terry raised his arms and said, 'I'm certain your performance today will reflect further glory on the 91st and those who have gone before. I wish I could be going with you. Good luck men. He saluted us and marched out.'[4]

The raid – one of the few occasions on which the USAAF undertook a mass attack on a city centre – went ahead in the mistaken belief that the German Sixth Panzer Army was moving through Berlin by train on its way to the Eastern Front. It was thought that the Sixth Panzer Army would use the Tempelhof marshalling yards for the move. Lieutenant General James Doolittle, commander of the 8th Air Force, objected to the tactic of bombing the city centre en masse but he was overruled by General Carl 'Tooey' Spaatz, US Strategic Air Force commander in Europe, who was supported by the Supreme Allied commander

General Dwight D. Eisenhower. They emphasized that the need to attack Berlin was of great political importance in that it was designed to assist the Soviet offensive on the Oder east of Berlin and was essential for Allied unity.

At Bassingbourn, 23-year-old Lieutenant Colonel Marvin Dell Lord, who was on his second combat tour (as operations officer of the 91st Bombardment Group) but who had not yet been to Berlin and was eager to lead, would occupy the co-pilot's seat of the 1st Air Division lead ship which was normally occupied by Major Emmanuel 'Manny' Klette, one of the best pilots and leaders in the ETO. Klette would fly 91 combat missions in all, the most of any bomber pilot in the 8th Air Force. His first 21, beginning in March 1943, were as a co-pilot in the 369th Bomb Squadron, 306th Bomb Group. In July 1943 he was upgraded to "first pilot" and assigned a crew, flying seven additional missions before being seriously injured in a crash landing on 23 September. But today the daring and brazen pilot, who had led 1st Lieutenant Frank Lee Adams' crew on 24 missions, was on furlough in London. Adams, a 29-year-old Texan born in Randall County was living in Hollywood, California when he had enlisted. Lord was a Silver Star recipient from a previous combat tour, was near the end of his second, voluntary tour in bombers and was a former squadron commander and group staff officer. He had a wife, Evelyn and baby daughter, Marilyn back home in Milwaukee, Wisconsin. His cheerful, upbeat personality was a contrast to the sombre Klette, who would thoroughly study the details of bombing missions and had learned how to operate every piece of equipment on a B-17. Some who flew with him claimed he had a death wish. For the Berlin mission lead pilot Lord would have Adams and nine other crewmembers for company. It would be 23-year-old Tech Sergeant John Porter Holbrook, the radio operator's 79th mission, Tech Sergeants' David C. McCall, the engineer his 81st and George R. Zenz the waist gunner from Brown County, Wisconsin, his 105th. The 24-year-old bombardier, Nando 'Tony' Cavalieri from Cook County, Illinois, had learned that morning of his promotion to captain.

In the 34th Bomb Group at Mendlesham, Tech Sergeant Raymond H. Fredette the 24-year-old togg.lier from Massachusetts on the crew of *Fancy Nancy*, began the day knowing that someone had scratched *Fat Boy Hector* – referring to his girth and middle name – on the chin turret of his crew's Fortress. The day before, a crewmate had kidded him about his waist size in a way that may not have been meant badly but was not well received. 'It was not with great relish that I got up this morning", he wrote in his diary. This would be his 21st mission on the crew led by 1st Lieutenant John F. Schroeder of West Portsmouth, Ohio.

First Lieutenant Bob Des Lauriers, co-pilot on *Purty Chili* captained by 1st Lieutenant Dean Hansen, was down to fly his 12th mission. Painted underneath Des Lauriers' cockpit window was the name 'Shirley' in honour of his sweetheart, Shirley Marie McHenry, who he had met in Sioux City, Iowa during his military training months earlier. One story claims that the name was in honour of Chili Williams, a well-endowed Hollywood starlet. Another was that on one of *Purty*

Chili's first missions the co-pilot inquired of each crewman how it was at his position? Reportedly, the tail gunner's reply was always, *Purty Chili back here*! When Hanson's crew finished their tour on *Purty Chili* she was reassigned to 1st Lieutenant William H. Wilcox's crew who would fly the bomber right up until VE-Day. Harold E. Province, who flew most of his 19 missions as togglier on the crew, painted his girl's name "ILA", with black in letters about 3 inches high immediately above the P of PURTY just behind the left cheek gun.[5]

At Hardwick 1st Lieutenant William Lozowski's B-24 crew prepared to fly their 30th mission. Bill Lozowski had worked at AMPCO Metal while living in Milwaukee, Wisconsin before entering the service in 1942. He wanted to fly and graduated as a B-24 pilot while stationed in Fort Worth. While in training he met Iris Thompson of Waco and they had married on 9 July 1944. During flak leave at Tiverton Manor, Lozowski wrote to Iris telling her that he was anxious to return to Hardwick to complete his tour of 35 missions and he also looked forward to returning home as he and Iris were expecting their first child in April.[6]

In the pre-dawn hours of darkness, American-manned de Havilland Mosquitoes of the 25th Bombardment Group at Watton, Norfolk flew weather- and target-reconnaissance missions ahead of the main force and the force of 122 of the RAF's 'Wooden Wonders' returned from a strike on Berlin. The weather flights were identified by the code name 'Blue Stocking'. As fog and murk shrouded bases in East Anglia until sunrise, the 'Blue Stocking' Mosquitoes, flown by a pilot and a navigator trained in meteorology reported correctly that the day was going to be largely clear.

In the forenoon the massive American armada totalling 1,437 B-17s and B-24s and 15,000 crew members in 42 bombardment groups in three air divisions became airborne for attacks on Berlin and Magdeburg, the bomber stream stretching all the way from Holland to Berlin covered by 948 fighters. The Tempelhof marshalling yards were the primary target of just over 1,000 Fortresses and 434 Liberators were to strike the synthetic oil plant at Magdeburg. The B-17 bombardiers were to use the Friedrichstrasse Bahnhof as their aiming point.

Major Robert 'Rosie' Rosenthal of the 100th Bombardment Group, who was flying his 52nd mission, led the 3rd Air Division on this raid, General Earle E. Partridge having approved the selection of a squadron commander to lead the division. Rosenthal was a graduate of Brooklyn College and Brooklyn Law School and joined one of the largest law firms in New York City. When the Imperial Japanese Navy attacked Pearl Harbor on 7 December 1941 he was playing basketball with his best friend in a Manhattan park. He had heard the stories of the Nazi atrocities and it upset him terribly. He enlisted in the United States Army the following day and requested to be trained as a bomber pilot because he felt that was the best way of causing the greatest amount of damage to the enemy.

At Mendlesham Ray Fredette had encountered a problem as he went to load his .50 calibre machine guns in the chin turret. 'I had quite a bit of trouble since the spring forming the bolt that guided the ammunition to the guns' feed way, was disengaged. I ripped up my B-10 jacket as I reached down in the turret to put my right gun in such a condition that it would fire. After doing that, I discovered that someone had loaded the ammunition in backward with the single link of the belt on the receiver. My patience was almost at an end as I changed the ammunition and reloaded. When I found the ammunition for the navigator's gun put in the same wrong way I was raving mad. I assisted the navigator in changing his ammunition.'

At 0807 hours *Fancy Nancy* had taken off from and crossed the North Sea in 'an endless procession of planes neatly arranged in battle formation,' wrote Fredette. 'The number of bombers was something beyond the imagination.' He watched one of the B-17s in his combat box bouncing up and down. Turbulence was always a problem but he saw this as 'a case of a nervous pilot bouncing his crew around. "We hit the Dutch coast at Bergen an Zee just north of Altmark, carefully flying the plotted course top avoid flak defences in the vicinity." As the flak opened up it crossed Fredette's mind that an infantryman would never charge into an artillery barrage, yet B-17 crews flew directly into exploding shells on every mission.

The bomber stream was at 27,000 feet when it passed over Holland. It would take three hours for all the bombers to pass overhead. In the 398th Bomb Group formation 24-year-old 1st Lieutenant Perry E. Powell, of Grand Island, Nebraska, had taken his B-17 off from Nuthampstead and was en route to the target when near Lemke in Holland his B-17G slewed out of control, veered right and broke in half. The two halves slammed into *Maude an' Maria* flown by 26-year-old 1st Lieutenant John R. McCormick of DeKalb, Illinois, tearing a 20 ft slice of metal skin from the left hand side of the bomber and leaving a gash through which others in the formation could see the inside of the aircraft. Tragically, the 23-year-old navigator, 1st Lieutenant Ray R. Woltman, who not wearing a parachute was catapulted into the open sky. McCormick tried to help his 26-year-old co-pilot, 1st Lieutenant William Feinstein remove the entry (and exit) hatch below them but the parachute belonging to the 21-year-old engineer-gunner Tech Sergeant Marvin Gooden had burst open inside the Fortress and billowed around them, impairing both vision and movement as they struggled to bail out amid howling wind and flying debris. Once the hatch was gone, McCormick watched Feinstein thrown upward and out, just as the Fortress careened abruptly to the left. The No.2 propeller blade slashed into Feinstein's body and threw him into the wing, tearing off an arm. Feinstein's parachute never opened. McCormick, who was tossed out of the open exit hatch and lived to tell the tale, was captured. The 25-year-old togglier, Staff Sergeant William G. Logan, who bailed out through a door in the nose of *Maude an'Maria* was the only other survivor. He was captured three days' later in Rassen (Uelsen) in

Germany, sent to Oberursel for interrogation and ended the war in a PoW camp. On 4 April 1945 Bill Logan was killed by friendly fire from P-47s on a forced march, south of Nürnberg. He left a widow Mary in New York who had waited in vain for his return.

Staff Sergeant Joseph 'Dave' Bancroft the 23-year-old tail gunner from Louisville, Kentucky was the sole survivor on Powell's B-17. He was alone at the instant of collision. When his aircraft began to break in half, Bancroft saw a pair of hands, probably the waist gunner's, reaching toward him just a few feet forward in the fuselage. Bancroft grabbed the hands but was unable to pull the other crew member back to his tail-gun position. The front part of the B-17 fell away and the hands disappeared. Alone in the tail section, Bancroft plummeted downward. He struggled against centrifugal forces to open the tail-hatch door but it was jammed. He kicked, wrestled, pushed and, after almost giving up, the door suddenly fell out and he bailed out. Bancroft, Logan and McCormick were the only survivors out of eighteen men on the two B-17s that collided.

When the first wave of Flying Fortresses reached 'Big B', the last Fortress was still over the Zuider Zee in Holland. The stream of bombers, from one end to the other, was 360 miles long. Group after group arrived over Berlin. Altogether, fully 90 minutes would elapse while the bomber formation passed over the capital. For almost two hours, Fortresses approached and passed over Berlin.

'As we approached Potsdam' recalled Ray Fredette, 'there were large breaks in the clouds over the ill-fated capital. Large portions of Berlin were visible. Smoke was rising from the bomb hits scored by other bomb groups that had preceded us. Bomb bay doors were open now and there was flak up ahead. But for the first time I was more intent on the target than the flak. I felt exhilarated. It was a fairly long bomb run. I was fully aware of the entire situation – hundreds of bombers bearing down with tons of high explosives to be dropped on Berlin. My fingers twitched as I held the toggle [bomb release] switch. My eyes were glued on the lead ship. Then its bombs dropped along with two white smoke markers that hurtled downward. This was it. I struck the toggle switch and two tons of explosives in *Fancy Nancy*'s bomb bay fell away.' *Fancy Nancy*'s journey out of Berlin was 'exhausting.' Yet the crew never saw a German fighter.

Robert Des Lauriers, co-pilot on *Purty Chili* noted in his diary that his crew was in the air for 8 hours 30 minutes. He thought he saw German fighters in the distance. He noted that the German flak was 'exceedingly accurate.'[7] As they flew toward the target, each succeeding battery of flak bursts moved closer to the formation. This was when the sweat begun. Every crewmember wondered if they would reach 'bombs away' before the anti-aircraft gunners made the final correction that would put their bursts in the middle of the formation.

In the lead ship in the 91st Bomb Group formation Tony Cavalieri engaged his Norden bombsight at the start of the bomb run before releasing the high explosive bombs and smoke marker bomb, which was the signal for the bombardiers in the other ships to pull a toggle switch releasing their aircraft's bombs. Immediately after 'bombs away' and before Adams could begin his evasive turn, the lead ship received a direct hit from an anti-aircraft shell in front of the radio operator's position, right where the trailing edge of the wing met the fuselage and was blown cleanly in half. The nose section went immediately into a dive with engines still under power and exploded throwing debris and crew all over the sky, the main wreckage falling onto Bellevue-Allee in the Tiergarten near the Brandenburg Gate. The tail section appeared to fly along with the formation for a split second before fluttering back over the top of the rear element, slowly tipping over before spinning downward and was soon lost from sight. Marvin Lord and all ten crew members on Frank Adams' crew were killed.

The B-17s dropped 2,267 tons of bombs into the Friedrichstadt and Luisenstadt and the Mitte and some other areas, such as Friedrichshain. The bombs used in this raid consisted mostly of high explosive ordnance and not incendiary munitions. The togglier on *Supermouse* in the 388th Bomb Group at Knettishall wrote in his diary: Berlin, Saturday. Barrage flak, weakening as each group went over. No damage to ship. Visual! 5 x 1,000 pounders. Shacked women and children!

The bombing was so dense that it caused a city fire spreading eastwards, driven by the wind, over the south of Friedrichstadt and the northwest of neighbouring Luisenstadt. The fire was to last for four days until it had burnt everything combustible in its range to ashes and after it had reached waterways, large thoroughfares and parks that the fire could not cross. 'Gigantic clouds of smoke hang over the whole city' wrote Hans-Georg Von Studnitz. 'The Adlon received seven direct hits, which destroyed the two upper floors and annihilated a cinema opposite. The hotel shelter is a foot deep in water that has leaked through from the melting snow above. Many people had to wade about underground for two hours in icy water. Under the heavy explosions the massive shelter swayed and shivered like the cellar of an ordinary house. Finally all the lights went out and we felt as though we had been buried alive.

'The Schlöss, the Esplanade and Fürstenhof hotels and the newspaper district were all burning. The German Office of Information and the Transocean Agency have been put out of action and the Antiques Section of the AWAG (formerly Wertheim) Department Store, now located at Lennestrasse have been destroyed. Unexploded bombs and huge puddles of water fed from burst mains have made the streets impassable. Above this scene of desolation, hangs, night after night, a moonless sky, tinged with streaks of blood-red and sinister, pale yellow.'[8]

Herbe Granberg, Berlin correspondent of the Stockholm *Afton-bladet* sought safety in an underground railway tunnel, one of Berlin's 'safest' shelters. 'Thousands of people stood in clusters or sat in overcoats along the massive concrete walls – grotesque in the ghostly light' he wrote. 'The first bombs came. The ground heaved, lights flickered. It seemed the concrete walls bulged. People scrambled about like frightened animals. A girl in a group of Russian labourers began to sing mass. 'Shut up,' somebody shouted, but the girl sang on. Then came the next load, six or seven right above us and a string farther away. The light in the tunnel went out. We sat in the musty darkness. Some pocket torches were lit, but they proved useless in the cloud of chalky dust which came welling through the tunnel. It penetrated the eyes, the mouth, the nose and ears. People kneeled and prayed. After ear-shattering explosions there was silence. Air pressure increased in the tunnel and I held my mouth open to equalize the impact on the ear drums. A heavy bomb had crashed through the tunnel roof a couple of hundred yards away. A wave of cold air followed the dust.

'Quit smoking' someone shouted in the darkness and several hysterical, persons took up the cry. In the distance someone yelled for a doctor, but the clamour for help, taken up by many voices, was drowned in the next wave of bombs. The explosions shook the concrete structure. By the crash you could tell several bombs had pierced the upper floor of the elevated railway station. 'For heaven's sake stop it, put an end to this insanity, put an end to the war' a woman screamed. 'Shut up with that' broke in a man's voice and a stir ran through the tightly packed shelters.

'Four more strings of bombs tumbled down. Finally there was a long silence in expectation of the 'All Clear' signal. It was difficult to breathe in the dust. No one said much. Some men discussed in low voices the types of bombers above.

'In the elevated station there were dead. One man on a stretcher apparently had had his lungs crushed by air pressure.

'Hardly anyone rushing out of the tunnel paid attention to the dead. Everyone had his own troubles to take care of. In the square a hurricane of fire raged. Smoke and flames limited visibility to fewer than 100 yards. I was blinded by smoke and soot.

'Even before I arrived at my hotel I knew I had been bombed out for the fourth time. It was the Esplanada Hotel and it had been crushed by nine heavy bombs, of which six were direct hits.

'I experienced more than 700 alerts and at least half as many attacks during two and a half years in Berlin and this attack was unquestionably one of the war's worst. Deep bomb craters blocked the Bellevue Strasse and many buildings along it were burning, including the detested People's Court. Germans were rushing past with bundles and suitcases.

'It began to rain. Time-bombs started bursting. The detonations could be heard for two days. Every other street was blocked because of duds – waiting for life-time convicts to remove the charges.

'Water, gas and electricity were restored temporarily only after a long time and for over two weeks it was possible to telephone from only one sector of the city.'

Photo-reconnaissance later revealed that an area 1½ miles square, stretching across the southern half of the Mitte had been devastated, destroying 360 industrial firms, heavily damaging another 170. The area that suffered the greatest damage did not include railway main lines, which were more northern (Stadtbahn) and southern (Ringbahn), but did include two terminal stations of

Berlin (Anhalter and Potsdamer Bahnhof, the latter of which had already been out of service since 1944 due to bomb destruction). The German Air Ministry sustained considerable damage, the Chancellery was hard hit. A number of monuments, such as the French Luisenstadt Church, St. James Church, Jerusalem's Church, St. Michael's Church, St. Simeon Church and the Marcher Protestant Consistory as well as government and Nazi Party buildings were also hit. They included the Reich Chancellery, the Party Chancellery, the Gestapo headquarters on Prinz-Albrechtstrasse – previously untouched by the war – and the Third Reich's Volksgerichtshof or 'People's Court'. Among the dead was the President of the Court, Roland Freisler, the notorious 'hanging judge'. The Unter den Linden, Wilhelmstrasse and Friedrichstrasse areas were turned into seas of ruins. The death toll amounted to 2,894, fewer than might have been expected because the raid took place in daytime with relatively few incendiary bombs. A direct hit on the underground station alone killed 320 refugees from the East. The number of wounded amounted to 20,000 and 120,000 were left homeless or 'de-housed'.

The 8th lost 23 bombers over the capital and another six crash-landed inside the Russian lines. The B-17 flown by Major 'Rosie' Rosenthal, flying with Captain John Ernst, was hit in the No.1 gas' tank and the bomb bay a few seconds before 'bombs away'. Although his bomber was in flames 'Rosie' continued to the target to drop his bombs and then stayed with the plane until after the rest of the crew had bailed out, just before it exploded at only 1,000 ft altitude. Ten of the crew reached the ground safely. The bombardier was killed. Ernst caught his leg on a jagged edge of the bomb bay while baling out and he later had the leg amputated. Rosenthal landed in Soviet territory and he was later reported to be in Moscow. Four other B-17s in the 100th Bomb Group failed to return. *White Cargo* piloted by 2nd Lieutenant Jesse Wofford was hit at 'bombs away' and immediately fell, possibly 5,000 ft, (although Lieutenant Leonard Furmin the 24-year-old navigator estimated 1,000 ft) but although badly damaged, the crew made it home. Wofford received the DFC for the effort.

Bill Lozowski's B-24 in the 93rd Bomb Group developed engine problems and had to leave the formation. The co-pilot, Lieutenant Frank C. Glut, born Chicago, Illinois, shut off the engine but too much oil had been lost and the propeller would not feather. The wind milling caused drag and they began to lose altitude rapidly. Suddenly, they took a flak hit and Lozowski gave the order to bail out. Lieutenant Arthur Schleicher, bombardier, Tech Sergeant Seymour Weisman, top turret gunner and Staff Sergeant John Corradetti, bombardier managed to bail out safely. Cornelius Carter the tail gunner, Paul Colby, radio operator and James Seger, right waist gunner, who were wounded, were found in the aft section of the Liberator. Frank Glut, Lieutenant Anthony Marulli, navigator and Bill Lozowski were too near to the ground for their parachutes to open fully. They died on impact in a farmer's ploughed field. The deceased were buried in the town of Benthe. Later they were temporarily buried in Belgium and finally laid permanently to rest back home. Julia Glut, the co-pilot's widow, learned that in the wreckage a pair of baby shoes had been found. She knew that Frank had always taken them along with him on missions for good luck, as they belonged to their son Donald.[9]

Among the other losses was *The Birmingham Jewel*, a B-17 in the 379th Bomb Group at Kimbolton in Cambridgeshire, which had flown its 100th mission on 10 November, and was due to set an 8th Air Force record of 128 missions on 3 February. The original pilot, 2nd Lieutenant Walter W. Smith had named the bomber after his wife Jewell, and his hometown, Birmingham, Alabama. The words *The Birmingham Jewel* were written over a diamond on both sides of nose. Upon losing an engine 50 miles from Berlin the Fortress had to drop out of formation. 1st Lieutenant William A. Webber of Topeka, Kansas and his co-pilot, 2nd Lieutenant James T. Kiester from Tacoma, Washington tried to get the bomber back to England on its own but near Rendsburg three Bf 109s shot the plane down and it crashed at Ilvenstedt killing Webber, Staff Sergeants' Ray Weatherbee, nose gunner and Bill Walls, ball turret gunner and radio operator Tech Sergeant Carl McHenry on the nine man crew.

The B-17 flown by 2nd Lieutenant Daniel G. Shoemaker in the 305th Bomb Group, which had been briefed to bomb the Tempelhof marshalling yards, had been brought home to Chelveston on 18 July 1944 by Cecil Tipper after a 500 lb bomb smashed through the nose of the aircraft over Peenemünde which killed Lieutenant Louis J. Simpson the navigator. Shoemaker's crew reached the IP, turned off the Tokyo tanks and started throwing out chaff. When they began their bomb run flak was bursting around the Group ahead. Just before 'bombs away' a burst of flak knocked out the pilots' windshield. Then the tail gun position was hit and Sergeant Galeyn Snyder's leg was shot off at the knee and only held on by what appeared to be tendons and skin. The top turret had a flak-hole dead centre in the top of the dome. There were about 16 holes in the radio room and Staff Sergeant Raymond J. Benton had three wounds in his left leg. Flak had knocked out the windshield and stunned Shoemaker who slumped over in his seat. He revived and went down in the nose to keep warm but called back to say that he was still cold. Co-pilot, 2nd Lieutenant Roy F. 'Fred' Moullen, meanwhile, had taken over flying the B-17. When the fire got more intense and the heat was starting to curl the skin he ditched in the sea at 200 mph. Moullen and Sergeant Ira Roisman the engineer were the only survivors. They were picked up by a rescue boat and put ashore at Great Yarmouth where they were taken to the Royal Naval Hospital and given further medical aid.

The 306th Bomb Group diary at Thurleigh read: No enemy fighter opposition was encountered. Intense and accurate flak tracked the group for eight minutes in the target area.' The 'Clay Pigeons' Squadron took the brunt of the assault; all three Fortresses that were missing were from the 367th Squadron. One of these was the *Rose of York*, a 62-mission veteran piloted by 1st Lieutenant Vernor Frank Daley Jr., a 26-year-old Texan, born in San Antonio who had enlisted on 24 September 1942 with several crewmembers who were completing their tours. Named for the then Princess Elizabeth Windsor (now Queen Elizabeth II) the *Rose of York* was originally named *Princess Elizabeth* but that did not meet with any official approval. The aircraft was renamed *Rose of York* instead and was christened by the Princess on her royal visit to Thurleigh on 6 July 1944.

Daley and his crew also found room for 26-year-old Guy Byam of the BBC and W. E. West of Associated Press. Guy Byam-Corstiaens (later known as just Guy Byam) had joined the Royal Navy and was among the 68 survivors of the 254 men on board HMS *Jervis Bay* which was sunk on 5 November 1940 in the North Atlantic. Byam had swum through oily waters before being rescued and that cost him the sight in his right eye. He was thus relieved from duty and started working for an engineering company before joining the BBC French Service in November 1942 as a sub-editor. In April 1944 he started working for the BBC's War Reporting Unit and jumped with the airborne troops on D-Day, 6 June 1944 and in Operation 'Market-Garden' in Holland in September 1944. His reports made him a household name. One engine on *Rose of York* was shot out over the target and another was streaming gasoline. Daley lagged behind the formation on the trip home. About two-thirds of the way across the North Sea Tech Sergeant Porfirio J. Marquez the 24-year-old radio operator from Tyrone, New Mexico radioed the air commander that they had one engine out and another trailing gasoline. The plane was last heard heading for the English coast. Daley radioed that he thought he could make it back to England but nothing more was heard and the B-17 and its crew were never found. A listener wrote after Byam's death: 'All looked forward to hearing his enthusiastic and youthful voice in the 9 o'clock news.'

Ninety-three bombers returned with varying degrees of major flak damage. Many carried men wounded in action. Then there were the unlucky ones. Among those that returned safely from the tumult over Berlin was *Blue Grass Girl* in the 486th Bombardment Group at Sudbury in Suffolk, piloted by 1st Lieutenant Lewis K. Cloud a 23-year-old Texan living in Louisville, Kentucky. All the crew were on their 35th and final mission were looking forward to receiving their 'Lucky Bastard Club' certificates and going home. No one will ever be able to say with certainty how the B-17 suddenly caught fire but the whole of the rear fuselage was soon engulfed in flames. The fire could have been caused by coloured flares fired from a Very pistol out the waist-gun hatch to celebrate their homecoming. *Blue Grass Girl* dropped away from the formation and only four parachutes appeared before the Fortress crashed into a field at Church Farm, Reydon not far from Southwold with Cloud still at the controls. Staff Sergeant 'Johnnie' L. Jones the ball turret gunner bailed out but by then the flaming bomber was too close to the ground and his parachute did not open.

At Mendlesham that night, Saturday, 3 February, Ray Fredette on *Fancy Nancy* wrote in his diary: 'Berlin! Berlin! The very name of this city pounded on my brains. This was the heart of Nazi-land. This was the city where Hitler had preached his defiance to the world. This was the city where the throngs had shouted 'Sieg Heil!' but today it was the shriek of falling bombs and the rocking explosions that were heard throughout Berlin.' After flying six 'Chowhound' mercy missions to Holland in *'Bottom's Up'* in early May, on 24 June 1945 his crew flew *Fancy Nancy* back to the United States.

Three days after the attack on Berlin strategic missions resumed and they became the order of the day throughout February when, weather permitting, many hundreds of heavy bomber sorties were flown each day against marshalling yards and synthetic oil and benzol plants in the ever diminishing Reich. On 21 February over 1,200 B-17s and B-24s protected by nearly 800 fighter escorts were dispatched to the marshalling yards at Nuremberg. There were no bomber losses but seven fighters were shot down. Next day, General Carl Spaatz unleashed Operation 'Clarion' during which 3,500 bombers and nearly 5,000 fighters attacked 200 German communication network targets in an attempt to destroy all enemy transportation. During these attacks when some of the American bombers were unable to see their targets they dumped their bombs on targets of opportunity. On 23 February in the vicinity of the great Bavarian castle of Mad King Ludwig lay Ellingen, a small town of 1,500 inhabitants, most of them farmers and of no military value was picked out for none other reason than it had a road running through it. Twenty-five bombers dropped 285 high explosive bombs on the town which killed 98 villagers and left 120 bomb craters. A note by General Frederick Anderson, deputy commander of the US Strategic Air Forces in Europe under Spaatz to his press office said that such operations were 'not expected in themselves to shorten the war... However, it is expected that the fact that Germany was struck all over will be passed on, from father to son, thence to grandson; that a deterrent for the initiation of future wars will definitely result.'

His views were echoed by Portal and Harris, who, though German defeat was clearly imminent, had further advocated even more destruction being visited upon cities such as Chemnitz, Dresden and the rest of Berlin to cause confusion in the evacuation of refugees fleeing from the Red Army in the east. Operation 'Thunderclap' which had been planned to cause as much confusion and mayhem in Berlin, Leipzig, Chemnitz and Dresden as possible had gone ahead on 13/14 February with a devastating raid on Dresden. The Associated Press finally admitted that 'the Allied air commanders have made the long-awaited decision to adopt deliberate terror-bombing of the great German population centres.'

On 26 February 1,204 B-17s and B-24s escorted by 15 fighter groups totalling 726 Mustangs and Thunderbolts were sent to hit three rail stations in Berlin. In the 305th Bomb Group at Chelveston 19-year-old Staff Sergeant Leon G. Mehring, the B-17 engineer/gunner on *Miss Dee Day* was awakened about 8 am for his first mission. 'There was light ground fog but heavy cloud cover" recalled Mehring, who was born in Butte, Montana and was living in Cedar Rapids, Iowa. "We ate breakfast of fresh eggs and then went over to briefing. A moan went up amongst the men, as we had been to Munich the day before. We were told, 'You will have a big tail wind (over 100 mph) all the way to Berlin after assembly. Because of the wind you will fly straight to Berlin'. In fact we made Berlin in three hours. This was my first sight of heavy flak; it was all around us, on both sides of us, below us, just everywhere. I was sure I would meet my maker this day. I was terrified but luck was with us. Bombs away and we turned and headed for home, now straight into that 100 mph wind. Six hours and 15 minutes to get back to base. Fuel consumption was heavy and it seemed we were getting nowhere. After a couple of hours our Group commander told us all we were to drop to 10,000 ft to see if the wind would be less. However, it turned out to be not so.

'At 10,000 ft we were off oxygen, took off our gloves and had a bit more freedom. We were sitting ducks at our slow ground speed but for some reason they never attacked us. We were ordered to throw out everything to make the plane lighter – flak jackets and helmets and ammo for a start. After helmets were gone I opened my gun cover and my luck ran out. A 50-calibre shell exploded and my hands and eyes were burned from the powder. I was temporarily blinded and that's all I could remember for a while. The rest of the crew completed my job and I was taken to the radio room. The engineer came back and poured sulphur powder on my face and hands. We must have made it back to base as the next thing I remember I was being put in an ambulance and taken to the base hospital for treatment.' Leon would complete his 11th and final mission of the war on 24 April 1945.

At Rougham Doug Sharp, a ball turret gunner in the 331st Squadron, whose wife was expecting a child, had been up since 0300 hours for what would be his 23rd mission, knowing Berlin was always a 'tough cookie'. 'But, everything went our way' he wrote. 'The sky was covered with clouds and we buzzed across Berlin and dropped our bombs. The flak was moderate but very inaccurate. The mission took about nine hours. We were on oxygen about five hours and saw no enemy fighters.' Even the normally notorious flak defences in Berlin could shoot down only five bombers."

In all, 1,066 sorties were deemed 'effective' with 363 Fortresses of the 1st Division aiming for the Schlesischer Ostbahnhof (Berlin East) and dropping just over 895 tons of bombs and 418 B-17s of the 3rd Division aiming for Alexanderplatz station in the Mitte dropped just over 1,250 tons. The Liberators aimed for Berlin Nord bahnhof (North Station) in Pankow, dropping 650 tons of bombs. Forty-six bombers dropped their bombs on Osnabrück, Eberswalde and other targets of opportunity. One aborting B-17 crashed in France and two B-24s were abandoned over Soviet-held territory. For just three Fortresses shot down, a total of 1,135 bombers dropped 2,886.2 tons of bombs on the raids, which left another 80,000 people homeless.

Notes

1. See Joe R. Urice's complete story on the 100th Bomb Group Foundation website.
2. *A Real Good War* by Sam Halpert.
3. *Miss Green Bay* by Jack Rude with Richard Wagner (Independently published, March 2020).
4. *A Real Good War* by Sam Halpert.
5. The June 1992 issue of *Mendlesham Memories* and *B-17 Flying Fortress Units of the Eighth Air Force* (Part 2) by Martin W. Bowman (Osprey Combat Aircraft 36 2006).
6. *A Tribute to Uncle Bill* by Carol Kozowski Gerard, *2nd AD Journal, Vol. 36 No.3, Fall 1997.*
7. Des Lauriers survived his missions and in 1949 he graduated from the University of Colorado at Boulder with a BS in Architectural Engineering. Altogether he spent 6 months flying 33 missions. On VJ Day, following an Honourable Discharge he married Shirley Marie McHenry in Sioux City, Iowa where they had met during his military training months earlier.
8. Ibid.
9. *A Tribute to Uncle Bill* by Carol Kozowski Gerard, *2nd AD Journal, Vol. 36 No.3, Fall 1997.*

Chapter Ten

Zossen

'...the German Officer Training groups that were housed in tents wouldn't enjoy their reveille call consisting of 250 lb bombs raining down and through their housing facilities.

Lieutenant Henry 'Hank' Wentland, a B-24 Liberator pilot in the 564th Squadron, 389th Bomb Group 'Sky Scorpions' at Hethel near Norwich, 15 March 1945. Starting in 1937, the German Army began building a command centre at Wünsdorf south of Berlin. The first sector completed was code named 'Maybach I'. The complex of 12 three-storey buildings, connected underground with reinforced bunkers served as the HQ of the Army High Command. In 1940 the second sector, 'Maybach II', was completed and was populated by the operational staff of the High Command of the Armed Forces (Oberkommando der Wehrmacht, or OKW) and was separated from 'Maybach I' by tall fences and barbed wire. Post-war western parlance often referred to the entire command centre as Zossen, named after the city nearby.

Born in Savannah, Georgia on 11 June 1923, by 1941 William Whitfield Varnedoe Jnr. was a student at Georgia Tech. When the US entered the war the school went to year round classes, squeezing a semester into the summer so that by November 1943 he was already making choices for his junior year. "There never was a question of whether I would go to war; it was just a matter of how and when. After Pearl Harbor took place in my freshman Sunday make-up drafting class, I knew that I was destined to fight." He started combat at Great Ashfield as a navigator in 2nd Lieutenant George H. Crow's crew in the 550th Squadron, 385th Bomb Group who took the nickname "Van's Valiants" after their first Commanding Officer, Colonel Elliot Vandevanter. Varnedoe's B-17 was called *Possible Straight*, because the last three numbers on its tail were '123'. Varnedoe would fly 26 missions in 1945 beginning on 1st March when the target was a railroad marshalling yard at Ülm. "It was our first mission as a full crew. We flew left wing off Lieutenant Alexander Rusecky's crew [in *Sugar-Jo*]. Chuck Armbruster's crew in *Mr. Lucky* was above and to the right of us. After assembly over England, we headed out over the Channel and began to climb to our cruising altitude en route. As we approached the Belgian coast, we also reached 10,000 ft and went on oxygen. There was a cloud deck just below the

Group. It was mostly flat and smooth on top, except that there were occasional humps of cloud here and there. Just as we reached the Belgian coast Rusecky passed into one of these humps and came up out of it in a steep climb just over us and into Armbruster's Fort. *Mr. Lucky* was contacted by Nos.1 and 2 engines of Rusecky's B-17, which cut into *Mr. Lucky* about the rear of the radio room. Rusecky slid back chewing up the waist section of Armbruster's plane, which was now in two separate pieces.

'I lost sight of Rusecky's Fort and the tail of *Mr. Lucky*, as I focused on the front half which was sliding to the left and dropping and was now mighty close to us on our level. I could clearly see Armbruster, looking back over his left shoulder trying to see what was happening. As he continued to slide toward us, Crow pulled us left, out of formation, or there would have been three planes in the collision. Armbruster's front half went into a flat spin and disappeared into the clouds, so near below. We then edged back into the lead slot, where Rusecky had been moments before. It was very eerie seeing all that metal ripping apart only yards away, but without making a sound as if in a silent movie. The constant, deafening roar of our own engines drowned out everything. Another lasting image was the sight of the radio operator falling out of Armbruster's plane – without his parachute. The whole thing was over in less than 15 seconds. Later we learned that Sergeant Stanley Lejkowski, the waist gunner of Rusecky's crew, who bailed out, and Joe Jones the tail gunner on Armbruster's crew, had survived. Jones tried to bail out his tail hatch, but it was jammed shut; he tried to go to the waist, but twisted metal blocked the way, so he sat back down in the tail. Joe popped his chute and tried to stuff it out of a broken window, but the air rushing by was too strong and this came to naught. In the end he just sat down and had a smoke, waiting. Six days later he woke up in a British hospital!"[1]

Next day, *Possible Straight* was part of a formation being pummelled by enemy fire on the mission to Ruhland and Dresden by 455 B-17s in the 3rd Air Division which cost eight Forts. Bill Varnedoe had lined up a machine gun on an enemy fighter, but nothing happened when he pulled the trigger. He used gloved hands to open the ammunition box. It was 40 degrees below zero at altitude so he could not touch metal with bare skin. He found a bent link in the chain of bullets that fed the machine gun, fixed it, and within a moment had turned his attention back outside the plane. "They had shot down both of my wingmen" Varnedoe said" and also the plane that had been in front of his. Altogether 'Van's Valiants' lost four B-17s including *Jeanie Beanie, Perry's Pirates* and *Leading Lady* in the attacks. "The war wasn't over yet" Varnedoe wrote.

Lieutenant Hank Wentland had also flown his first mission on 1 March, to the marshalling yards at Ingolstadt. 'Immediately after the debriefing session of our first mission (and while the jigger of medical libation still addled my brain), I thought to visit the CO of the 564th and ask for a transfer back to Stateside. My reason was that Mission #1 had made me as expert on aerial warfare as I ever would be. Consequently, I felt I would be of more value to the war effort back home at some Advanced Training Center preparing new crews for the realities of aerial warfare. However, the bike ride back to the 564th area must have cleared my brain somewhat because I didn't stop at Squadron HQ after all. You see with a clearer head I reasoned that our CO just wouldn't have grasped the significance of my request.'

All the occupants of his Quonset hut were agreeable in his eyes, even if 'Chuck' Dearing could not be convinced of his 'very audible breathing' (snoring) during the night. The arrival of a package containing edible items such as cakes, cookies, candy, or the like was normally shared with all. One day Hanks received a package, which he eagerly tore open in anticipation – only to find that the wrapping concealed a sealed box of Lux soap powder. 'What the heck am I going to do with this?' I uttered. 'You can always help me to do my delicate undies' – to which I replied, 'Wise guy. I'll share it out with the others by putting it in the latrine.' Returning to my sack, I felt a bit benevolent at sharing my gift. After all, this was really a generous present, since soap of any kind was in short supply back home.

'A week later I received a letter from home written by my elder sister. Besides bringing me up to date with the goings on at the home front, she asked a question; 'Did you or your friends enjoy the pint of libation I had carefully placed within the box of Lux soap powder?' After coming down from climbing the walls, I changed my view of believing that all members of the 564th Bomb Squadron were 'wonderful sharing types!' One among them (or an outsider) who had the cleanest laundry around also fell heir to a community pint of firewater!

'On 15 March during briefing, a large groan erupted when the map of our mission was uncovered and we saw a long red ribbon heading straight to Berlin! Our concerns were not assuaged when informed that we were not really going to Berlin but to a small town five miles south of 'Big B'. Wow, hope the Germans understand this! In closing the briefing for Zossen we were told our Command Pilot for this mission would be Lieutenant Colonel 'Jimmy' Stewart, who was in the back of the room. We turned and saw him, a tall, lean figure, nonchalantly leaning against the doorjamb. Oh, we caught the wrath of every 88mm battery on the way in. And before we reached the Initial Point Stewart came on the radio and said, 'OK f-f-fellas…let's pull it in real t-t-tight!' Having heard the actor Jimmy Stewart stutter occasionally in pictures, I thought it was a cute affectation and now realized he had a real little verbal glitch. Anyhow, the German Officer Training groups in Zossen that were housed in tents wouldn't enjoy their reveille call that morning consisting of 250 lb bombs raining down and through their housing facilities.'

"There were screams and moans that were loud and numerous' on American bomber bases when at briefing, the curtain was pulled and the lines on the map ran straight to 'Big B'!' So wrote Staff Sergeant Donald L. Becker, tail gunner in Lieutenant Bernard L. Painter's crew in the 'Bloody Hundredth' at Thorpe Abbotts. 'Berlin was the terror of the heavy bombers because it was so well protected. But our target (Wittenberg) was 15 miles north of Berlin, just missing their 400 flak guns, but still remained the terrific fighter menace with the 'Defence of the Reich Staffel' up against us.'

At Old Buckenham 2nd Lieutenant Wesley J. Bartelt's crew in the 732nd Bomb Squadron, 453rd Bomb Group were scheduled to fly their 22nd mission; so it was up early, with a breakfast of powdered eggs and the usual coffee and off to briefing. Bartelt's crew were in all probability like hundreds of other bomber crews. 'We came from all parts of the country' recalled the 21-year-old half Polish pilot born in Milwaukee, Wisconsin, who had flown three Battle of the Bulge missions. 'We were a mixture of ethnic backgrounds and religions. Staff Sergeant James W. Provo, my nose gunner, was a Frenchman from Chicago; William Carlson, my radio operator, a Scandinavian from the San Francisco area; Tech Sergeant Franklin Pepper the engineer was English and a rebel from Athens, Alabama – to him I was a 'damn Yankee'. Myron Foster the bombardier who hailed from Boston was of Jewish heritage; one waist gunner, George D. Tatar, was an Italian from Michigan; Ken Olsen my tail gunner was a Swede from New Jersey. The co-pilot, Charles Parker, came from Baton Rouge; he was a Duke's mixture. One crew member was distinctive and that was my navigator, Lieutenant Hans Nüchell. Tall, blond, blue eyed, born in Munich, he came to America at age four. He always told us he had two first cousins flying with the Luftwaffe. We were grounded for almost three weeks after being ready to fly combat. 'Bob' Harper in Intelligence recalled that they were rechecking Hans' records as he was being considered to lead a mission to bomb a camouflaged target in Munich, his birthplace. It may have been more of a loyalty check to get his reaction to such an assignment. After a short discussion with Wing S-2, it was clear that Hans was not only loyal, but a very good navigator and a competent photographer. We were finally cleared and went on our first mission in November of '44. From that mission on it became a running joke that someone on the crew would call Hans, up in the nose, as we crossed the Zuider Zee and yell, 'Hey Hans, get on the horn and tell your cousins we are up here today and to leave the 453rd alone.'

'Our luck continued to go well, even with the zero-zero take-offs in the dark for the Bulge missions, a few flak holes and now and then, a near-miss with some clown flying a reverse course around the Buncher. On our third mission, we took the lead of the 732nd Squadron. That day we were flying in the 'Coffin Corner', but were the only ship with a bombardier and a bombsight that was working. The months moved on, December, January, February and March and our mission count grew to 21. One week before our 22nd mission, I was called into Squadron Operations and was told to take up a new B-24L [*Never Mrs Too*] that had come to the Group. It was the latest model and I was to take it up and check it out. It had a formation stick which worked with the autopilot and a new type of 'Mickey' equipment set on the flight deck behind the top turret. It sure didn't give us much room to move around. I took it up on two flights around Norwich and everything seemed to be working well. I gave my report to the Squadron Operations Officer and was told it was going to be the CO's personal ship.

"As my co-pilot and I listened at the briefing on 15 March we couldn't believe that we were going to fly deputy lead for the Group and that our plane was the new bird we had just checked out. The target was Zossen, 20 miles south of Berlin, headquarters for the German Army. This would be our third trip to Berlin.' Altogether, 1,282 American heavy bombers covered by 14 fighter groups were dispatched to various targets, including a marshalling yard at Oranienburg on the banks of the Havel River, 35 kilometres north of the centre of 'Big-B' and the German Army Headquarters at Zossen about 20 miles south of Berlin. The Germans kept the location of this headquarters a closely guarded secret, but by late 1944 or early 1945 the Soviets had learned of this location and had requested the US Army Air Forces to dispatch long range bombers to disrupt its operations. The USAAF obliged, attacking the complex several times.

'With briefing over' wrote Wesley Bartelt, 'Parker and I headed for our hardstand. Shortly after, we loaded our gear and pre-flighted our 'New Baby.' Just as we finished, Hans came along with another crew member whom none of us had ever seen. We all gathered under the wing and met bombardier and 'Mickey' operator, Lieutenant Julian L. Clark.

'Well, it was time to load-up and move out. Everything seemed to be normal. We took off, formed and headed for the coast, then across the Channel and over the Zuider Zee. There was the standard intercom chatter. My nose gunner was complaining how cold he was; my tail gunner would tell me to quit swinging him from side to side, he was getting sea sick. Everything seemed to be going great. Now, the formation was well inside of Germany and the crew got on Hans again about his cousins, even though we hadn't seen any German fighters for several missions.

'Flying off the right wing of the lead ship, I did most of the flying. I was concentrating on flying formation because I was using the new formation stick. Suddenly, my ear drums were nearly blown out with the words, 'Fire on the flight deck!' I called for someone to give me a report. The 'Mickey' set was on fire. The cabin was filling with smoke so I opened my window to see and to ventilate. Parker did the same. Carlson got a fire extinguisher and helped Clark and Pepper with the fire. It seemed like hours. I kept asking Parker, who was watching everything, to keep me posted. I was worried about the oxygen in the cabin blowing us up, so I opened the bomb bay doors as a precaution. The word came that the fire was out and so was the 'Mickey' set. With that, I relaxed and we closed everything up. I don't remember how close to the bomb run we were then, but things seemed OK and then the cabin started filling up with smoke again. I remember hollering to get the damn fire out, thinking it was the 'Mickey' set again.

'At that time, I was too busy flying formation and not looking around; with that, my co-pilot hit me and yelled, 'The smoke is coming from behind your instrument panel:' With more profanity I said, 'What next?' Little did I know what else was in store for us before the day was over? By this time, the smoke was coming out on Parker's side, too. Again, I opened the window and so did Parker. Whether we talked or just acted automatically, I don't know. I signalled for Parker to take over the controls and then I started unbuckling, threw off my flak suit, got out of my parachute harness, ripped off my right hand glove and pulled out my oxygen hose. While Parker flew, I went under the controls and reached behind the instrument panel with my bare hand. I knew that if I touched -40° metal with my warm hand, it would stick and burn, so that would not be the area of the fire. After touching a few times and pulling skin off to get my hand loose, I hit something hot and my hand did not stick, so I grabbed a handful of wires and pulled and looked for more hot spots. By this time, I needed oxygen and Pepper was there with the walk-around bottle. I took a few fast breaths, unplugged again and went back under the panel looking for more hot wires and found them. As soon as I pulled them loose, the smoke seemed to diminish and the cabin was clear once more.

'By this time we were on the bomb run. The lead ship called 'Tuck 'em in;'The speed with which one can work to get buckled up with all the gear is something else. Now it was up to me to fly the run. As I remember someone remarked, 'Two down and three strikes, you're out;'There was a quick reply of, 'Knock it off with those damn superstitions;' I was to find out later that Clark, the new man, had parachuted once and on another mission had crash landed in some trees from which he had spent several weeks in the hospital. This was his first mission since that accident. The flare dropped from the lead ship and Hans started the countdown. Then I noticed I was pushing full right rudder and was still skidding left toward the Leader. Out of the corner of my eye I could see our two port engines windmilling. By this time we were no more than 25 ft from the Leader. I jammed the wheel forward and we slid right under the lead ship. Hans was still counting as I heard, 'six, five, four'. All I could see above me was an open bomb bay full of bombs. Instinctively, I pushed the controls forward and turned to the right to get away from the formation before they dropped their bombs!

'Now, there we were, out of formation and down to 15,000 ft and heading east to Poland. The crew was busy throwing out flak suits and loose gear, but we kept the guns loaded since we were not sure where the Russian lines were. A fast check with Hans and he gave me the headings to Łódź, Poland, which was one of the fields designated. Parker and I were busy trying to fly on two engines and maintain as much altitude as we could, but we were slowly settling. The one thing that bothered us was that our altimeter was set in England so we had no idea how much the altimeter setting would be off when we reached Poland. We had salvoed the bomb load after leaving the formation in a dive. While Hans was working on headings and giving me information on the two available airfields, all the gunners were watching for any sign of enemy fighters. The feeling of being over enemy territory all alone without the P-51s or 47s to keep us company was a scary time. We would have welcomed their escort, but we knew we were going in the wrong direction.

'Parker was using the escape map from his jump suit pocket and giving us the distance to the Polish border; 100 miles of enemy territory and then another 150 miles over Poland to Łódź. We had plenty of fuel. The big worry was, why did the two left engines stop and would the other two get us out of Germany? Our air speed dropped to 130, so that meant two hours flying if we didn't have a head-wind. We kept busy checking everything, but it still seemed like forever. It wasn't long before Hans called, 'there's a fair sized town ahead and to the left.' Soon we could see the airfield, so I called to Pepper to ready the Very pistol with double red flares. That was the briefing signal for the day. By this time, we were down to what we figured to be about 1,500 ft. We came over the airfield on which there were a number of fighters with big red stars on the wings. Provo called and said that some of the fighters were taking off. I then called the crew to clear their turrets and we would try to hold our altitude as long as we could. We were thinking that they were coming up to escort us in. I cautiously turned into the good engines and levelled out on my downwind leg. The co-pilot started the landing checklist; gear down, 10° flaps; that's when we started losing altitude fast. At that time, two fighters roared over the top of us. They were so close I could see they were Bell P-39 Airacobras. The engineer was still firing double red flares.

'Suddenly, all hell broke loose. Someone called, 'I see tracers coming at us:' Parker looked up and two P-39s were coming straight at us from 12 o'clock level. By now we were below 1,000 ft and someone (I never found out who) hollered 'Bail out!' With that I screamed, 'Don't jump, we're too low!' Russian bullets and shells were coming in everywhere. They were even hitting the controls because the wheel was jerked right out of my hand.

'At that time I yelled to Parker, 'Gear up!' While he was trying to get it up, I ran the servo power all the way to ten. It was either burn out the engines to get enough altitude for bailout, or dive for the airstrip. Either way, should the bastards make another pass at us and hit our gas tanks; we'd all buy the farm. Everyone was watching for their next pass. There were four P-39s after us. All that ran through my mind was 'what kind of allies are they?' I watched my rate-of-climb, it was slow and then Parker said 'the gear is stuck, it won't come up:' with that I got on the intercom, 'Bail out on the bell, don't even count, open your chutes as soon as you clear the ship. We'll try to get more altitude and if they turn back, that's when we go:' I looked at Parker and said, 'How high do you think we are?' The altimeter showed a little over 1,000 ft. He said he thought that was pretty close.

'The fighters turned and headed toward us again. I hollered, 'Good Luck' and rang the bailout bell. The bomb bay doors had been opened by Parker while I kept trying to climb for more altitude. We had always talked about bailing out at high altitude and also what to do at low altitude. I also told my crew that I would count to 15 and then I was going and they had better be ahead of me. With all the extra power on the two right engines, it took both Parker and me to hold full right rudder so that we wouldn't roll over. The countdown to 15 was over and I signalled Parker to leave. At the same time, I was unbuckling as he headed for the bomb bay. I started to pull back the throttles on the good engines, rolled in some trim, but when I took my foot off of the rudder, it still wanted to roll. The only way out for me was to cut back the power and trim for a glide. As I climbed to the catwalk, I saw some cows go under me. They were BIG as hell! I was way below bail out altitude. I knew there was no way to land and no way to get out except jump, so I dove out and pulled my ripcord at the same time. I remember my foot hitting the centre bulkhead and as the rudders went by, I could see the chute coming out and I was parallel with the ground. When it opened, I swung 180° like a pendulum. I remember looking at my ripcord and my fingers gripped tight around it. The thoughts raced through my mind that we were told that we had to bring it back or pay for it; the crazy stuff that passes through your mind when you think you're going to die. I thought you were supposed to see your whole life pass before your eyes and not the price of a ripcord. With that, I threw it away and grabbed both risers as I was starting to swing back in the other direction. Unfortunately, the ground came up to meet me on that swing. I slammed into the ground, but luck was with me. I hit in a marsh and my legs went in all the way to my hips.

'After crawling out, I was met by four men in drab uniforms with no markings, but each had a rifle that looked six feet long. They started to speak what I recognized as Polish. Oh, how I wished I had listened to my Grandmother, who tried to teach me her language. With my hands up, I pointed to my leg pocket and with a slow move I pulled out a pack of cigarettes and the American flag armband which I showed them. I gave them my cigarettes and then they marched me to a small town and into the local pokey where I found my co-pilot. They held us a day and by that time, we were both hungry.

'About noon the next day, they brought us a bowl of jellied meat with vegetables and black bread. It was the best they had and after 36 hours, we were both darned hungry. That night, we were taken from the cell and put into an old army truck with a red star. We bumped along very slowly for an hour or two and then pulled up to an old barn. It was dark; we weren't sure where we were. As daylight broke, we could see that it was an old barn with wide cracks between the boards and some straw scattered on the floor. We also had company. There was a B-17 crew that had landed on the strip, only to have the machine gun emplacements open fire on them. The barn we were in was a part of the airfield. We introduced ourselves to the other crew and traded stories. It seems that the Russians would shoot at anything that didn't have a red star on it.

'The next day, two more of my crew showed up. We talked over the events of the day before and they didn't know if everyone had made it. Then two days later, the last of my crew was brought to the barn. I should add that the barn was constantly guarded by the Russians with automatic type weapons. That's when I learned the heart breaking news that Hans Nüchell and Ken Olsen were both dead. Provo, Staff Sergeant George Tatar and Carlson had attended their funerals in a small town. They told us that they were both given a High Mass funeral as they were both Catholics. After the shock was over, we tried to figure out what had happened. Both were found with their chutes fully strung out, but they had not opened. Further speculation as to what happened would not bring them back. I still had one more man missing, no one but the engineer had seen him and it was confirmed that his chute opened but he disappeared behind a ridge of trees. That was my other waist gunner, Russell Hughes. It seems he landed behind a hill, near a road and before he got out of his chute, several Russian tanks came up, stopped, pulled him up into one and off they went to the front lines.

'In all probability, we were the only B-24 crew in the 2nd Air Division to be shot down by American-built fighter planes flown by Allied pilots. Or were they really our allies?'

'It was a gruelling nine hour flight, five of which were on oxygen at 25,000 ft and 50 degrees below zero" wrote Staff Sergeant Donald L. Becker in the 'Bloody Hundredth' formation. "Our primary target was obscured by low clouds, so we had to go to the secondary target, Wittenberg which had eight flak guns. We were much relieved when the lead crew radioed to Painter where we were headed. We were on the bomb run when all hell broke loose. We were hit once and my head crashed against the plexiglas window. I was stunned. Then we were hit again and again. I died four times. I was without a flak suit or helmet and a dead duck if shrapnel hit me. But then the light but perfectly accurate flak barrage was over and we were clear. When we landed we had ten hits on our ship, ranging from the size of a grapefruit on down. We were all OK although 'Mac' Painter, 'Rabbit' and I had had close calls. When we landed, the red flares (wounded aboard, bring ambulance) were going off like the Fourth of July as planes limped in with wounded, dead engines and severe battle damage. All-in-all in our squadron, four men were killed – eight wounded. My pal, another tail-gunner, had his leg blown off and bled to death. Of all the places we've been – it had to be a place with only eight guns to raise hell – passing all those at Berlin, Munich, Frankfurt and Hanover – now I'm really getting flaky!'

This proved to be the largest raid on Zossen, during which 25,000 incendiary bombs and 6,000 high explosive bombs were dropped; Chief of the Army General Staff Hans Krebs was wounded in this attack. All told, 308 B-24s of the 2nd Air Division and 276 B-17s in the 1st Air Division dropped over 1,370 tons of bombs on Zossen, for the lost of just one bomber. Another 61 bombers bombed targets of opportunity at Gardlingen, Parey and Stendal. Of the 149 B-17s in the 1st Air Division and 526 B-24s in the 2nd Air Division, that were given Oranienburg as their target, just over 660 sorties were considered 'effective' while 47 B-17s in the 3rd Air Division dropped their bombs on targets of opportunity. The flak came close and eight B-17s were lost.

Paul M. Montague, a B-17 armourer-ball turret gunner in the 487th Bomb Group at Lavenham in Suffolk flew his seventeenth mission on the Oranienburg mission. 'This was another long haul into and out of Germany. Captain William Sylvernal's crew in the *High Tailed Lady* had made it before. All went well until we approached the turning point toward the IP west of Berlin. We were flying at 24,000 ft when, suddenly, an accurate burst of flak hit our ship. The pilot was seriously wounded, one engine quit, the intercom functioned only sporadically and all the control cables on the port side, except the rudder, were severed. This caused us to bank to starboard at about 30 degrees. We dropped from formation, apparently unseen, lost altitude and turned toward Berlin. At only 12,000 ft over Berlin a second flak burst smashed part of the plexiglas nose, stopped a second engine, ruptured the oxygen system and started a fire in the bomb bay. Twelve 500-pounders stuck there would neither jettison nor toggle. Several crew members were hit by shrapnel. Our pilot gave us the alternative of bailing out or staying while he attempted to ride the *Lady* down to a crash landing in Poland. As we gazed directly down at the Tiergarten, no one had the nerve to jump! The fire in the bomb bay was finally extinguished and we managed to jettison our bombs into a lake below. Thankfully, we were alone. No German fighters appeared. As we crossed the Oder River at only a few thousand feet, our Russian allies fired on us but no hits were sustained. Our pilot did a magnificent job of approach to what appeared to be a level field enclosed on three sides by woods. We had no flaps, gear, air speed indicator and many other vital instruments but all the crew survived the crash landing.

The co-pilot and the engineer were later placed in a hospital for Russian wounded and the seven remaining crew were 'looked after' by their Russian Army hosts. The crew was disrobed by some Russian Army women who then proceeded to wash them with cloths and basins of water. Their uniforms were taken away and replaced with 'pyjamas' (the type worn in concentration and prison camps).

'Little did we seven suspect that everything would be pantomime for two ensuing weeks and these pyjamas would be our clothes. We were under constant guard. We were prisoners – not guests of our 'allies.' Just as we were falling asleep several of us heard the unmistakable click of the lock in our door. Next morning we had our first breakfast. I recall being very thirsty and I spotted a large cut-glass container of water in the centre of the oval breakfast table. After pouring a glass-full, I took a large swallow and my breath was whisked away! Pure vodka at 0530! I tried to warn the crew members but was speechless. A few others made the same error. The Russians roared with laughter. For the next two weeks we used vodka in our cigarette lighters; it worked marvellously like an acetylene torch!'

On 18 March 1945 a record 1,329 8th Air Force heavy bombers escorted by 1,184 fighters were assembled for another daylight raid on targets in and around 'Big B'. 'At Great Ashfield when the briefing officer pulled the curtain back for this one" wrote Bill Varnedoe, "we all 'Ooohed' and 'Aaaahed' for the black tape on the map led to 'Big B' – Berlin. The target itself was a railroad yard in the heart of downtown Berlin. Weather was to be clear. (It was).'

Just after 5 am, as the huge formation of B-17s and B-24s was assembling over London, at Parchim airfield in Mecklenburg east of Hamburg, Jagdgeschwader 7 'Nowotny' which had relocated there for operations against US bombers, went on alert. JG 7 was equipped with Me 262 Schwalbe ('Swallow') jet fighters each armed with 24 R4M (Rakete, 4 kilogram, Minenkopf) 55 mm rockets beneath the wings on specially designed wooden racks fitted with sliding lugs to hang freely from guided rails. (The first launching rails were made from curtain rods). When fired, these missiles travelled up to 1,700 ft per second and packed a 1.1 lb, impact-fused warhead, which could easily vaporise a bomber. The probable target, the unit's seven pilots were informed, was Berlin. Oberleutnant Günther Wegmann, the 9th Staffelkapitän, credited with many aerial victories, including eight while flying the Me 262, was well suited for the task that morning. Involved in the early experimental stages of the Me 262 he had been assigned as adjutant to the late Major Walter Nowotny, the first commander of JG 7, the world's first operational jet fighter unit, on 8 November 1944.

'The day was as bright and crisp as I have ever seen; more like a Technicolor movie than real life" recalled 2nd Lieutenant William C. Stewart Jr., a B-17 ball turret gunner in the 92nd Bomb Group at Podington. "There were a few small wisps of white cotton clouds interspersed through the picture but mostly it was clear. The sun glittered back from reflections of the shiny aluminium skin of the other ships in the formation. Before we reached the IP I could see the stretch of this great city. The streets were like a checkerboard beneath us and once in a while, an ant-like motor vehicle appeared on the streets. The movement of the scene below was unbearably slow and it seemed as though we were motionless. The black bursts of flak were also hanging ahead and right at our altitude the sky was completely peppered with the stuff. As I looked ahead, I said to myself, 'And we're going to have to fly through that?'

'I turned the ball turret to the right, at about the 3 o'clock position and could see the lumbering hulk of a Fortress, which was probably from another squadron, about 4,000 ft below us going in the opposite direction. Its nose was pointed downward with its right wing toward my left. Its right outboard engine was engulfed in red-orange flames streaking back about ten feet. There was no doubt that the plane was going down. I watched the scene transfixed and uttered silently to the crew of the plane, although really to myself, 'Get out. Get out!' As I watched one, two, three and then four small white blossoms appeared behind the craft. Some had made it out. I changed my gaze to one of the small white parachutes in the air with something hanging below; an airman, another American. As I watched small black puffs appeared around him as he slowly floated downward. The Germans were shooting at him with anti-aircraft fire. They could have used the 88 mm ammunition better by going after the rest of us still flying. As we proceeded over Berlin the ship lurched and twisted from impacts but we kept going and finally unloaded our bombs onto a railroad station in the heart of the city. Once away from the city, the flight back was uneventful. When I turned my turret to about 2 o'clock I could see strips of aluminium skin peeled back from the right wing. When we landed we found we had taken what must have been a 105 mm anti-aircraft shell through the wing. It left a hole that a man could put his head through near the inboard end of the 'Tokyo' gas' tank. There were hundreds of smaller holes throughout the main body, wings and tail sections but no one was hit. I had learned what accurate and intense flak was.'

On the climb to altitude the No.4 engine's supercharger on 2nd Lieutenant George H. Crow's B-17 refused to work. 'At low altitude it was a good engine' recalled Bill Varnedoe "but up where we were going, it would draw only 12 inches of vacuum, about the same as if it were feathered (shut down). But since we could keep up with the formation, we elected to go on. Flak was very heavy and quite accurate and was responsible for the loss of *Kentucky Winner* piloted by Lieutenant William H. Cocke and Lieutenant Hubert I. Bloom's B-17. Once I looked out to the left and saw a cluster of six flak bursts at our level. Shortly, there were six more, closer. The next six were very close and I could see the following six would intercept our flight path. But we were on the bomb run and could not take any action. I just tried to make myself as small a target as possible, a thing hard to do when you're hiding behind 1/16th thick aluminium! The next six came on time and although we never heard the actual explosion, the shrapnel hitting the B-17 sounded like someone throwing gravel on a tin roof. It did us no serious harm, however. A piece knocked the handle off the front exit hatch and other punctures hit nothing vital.

'After 'bombs away', the Group made a sharp, diving turn to the left. This was normal to throw off that tracking flak after the straight bomb run. However, this evasive action turn was so tight, that with our right outboard engine not functioning, we could not turn that sharply to the left. (We were on right wing of our element). We were literally slung out of the formation! However, the turn was sharp enough to carry the Group right back through the flak zone again. But thanks to our bad supercharger we missed that and finally caught up with the Group. Also, fortunately, there were no enemy fighters in the immediate area. Solo bombers were prime targets for them. Ira Barnes, our ball gunner, said: 'I must confess that until Berlin I was confident that if some fate occurred in our Group, it would affect the other crew; but, now and I don't want to sound too melodramatic, I suspected that misfortune could dial our number at any time and I think that conviction remained with me for the balance of our missions.' However, all ten crewmen all made it to the end of the war and they had a pact to reunite every five years for as long as they were able.[2]

JG 7 Kommodore Major Theodor Weissenberger attacked an isolated diamond of four B-17s in the 'Fireball Outfit' from the rear. Three of the B-17s were damaged, but escaped into the contrails and clouds *Lady Be Good* was severely damaged. However, Lieutenant Craig P. Greason, who was from Garden

City, New York managed to put the Fortress down near Langemark, Belgium. None of the crew was injured and all returned to Glatton. On 21 March 1945 Greason and his crew bailed out when *Rene III* was crippled by enemy action over the Ruhr around Essenin. Initially this B-17, the 1,000th Douglas-built Fortress produced, was called *Pistol Packing Mama* by the workers at the Long Beach plant who built the aircraft but after she was flown from the United States to Glatton by Lieutenant Colonel Luper and his crew, Luper had her named *Rene III* in honour of his wife. Over the next year, *Rene III* completed fifty-three missions before her demise. On 7 October 1944, on the mission to Pölitz, Luper and his crew on 44-8046 were shot down by flak on the mission to Politz. He and four of his crewmen were taken prisoner. The other six members were killed in the attack. At the end of the war *Lady Be Good* was flown home to the USA and to Kingman, Arizona where she was ultimately scrapped with thousands of her kind.

Unusually, Weissenberger then led a second pass, right over Berlin, which hit *Lady Jane II* in the 401st Bomb Group piloted by 2nd Lieutenant David E. Vermeer, who had turned 21 years of age three days before. After being hit, the B-17 continued over the target and then fell off on one wing out of the formation. However, Vermeer was able to make it most of the way out of Germany but was again attacked by Me 262s after American escort fighters had left. Vermeer then gave the bailout signal and six of the nine crew members parachuted to safety and into captivity. Vermeer, his togglier Ernest J. Butlin and Milan Basara the radio operator did not exit the ship and were killed in the crash.

A second formation of a dozen Me 262s was led to a disorganized section of the 3rd Air Division stream by Oberleutnant Günther Wegmann. He picked out a formation of about sixty B-17s and led his wingmen in a loose formation toward the incoming bombers. To his right was Oberleutnant Karl-Heinz Seeler (killed in action at a later date) and on his left was Leutnant Karl 'Quax' Schnorrer with Leutnant Oberfahnrich Günther Schrey on the outside in 'Yellow 2' From a distance of 3,000 ft, they fired nearly 100 rockets into the midst of the 100th Bomb Group formation, creating a scene of devastation, with pieces of aircraft and body parts and smoke and flame erupting all around the sky.

Wegmann shot off the left stabilizer of *Skyway Chariot* flown by 1st Lieutenant Rollie C. King from Seattle, Washington and co-pilot Lieutenant John S. 'Jack' Williams from Chicago, Illinois flying in the dreaded 'tail-end Charlie' position, the last and lowest in the squadron and the Fortress exploded. It was last seen going down into the contrails under control with the jets making another attack. 'Old hands' at the aerial warfare game, the crew had been together for many months. 'Shortly after 11 am 'all hell broke loose' recalled navigator Flight Officer John W. Spencer from Elizabethtown, Kentucky. 'Everything went well' until just after they turned on the IP when a Me 262 got practically the entire left horizontal stabilizer.' A second attack was fought off 'halfway down the bomb run with no damage done. Since being hit, we were gradually trailing the formation and by the time we were over the target area, the rest of the formation was approximately one-half mile away.'

Spencer said that the bombardier toggled the bomb load over a 'built-up' area of Berlin at about 11:25 am and approximately 15 to 30 seconds later 'there was a terrific burst that seemed to come from the rear of the plane. From where I was, in the nose, I could see smoke boiling up from under the pilot's seat. The condition of the plane then was that the controls had been shot out, as had the intercom system and the right wing was on fire. Up until we received this last attack, everyone in the ship reported they were all right. As soon as we were hit – since there was no communication – I looked through the astrodome into the cockpit and I handed my toggler his 'chute and then put on my own but still wasn't sure to bail out, so I looked through the astrodome again and saw both the pilot and co-pilot preparing to abandon ship. Then looking at the right wing, which was burning pretty badly, I decided it was time to leave. I bailed out, floated to the ground and was captured immediately.'

Spencer talked to fellow crew members when he ran into them two or three days later in Stalag Luft I. He learned that Sergeant James M. Baker the tail gunner from Lake Lynn, Pennsylvania was hit badly in the final attack. Later his unopened, bloody parachute was shown to the enlisted men of the crew and they recognized the number on it. The fate of Sergeant Robert Mitchell, the ball turret gunner from Galesburg, Illinois remains unknown. Sergeant Meyer Gitlin the waist gunner, who was to assist him in getting out of the ball turret in case of emergency, was also missing. Staff Sergeant Archie Mathosian the radio operator from Bronx, New York recalled that Gitlin bailed out ahead of him through a hole in the fuselage made by cannon shells from the Me 262 but he was not seen again. Spencer said that his suspicion was that 'if his 'chute did open, he may have been killed by Germans, for he was a Jew, had it on his dog tags and didn't seem to care who knew it.'

First Lieutenant Alfonso C. Guardino, born Hartford, Connecticut, the 26-year old pilot of *Patriotic Patty*, first saw *Skyway Chariot* being attacked by a Me 262, noting that the stabilizer broke off and the bomber then going down 'under control' with enemy aircraft making further attacks. Five days' later on the mission to Marburg on 23 March a flak hit registered on the side of *Patriotic Patty* as it left the target area; the right wing crumpled and the aircraft went into a spin and then levelled off for a moment before it went into another spin. *Patty* exploded on impact near Montabaur, Germany killing Guardino and his eight crewmembers.

Wegmann started for home when near Glowen he spotted another bomber formation in his path so he swung around to take a pass at them with his four 30mm Rheinmetall Borsig MK 108 cannon. In the head-on attack, the combined closing speed of about 720 mph was too high for accurate shooting, with ordnance that could fire only about 44 shells a second (650 rounds/minute from each cannon). Even from astern, the closing speed was too great so a roller-coaster attack was devised, the 262s approaching from astern and about 5,900 ft higher than the bombers. From about three miles behind, they went into a shallow dive that took them through the escort fighters with little risk of interception. When they were about 0.93 miles astern and 1,480 ft below the bombers, they pulled up sharply to reduce speed. On levelling off they were 1,100 yards astern and overtaking the bombers at about 93 mph, well placed to attack them. Wegmann swooped in from astern and closed to within 600 yards of one bomber before opening up with a staccato of fire that ripped away the cowling from one of the bomber's engines. The German was jubilant and began transmitting his victory to home base when a stream of bullets fired from a P-51 Mustang shattered his canopy and instrument panel and riddled the airframe with bullet holes, one of which struck his right leg. Reaching down, the wound was large enough for Wegmann to put his whole fist in. Günther Schrey was shot down and killed by a Fortress gunner. Oddly, Wegmann felt no pain as he streaked along at 18,000 ft above the German countryside before desperately pushing his shot-up jet downward. At 12,000 ft he saw flames leaping from his starboard Junkers Jumo turbojet engine. That quickly ruled out a crash landing that would turn his jet into a giant fireball. He pushed the control stick forward, disconnected his seat straps, removed the retaining bolt from the canopy and was sucked from the cockpit at 250 mph. Wegmann bounced off the jet's tail and fell free. He counted five long seconds before pulling the release cord of his parachute and drifted downward toward the town of Wittenberge 60 miles northwest of Berlin, which he recognized from the air, having flown over it many times. He brushed the tops of pine trees and managed, just barely, to land in a small meadow.

'German pilot!' he shouted loudly as an elderly woman made her way to him. He was nervous because he was wearing a leather flight jacket obtained from a downed American flyer. If the villagers thought he was an American pilot, he might have been beaten or possibly killed. Wegmann's luck held. The woman was a nurse who quickly bound his thigh above his right knee and applied a tourniquet. Within four hours he had been rushed to a hospital where his right leg was amputated.

Sweet Nancy II piloted by 2nd Lieutenants' Edward 'Duke' Gwin of Whittier, California, and Donald H. Reichel from Milwaukee, Wisconsin, had two engines on fire and the B-17 dived away from the formation and then nosed up and the tail fell off and the doomed bomber went down spinning. Of the ten men on board, Gwin, who had named the Fortress in honour of his wife, and three of the crew were killed. Six men including Reichel were taken prisoner. All told, the 'Bloody Hundredth' lost four B-17s, one of which, badly damaged, made it to Russian territory and landed at Kostian in Poland. Another 15 bombers force landed inside Russian territory.

Doug Sharp, who was flying his 30th mission in the 94th Bomb Group, said: 'It was a rough one and we knew it from the beginning. Up at 0430, take off at 0800 and back at 1600. We were on oxygen 4½ hours. We flew another new plane and it was pretty nice. The flak was pretty accurate because they could see us. We didn't lose any planes out of the squadron nor the group but many groups weren't near as lucky. I saw about eight chutes floating down over the target. Poor devils. I know the civilians mobbed them when they hit the ground if they weren't shot before they hit.'[3]

'Things didn't go right from the start' recalled Staff Sergeant John E. 'Jack' Bode, a man of many talents – right waist gunner, photographer and assistant engineer – on *Doodle Bug* in the 392nd Bomb Group flown by 23-year-old Lieutenant William E. Meighan of Morgan Township, Pennsylvania. 'Just after the French coast a B-24 got into prop-wash and collided with another. I watched both planes all the way down with my binoculars but saw no 'chutes open. Heard later one man did get out. It was his first mission. As we neared the target I could see the Alps in the distance, but my attention was soon drawn to the biggest mass of flak I was ever to see. To jam the gun-laying radar I had to throw 'chaff' out. The Germans had us bracketed and we were hit in several places. Our bombardier was hit in the face and blinded; he screamed over the interphone. Looking out I was appalled to see five B-24s falling at once over the target – just like fingers on your hand. As the wounded bombardier was being removed from the nose turret I saw a gaggle of about 40 fighters flying parallel on our right at 3 o'clock. Looking through my binoculars I recognized them as a mixture of 109s and 190s, although our pilot at first suggested they might be our escort arriving. A moment later the air around us was full of white puff-balls. I wondered if they were a new type of flak but the pilot yelled, 'Here they come!' and sure enough outside my waist window an Focke Wulf 190 flashed by from the front, doing a roll between us and the nearest B-24.

'By now I felt it was only a matter of time before they got us as we were already crippled. I tried to swing my point-50 after other Jerries as they streaked by. Our top turret was doing most of the firing and the ball turret gunner was trying to get into the damaged nose turret. A fighter started pumping 20mm shells at us from behind and though the tail gunner replied, the recently installed link chutes in his turret caused the guns to jam intermittently. Next thing I saw was a B-24 upside down and then to my amazement a Me 109 about 100 yards or so below us on my side going in our direction and not much faster. He was probably shooting at a B-24 ahead of us and may have assumed our plane abandoned; at any rate he acted as if we didn't exist. I aimed my gun almost straight down, sighted point blank and fired 30 to 40 rounds into his wings, engine and cockpit. His glycol sprayed but I'm sure I must have killed the pilot as the plane rolled over and went straight into the ground 20,000 ft below. Our fighters finally came to the rescue of what was left of our formation. We now had two engines out but though we were losing altitude fast we managed to make a Spitfire field on the English coast. We had one flap shot away, a bad wheel and, as the hydraulic lines were cut, no brakes. We went off the end of the runway but out pilot brought the plane to a standstill without further hurt to us.'

Final assessment showed that twelve B-17s were lost to flak and flak damaged half of all B-17s of all groups on the mission. *Southern Clipper* in the 467th Bomb Group at Rackheath that was hit by flak in the bomb-bay area over Berlin and killed three of the crew was the only Liberator that was lost from the 347 Liberators that had set out for Berlin. First Lieutenant William E. Shinn of San Francisco and his co-pilot, Flight Officer Kenneth C. Micko of St. Paul, Minnesota and five others bailed out safely but Sergeant William B. Wilson struck the ship below while bailing out and later died from his injuries. The lead ship of the second squadron was also hit by a flak burst which blew out the underside half way from the bomb bay to the nose. The engineer holding the doors open blown out of the ship and the navigator was killed. The parachute belonging to Bill Yarcusko who was riding as bombardier was half in the Liberator and half hanging into space. He was almost afraid to reach for it, but finally got it on and jumped. "Aside from a little trouble with the Russians – a Cossack rode up, pointed a gun at one man's head and pulled the trigger three times without the gun firing – they were OK" said 1st Lieutenant Charles E. 'Chuck' Huston, pilot of *The Honey Wagon* in the 467th Bomb Group formation and one of 16 bombers that force landed inside Russian territory. "Yarcusko spoke Russian and he soon convinced the Reds that they weren't Krauts and the treatment was good after that. About the third ship behind us had the nose wheel shot out and slid about a half mile on the wheels and the nose. They changed runways and the second ship in had a tyre gone and went spinning away through the dirt. Another pilot crash landed and washed a ship out at an emergency field. Every person was thoroughly shot. I didn't see anyone smile as they got off of the truck for interrogation. The locker room was quiet. No one that I know of passed up their shot of whiskey that day. We hated like heck to go back to the barracks that night. We didn't know what to do. We knew that Micko's baby was expected any day, and we thought maybe we should see if the missing message could be held up just a couple of days to see if maybe he had got down OK somewhere, and yet it didn't seem right to hold up the message. The chaplain said he couldn't do anything about it anyway, so that solved our problem."[4]

The appearance of the jet fighters of the Jagdverbande had caused quite some concern since they could out-fly anything the 8th had. Thirty-seven Me 262s had attacked the massive bomber formation and shot down several bombers and fighters for the loss of only the two jets flown by Wegmann and Günther Schrey. By the end of the month the 8th was to lose thirty bombers to the German jets. The jet menace became such a problem that, beginning on Tuesday, 21 March, the 8th flew a series of raids on airfields they used. The raids also coincided with the build-up for the impending crossing of the Rhine by Allied troops. For four days the heavies bombed jet airfields and military installations. On 22 March the heavies were requested by SHEAF headquarters to bomb the Bottrop military barracks and hutted areas directly behind the German lines. Next day the 8th struck at rail targets as part of the rail interdiction programme to isolate the

Ruhr and cut off coal shipping. Since the loss of the Saar Basin, the Ruhr was the only remaining source of supply for the German war machine.

An historic 15th Air Force operation mission occurred on Saturday, 24 March when 169 B-17s in six groups in the Fifth Bomb Wing at Amendola, Tortorella, Lucara, Celone and Sterparone in Italy struck at the Daimler-Benz tank assembly factory in Berlin over 1,600 miles from Foggia in southern Italy. The 'Forgotten Fifteenth' had never attacked the German capital before and the Fortresses and their four groups of Mustang escorts and one of Lightnings had never flown so far before on a mission. The mission began well. The weather over the Alps was clear and continued that way to the target. The escort was visible in abundance. But around Ruhland serious flak was encountered and groups took evasive action. By the time the Forts reached the IP, dogfights had broken out and many of the bombers were damaged by flak. Only 148 B-17s made it over the Berlin. Eleven returned early. Some of the fighters turned back early too but 241 of the fighters proved effective escorts. In just thirteen minutes the force dropped 356 tons of 1,000 GP and cyclonite bombs in visual conditions from altitudes ranging from 25,000 to 28,300 ft. As many as thirty Me 262 jets attacked using the sun and the bombers' vapour trails to conceal their approaches and they shot down ten of the 14 bombers and five fighters that failed to return while the Mustangs claimed eight jets downed.

February and March saw the most intense bombing destruction when German defences were minimal or absent and the war was all but over. Up to the end of March 1945 there had been a total of 314 air raids on Berlin, with 85 of those coming in the last 12 months. Half of all houses were damaged and around a third uninhabitable, as much as 16 square kilometres of the city was simply rubble. Estimates of the total number of dead in Berlin from air raids range from 20,000 to 50,000; current German studies suggest the lower figure is more likely.

Raids continued until April, when the Red Army was outside the city. In the last days of the war the Red Air Force also bombed Berlin, as well as using Ilyushin Il-2 Shturmovik and similar aircraft for low-level attacks from 28 March onwards. By this time Berlin's civil defences and infrastructure were close to collapsing but civilian morale held. After the capture of Berlin, Soviet General Nikolai Bersarin said, referring to the Red Army's artillery and rocket bombardment, that: 'the Western Allies had dropped 65,000 tons of explosives on the city in the course of more than two years; whereas the Red Army had expended 40,000 tons in merely two weeks'. Later, statisticians calculated that for every inhabitant of Berlin there were nearly 39 cubic yards of rubble.

By now the situation in Germany was one of utter desperation. On 7 April young and inexperienced pilots who had volunteered for the Sonderkommando Elbe tried one last-ditch effort to halt or at least interrupt the constant daylight air attacks on the doomed Reich by ramming the heavies in the 8th Air Force formations. "We were flying high squadron" recalled Jack Rude in the 493rd Bomb Group 'and no one knew it was coming. Co-pilot Robert R. 'Smitty'

Smith from Illinois had just told us over the intercom that German bandits were in the area. As I looked down, about six or eight close-formation Bf 109s were flying at 6 o'clock level coming toward the low squadron. They never fired their guns and broke left in a big hurry as four P-51s were on their tail.

"As I looked up, another Bf 109 was at 5 o'clock a little high. I was looking at his prop spinner before I knew he was near. In an instant, other gunners from our squadron worked him over. He never fired a round but went by us so close I could have hit him with a slingshot. As he went by, his head was down very low in the fighter.

"We were flying on the right wing of our element of B-17s. The Bf 109 rolled over, and as he dove under the tail of the B-17 flying on the left wing, he hit and damaged the B-17's right hand elevator. Now, diving straight down and about a hundred yards away from us, the Bf 109 blew up, just a puff of smoke and many small pieces that included the German pilot. In just a few seconds, it was all over. Although 17 bombers were reported lost, 188 bombers damaged and 142 airmen missing, losses caused by the Sonderkommando Elbe are unknown.

"The temperature in our plane was probably about 50 degrees below zero, but the palms of my hands were sweating. After my heart slowed down and my eyes went back where they belonged, that incident was all over. The rest of the mission was similar to past missions. The 493rd Bomb Group lost one bomber that day. It was damaged by a German fighter, and the crew tried to make it to Russia, but, when the B-17 couldn't make it any further, the crew bailed out over Germany, landed safely, and became PoWs."[5]

Over 1,300 B-17s and B-24s took part in the bombing missions on 7 April and there no let up in 1,000 plus bomber raids on German targets during the next few days. On 10 April 1,315 B-17s and B-24s were dispatched against primary targets such as the German Army HQ at Oranienburg and several airfields that included Rechlin, Neuruppin, Parchim and Brandenburg/Briest and marshalling yards at Wittenberge and Stendal. Nine B-17s in the 1st Air Division were shot down on the Oranienburg mission. Eight B-17s in the 3rd Air Division were lost on the Brandenburg strike, one of which was *Miss Purty* in the 34th Bomb Group headed by Lieutenant Paul E. Roscher which was struck in several places on the bomb run. Roscher had become well known at Mendlesham when the pilot had featured in press coverage posing with his B-17 which he had named *Gotta Haver* with the best wishes of the movie starlet who was glad to grace the bomber with pin-ups she sent its pilot. On the bomb run heavy flak struck *Miss Purty* in several places but it held on its jolting course to drop the bombs on the railway yards below while seats were blown from under crew members and fires started inside the Fortress. The bail-out order was given and the entire crew parachuted out. Roscher, last to leave, was badly burned passing through the fire in the bomb bays. The crew landed after several were fired on by waiting Germans on the ground and all were eventually captured. Ball turret gunner Staff Sergeant Glen R. Lyon and tail gunner James N. Johnson led their armed captors a chase and Flight Officer Roger A. Revay the co-pilot, was severely beaten with clubs wielded by angry civilians who climbed from air raid shelters to round up the flyers. Although each man had a different adventure before being captured, ranging from arguing with SS troopers not to kill them, evading civilians eager for their lives, to being patted on the shoulder sympathetically by a frau, the whole crew found themselves imprisoned on a Luftwaffe airfield with other Americans. Here an air force colonel persuaded their prison guards to aid their escape by marching them out of the airbase to a barn hideout from which they were liberated three days later by advancing American mechanized units. They all recovered from their serious and minor injuries.

On the weekend of 14/15 April 1945 the race to Berlin began between the Soviets and Western Allies. The British 11th Armoured Division liberated Bergen-Belsen concentration camp pursuant to a 12 April agreement with the retreating Germans to surrender the camp peacefully. There they found 60,000 ill and emaciated prisoners and more than 13,000 corpses strewn about the camp. The 1st Canadian Army captured Arnhem. Franklin D. Roosevelt was buried at his family estate in Hyde Park, New York. Nazi Gauleiter Joachim Albrecht Eggeling committed suicide and General Friedrich von Rabenau was executed at Flossenbürg concentration camp shot on Himmler's specific orders for opposing the Nazis. On 16 April Orders of the Day No.2 from General 'Tooey' Spaatz ended the strategic mission of the 8th Air Force and only some tactical missions remained, though on 18 April 1,211 American heavies escorted by more than 1,200 fighters were sent to attack Berlin. Forty Me 262 jet fighters shot down 25 bombers with rockets. It was the final challenge by a dying enemy and an unnecessary show of strength by the Allied air forces. The Luftwaffe was finished, destroyed in the air and starved of fuel on the ground but Hitler had repeatedly refused to fall on his sword until the inevitable happened. The Allies too, had prolonged the conflict longer than necessary. As General Frederick Anderson, deputy commander of the US Strategic Air Forces in Europe had said, Allied raids on German cities had been allowed to continue for no other reason than to teach the Germans a lesson.

It was people like Gerda Kernchen, born 1927, who lived with her parents in Wittenau on the northwest edge of the capital, who were now the victims of that lesson and not only had to endure constant bombing around the clock but were also about to suffer under Soviet occupation. Gerda worked in a factory where she sewed uniforms for the Luftwaffe.

'When daylight bombing began in March 1944, the factory workers had to leave their jobs during the day and run to the nearest shelter. The alarm would sound and then swarms of people would start running from all directions towards the Humboldthain bunker. This was the biggest one in Berlin, five storeys tall, with room for thousands of people. There were anti-aircraft guns on the roof and when they were firing the whole building would shake, which was very nerve-wracking.

'One day there was a daylight raid and we went to the bunker. When we returned to work, we found that our factory was a pile of rubble. There was no transportation, so I had to walk home. The entire street was on fire – every building on both sides of the street – and the air was so hot that people could stand it only if they walked down the centre of the street. The phosphorus from the incendiary bombs was running down the outside of the buildings and catching fire. They looked like snakes of fire. The worst thing was that I could hear the screams of people inside the buildings who were trapped and burning to death. It was terrible. I can still hear their screams when I think about it.

'Every apartment building had reinforced bomb shelters in the cellar. The buildings were connected by tunnels, so that if your building was hit, you had a chance of escaping to the next building.

'But there were always people who refused to go to the shelters, or couldn't make it in time. Those were the people who died.

'There was a very well-organized system in place for dealing with the homeless. The goulash wagons arrived quickly, like the food trucks used in the army. The most important thing for people was food. As long as you had something to eat, you could survive. They would hand out slices of bread with margarine and jam and noodle soup.

'You were just trying to survive. You only thought one day ahead. There were no official funerals, because there was no material for coffins. Everyone was cremated. There were so many people killed, that there was no time for ceremonies.

'All the restaurants were closed and there was no dancing or night life. The only things that were still operating were the movie theatres. They continued to make movies throughout the war and showed them right until the last day.

'We were really kept in the dark as to the progress of the war. We listened to the radio, but it was all propaganda. About ten times every day, there would be a special bulletin – always positive, announcing some German advance or some victory.

'At my workplace, there was a group of women who sat apart and whenever you went close to them, they would stop talking. I believe now that they were saying negative things about the Nazis and didn't want anyone to overhear.

'We asked the soldiers who came home on leave what was happening, but they only knew about their own small part. They also had to be careful about whom to trust, because any mention of losing the war was treasonous. The soldiers all said the same thing: they would rather be at the front than be at home, getting bombed. At least on the front, they could fight back. They felt so sorry for us and worried sick about their families at home.

'By April 1945 people were becoming very frightened. We knew that the Russians were marching towards Berlin and there was no hope of salvation. 'We began to hear some awful stories about what was happening to the German people in the east as the Russians advanced. During the final weeks, we could hear the big guns firing in the distance as the Red Army drew closer and closer to the city.'

We wanted to surrender to the Americans, who were advancing from the west, but it appeared that the Russians would arrive first.'

On 6 May 1945 the BBC interrupted a *Music While You Work* programme to announce: 'The German State Radio has just announced that Hitler is dead.' The Reich capital capitulated to the Russians the following day. Two days' later Britain and the rest of the free world celebrated Victory in Europe Day.

Notes

1. Correspondence with the author. See also, *The Story of Van's Valiants of the 8th Army Air Force; a history* by William W. Varnedoe.
2. In 2019 only Varnedoe and one other crewmember were still living.
3. Doug Sharp flew his 31st and final mission the next day, 19 March, when the target was Plauen near Dresden. "After each mission the crew was given two shots of whiskey and a peanut butter and jelly sandwich. The crew of *Seven Come Eleven* saved their whiskey after each mission and threw a party after their last mission.'
4. The foregoing account by Chuck Huston is adapted from his letter to Kenneth C. Micko on 17 November 1945.
5. *Miss Green Bay* by Jack Rude with Richard Wagner (Independently published, March 2020).

Index